Still We Danced Forward

World War II and the Writer's Life

By Rhonda Sonnenberg

Brassey's

Washington • London

Brassey's Editorial Offices: Brassey's Order Department:
22883 Quicksilver Drive   P.O. Box 960
Dulles, Virginia 20186   Herndon, Virginia 20172

Brassey's books are available at special discounts for bulk purchases for
sales promotions, premiums, fund raising, or educational use.

Library of Congress Cataloging-in-Publication Data

Sonnenberg, Rhonda, 1959-
      Still we danced forward : World War II and the writer's life / by
   Rhonda Sonnenberg.
         p.   cm.
      Discusses Thomas Mann, John Steinbeck, Virginia Woolf, Colette,
   Ernest Hemingway, and Ezra Pound.
      Includes bibliographical references (p.   ) and index.
      ISBN 1-57488-013-6
      1. War in literature. 2. Literature, Modern--20th century-
   -History and criticism. 3. World War, 1939-1945--Literature and the
   war. I. Title.
   PN56.W3S58 1998
   809'.93358--DC21   96-40039
                                                       CIP

Designed by Innodata

First Edition
10 9 8 7 6 5 4 3 2 1

Printed in the United States of America

For Peter
worldly wisdom hidden in youth's absent glee

For Charlie
proud boy delight of the day

And for Norma Sweat
the great resuscitator

"I dont think I was alone for 3 days for one moment; and each brought a little jab of war—each time the door opened or the telephone rang it was war and war—and 'still we danced forward.' "

Virginia Woolf, June 9, 1940

Table of Contents

Acknowledgments

I first conceived of a book about the effect of World War II on writers of the era in 1988, while reading the published letters of T. S. Eliot. As with many special books in my library, this was a gift from my husband, Peter Golenbock. His love and ceaseless encouragement have sustained me during this long and difficult project. My moods have not been easy to withstand. I endured Colette's dread of imminent catastrophe, Ernest Hemingway's fear of failure, and Virginia Woolf's self-criticism for writing biography honestly and accurately—and alas, without the benefit of their astounding gifts. I wavered between passion for the work itself and black despair that I was not up to the task, and each day began with Peter scolding, "Just do your work," and each day ended with Peter murmuring gently, "Just do your work." And so it is done.

I want to thank my editor, Don McKeon, who for three and a half years closed each correspondence with similar words of encouragement, "Keep going"; and Frank Coffee, who has believed in me since those early Jersey days. I especially want to thank Neil Reshen and Dawn Reshen-Doty, a divine duo, whose extraordinary caring, intelligence, and humor are precious to me each day. Thanks also to Professor Robert Cording for his important editorial contribution.

I would like to thank the army of local librarians here in Florida who provided me with invaluable assistance in obtaining hard-to-find materials: Richard Cassola and his crackerjack staff of book detectives at the Pinellas Park Public Library; Kevin McGinn and Alicia Ellison of the Tampa University Library; Sue of the Humanities Department of the Tampa Public Library; and Elaine Birkinshaw and David Riccio and their reference staff at the St. Petersburg Public Library. Joseph Rothberg, Ph.D., of the U.S. Army/Walter Reed Army Medical Center was most generous in imparting some of his vast knowledge on the subject of wartime depression and suicide rates. Other people who graciously gave of their time and expertise include Ronald Hudson of The Royal Bank of Scotland and Juliana Avanzini of Crédit Suisse, both in New York; also Sharon Culley, Holly Reed, and Janita Dixon at the National Archives II in College Park, Maryland.

Many friends gave me absolute support during this project. I especially want to mention: Kate Agmann, Gini and Peter Benin, Vida and Jim Rothchild, Vivienne Sohn, and Lori Pearson-Wise. I will never forget the contribution of my special friends, Betty Grice, who personifies the rarest human gifts of kindness, balance, and generosity, and Leah Mainzer, friend for life.

Lastly, Charlie Golenbock, the apple of my eye. You dutifully, if begrudgingly, shuffle away from my desk when I scream at you to leave me alone, and you await me smiling when work is done. Your love and cooperation made this book possible.

Introduction

A writer's talent is a fragile and at the same time indomitable creature. It requires the opposites of calm and stimulus, so that even when the writer feels the impulse to withdraw from tumult, he cannot help but respond to forces outside himself. By virtue of his susceptibility to infinitesimal changes in the world around him, he is, even if against his will, uniquely society's mirror, interpreter, critic, parasite, and victim. In wartime, his natural skepticism, demand for truth—especially in writing—and mistrust of authority may prevent him from seeing the value of the basic necessities of winning a war, such as patriotism and propaganda, and thus put him at odds with his peers and public. His intellectuality and individualism may make him seem unempathetic and selfish; his acute sensitivity may render him empathetic and weak. And his love and need for art during such a time of misery as war may lead him to the painful hunch that art, the essential benchmark of civilization, is unimportant and dispensable, or worse, an absurd narcissistic indulgence. No matter what one's political color, it becomes difficult to justify spending one's days shaping ideas into pretty words when one's son or brother is being held in a prisoner-of-war camp or one's daughter is aboard a refugee ship being torpedoed by the Nazis.

The Second World War presented a monumental threat to writers, whose lives even in the most peaceful times are rarely characterized by equilibrium. Certainly, for the entire populace of nations at war, stable lives are disrupted by separation, dislocation, financial loss, and death, but World War II's enormous global impact and dark shroud of evil, coming a mere twenty-five years after World War I, entrapped writers in a unique web of suffering, intellectual conflict, and inconvenience, affecting their lives and work, often permanently. Many writers, including all of those featured in this book—Thomas Mann, John Steinbeck, Virginia Woolf, Colette, Ernest Hemingway, and Ezra Pound—wondered whether in the face of menace, death, cruelty, and destruction there was a place for them as artists, and under the strain of the question fought against the invisible enemy of writer's block.

And yet, for most of the writers in this book, World War II provided the backdrop for an extraordinarily fertile period in their lives. They endured emotional chaos, depression, marital discord, grief over lost loved ones, ideological disillusionment, and the simple hardship of facing each day in a world turned upside down, and in many cases produced the major works of their careers. Their common doubt as to whether novels and poems still held any value gave way to their indomitable belief in themselves as artists. Except for Virginia Woolf, who killed herself in 1941 rather than face an invasion by the Nazis, they all ultimately recognized that they must continue to create—if not for others, then solely for themselves. They achieved what Thomas Mann called the artist's "unity of the All and the Nothing," by holding fast to the safest harbor they knew, the written page. They overcame economic hardship as the public stopped buying books, foreign assets were frozen in bank accounts, postal services became unreliable, and treasured food supplements from friends in the countryside failed to reach them in the cities. Breaks in lines of communication and transportation caused particular suffering, because as society's outsiders, they relied desperately on close circles of friends for affection and acceptance. They clung ferociously to their homes as refuges, and treasured souvenirs collected over lifetimes took on even greater dramatic importance, especially when war forced them to become itinerant, or worse, refugees. They felt the horror of war and the simultaneous thrill that it was providing them with material for future work, feeling themselves "untouchable," even when shells or bombs exploded dangerously close to them. And whatever anxieties, fears, idiosyncrasies, ethnic prejudices, and obsessions which had been framed in youth and had characterized their previous work were magnified exponentially under the strain and insecurity of war as it progressively unmasked their true natures as individuals. Ernest Hemingway could never forget his parents' bitter arguments over money, nor could Virginia Woolf dim the excruciating memory of her father's Monday morning hysterics about going broke as he surveyed the family's "books." Hemingway and Woolf particularly suffered from fear that the war would render them penniless, whereas Thomas Mann, who had been reared in wealth and comfort, was brought to tears at the possibility that exile from Hitler-held Germany would lower his lifestyle.

Regardless of their differences, all documented their mad scrambles for safety—for themselves and their manuscripts—their anxiety over the fate of mankind, and their own ideas to vanquish the enemy. In letters of lush prose or lean text echoing their characteristic writing styles, writers recorded the horror of gunfire or bombs bursting above their heads and the simultaneous thrill of witnessing catastrophes in shocking vividness, as well as the more prosaic, but dogged struggle to survive financially.

When World War II broke out exactly one year after the Munich Pact's false promise of peace, Europeans were already exhausted in the wake of a hundred and fifty years of political, social and philosophical crisis. World War I was a vivid and brutal memory to the middle-aged and elderly, but the era's rabble-rousing about freedom and independence from the stranglehold of the ruling, monied aristocracy was a legacy of hope and optimism rooted in yet a far earlier time. For artists and intellectuals, World War II posed a staggering challenge to the social philosophies which had indirectly inflamed and inspired them since the French Revolution in 1789, the July Revolution in 1830—bringing about the overthrow of King Charles X and resulting in the most liberal constitution in Europe—and German Republicanism of the 1840s. Explosive eighteenth-century Enlightenment ideas about intellectual, religious, and political freedom had been implemented as effectively as their republican supporters could hope against entrenched Church and aristocracy, but if modern Europe had been born out of these whisperings of freedom, zealous nationalistic passions took their breath and gathered frightening momentum. Not since Napoleon had one man, Adolf Hitler, killed so many, so grotesquely, so far afield, in the name of national honor and justice.

What had gone wrong? Had not the flowering of the truly breathtaking new technology on the eve of the twentieth century ushered in a modern age which promised the permanent end of human despair and suffering? During the First World War, it seemed bizarrely incongruous (and awe-inspiring) that the nearly brand-new "aeroplane," invented to make men's spirits soar, was being used by the likes of Baron von Richthofen and Eddie Rickenbacker to wage war, and now a quarter century of stunning modernity later, war remained the preferred choice among nations for settling power struggles, ancient territorial disputes, and all-consuming hatreds. Where was modern man's ability to think and reason for a higher purpose than mere invention? Time and again intellectuals shook their heads, commenting that "modern warfare" was an absurdity, an oxymoron, as though somehow Thermopylae or Hastings was acceptable, but war in the twentieth century was not. "Modern warfare" defied a romantic notion about war, as though a machine gun or bomb was a less honorable means to kill than a leather-sheathed truncheon or a saber with a handsomely carved ivory handle.

In this tide of violent confusion and anger, writers suffered great turmoil over their political ideology. In just two short decades since the Bolshevik Revolution, communism had shown disappointing, if not tragic, flaws in the Soviet Union. Fascism won over intellectual minions who sought a panacea for society's ills with a platform that emphasized culture, education, and technology. Followers pointed to the successes of Mussolini in Italy and Hitler in Germany in transforming societal chaos into sleekly running human machines. But when philosophy turned to brutal reality, fascism, too, proved to be an inadequate solution to entrenched poverty and national impotence, and in fact nothing more than a dictator's instrument for mass domination and murder. And because neither communism nor fascism was palatable to writers who shunned their precepts out of skepticism, lack of interest, or passionate hatred of war as pointless killing, a strong pacifist movement arose between the two wars. Its followers became engulfed in personal and professional conflicts, however. Colleagues were pitted against each other as pacifists accused nonpacifists of being hawkish spendthrifts of human life, or conversely were themselves accused of being "ivory tower snobs," "traitors," "naifs," and "communists," unwilling to help rescue the world from evil.

As these conflicts spread out beyond the men's clubs and cafés, World War II severely tested the tricky relationship between the writer and society. The writer's stalwart individuality and frequent endorsement of nonmilitary solutions to international crises made him vulnerable to attack. Against rampant flag-waving, World War II tried the writer's belief in himself and the moral correctness of his work at a time when the world seemed to be crumbling around him. Writers wondered whether they could remain strictly observers of humanity, looking inward for satisfaction at a time when humankind was under assault, or whether their capacity to sway the public with their words gave them a moral obligation to forsake personal concerns and look outward, to change the world for the better. Ardent pacifist Virgina Woolf, who never recovered from World War I and spent her life repudiating the charge she wrote from the vantage point of an "ivory tower," believed that writers should never become political and viewed war solely as the heartless conceit of male politicians, who waged war merely to satisfy their roguish lust for power—a view precisely shared by Colette across the English Channel in France.

Particularly in America, where war bureaucrats frantically labored to meet the challenge of Joseph Goebbels's ingenious propaganda machine in Germany, propaganda became one of the most heated sources of conflict for American writers like John Steinbeck and Ernest Hemingway, who had rejected the "American Way" long before the war broke out. The war called into question their commitment to fight fascism, their patriotism, and the extent, if any, to which they wanted or were willing to be used for propaganda purposes. The U.S. government itself hardly knew its own mind in this area, either. The FBI maintained dossiers on writers hired by other federal agencies, labeling many of them "Communists," because they had leftist or suspected leftist histories. After the war, when communism replaced fascism as the nemesis of the Western democracies, and writers were no longer needed to fight a war, these secret dossiers came back to haunt them.

The writers included in this book have been selected in part on the basis of nationality and geography. The war surely presented different challenges to a writer like Colette, living in Nazi-occupied Paris, as opposed to Hemingway, living in Cuba. Nevertheless, their common experiences in lands as far afield as Belgium and Paris, China and Spain, Santa Monica and Rapallo, convey both the global omnipresence of World War II, as well as the simple fact that war metes out common punishments no matter who one is, where one is living, or what one's politics or position on war is. Because these writers observed the key historical events and political issues of the time, each chapter is intended to form one piece of a broader picture of World War II and its effect on the creative process.

None of the writers selected for this book fought in the war as soldiers, either because they were too old or otherwise ineligible to fight. I purposely steered away from younger writers who used their experience in combat to launch their careers, such as Norman Mailer, Italo Calvino, Heinrich Böll, and Gunther Grass, because I was searching for the hidden rather than the obvious. All of the writers included had established their international fame well before the war. Most possessed firmly established, even rigid, codes about art and life at the time war broke out, and most were linked to a larger group of eminent artists and intellectuals whose beliefs supported their own. As I discovered, the war's effects on these beliefs were often very subtle, even imperceptible, if not understood in the context of both the time and the writer's own life. The impact of World War II on the work of most of these writers is not generally appreciated, because it did not produce outright "war" novels and stories, either during or after the war. One is not likely to identify Colette's most widely known work, the Belle Epoque Cinderella story of a young Parisian filly named Gigi, as her "war" novella, nor will one readily recognize John Steinbeck's scientific exegesis on tide-pool life off the coast of Baja California, *The Sea of Cortez*, or his harrowing story of a man hunted, *The Pearl*, as his "war" books. Yet, all three were the direct result of the effects wrought by war on these authors' emotions and consciousness.

Those of us who did not endure that bleak time can only marvel at the strength of those who did survive and flourish, for there is no question that the world was a dark, difficult, terrifying place. The example set by writers like Ezra Pound and Colette are all the more astounding since they continued to create under the direst of circumstances. Pound wrote his finest poems, *The Pisan Cantos*, while imprisoned in Italy on a treason charge by American military forces, and Colette wrote

Gigi while fearing that Nazis would find her Jewish husband's secret hiding place in the garret atop their Paris apartment building and take him to the Auschwitz concentration camp and all but certain death. Colette, whose brand of political philosophy ran to how to select the proper garter or rouge, had spent her life expecting the cataclysmic to occur at any moment, shattering whatever meager drop of pleasure, love, and happiness she could manage to squeeze out of it. For her, World War II was simply her worst nightmare come true.

At the opposite extreme was Ernest Hemingway, who shed his correspondent's insignia and donned a military mien when he led a group of French resistance fighters clearing the countryside of Nazis on the way to Paris before the Liberation in August 1944. For him, World War II was the magnificent realization of a lifelong dream to be a soldier heroically leading a command. Haunted by the prospect of his own death, and worse, of dying alone a failure and a coward, Hemingway never felt so alive and useful as when in the company of soldiers in France in 1944. Because war gave a man license "to think about nothing," war— better than the stiffest whiskey or absinthe—allowed the oft-besotted Hemingway to forget the dirty business of a marriage whose bloom had faded too soon, financial burdens, and a writer's bondage to his work. Though he denounced war for its cruelty and pointlessness, Hemingway loved every moment of it. The unfettered happiness he experienced in Europe was to be his last. In the years after the war he submerged into depression, alcoholism, and illness, and committed suicide in 1961.

Confronted by the overwhelming evidence of evil in man and his seeming bent toward self-destruction, some writers experienced an intensified communion with nature. John Steinbeck and Ernest Hemingway had shared a reverence for the natural world and, after the fighting began, became more convinced than ever that nature's enduring beauty, goodness and rationality made it the only alternative to the sinister and capricious world of man. Steinbeck's longtime interest in human and animal biology led him to the conclusion that warmongering was an inevitable product of the inborn, natural self-destructive instinct that humans share with other animals. Although Steinbeck's career rested on his wrenching, minutely-detailed portrayal of the suffering and injustice borne by common Americans, and his novel *The Grapes of Wrath* had just won him a Pulitzer Prize, his disgust with man's bellicosity led him to reject humanity as a source of study. Nevertheless, Steinbeck eventually joined the American government's propaganda effort under the passionate conviction that Hitler and fascism must be defeated. As with the most talented artists and writers sought by the United States government, Steinbeck's individualism made him essentially incompatible with institutional bureaucracy, and eventually, frustrated and angry, he quit to cover the war in Europe as a correspondent. But what had beckoned as a solution to inaction proved to be a hell. Steinbeck never recovered from "the nightmare" of war or his despair that men had chosen the atomic bomb, capitalist greed, and communist power-lust to settle their differences, rather than basic human morality.

Steinbeck and the other moralist of this book, Thomas Mann, despaired that man had taken what they viewed as God's gift of free choice and chosen evil over good. Because both writers saw the period as the symbolic death of the nineteenth century, a time which they profoundly believed had embodied superior values of justice, decency, and humanity, extraordinary similarities emerge between these two outwardly different men. (Colette and Woolf also mourned the end of the nineteenth century, and translated their sadness into symbolic terms readily understood by their women readers: the end of a time of madeleine cakes, brocade, and "perfect gloves.") Though Mann had been reared in a wealthy, refined, intellectual German bourgeois setting and Steinbeck in Victorian Salinas, California, around ranches, farms, and lumber mills, they both idolized the written word, treasured a life rich in imagination, feeling, and mysticism, and drew exciting moral and creative inspiration from the Bible. (In one of those ineluctable literary coincidences, Steinbeck's postwar *East of Eden* explores essentially the same biblical territory as Mann's Hitler-era adaptation of the Old Testament Joseph story.) Both men were preoccupied with the idea that man's uniqueness resulted from the duality between good and evil, and were fascinated by the idea of repetition of human patterns of behavior and regeneration. Both had an uncanny grasp of mob mentality in an era of mob hysteria and madness, and later, in the postwar atomic period, both viewed the cheapening of human life with tragic despair. No matter in what direction they looked, man had lost his nobility, moral purpose, and the spiritual links that bind one man to another. Having idealized America during the Nazi period and become an American citizen in 1943, Mann's lament that America had become a monster driven to buy the world was no less sincere than Steinbeck's sorrow that America had been drawn into a deep pit of crass consumerism and corruption by the lure of easy money. Mann spent the last decade of his life still hoping that man's intellect and inherent humanity would awaken to lead him to do the right thing, and yet at the same time deriding man's latest bent toward easy, "mathematic" solutions to moral dilemas. For these reasons, both he and Steinbeck dreaded the coming of a third world war, more terrible than any that had come before.

Though Thomas Mann believed that man's dual nature was the explanation for his troublemaking, he refused to equate evil with self-destructiveness as did Steinbeck. Deeply if iconoclastically Protestant, Mann steadfastly rationalized evil as the necessary ingredient for man's inherent goodness to emerge. Thomas Mann's rare moral conscience, coupled with his dynamic natural aptitude for politics and his overriding sense of mission to sway the German people back to goodness, catapulted him into the international spotlight. First as an exile in Europe and then in America, Mann mobilized himself to action—speaking out against Hitler, calling on Western democracies to take action, organizing refugees—on a scale matched only by a national leader. Indeed, throughout the Hitler era, German intellectual exiles mentioned him as the likely future leader of Germany. Mann's disgrace among his German colleagues after the war when even antifascists yearned to forget German national sin, followed by his resounding fall from grace in "Red Scare" America, make his story the microcosm of the entire prewar, war, and postwar era. His birth in Germany four years after the end of the Franco-Prussian War, his horrified witnessing of Germany's fascist takeover, and his ultimate return to Europe in 1952 from America, reflect the broader historical context of the Second World War. Mann's story is the story of fascist Germany, but it is also the story of the American legacy of World War II—the Cold War and McCarthyism.

Thus, the book begins and ends with Thomas Mann. The first chapter takes him from his early days as an exile in Europe after Hitler assumed power through the height of his period as an antifascist campaigner in America and, of course, as one of the century's towering writers. The last chapter begins with the death of President Roosevelt, which marked the beginning of the transfer of the reins of power in America from New Deal liberals to right-wing conservatives, and ends with a deeply disillusioned Mann nevertheless triumphing as an artist with his greatest success, *Confessions of Felix Krull, Confidence Man*, published in 1954.

Disillusionment came in many shades and degrees, especially when the New Order, promising and alluring, turned out for many to be even more bleak and more horrifying. In general, those writers who were less ideological and intellectual were the ones who enjoyed greater protection from the stark pain of disillusionment. Colette best personified Hemingway's "active doer" who does best to avoid thinking too much. In fact, she did much better than Hemingway himself. Her pragmatic, apolitical, narrow yet intensely sensual horizon of interest included only herself, her husband, beloved friends, and pets, and she survived Nazi occupation and the omnipresent threat to her Jewish husband by absorbing herself solely in their survival.

Unfortunately for Ezra Pound, he set his sights on saving the world. An elitist who embraced fascism as the perfect response to humanity's gross mediocrity, he thought too much, placing his intransigent, perhaps insane, faith in an ideology which failed monumentally and a dictator, Benito Mussolini, who turned out to be a fool and a coward. Because Pound was incapable of seeing that his faith cost him too much, his disappointment and frustration resound with a sadness which surpasses even Virginia Woolf's last attempt to ward off mental demons or Mann's all-consuming lament for Germany. Pound was doomed by his own naive, obsessive, demented idealism. He suffered from a mind simultaneously effulgent and hermetic, and the real world—even run by his hero Mussolini— could never measure up to the perfect intellectual world he concocted.

It is fascinating to note that Pound and Mann, the two most politically and ideologically fervent writers of the era, also became the most tragic literary victims of postwar right-wing hysteria in America, although Mann's illustrious reputation enabled him to continue living and working in relative freedom, whereas Pound remained imprisoned in a Washington, D.C., mental institution for twelve years. The gargantuan divide between these two writers in essential nature, background, and outlook accounts for their respective embrace of democracy, in Mann's case, and fascism, in Pound's. Whereas Pound accepted no less than perfection in individuals—an impossibility—Mann expected kindness and justice, perhaps equally impossible. And whereas Pound, like fascism itself, saw people as weak, stupid, and needing to be led, Mann credited them with the intelligence, reason, and compassion to rule themselves fairly. As a result, Pound saw Mussolini as a rare leader of refined sensibilities and intelligence, those very qualities Mann praised in Roosevelt. Since both men proselytized their ideologies with equal fervor, had the Axis won, Mann would surely have found himself in Pound's shoes, if not worse. Of the writers under consideration here, the disillusionment brought by World War II was perhaps most wounding for these two men. Yet, like their peers who came to recognize their powerlessness to transform society, they survived and flourished as artists. All of these writers' determined pursuit of self-illumination in the face of humanity's apparent unwillingness to delve more deeply into itself to find peace and harmony was not an admission of defeat or self-sacrifice, but rather a narrowing and deepening in their definition of themselves as human beings and artists. Bereft of a loftier mission, they hunkered down and simply wrote for no other reason than it was what they were born to do. In recounting the writers' tenacity during wartime, this book is as much about the pure creative struggle as it is about war and the writer's life.

There were many surprises for me during the three and a half years of writing this book. I delighted in the discovery that Ernest Hemingway and his early mentor Ezra Pound drew opposite conclusions about the authority of the state and fascism, despite their common Midwestern roots, anti-Semitism, and contempt for the rich and powerful. Hemingway and Thomas Mann, on the other hand, shared a consuming hatred for fascism although superficially the two were nothing alike. When Hemingway, fresh from observing the Spanish Civil War, delivered a speech at Carnegie Hall in 1937 declaring that no other form of government was as alien to the artist as fascism, he was echoing the words Mann had spoken for a decade. Both writers concluded that war resulted from the failure of the state to solve its internal social ills, both called fascists "cowards," and as sticklers for language and honesty in writing they specifically targeted propaganda as the fascists' nefarious tool for wielding power through deception. Hemingway's cocky confidence that he could correctly assess political situations, however, contrasts comically with Mann's pangs of guilt that he was too arrogant. Mann was ordinarily right, whereas Hemingway more often was wrong.

My research also provided me with humorous images—perhaps most notably that of Ernest Hemingway the vigilante, standing on the prow of his cabin cruiser, a Bahamian sponger's sombrero atop his head, binoculars in hand, scouring the Cuban coast for Nazi subs on patrol missions subsidized by the U.S. Navy. Hemingway's and Steinbeck's wartime boating experiences hilariously point up their diametrically opposite natures. Whereas in 1940 Steinbeck launched a scientific expedition to study marine biology off the Baja coast, relieved to be away from Western civilization and war, Hemingway, who loved soldiering though never a soldier, reveled in his spy-play with a coterie of ragtag alcoholics and cavorted drunk on his bogus expeditions. While Steinbeck's boat was equipped with microscopes, holding tanks, and tubs of formaldehyde, Hemingway's bore the Navy-provided cover of "Museum of Natural History," and was armed with bazookas, machine guns, and grenades. And whereas Hemingway was greatly amused by his "scientific" ruse to conceal covert activity, when Mexican officials suspected that Steinbeck's expedition was really a spy mission, Steinbeck took pains to explain that the mission was strictly scientific.

The comedy, however, is brief. Though Steinbeck and Hemingway after the war enjoyed their greatest financial success and both won the Nobel Prize for literature, the war represented for these men a terrible transition from youth to old age, as though catapulting them over a middle age which might have eased them into the battle against physical and creative weakness. As Steinbeck and Hemingway strove after the war to find a new form to express everything they had ever learned, they became bogged down in fear and anxiety, and writing became a tougher fight than anything they had ever confronted on the battlefield.

More affecting images that linger in my mind are of Ezra Pound, sitting in a prison camp cell, bewildered and confused yet beginning the best poetry of his life; of Colette, discovering that a familar streetwalker near her Palais-Royal home has returned from a long disappearance wearing the scars of her Nazi tormenters; and of Thomas Mann's wife, telling her husband to move from his window seat as their tiny plane was escaping Sweden, because the pilots of Nazi junkers were looking to see if he was on board.

It is sadly ironic that of all the writers included in this book, Virginia Woolf is the one individual who did not "dance forward," when it is from her writing that this book derives its title. Woolf did not, because she could not. But for the mental illness which she had fought against for a lifetime, Woolf was a brick wall who withstood considerable pain and criticism throughout her life. She would have put up a tough fight against the Nazis, had not her illness, over which she had no control, won out.

Finally, in the case of Thomas Mann, I believe no accolade is tribute enough. Mann simply astounds. Torn from the country he loved and fearing for the safety of friends and family stranded in Germany, he spoke against fascism and Hitler from an international pulpit with the energy of a man half his age, and with a moral conscience and sensitivity so deep it would have sunk most men during such a tragic time. His brutal candor about German national sin and paeans to human freedom and decency made him persona non grata among German intellectuals who embraced Hitler as well as German antifascists who nevertheless resented having their dirty linen aired in public. With all the attacks and interruptions to his peace and tranquility, but for a few intermittent periods during the war, Mann put pen to paper each day and continued to create works of breathtaking depth and vision. Lesser men might have been crushed by the burden of a seer's foresight about fascism, Hitler, and the failure of the Western democracies to halt his power. Mann, however, continually overcame emotional chaos by drawing strength from his monumental creative powers. Despite Mann's eventual realization that the artist was impotent to bend society to his message—the conclusion to which all the disparate writers of this book came—his extraordinary example of creativity as embodiment of a supremely powerful, natural life force resounds magnificently like the single lingering musical note in his wartime novel, *Doctor Faustus*. Mann's persistent will to make art against all odds is in the end the strongest and perhaps the only evidence that there is some inalienable part of man which must reach beyond the simple, sunlit world of nature to the life of the mind and the heart, even when the world of men seems nightmarish. Perhaps there is no reason why, but what better argument for the beauty and preciousness of life than the artworks these writers created out of their experience during such a horrible time of war. For when war was over, though John Steinbeck despaired at the corruption and narcissism of his world, his worst nightmare was that he had lost his power to write.

CHAPTER ONE

Thomas Mann

ON A MISSION FROM GOD

Our "thousand-year" history, refuted, reduced *ad absurdum*, weighed in the balance and found unblest, turns out to be a road leading nowhere, or rather into despair, an unexampled bankruptcy, a *descensus Averno* lighted by the dance of roaring flames.

Doctor Faustus, Chapter XLIII, 1947

When Archduke Francis Ferdinand, heir to the Austro-Hungarian Empire, and his wife were assassinated in Sarajevo by a Serb gunman on July 28, 1914, Germany's leaders gloated at their good fortune. Ever since the end of the Napoleonic wars a century before, Germany had been looking for an excuse to drive eastward into Asia. On August 1, the Germans launched *Drang nach Osten*, their dream of wealth and power, and joined Austria-Hungry in her war against Serbia and her ally, Russia.

Upon the outset of World War I, Thomas Mann, then recognized as one of Germany's foremost writers, immediately became an outspoken advocate for German military might. He lauded Germany's march against Russia, expressing "deepest sympathy" for her attempt to "smash the most despicable police state in the world," and characterized the war as "great, fundamentally decent."[1] At age thirty-nine, Mann was utterly confident that Germany would win the war. In an article, "Thoughts on Wartime," printed in the November 9, 1914, issue of the cultural journal *Die Neue Rundschau*, Mann called upon the intelligentsia to uphold its moral role to "ennoble" the German war effort.

Mann maintained an almost cheery optimism that the war would build Germany's moral character, making her "stronger, prouder, freer and happier," but the war's enormous toll eventually made breezy, moralizing explanations less comfortable for him.[2] Two million Germans were killed in the fighting and more than four million were wounded, not counting hundreds of thousands more who died from starvation and disease. Mann's wife's twenty-year-old cousin was killed on the Russian front, and her brother, a physics professor, was interned in Austria. But almost worse than this for Mann, his support of the war had set off a firestorm among German pacifists and left-wing intellectuals, who bitterly attacked his nationalistic position. Mann felt himself wronged and besieged. The war, he wrote in 1916, had "turned the world into an intellectual witch's cauldron."[3]

Mann's personal cost was a family literally torn apart by politics and bickering. His older brother, Heinrich, also a novelist and essayist, was as ardent a pacifist and critic of German politics and society as Thomas was Germany's great defender. Heinrich's novel *Professor Unrat* (*Small Town Tyrant*) sounded the alarm for Germany's future when it appeared in 1905, and his wartime alliance with the international circle of pacifist intellectuals surrounding Nobel Prize–winning French writer Romain Rolland brought Heinrich even wider recognition.[4] As the brothers were equally zealous on diametrically opposite political sides, it was not surprising that the war became the catalyst for a messy, wounding, public feud. Although the battle was long in coming and unearthed deep fraternal jealousies and resentments, the ensuing rift deeply anguished Mann and lasted until Heinrich came close to dying in 1922.

Mann felt he was viciously, unnecessarily attacked in his fight with Heinrich and privately grieved for the wrong committed against him, agonizing about fraternal love and hate. After Thomas Mann had sufficiently recovered, he distanced himself, quelling his emotional turmoil with a Herculean effort. Strict rational analysis followed in the shape of a long written work. When Mann began to write *Reflections of a Non-Political Man* (*Betrachtungen eines Unpolitischen*) in late 1915 as a fillip to his brother and the rest of his critics, he framed the antagonism between himself and Heinrich as "an opposition of principles." He himself was more like his father, a stoical "Nordic-Protestant," Mann explained, whereas his brother was like their emotional Brazilian-born mother, a "Roman Catholic."[5] Mann wrote that he had come to see Germany's "fate symbolized and personified in my brother and myself."[6]

Bruised and scarred, Mann surrendered his earlier optimism to a less certain view of Germany's future, her troubled attempt at democracy, and her fragile unity. In *Reflections of a Non-Political Man*, Mann jeered and lamented that the world was heading for "democratization," and he lashed out at those who saw a natural fusion between art and politics, terming this "the enslavement of intellect" by politics. He argued that in order for the "German spirit" to live, there must be an absolute division between German politics and culture.

When it appeared in October 1918, *Reflections of a Non-Political Man* provoked outrage among left-leaning intellectuals as Germany's all-but-defeated military commanders were negotiating the terms of their ignominious surrender. Though privately Mann had been mired in anguish, publicly he was an ironclad cannon, taking aim at pro-entente Germans like his brother Heinrich who condemned the German national character and blamed their country for the war. A week after a vanquished Germany submitted to the punishment of the Treaty of Versailles on June 28, 1919, Mann vented his disdain for such Germans: "That the great tradition of Germanism from Luther to Bismark and Nietzsche should be refuted and discredited—this is the fact which is hailed by many among us, the fact which is laid down in many a carefully considered paragraph of the peace conditions."[7] Like many critics of the Versailles treaty's peace terms, Mann predicted it would bring bitter turmoil to Europe. Nevertheless, he remained optimistic that Germany would find strength in her essential humanity and culture to become an ever healthier, more moral civilization.

"I was very much interested in your remark that before too long the conservatives will again have the greatest say in Germany," Mann wrote on January 18, 1920, to Count Hermann Keyserling, a writer and philosopher. "I too believe that; in the end nature restores the balance somehow, and 'the German IS conservative'—Wagner will prove to have been forever right in that regard. . . . what is at stake is nothing other than the celebrated 'reunion of intellect and soul.' "[8]

During the coming decade of the 1920s, the rapid growth in Germany of right-wing extremism dramatically changed the traditional definition of the German "conservative" with whom Mann had aligned himself morally, philosophically, and artistically. Throughout his life, Mann identified himself solely as a patriotic German of the nineteenth-century "bourgeois era," and he clung passionately to his ideal of that century, when for a brief interlude Germany was Europe's cultural leader. But it was only after the horror of World War I that Mann fervently championed Germany's nineteenth-century political dream of a democratic German Republic, flimsy though it was. Until then, democracy for Thomas Mann constituted a strictly aesthetic ideal, linked with "aristocratic" absolutes of freedom, decency, equality, and above all, humanity.

Democracy in nineteenth-century Germany had been the ambitious dream of those few politicians who sought to avert a French-style revolution and to unify an ethnically diverse people by implementing the same democratic changes in Germany which had already come to France and England. After the so-called German Revolution of 1848–49, liberal and democratic politicians stepped up their efforts to bring social change to the loose confederation of German states, but they were a fractured, impotent minority, fighting against an entrenched landed aristocracy and military, and a burgeoning business class. Their effort, though sincere, was feeble and unsuccessful. When in 1862 new Prussian Chancellor Otto von Bismarck proclaimed that Germany's Second Reich would sign greatness in "blood and iron," rather than in freedom, the bellicose leader turned his back on the republican dream of democracy for the rest of the nineteenth century and beyond. In 1871, Germany crushed France in the Franco-Prussian War, and Bismarck and his successors thereafter reigned with a military autocracy over the huge conglomeration of Prussian and German lands which formed the German Empire. A German Republic representing an inviolable moral bond uniting God and the Germans in equal partnership with a greater Europe would have to wait.

On into World War I, Thomas Mann, who was born four years after the formation of the German Empire, maintained a roseate vision of Germany's bond with freedom. He continued to see Germany as a great lover of democracy because it had produced so many revolutionary artists and philosophers, and like millions of Germans embittered by their defeat at Versailles, Mann angrily believed that the war's victors were only interested in an impotent Germany made to "grovel."[9]

When World War I ended, Mann put his profound hopes for a strong Germany into the new Weimar Constitution which was signed on July 31, 1919, just one month after the stinging Versailles treaty. The Weimar Constitution was the most democratic in all Europe, guaranteeing complete freedom to all Germans, and proclaiming that "Political power emanates from the people." Mann hailed the Constitution and expected it to be political salvation for Germany's social and intellectual chaos.

Yet, World War I had not even ended when Bolshevik fervor consumed large numbers of German intellectuals. The Bolsheviks condemned their peers for disregarding the troubles of the proletariat and called for a communist dictatorship to represent the underclass. Bolshevik support was so great in 1918 that a Soviet German Republic based in Berlin was a real possibility. In January 1923, after Germany defaulted on a repatriation debt, French troops occupied the Ruhr Valley, Germany's richest industrial region, and the German mark, already dangerously devalued, became worthless. The disaster for working-class Germans might have been the perfect inspiration for a Bolshevik revolution in Germany had not the real power after the war remained with Germany's antirepublican, antidemocratic and, especially, anti-Bolshevik military and industrialists. Millions of Germany's lower and middle classes were ruined by the postwar economy, but the German state and the very rich landholders and industrialists benefited, because they could repay their war debts in worthless marks.[10] To prop up the ruined German economy, enormous international loans were extended at high interest rates, largely guaranteeing the European economic debacle which Thomas Mann had predicted.

No matter what one's political persuasion, a consensus took hold among German cultural observers that Weimar democracy was "degenerate," a sham order, built on foreign money, masking lies, chaos, impotence, and internal German self-ruin. Morbid pessimism festered and spread. Especially in Berlin, the mood was anti-intellectual, antiacademic, reactionary, and morally decadent —among Berlin's female Jewish elite, blond hair became the vogue even as rightwing reactionaries were calling Jews the scourge of Germany and "vermin." Many of those very writers who had attacked the bourgeoisie right after the war hailed old-fashioned Prussian discipline and the new German industrialism as the antidote to moral chaos and postwar economic disaster.

This atmosphere sparked artistic and literary works full of terror, foreboding, angst, violence, and death. German Expressionism presented images of the chase, dark narrow alleys of terror and subjugation, and ghoulish death-in-life—humans with long angular bodies and still longer nails for drawing blood from innocent victims. Artists who shared a taste neither for ideology nor for military-style behavior ventured into this morass, writing "low-brow" pulp novels and musical comedies condemned by intellectuals as trivial and vulgar. Writers such as Hermann Hesse, who after World War I reached for peaceful answers in Buddhist philosophy and consciously stayed above the political fray, became disillusioned for a lifetime. In 1919 the author of *Demian* and later *Siddhartha* took up permanent residence in a mountain refuge in Montagnola, Switzerland, unwilling to live in what he perceived to be the increasingly chilling atmosphere of Germany. Hesse removed himself from German society, extinguished "the sentimental streak" in his love of Germany, and turned instead to "organic" nature, confident that his "individualism and . . . rejection and hatred of certain Germanic attitudes and phrases to be functions in the exercise of which I serve not only myself but my people as well."[11]

By the mid-1920s a bloodless civil war was being fought among German writers in their newspapers, literary magazines, and journals. The battle lines were less clear among the suffering German masses who clamored for solutions rather than rhetoric to their gargantuan economic problems. Writers divided into two major camps: devout pacifists and/or antinationalists like Hermann Hesse and Heinrich Mann, and pro-German nationalists represented by writers such as Hanns Johst and Hans Grimm, whose 1926 novel *Volk ohne Raum* (*A Nation without Room*) furnished the Nazi slogan for world conquest.[12]

The right-wing nationalists saw hope, vivacity, and strength in fascism, and defined it as an ideal which spoke to the younger generation. They chose to ignore or disregard the systematic violence committed by radical right-wing youth and instead praised fascism's "healthy, creative spirit."[13] Known as *Blut und Boden* (blood and soil) writers, these nationalists aimed their repugnance at the Left, which they claimed would bring class warfare to Germany and thus was Germany's "real enemy." In retrospect, this all-encompassing "Left" was a deftly crafted abstraction used by the radical Right to divide Germany into a nation of self-righteous monsters and their victims.

Thomas Mann was the most visible and highly esteemed among those German artists who had staked Germany's future on peace, freedom, and justice, predicting it would be the legacy of World War I. His fierce love of and faith in Germany and German culture seemed to render him invulnerable to both disillusionment and criticism from reactionary peers. Indeed, as the threat to German democracy grew through the frantic, violent 1920s, so did Mann's resounding faith in Germany's innate humanity. German republicanism, together with bourgeois pride, had become the unshakable essence of his German identity.

Mann's "apolitical humanism," as he called his message, was widely attacked in German newspapers and magazines for being anti-German, but Mann was undaunted by the criticism. By now he had forged an unswerving belief in the unity of humane man and his state. He took this political vision to an international audience with the publication of *The Magic Mountain*, a novel he began before the war and finished in the winter of 1922–23. At a Swiss sanitorium symbolizing prewar decadent Europe, Mann's Hans Castorp is facing death from tuberculosis, when he reluctantly realizes that man is a "sublime structure," capable of exalted, "mystical," "metaphysical" joy and sensuality, if only he acts kindly and freely. He rejects decadence and death and chooses life and service to humanity.

The Magic Mountain was published in 1924 to resounding applause among Germany's educated class and abroad, but German nationalists, who had thought Mann one of them, felt betrayed. In the increasingly hermetic, zealously self-guarded world of German society, a writer like Mann, who envisioned the true

German patriot as a kind of universal, free-thinking aristocrat, aroused enemies among right-wing observers who lacked those very characteristics, yet whose power was building exponentially at the end of the decade. When Mann rejected a bid to join the German Nationalist Party in the summer of 1928, even bourgeois writers preached to Mann that he was making a big career blunder. Old critics emboldened by the times lashed out as never before, accusing him of holding himself above his peers because he was rich and famous.[14]

Indeed, as the 1920s drew to a close, Thomas Mann had achieved the kind of rarefied fame grasped by only a handful of novelists. *Buddenbrooks, Tonio Kroger, Death in Venice*, and *The Magic Mountain*—all intensely intelligent, sensitive, psychological, and gorgeously constructed novels, novellas, and short stories—were translated and in print around the world. Mann was a literary virtuoso, delivering speeches throughout Europe which were paeans to his philosophical, literary, or musical idols—Goethe, Schiller, Wagner, Nietzsche, and Schopenhauer. Then in 1929, at the age of fifty-four, Thomas Mann won the Nobel Prize for literature.

That same year Mann's beloved Germany exploded apoplectically, rent by a decade of political reactionism, economic despair, and an identity crisis at all levels of German society. Mann was at work on a humanistic adaptation of the biblical story of Joseph when the world's worst economic crisis left millions of Germans unemployed and hundreds of thousands on the verge of starvation. The president of the Weimar Republic, Gustav Streseman, died, and the Republic seemed to be drawing its last breath as well. By guaranteeing political freedom to a people in chaos, the framers of the Weimar Constitution had sown the seeds of their own demise. In the national elections of 1930, twenty-eight political parties were listed. By 1932, the National Socialist Party (Nationalsozialistische Deutsche Arbeiter-Partie), led by Adolf Hitler, had become the largest single political party in Germany.

Thomas Mann ventured forth into the dangerous waters of reactionary Germany emotionally armed and shielded like his biblical Jacob, "the man of the blessing," as Mann called him, who "by nature, rank and inheritance, as son of his fathers," is prepared to battle all forces of opposition.[15] Mann's ability to immerse himself in his fiction no matter how the world teetered around him, how critics skewered him, or how anxiety shook his equilibrium was a gift of infinite bounty. From the beginning of his career, artistic creation was for him a bulwark against suffering from external as well as internal causes.

Intensely emotional, Mann nevertheless had acquired extraordinary personal resources as the pampered son of a wealthy council senator of prosperous Lübeck, then a free state in northernmost Germany, and for centuries the capital of the Hanseatic League. Mann's father was the scion of an old Lübeck merchant family, and Mann was reared amidst beauty, refinement, and culture. His family's large patrician home was filled with art, music, literature, lively political conversation, good food, drink, and fine clothes—all the best that nineteenth-century European bourgeois life had to offer.[16] In 1901, at the age of twenty-six, Mann had shattered the crystalline surface of the German bourgeoisie in his first novel, *Buddenbrooks*, which, after initially slow sales, catapulted the young writer to fame and a small fortune. The novel depicts a world so obsessed by tradition's strictures and pretensions that its victims wither in a stifling life of preordained successes and hardships, births and deaths. For those truly unlucky ones with an artistic calling, this life becomes a emotional minefield of misery, sickness, and finally, death.

Even in this early novel, Mann demonstrated his predilection for showing both sides of the coin, or at least to balance one thought or feeling with its opposite. Wealth and tradition may have suffocated many a rich man in Mann's early observation, but *Buddenbrooks* also showed that the bourgeois world unquestionably offered its select membership character-building gifts to temper the pain of life. Unshakable values of family, home, and tradition, combined with financial ease and cultural plenty, imbued Mann with a powerful sense of invulnerability, specialness, success, and security. "Had not this carefree childhood known the best of both worlds—the perfection of culture as well as almost perfect freedom," Mann's son Klaus wrote in a veiled description of his father's early life in his novel *Mephisto*, published in Amsterdam in 1936, after Klaus fled the Nazis.[17] As Mann passed from middle into old age through the German national crisis and ensuing debacle, he clung more and more to his sense of unassailable tradition and ancestry—an ideal inseparable from justice and decency, which he believed the German people must never forsake.

A defining schism grew within the German literati in the fall and winter of 1930–31, when the head of the prestigious Prussian Academy of Arts, archnationalist Wilhelm Schafer, organized ninety-three members to sign a proclamation calling for the resignation of "less active members"—their euphemism for non-nationalists. Hermann Hesse, who had been an ambivalent member of the Academy's Section of Literature since its founding in 1926, felt he was witnessing a bizarre reprise of the German madness which had driven him away in 1919, and he resigned from the Academy.[18] He predicted that only the "Bolshevization of Germany" would solve the country's economic, social, and political problems, and since that could not happen without a terrible fight, the very worst was yet to come.[19]

A little more than a month after his resignation, Heinrich Mann, who had just been elected president of Section for Literature, also resigned. Yet, unlike Hesse and his brother Heinrich, Thomas Mann retained his membership in the Academy, as well as in other cultural organizations which had also begun to acquire a nationalistic shading.[20] Mann was repulsed by the nationalists and considered himself far more patriotic than those who spewed their steady stream of nationalist rhetoric, but he was not willing to align himself on the other side, with pacifists and "bolsheviks." His allegiance was strictly and passionately to the German Republic of the pre-extremist bourgeois era. In October 1930 Mann had warned of the dangers of Nazism in his address, "An Appeal to Reason." He had told his audience in Berlin's Beethoven Hall that responsibility for German's future rested upon its bourgeoisie, who must unite with the socialist working classes to fight national socialism. Nazi hecklers in the upper gallery unsuccessfully tried to stop the speech, a near-riot ensued, and Mann and his wife were forced to flee the hall through rear passageways and escaped by jumping into a waiting car.[21] Nevertheless, Mann still believed there was no need to take strong action; German national character would set things right without his intervention.

In part, Mann's feeling stemmed from an acute self-consciousness as the winner of the 1929 Nobel Prize—an award he viewed both as a great triumph and terrific burden. Mann felt strongly that his voluntary rejection of honoraria and honorary posts in protest of German right-wing reactionism would convey his stinging indictment of Germany to the world at large. Mann dispelled any suggestion that he make official public protest out of his deep sense of German honor, cultural heritage, and hope for rebuilding the German future, which in his mind dictated a responsibility to safeguard the old, rather than rebuke the new.

In this frame of mind, Thomas Mann, who had known Hermann Hesse since 1904, when they were introduced by their mutual publisher, Samuel Fischer of Berlin, tried to win his friend back to the Academy, appealing to his sense of "social obligation."[22] Hesse told Mann he mistrusted the German Republic too strongly to rejoin. He recalled vividly the rampages in 1919 in Berlin when right-wing nationalists murdered German Communist Party founders Rosa Luxemburg and Karl Liebknecht, and Bavarian Republic founder Kurt Eisner. He cited the murder in 1921 of Catholic politician Matthias Erzberger and the assassination in 1922 of then–foreign minister Walter Rathenau, a Jew accused by nationalists of selling out Germany in war reparations. Hesse believed that all of this had transpired "with the approval of ninety-nine percent of the population."[23] Unlike Mann, he saw honorable republicans as helpless against a German public which refused to acknowledge guilt for World War I, or even that they had "signed the Treaty of Versailles." Hesse told Mann he found circumstances in Germany "absurd" and could no longer stand to read a German newspaper.

Though Mann would later hail Hesse's extraordinary foresight, at the time he merely respected his colleague's decision. The men continued their correspondence, commiserating with each other over "hate letters" they received from right-wing reactionaries and nationalists. In the summer of 1932, a young man from Königsberg sent Mann a charred copy of *Buddenbrooks*, alleging Mann had written something derogatory about Hitler. Undoubtedly the man's reference was to Mann's comically scathing depiction of the beer-guzzling, loden-jacketed Munich hops dealer, Herr Permaneder, a southern German buffoon who uses German idioms rather than the more dignified standard German of the north. Mann of course wrote *Buddenbrooks* in 1900 and set the story deep in the 1800s, before Hitler was born. Mann saved the charred remains of the book, declaring in late December, "someday they will bear witness to the German people's state of mind in the year 1932."[24]

Mann still felt he had cause to be hopeful that Hitler's popularity was a passing fad. He never believed Hitler would wield power. In the final months of 1932 Mann seemed to be taunting Hitler, declaring in print and speech his belief that Nazism was a "national disease." Citing the recent elections of November 6 in which the Nazi party lost thirty-four seats after their stunning win of 230 seats the previous July 31 (37.4 percent of all those who went to the polls), Mann wrote Hesse, "The worst is over, I think. The madness seems to have passed its peak, and if we live long enough we shall witness happier days."[25]

In December 1932 and January 1933, Mann set aside work on his second Joseph novel to write a lecture on Richard Wagner, the revolutionary and controversial creative force behind the operas *Tristan und Isolde, Lohengrin,* and

The Ring of the Nibelungs, and one of Mann's artistic heros. Wagner's music—big, loud, passionate, threading together ancient German cultural myths in a fever pitch of love, hate, war, and death—inspired fidelity and fascination in Mann decades before Adolf Hitler fell in love with the composer and adopted him as the artistic symbol of the Third Reich. Mann, who increasingly found himself defending his loyalty to the composer to incredulous friends, had maintained an ambivalent devotion to Wagner, as though he had been a childhood best friend who had hurt everyone else, but had remained true to him. Inherent in Wagner's greatest artistic strengths, his passion and naturalness, lay his most terrible artistic weaknesses, according to Mann—"swagger and histrionics," for which Mann only slightly forgave him. But Mann categorically denied the charge that Wagner, an anti-Semite, was also anti-intellectual. To the contrary, Mann, who borrowed much of his recurring leitmotif technique from Wagner, argued that Wagner was a supremely intellectual composer, employing a brilliant and revolutionary interplay of psychology, myth, and music to portray "the first and furthest of our human picture-dreamings."[26] Mann even went so far as to assert that *The Flying Dutchman*, with its evocation of the mother complex, sexual desire, and fear, made Wagner the equal of Sigmund Freud, who as revolutionary psychoanalyst and Jew, had become an "enemy" of the Fatherland.

Mann clearly understood why Wagner's bombastic grandeur and use of German myth had been seized upon by right-wing German nationalists. Nevertheless, he was deeply offended and contemptuous of the Nazis' embrace of his icon, and intended through this essay to shatter the false Nazi imagery built up around the composer and thereby reveal the "true" Wagner—an artist firmly planted in the bourgeois epoch, who viewed art as a means of salvation for a corrupted society. Mann charged that the nationalists, out of their own anti-intellectuality and self-interest, had twisted Wagner into a standard-bearer for German world ascendance, when in reality, according to Mann, Wagner inhabited a purely creative sphere and was completely removed from politics, indifferent to the idea of a powerful German state and feeling no "ulterior patriotic emotion."[27] Mann asserted that Wagner's interest in history was, like his own, an interest in greater humanity and its primitive foundations, and that his interest in myth was in the universal and not the narrowly nationalistic. In an especially stinging rebuke to Hitler's hypocritical contempt for bourgeois comfort, Mann quoted the composer's personal letters describing his happiness during an exceptionally creative stay in an elegant asylum near Zurich. In truth, Wagner was an inveterate high-liver and overspender, and once fled Vienna to avoid debtors' prison. Mann wrote in his essay that the bourgeois Wagner needed "degeneracy to create the myths which gladden the German youths' heart."[28]

The lecture Mann was preparing was astonishingly bold in the context of the day—a literary whipping of German nationalists—though Mann had no idea when he wrote it in the last days of the German Second Reich that it was dangerously so. Indeed, Mann was sanguine enough that the Social Democrats would hold onto the government that he took his usual rest before embarking on a lecture tour in the Bavarian Alpine resort village of Garmisch-Partenkirchen, just north of the Austria border. Mann was in Garmisch when, as he was later to describe Hitler's legal election on January 30, 1933, "the catastrophe struck," stunning him and millions of other Germans.[29]

Mann delivered the lecture "Sufferings and Greatness of Richard Wagner" at the University of Munich on February 10, 1933, the fiftieth anniversary of the composer's death. Accompanied by his wife, Katia, Mann reprised his performance in Amsterdam, Brussels, and Paris. After Paris, the couple arrived on February 26 in the village of Arosa in the Graubunden region of western Switzerland for what had been planned as a rest before returning home to Munich. The rest lasted all of a day. On the night of February 27, the Reichstag building in Berlin, home of the German legislature, was gutted by fire. Hitler charged that the fire was set by a twenty-four-year-old Dutch, card-carrying Communist and his accomplices, though it has always been suspected that Hermann Goering and Joseph Goebbels, Hitler's top henchmen, orchestrated the fire as a pretext for the massive arrests of Communists which were immediately carried out with especial brutality.[30] Moreover, Hitler used the Reichstag fire as his excuse for the suspension by emergency decree on February 28 of all constitutional guarantees of individual freedom, freedom of the press, post, and private property.

Overnight, Berlin looked like an armed camp, as hundreds of armed Nazi soldiers were dispatched to police the streets, arbitrarily assaulting, arresting, and even murdering citizens. Mann and his wife were warned by friends not to return to their house in Munich until the atmosphere calmed down. But there was to be no calm, and the Reichstag fire remained for Thomas Mann the seminal, symbolic event of the entire epoch. Mann often referred to it in later years as the "swindle" and "foul deception" upon which the Third Reich was founded.[31]

And thus, Hitler's Reich wrote its law, and so began the long term of Mann's wandering, like Joseph and his father, Jacob, before him. Left behind in Munich were a life's worth of personal papers and diaries, which, among many inflammatory and excruciating intimacies, documented Mann's homosexual yearnings.

Despite Mann's initial expectation that circumstances in Germany would swiftly be restored to some semblance of normalcy, it very quickly became clear that things were only going to get worse. Especially in the cities, confusion reigned. Many whose race, religion, politics, or work rendered them the slightest bit suspect to the Nazi authorities, fled in desperation, without plan or destination. Passports of Jews were revoked, while others were held in frantic limbo as the government intentionally failed to act on requests.

Bavaria, Mann's state, had fiercely resisted a Nazi takeover longer than any other, through its Catholic Bavarian People's Party, but on March 9, 1933, Hitler sent armed detachments of privately trained storm troopers, called the S.A. (Sturmabteilung) and the S.S. (Schuztstaffel), into Munich, and a swastika was hung from the city hall tower. Longtime Bavarian Minister-President Dr. Heinrich Held remained stalwart, but his resistance collapsed under a general fear of civil war and the realization of powerlessness against such a formidable Nazi leviathan. Hitler invoked the February 28 Emergency Ordinance, forced Held to resign on March 12, and installed General Ritter von Epp, a longtime Hitler ally, as his Nazi representative in Bavaria.

In Switzerland, Mann received reports of "idiocies and atrocities" from his eldest children in Munich, and friends warned him that "recognizable members" of the Mann family might not be safe if they returned to the city.[32] Though Mann had every intention of returning to live in Munich, where fourteen-year-old

Michael and fifteen-year-old Elizabeth were still attending school, his single effort in those frantic months was aimed at renewing his passport, which was due to expire April 1. Mann feared that the Nazis would keep him from returning to Germany by refusing to renew, providing a legal basis for confiscating his house and possessions.

Katia's passport was still in effect, and Mann considered sending her to Munich to retrieve some of their belongings and apply for his passport renewal. But Katia, who was Jewish, had been warned not to return to Munich, partly because of her renowned outspokenness, and partly because the Nazis were confiscating passports of wives in order to force the return of their husbands. So Mann instead gave the task of arranging for the passports, as well as for the transfer of money to Switzerland, to his old family friend, Dr. Hans Feist, who had "personal connections with 'the Party,'" according to Mann.[33]

With little else that he could do, and far from Munich, Mann felt helpless and fearful of the future. His anxiety mounted daily as government-sanctioned atrocities surged that March and a death shadow fell over Germany. With the banning of opposition and left-wing newspapers and cultural periodicals like Berlin's *Das Tage-Buch* and *Die Weltbuhne*, Mann kept abreast of events, reading newspapers like the *Vossische Zeitung*, which had been turned into a Nazi propaganda sheet, spewing anti-Semitic, anti-Communist hate. From newspapers printed outside Germany, like *Neue Zurcher Zeitung*, a Zurich newspaper, Mann read in shock of arrests, deaths, "and other horrors"—the daily slanders against Social Democratic politicians, writers, and artists—anyone who was not a Nazi. Papers described the mistreatment of Jews, their removal from legal and medical positions, and the establishment of the Dachau concentration camp outside Munich for communists and socialists. At the end of March, German citizens became subject to "certificates of political reliability" in order to move freely.

By the middle of March, Mann realized it was dangerous for him to be anywhere in Germany, but he vacillated with frantic uncertainty as to where to go; hourly he seemed to entertain notions of new destinations. "I feel a rush of fear at the thought of being separated from my family," he wrote in his diary from Arosa on March 16. He declined a friend's invitation to visit in Italy, citing "the friendship between the German and Italian governments," but Austria, too, was out of the question, according to reports from friends who had been there. Austria "on the whole is sinister and to be avoided," he concluded. Mann still hoped he could return to Germany, perhaps in a year, though he probably knew it was a pipe dream, since he now believed it would take almost a miracle to bring down Hitler.

After a tumultuous process of elimination, the Manns decided they would wait for their passports in Lugano, in the very southern tuck of Switzerland, near the Italian border and within driving distance of Hermann Hesse's home in Montagnola, in the Ticino region. Mann's friends, writer Bruno Frank and seventy-one-year-old Ludwig Fulda—both Jews—had already fled to Lugano, but all three men considered it only a temporary holding station.[34] Mann was unsure where he would settle, but thought Locarno or Zurich might be the final destination.

When Mann departed from Arosa and headed for Lugano on March 18, 1933, his tears as he said goodbye hinted at the full-blown crisis of nerves he was experiencing. He was plagued by anxiety, sleeplessness, and despair. "Horrible sense of frenzy, helplessness, twitching muscles, almost a shivering fit, and feared losing my rational faculties," Mann recorded in his diary en route.[35] A local Hungarian-Swiss doctor prescribed a sedative, Adalin, which Mann took with peppermint tea in the evening. Before bedtime, he took Phanodorm, another sedative.[36]

On March 23, 1933, while the Manns were still en route, Parliament passed Hitler's Enabling Act, which structured local governments on the Reichstag model and consolidated Hitler's power over local government. Nationalists hailed the act as the long-sought attainment of German unity, since it abolished the power of the separate German states. In fact, it signified disaster for Germany, because it provided the legal basis for Hitler's absolute dictatorship. The act immediately targeted Jews, calling for the revocation of passports, a systematic boycott of Jewish-owned businesses, which were now to be designated with the infamous yellow Star of David, and the establishment of disproportionately minute quotas for Jews in the academic and legal professions, based upon the entire population. The chief Nazi Party newspaper *Volkischer Beobachter* carried a proposal by a doctor to have Jews sterilized.

Mann was incredulous that the German people had not only elected "an idiot" to lead the country, but also were now handing him further power. In fact, the act was passed by means of intense extortionist tactics by Hitler, who sent his S.A. and S.S. troops to parliament, where they hovered beside opposition benches, bore swastikas, and sang the national anthem at the end of Hitler's speech. The act immediately affected Mann, who had been told that his passport renewal was awaiting the signature of a "political review officer" of the police passport division. As a result of these events, as well as firsthand accounts of atrocities he received from friends in Germany, many of whom were Jewish, Mann tended to believe a Swiss newspaper writer who had written that if Mann were in Germany he would be "in the Dachau concentration camp by now."[37]

Meanwhile, his hatred for the Nazis continued to fester. Mann suspected that they were withholding his passport in order to "ruin" him. He privately boasted to friends that he was prepared to do everything he could to help bring about Hitler's downfall. "Intense desire for this," he wrote in his diary, "prepared to make every sacrifice, share any suffering. No personal ruin would be too high a price to pay for the ruin of this common scum!"[38] Mann was anticipating a personal struggle between himself and "the hostile, malevolent, threatening forces" which had taken over Germany.[39]

Occasionally for Mann moments of black humor arose from the gruesome hard-to-believe, as when in early April 1933, the Munich Rotary Club ejected him, the self-proclaimed "jewel of their organization." Mostly, the days were unremittingly grim and nerve-wracking. Until spring 1933 Mann had doubted that war would be necessary to end Hitler's seizure of power. Rather, he believed that economic crisis or foreign pressure would bring about his downfall. By mid-April, Mann had come to an understanding that Hitler intended to use whatever means necessary to stay in power. "I consider that the only effective means of toppling the leadership would be war," he confided in his diary.[40] No matter what the outcome, Mann envisioned tragedy for his country, and as he continued working on *Young Joseph* throughout the upheaval, Mann knew that he would write about Germany's pact with the devil in a work based on Goethe's *Faust* when he finished his Joseph story.[41] In these earliest days of the Third Reich, Mann possessed—though he did not realize it at the time—his complete personal and artistic vision of a long-term German future: "The baldly modern, fast-moving, futuristic approach put to the service of an anti-future, a philosophy devoid of all ideas, a mammoth advertising campaign for nothingness."[42]

Amid his fear and mistrust, Mann tried to fathom what his role was to be for this refashioned nation, its people, and its exiles. While it was true that Hitler moved fast to suppress voices of opposition within Germany, there was still dissent in the early days of the regime, but always at a terrific cost. Left-leaning or pacifist writers and defenders of the Republic disappeared, taken to concentration camps, or left dead on the street, as the S.S. went systematically down the long "blacklists" that the Nazis had been compiling for nearly a decade.[43] During the volatile 1920s, Thomas Mann had pretentiously assumed the role of German spokesman, rejecting off-center intellectuals whom he felt were unqualified to proclaim German democracy. He had judged his works to be definitively "German" and insisted that he was "genuine enough, has enough of a national 'nature' to be permitted to say a word or two, with specific and carefully considered motives, as spokesman for the 'world of intellect'—without tumbling into 'literary vacuity.' "[44] Mann wrongly believed, too, that he could be the spokesman for Germany's nationalistic youth.

Mann's willingness to oppose the Nazis' attack on freedom in these early days of the Reich was in practical fact little more than disingenuous self-martyrdom. He was in Lugano, more than six hundred miles from Berlin, and not planning imminent return; yet, on April 2 he proclaimed with monumental conceit that "no one in Germany feels my outrage and disgust at the truly swinish methods by which this 'people's movement' won its victory!" He asked himself, "Is my role merely that of an Erasmus vis-à-vis a new Lutheranism?"[45] (Erasmus tried to reform the Roman Catholic clergy, refusing to follow Martin Luther's revolt because he believed in the unity of Christendom.)

Mann's role seemed limited to his tortured observation of events taking place in Germany. He was not immolating himself on the streets of Berlin, but neither was he fabricating the utter failure of his fellow intellectuals, whom he asserted "showed an inadequate intellectual grasp of the situation."[46] Like millions of politically exhausted Germans who did not support Hitler, many intellectuals had believed that parliamentary methods and the Weimar Constitution would keep the Nazis in check. They fully expected the Reichswehr to assert its power and establish a military dictatorship or to form an alliance with the Catholic Bavarian People's Party, ignoring the fact that the army's commanders had taken no action when Hitler was appointed chancellor over their bitter objection. Mann expected nothing of the sort. He was devastated by the betrayal of so many intellectuals who went over to the Nazi side. Despite the fact that his Wagner lecture appeared in full in the April issue of the journal *Die Neue Rundschau*, Mann was aware of the suppression of outlets for expression and influence, and wondered how the intelligentsia could continue to "register its criticism, at least for history?"[47] He got his answer soon enough.

On April 16, 1933, Nazi authorities directed a public protest of Mann's Wagner lecture by prominent fellow artists and intellectuals. It now became clear that the

Nazis intended to ruin Mann, using many of his own Munich colleagues to do it. The "manifesto" against Mann appeared in the Easter issue of the *Münchner Neueste Nachrichten* under the title "Protest of the Richard Wagner City of Munich." Among the protest's illustrious signers were the composers Richard Strauss and Hans Pfitzer, whose best-known work, the 1917 romantic opera *Palestrina*, had impressed Mann as much as Wagner's operas when he first heard it.[48] The Bavarian cultural minister, the president of the Academy of Fine Arts, and the director of the Bavarian State Theatre were also among those who added their names to the protest. Mann, who was outraged, wrote a reply and submitted it to the *Frankfurter Zeitung*, the *Neue Freie Press*, the *Deutsche Allgemeine Zeitung*, and the *Vossische Zeitung*. All four newspapers published Mann's reply, but protests lodged in Germany by non-nationalist writers in Mann's defense were suppressed. The protest prompted an outcry in other European countries.

It was during this time of uncertainty and isolation that Hermann Hesse began to fill a major role in Mann's life. The two men had first been introduced in 1904 by their mutual publisher, Samuel Bermann Fischer, but for two decades their divergent lifestyles and political positions regarding the German Republic had limited their relationship to one of mutual professional respect. Mann was the bourgeois family man, upholder of tradition and law; Hesse had thrown over bourgeois respectability in countless ways and was the iconoclastic poet-dreamer and philosopher-anarchist. Hesse had turned to Jungian psychoanalysis and Buddhism for answers after suffering a nervous breakdown in 1916, and had concluded that political neutrality was the only sane tack a moral man could take. Mann, on the other hand, had turned to Goethe, Wagner and Nietzsche, confident that the German political process would always reflect credos of decency and fairness, finding the delicate balance between sterile reason and decadent spirit.

With the darkening of the German landscape, the two men were drawn to one another because, for both, life was inseparable from art and thought. Their kindred yearning was to understand, if not reconcile, man's daily, often tragic struggle to merge the life of the spirit with the life of the mind. Mann cherished in the poetic Hesse a rare love of truth, wisdom, conscience, erudition, and spirituality —those very same qualities which Hesse saw in Mann—and he now realized that his friend had won his spiritual freedom largely by detaching himself from German politics after World War I. A vibrant dream-nature simmered beneath Mann's granite veneer of intellectuality, and though Mann consistently tried to quell inner forces of opposition, he always failed in the end because at his core he was the same kind of gentle, mystical individualist as Hesse.

Thus, when Hitler's reign forced Mann to break with Germany as Hesse had done after World War I, Hesse uniquely understood the inner turmoil his friend suffered. During his time in Lugano, Mann visited Hesse regularly in nearby Montagnola. Hesse's tranquil dogma, as expressed in his 1933 poem "Taking Stock"—"not judgement and not hate,/But patient love/And patient tolerance lead/Us closer to the sacred goal"—soothed a brooding, angry Mann when he was most vulnerable.[49]

In late April 1933, Mann's house in Munich was searched for weapons, and his automobiles were confiscated. Fearing that seizure of his personal papers was imminent, Mann's housekeeper packed some possessions in a trunk, including his precious diaries, and gave them to Mann's Munich lawyer, Valentin Heins, who arranged a rendezvous with Mann at a hotel in Rohrschach-Hafen, near the German-Swiss border. When Nazi police were informed—presumably by Heins's chauffeur—that the suitcase had been smuggled to Switzerland, Mann, Heins, and the Manns's twenty-four-years-old son, Gottfried, devised a story that it had been stolen. Though now in possession of his diaries, Mann was scarcely comforted. Perhaps rereading them in this electric atmosphere of danger and secrecy made their bold sexual and political confidences seem all the more dangerous. Mann, sleepless and nervous, wrote in his diary: "My fears now revolve first and fore-most almost exclusively around this threat to my life's secrets. They are deeply serious. The consequences could be terrible, even fatal."[50]

Mann understood that the possibility of grave danger lay before him even away from Germany, and he felt trapped in a confusing web of bourgeois insecurity, nationalistic self-identity, and the more basic human antipathy for rootlessness. He despaired at the prospect of living away from his native country and particularly at the lower standard of living he would be forced to adopt. Initially, he had been reluctant to withdraw his cash and other assets, consisting largely of his Nobel Prize winnings, from his bank in Germany. The move had seemed too permanent and an act of disloyalty to a country Mann still loved. With the April "manifesto" against him, however, Mann realized that any more hesitation on his part could prove financially disastrous. The Nazis held a wide and powerful reach over Germans' finances; the payment of royalties to writers living abroad became ille-gal, as did the use of capital deposited in foreign banks. Under the advice of a Zurich financier, Richard Tennenbaum—"the little Jew Tennenbaum," Mann called him—Mann secretly transferred part of his estate to Switzerland. Nevertheless, with each week, Mann's German gold bonds lost a percentage of their value in Switzerland—60 per cent by mid-June—a loss compounded by the expense of living in hotels and eating in restaurants. Mann felt pressure to conserve the 200,000 Swiss francs (equivalent to about $60,000) that he had on deposit in the Crédit Suisse and to come to some decision about a residence. Yet, when he inspected rental property in Basel, he was thrown into a state of nervous despair.

"I was not feeling well and the impression the house made on me of a ghastly and dreary déclassé existence so aggravated my state that back at the hotel my nerves collapsed, bringing on tears," he wrote on May 3.[51] The previous two days had been among the most trying. In Germany, Hitler had turned the traditional May Day festivities into a diabolical farce, offering workers a paid holiday and lulling one hundred thousand of them and their leaders at a "Day of Labor" show at Berlin's Tempelhof Airfield into thinking he was on their side. The following day, Hitler dissolved all trade unions, ordering their funds confiscated, and their union officials arrested. (This was a political reprisal against the one hundred thousand workers who demonstrated in Berlin on January 29, 1933, against Hitler's becoming chancellor.) But there was more. The Nazi authorities sus-pended twenty-nine university professors in Berlin and Cologne, including Katia Mann's brother, Peter, a well-respected physics professor.

With the pressure increasing on Mann to come to a decision as to where he would live, his vacillation became tortured, and ultimately he rejected Basel, at the convergence of the French, Swiss, and German borders, as well as inland

Bern. The Manns decided not to settle anywhere for the time being, preferring to remain mobile and near friends. Since France had agreed to grant Mann a residence permit, and Heinrich Mann had already settled in Nice after his Munich home was "sequestered" and his Berlin assets were confiscated, the Manns decided to ride out the summer on the Riviera. Possibly they would return to Basel in the fall, although Mann dreaded the thought.

Still without a valid passport, Mann and his family arrived in southern France on May 6. They lived in hotels in a variety of small coastal towns near Toulon for more than a month until they moved into a rented villa in the village of Sanary-sur-Mer, a few miles west of Toulon. The villa, ironically, was named "La Tranquille." Back in Germany, Hitler's intensified barrage against seemingly untouchable German cultural icons made even more remote the prospect of Mann's return at any time in the foreseeable future. On May 10, Goebbels' Propaganda Ministry staged a book-burning on the Opernplatz in Berlin and in public squares all over Germany. Blacklisted were works by leftists like Marx and Trotsky, democrats like Hugo Preuss, the father of the Weimar Constitution, and Jews like Kafka, Albert Einstein, and Sigmund Freud. Their writings were reduced to ashes, as were "degenerate literary works" by Bertolt Brecht, Alexander Doblin, Hermann Hesse, Heinrich Heine, August Strindberg, and Thomas and Heinrich Mann.

A sense of desperation and danger swirled around the Mann family. Mann's son Gottfried, nicknamed Golo, had already fled to Berlin after the Nazis confiscated his car, and on May 10, Mann received word that the car had been left stripped in front of the family's Munich home on Poschingerstrasse—"obviously a provocation," Mann wrote astringently.[52] Mann asked his friend Felix Bertraux to convey ninety thousand marks (about $27,000) out of Munich secretly as soon as Golo and Mann's twenty-three-year-old daughter Monika had arrived in France safely.

Mann felt shipwrecked. Under no circumstances did he want to become an exile, and exile loomed before him like an interminable sentence. In a letter to Albert Einstein, who had also been out of Germany at the time Hitler came to power, Mann wrote on May 15, 1933, "the breach with my country, which is almost unavoidable, fills me with depression and dread—a sign that it does not fit my nature which has been formed by electment of the Goethean tradition of representation, so that I cannot feel I was destined for martyrdom. For me to have been forced into this role, something thoroughly wrong and evil must surely have taken place."[53]

Considering that imprisonment or death likely awaited Mann in Germany, the Manns fashioned a pleasant, if nervous, existence on the Riviera. Many German intellectuals had relocated to southern France and in these dark days after Hitler's rise to power Mann's acquaintance with such men as banned novelist Lion Feuchtwanger, pacifist magazine editor Réné Schickele, and art historian Julius Meier-Graefe flowered into abiding friendships rooted in a common, uniquely German bond of misery, uncertainty, alienation, and outrage. In *Joseph in Egypt*, Mann would write: "the content of kinship is always the same: it is the idea of a catastrophe, the invasion of destructive and wanton forces into an ordered scheme and a life bent upon self-control and a happiness conditioned by it."[54]

In the evenings after work, visitors like Aldous Huxley read from their works-in-progress. Buoyed by clear blue French skies, sunny mornings, and cool, breezy afternoons, the exiles attempted to carry on life as usual, taking scenic drives through the sensuous coastal towns and lunching at cafés, but their efforts were marked by grief and restlessness. They remained glued to news of events back in Germany, praying that if they remained patient and calm, sanity would be restored, and they could go home. But they had no illusions. As though in freeze-frame they saw the "new" Germany: the ascendance of the uneducated, uncultured lower-middle class spewing race-hatred in the streets; Nazi thugs wreaking unremitting terror; trumped-up "corruption" trials; a swollen bureaucracy, based in violence and extortion—"the rule of simple force, which makes mockery of all legality," as Mann wrote.[55] He no longer likened the German revolution to the political and social upheavals underway in Italy and Russia, but saw it as the unique and sinister tyranny of a demonic megalomaniac.[56]

Mann rested easier once Katia had finally obtained a valid passport covering herself and their children through the German consul at Marseilles, although by now they had no intention of her returning to Germany for money or property. With the grace period for withdrawing funds from Germany due to expire September 1, 1933, at which time Germans living abroad were summoned to return or face confiscation of property, Mann faced the bitter finality he had tried to avoid since January: confiscation of his house, assets, and most important, German citizenship. Mann wavered between feelings of hopefulness about his work and new life and gloom that he would become "weary of life" as it lay uncertainly before him. This was not the expression of a suicidal nature, but of a man who had turned fifty-eight on June 6, 1933, whose beloved country had been seized by an "idiotic" madman and who was gripped by the painful disparity of youthful hopes and dreams and the disappointing reality. Mann acknowledged that he had been fortunate in his life and that many of his dreams had come true, yet he felt an overwhelming sense that "not much ever changes."[57] This was one of the central themes of his Joseph story, in which life-experience—both good and evil—repeats infinitely down through the generations. In *Young Joseph*, the second volume of his story, Mann had written that even "world revolutions" represented "repetitions of the past" and "everlasting recurrence."[58] Now, in a decidedly more vicious reprise of the "bottomless" past, it seemed not a week passed without Mann's nationalist colleagues denouncing him on patriotic as well as artistic grounds. Perhaps the most dangerous accusation was leveled by the Reich Agency for the Promotion of German Literature on October 10, 1933, alleging "pacifistic excesses" and "intellectual high treason," as a result of Mann's contribution to his son Klaus's literary and political journal for exiles, *Die Sammlung (The Collection)*, which had begun monthly publication in Amsterdam that previous September, with sponsorship from André Gide and Heinrich Mann. This charge, which seriously threatened the publication of *Tales of Jacob*, was subsequently rescinded after Mann's publisher submitted a statement in which Mann distanced himself from his son's journal.[59]

The summer of 1933 marked a decisive point in Hitler's consolidation of power in Germany as he moved to eradicate those organizations which had lingered feebly until now to oppose him. The tenacious Catholic Bavarian People's Party had dissolved itself after being ejected from the government on March 9. Then, on June 21, the S.S. closed the offices of the pro-business, pro-army German National Party, which had helped Hitler ascend to the chancellorship the previous January. On June 22, the Social Democratic Party was dissolved. These moves culminated in Hitler's July 14 decree announcing: "The National Socialist German Workers' Party constitutes the only political party in Germany." By the end of July, after months of indecision, Mann decided once and for all he could not return to Germany.

Though just weeks earlier he had deemed Switzerland dangerous, calling it "German" Switzerland, his feelings of nostalgia for his homeland now led him to reconsider the country precisely because of its "atmosphere of German culture and language." After obtaining Swiss citizenship—under the official condition he observe "silence"—the family moved to Kusnacht, a suburb of Zurich, in late September 1933. Mann expected that this move, too, would be only temporary, since Zurich was expensive and he disliked the dark winter sky and the "fohn wind" which he complained "affects the nerves."[60]

The real waiting game had begun. As in countless instances, Mann's prescience about Hitler's war aims was remarkable, considering how many men of merit, intelligence, and humanity were fooled—either through politics, ideology, fear, or hatred of war—into thinking that Hitler could take Germany through a fascist revolution without smashing the false, post–World War I peace into razor-edged bits and pieces. In those instances when Mann was later proven incorrect, his flawed conclusions were rarely the result of an inaccurate analysis of events, but rather the result of wishing so desperately that things were different.[61] He was by nature an optimist, although he always spoke of his "attraction to death." Well into the fateful summer of 1933, Mann felt a qualified confidence that the international community, acting through the League of Nations, would take decisive action by the spring against Hitler's buildup of arms, which was in direct violation of the Versailles treaty. Mann, however, considered war "unlikely."[62] When British Secretary of State for War, Lord Hailsham, warned Germany on May 11, 1933, that it risked reprisals for rearming, Mann, unlike many others living in Germany at the time, did not expect the British to invade. Mann had been among the most vociferous opponents of the Versailles treaty, and he viewed Germany's blatant rearmament, as well as the world's failure to intervene, as proof of the treaty's impotence. In addition, the world seemed genuinely unwilling or unable to fathom the real threat of Hitler's "revolution" to Germany and the world. After all, many nations, including the United States, had received Hitler's spurious "Peace Speech" of May 17 with voluptuous praise, taking note of the Fuhrer's calls for peace and disarmament, while ignoring his veiled aggression. With so many intellectuals all over Europe hailing Germany's spiritual awakening and calling for similar revolutions in their own nations, how strong was Europe's will to challenge fascism? Though it would take until 1938 for millions of Germany's educated citizens—its professors, judges, clergymen, artists, and even many members of the military—to realize that Hitler intended to lead the German Reich into war, Mann recognized as early as September 1933 that if Europe lacked the will to intervene, Hitler would write a bloody history of aggression which would make make "prewar imperialism [appear as] innocence itself."[63] Mann was convinced that Hitler's spiritual isolation of the German masses, quelling of opposition, and stirring of fanatical support which would blindly follow him were all part of the dictator's long-range war plans.

On September 7, 1933, almost six years to the day before Hitler's unspoiled reign of trickery and extortion ended in his march on Poland to begin World War II, Thomas Mann entered into his diary this startling summation of Hitler's German "program" for war:

> This prince with the soul of a waiter assures us that Germany will organize Europe as peacefully as she achieved power internally "in accordance with the Constitution." But this is the only nation in Europe that does not fear and abhor war; rather it deifies it, has nothing less in mind in all that it has done in the past six months, has prepared for nothing less than war, which perhaps it does not consciously desire, but which its background and nature dispose it to desire. . . . What comes then no one knows; it cannot be predicted, and they deny that it is what they want. But secretly they hope for it, long for it as their beloved Chaos—a love that entitles them to political dominion over the entire world.[64]

Earlier that day Mann had received an anonymous card from Munich, signed "a National Socialist." The card warned him "never to set foot on German soil again."[65] Like Mann's own mythical Jacob, blessed by Abraham to lead his people to godliness, but forced out of his home by jealousy and evil, Mann himself, in leaving Germany, "had saved his life . . . but at what price."[66]

Thomas Mann once described his "life plan, which was always a plan of work," and indeed, he continued writing the second installment of his Joseph story, *Young Joseph*, with remarkably few interruptions throughout those terrible first months of Hitler's rule.[67] When Mann began the work in December 1926, he had been attempting no less than to explore the essential nature of humanity and its relationship to its origins and future. Mann used the Old Testament tale of fraternal jealousy and power-hungry hate and greed to show how myths become truth as they are ingrained in a culture. At a time when nationalists fervently invoked a kind of scripture of German myths to justify their bigotry, violence, and national ambition, Mann told the story of man's "bottomless past," in which cultural destiny forces children to repeat the sins of their fathers.

Hitler's ascension was six years in the future when Mann began the work, but by the summer of 1933, what Mann had already written of Jacob and Joseph's exile and their hazardous mission from God was strikingly parallel to Mann's own pilgrimage. As history unfolded, Hitler's march on Europe was spreading itself before Mann like a biblical event. The Nazi takeover had all the requisite components: archetypal evil, blind followers, and a righteous and vanquished hero. From his Nuremberg podium, Hitler declaimed to the German people that he would lead them out of their deep suffering into a great and majestic future—a skewed echo of Abraham's prediction of the "day of God's apotheosis, day of Promise, expectation, and fulfillment," which Mann described in *Young Joseph*.[68]

Mann acknowledged during its writing that the Joseph story represented a major change of direction in his work, marking the end of the period in his life when "the artist-bourgeois problem was my most dominant concern."[69] He sensed that he was leaving something behind of his old psyche and life, going from "bourgeois individuality" to the "essentially human." For the first time in his career, he worked without actual human models, preferring to link his characters to broad cultural myths and ideas. Yet, Mann's biblical models served as rich material for a writer who felt that his own life had been tainted by fraternal hate, competitors' jealousy, greed, and false slander. In telling this ancient story of forced wandering and the moral man's burden, of a blessed man sent out to spread the word of God, but resisted, resented, and denigrated by his own people, Mann in fact became the scribe of his own morality tale, writing his own autobiography as his life was being lived, and in some instances, even before it was lived.

Joseph's love of beauty, wisdom, and knowledge, like Mann's, leads him to worship the art of writing and to seek transcendence through the written word. In *Young Joseph*, Mann described the word's power not simply to move whole masses of people, but to give rise to life itself, in concert with the one almighty God.[70] But Joseph—"the dreamer," "the artistic personality," the anointed one who is singled out for special treatment—not only possesses enormous, often mystical power, but is also supremely arrogant. He is taken with his own myth and assumes that the world will love him as much as he loves himself. However, Joseph has a rude awakening. Feeling extremely deserving, he receives his coat of many colors, the symbol of his anointment by God and his father, only to be nearly murdered by his jealous brothers. Like Mann's Nobel Prize, Joseph's coat epitomized his specialness and separateness, but was also a burden that hinted at trouble, and even death. As Joseph lies wounded in a dark pit, he tries to fathom the nature of his arrogance and his blessing. Mann completed *Young Joseph* during the excruciating early months of Hitler's regime, when he felt not only a sense of siege and humiliation, but conversely a heightened awareness of his own arrogance. While, collectively, the Joseph novels are possibly among the greatest literary works of the twentieth century, displaying a remarkable intellectual brilliance and emotional richness that defies description, *Young Joseph* can be distilled as a study of arrogance in an extraordinary human being. Thomas Mann was writing about Hitler, but also about himself.

In the months after Hitler's ascension to power, most writers of widely diverse ideological platforms living in Germany shed their former ideas—out of terror or sheer pragmatism—and became representatives of the Third Reich, united in ambition to restore the Fatherland to greatness. Apolitical writers suddenly swore devout loyalty to the party and attempted, sometimes desperately, to prove their racial purity.[71] Even formerly devout Communist writers suddenly took a hard Nazi line. They renounced their past "sins" to prove they had "abandoned such a reprehensible outlook in favor of a heroic conception of the world."[72] A good word from a high-ranking Nazi might persuade the Reich leadership that a former affiliation was only the meaningless folly of a flighty artist. Thus, friendship with a highly placed Nazi could mean the difference between life and death for a writer. Patriotic tragedies became pablum for the Nazi public, and writers who presented the image of a noble Germany were awarded money, rank, and prestige. And in Prague, Zurich, Geneva, Vienna, Paris, London, Madrid, and New York, German writers who had fled immediately upon Hitler's success sat huddled around café tables, predicting their future and the nation's, and wondering about the fate of their vulnerable friends and colleagues who had stayed behind.

In January 1934, the Reich demanded that all German writers sign a declaration of loyalty issued by the new compulsory government-controlled writers' organization, the Reichsschrifttumskammer.[73] The oath guaranteed that writers would spread a literary vision of German ascendancy, filling Hitler's demands for "German art," and prohibiting what he called "Gallic" and "Semitic" works. Any writer who refused to sign the oath was banned from publication in Germany. Mann refused to sign the Reichsschrifttumskammer oath. His act of defiance prompted attack and condemnation in the German nationalist press.[74]

That same month Mann left his new home near Zurich for a ten-city tour of Switzerland. Eleven months had passed since he had left his home in Munich to deliver his infamous Wagner address. The tremendous success of *The Tales of Jacob* in Germany was a slap in the face to Hitler, and in April 1934 in Locarno, Mann made another of his thinly veiled repudiations of the Fuhrer by redelivering the Wagner address. The timing of the lecture made it all the more inflammatory, since Hitler himself had delivered a speech hailing Wagner the previous month at a Nazi-inspired Wagner tribute in Leipzig.

Mann's veneer of the self-possessed intellectual giant belied his persistent, debilitating sadness, depression, and gloom. He seemed surprised that the Nazis still refused to grant him his passport, as though he thought that by using Wagner to indict fascism indirectly, he could avoid antagonizing them too much.

Hopeful that a forthcoming trip to America might pressure the German authorities into granting the passport, Mann left Zurich on the R.M.S. *Volendam* on May 19, 1934, using Swiss and French travel papers. Alfred A. Knopf, Mann's American publisher since 1916, had scheduled the publication of *The Tales of Jacob* (*Joseph and His Brothers*) to coincide with the author's first visit to the United States. The festivities, which were widely reported in the American press by the likes of H. L. Mencken and Dorothy Thompson, culminated in a testimonial dinner at the Plaza Hotel on June 6, Mann's fify-ninth birthday. Two hundred and fifty guests attended the dinner, including New York Mayor Fiorello La Guardia.

This brief respite was shattered by a new surge of horrors in Germany. Beginning on the night of June 30, 1934, and continuing for two more days, Hitler carried out a purge of S.A. troops and their officers who had probably set the Reichstag fire on orders from his high command. The National Socialist press told the German public that the murders were done for their benefit to stamp out Bolshevik "conspirators" among the senior ranks of the S.A., whose numbers now exceeded three million, when in truth Hitler had merely vanquished potential enemies who possessed more power than he found tolerable. Among the more than one hundred murdered during the three-day purge were S.A. leader Ernst Roehm, Hitler's ally from Munich since 1919, and former chancellor General Kurt von Schleicher, who had called for a socialist regime to follow a brief military dictatorship. Schleicher had been chancellor all of fifty-seven days when President Hindenburg dismissed him on January 28, 1933, in order to replace him with Hilter.

With the S.A. now under his power, Hitler went after bigger targets. On July 15, Austrian Chancellor Engelbert Dollfuss was murdered by National Socialists in Vienna. Two weeks later, anticipating the imminent death of eighty-seven-year-old Reich President Hindenburg, Hitler ordered the Reichswehr on August 1, 1933, to take an oath of "unconditional obedience" to him rather than the country or the constitution. The next day Hindenburg died, and Hitler combined the offices of chancellor and president, and in one terse, absolute move, seized the powers of head of state and commander-in-chief of the armed forces. After August 2, Hitler was henceforth known as Fuhrer and Reich Chancellor.

Not since the first days of Hitler's election in January 1933, when Mann's son Klaus remembered his father sitting silently for hours gazing with a blank stare, had Mann been too upset to work. Suddenly, work on the third Joseph novel, already titled *Joseph in Egypt*, came to a halt. Mann admitted to being depressed and filled with a sense of personal failure—"psychologically a most difficult and dangerous thing for me."[75] He felt an overriding ambivalence about his public role. Mann confided to Hermann Hesse on August 7, 1934,

> I am so plagued by the happenings in Germany, they are such a torment to my moral and critical conscience, that I seem to be unable to carry on with my current literary work. Perhaps the time is ripe for a political statement, which would have to be uncompromising and, of course, deal at length with my own inner development. On the other hand, it pains me to neglect my novel, and I am tortured by doubts as to the usefulness of such a risky step. In short, I am unable to make up my mind. I wish I could talk it over with you, but, alas, you are far away.[76]

Mann's decision to maintain public silence was another one of his overwrought calculations which masked a deeply emotional conflict. Privately, he was bold in confronting old friends like Ernst Bertram, chastizing him for adopting Hitler, "the most repulsive scarecrow begotten by world history for the 'savior.'"[77] Nevertheless, Mann's raging opposition remained essentially private, painfully suppressed, poured out only to his closest friends, and even more intimately, in nervous, angry, often desperate diary entries. His silence troubled him, but the idea of public retaliation daunted him more. He shamefacedly accepted Katia's criticism that in silence he had let himself be "led around by the nose with regard to [his] property," as well as her caution that when the Reich fell, he would regret his "outward passivity."[78] Still, he could take no direct public action.

During the next year and a half, Mann channeled his inner turmoil, indecisiveness, and self-doubt into the Joseph story, finally resuming work on *Joseph in Egypt* in November 1934.[79] His quandary was whether by speaking out he would be thinking only of himself, his image, and satisfying an inflamed ego. In *Young Joseph*, Joseph is victimized by his arrogance and becomes sidetracked on his mission to spread the word of God. In *Joseph in Egypt*, Joseph recovers a virtuous sense of his allegiance to God, and by resisting the forces of evil which tempt him, he moves closer to his anointed role as leader of his people.

As Mann continued work on *Joseph in Egypt*, his expectation and hope that Hitler would be swept out by a magnificent tide of German humanism became not only remote, but patently ridiculous. Antiaircraft testing began in the skies over Berlin in January of 1935, a prelude to the reinstitution of military conscription on March 16, in direct violation of the Versailles treaty. Hitler's promise to France that all territorial claims stemming from Versailles were satisfied by the peaceful return of the coal-rich Saar region on March 1 appeared as hollow as all his other promises, and yet the British response was to sign a secret naval accord with Hitler in June, granting Germany an enlarged navy one-third the size of Britain's.

Mann remained certain that Hitler was preparing for war and that England actually seemed to be helping him. Eventually, like a cancer gradually making itself felt, the awful truth became clear to Mann: a huge cadre of Germany's writers and professors had fallen under Hitler's spell and willingly defended his policies, becoming accomplices to the atrocities. Whereas in the past, Mann partly blamed political confusion and naiveté for his colleagues' endorsement of National Socialism, by 1935 there could be no mistaking Hitler's intentions or his deadly modus operandi. Ultimately, Mann's public expression would arise out of the need to excise a malignancy in order to live with himself.

To understand the tragedy of Hitler's Germany as Thomas Mann saw it, one must understand the century into which he was born and which he loved. Goethe, Schiller, Beethoven, Brahms, Wagner, Hegel, Nietzsche, and Schopenhauer all were nineteenth-century Germans, masters who embodied immense creativity, intellectuality, and deep suffering. They rebelled against the eighteenth century's credo of strict rationalism, and believed instead that reason needed spirit and nature in order for man to be truly alive. Although anti-Semitism and nationalism (which implied anti-French feeling) were well entrenched, they were moderated by an intellectual aestheticism which allowed for human flaws and weakness. Art could redeem society.

This romanticized Germany—Mann's Germany—was the Germany admired by the elite sons and daughters of the British Empire who would be blindsided by Hitler until the day their sons took up arms against him. When Victorians like Matthew Arnold and John Ruskin expressed a vision of art as the foundation for a great humanist civilization, they were invoking the nineteenth-century Germanic vision. The state, justice, decency, and a passion for truth and beauty formed the intertwined ideals of the European bourgeois intellectual elite. "[T]o come close to art means to come close to life," Mann wrote in 1938, expressing precisely this view, "and if an appreciation of the dignity of man is the moral definition of democracy, then its psychological definition arises out of its determination to reconcile and combine knowledge and art, mind and life, thought and deed."[80] For Mann and thinkers like him, this determination rested solely in the artist, who combined intellect and spirituality, reigning above humanity in a sphere close to God, perceiving what was essential and decent for his less-inspired brethren.

Thomas Mann's sense of ownership of his esteemed German culture, rooted in his Lübeck childhood, implied responsibility and guardianship as well. Such a duty was a valiant, even godly, burden which its children were honored to bear. Mann's great success as the writer of his time and culture was only partially due to his awesome mastery of literary form and description, although this alone would have guaranteed him a place of literary distinction. More importantly, perhaps, his style enclosed the quintessential philosophical dialectic of modern Europe: intellect/reason versus nature/instinct. What made Thomas Mann's work so appealing to his countrymen was that its intense intellectuality was threaded with a distinctly Germanic sense of tragedy, darkness, religion, suppressed sexuality, and swelling emotion which despises itself at every turn. As a result, the German reading public proudly proclaimed Mann its own, until totalitarian fascism snuffed out all literary and philosophical debate in Germany. Ultimately, one of the charges leveled against Mann by the extreme Right was that his work demonstrated "unhealthy eroticism."

The intellect versus nature debate had exploded in the 1700s with Enlightenment writers such as Voltaire, Hume, and Kant, who consumed Mann's artistic idols, Goethe and Schiller, in the late eighteenth century, and his other idol, Friederich Nietzsche, in the late nineteenth. In Nietzsche, a philosopher with the nature of a poet, the debate took an intensely personal twist. His *Ubermensch* or Superman theory arose strictly from his vision of a noble, sexual, generous, and creative man who yearns for power over himself and creative mastery. In works like *The Birth of Tragedy, Thus Spake Zarathustra, Beyond Good and Evil*, and *Ecce Homo*, Nietzsche proclaimed that there was no life beyond the here and now—as opposed to the teachings of Christian dogma, which he despised. Nietzsche decried seeking revenge against enemies, was fiercely opposed to German nationalism and militarism, and looked to Greek ideas about man.

The Nietzsche whom Thomas Mann prized was the archetypal artist cut from the same golden, flowing, humanist German fabric as Goethe: a truth-seeker willing to sacrifice his life for the sake of his art. Together they were, Mann wrote, "the great teachers of Germany—Goethe and Nietzsche—who knew how to be antiliberal without making the slightest concession to any kind of obscurantism, without abandoning an iota of human rationality and dignity."[81]

Unfortunately for Mann, Germany, mankind, and the reputation of Nietzsche himself, Nietzsche's work appeared in the 1870s and 1880s, just as German nationalism and anti-Semitism were gaining momentum under Bismarck's Prussian leadership. The philosophy to which the Nazis partly attributed their platform of Aryan supremacy was actually a trumped-up, cut-and-pasted version of Nietzsche's writing, made to suit their perverse needs, disseminated in expurgated texts by Goebbels's propaganda ministry. A syphilitic who spent the last years of his life in an insane asylum, Nietzsche, like Wagner, was anything but the model Aryan Hitler lionized.

It pained Mann viscerally that German nationalists had warped his icons of art and philosophy into puny, one-sided thinkers, appropriating them for their own demonic purposes. It was bad enough that Hitler compared himself to Wagner: "The repugnant traits of Wagner, but only these to be sure, are precisely mirrored in Hitler," Mann averred.[82] The fact that artists could subscribe to Hitler's cooked-up mythology struck Mann as his most sinister manipulation of Germans' "lust for everything misty and vaporous."[83]

For Mann, the political principle of fascism violated the artist's essence, because it symbolized repression and lies, whereas freedom and truth were the artist's food and air. Fascism, he would write in 1938, showed "contempt for pure reason, the denial and violation of truth in favor of power and the interests of the state, the appeal to the lower intincts, to so-called 'feeling,' the release of stupidity and evil from the discipline of reason and intelligence."[84] Perhaps the uneducated, uncultured, and self-seeking could twist Nietzsche, Wagner, and others, but how was it possible for artists and intellectuals to do so? Mann simply could not fathom how friends and colleagues who had once shown liberal or republican tendencies could embrace fascism. To Mann's mind, any artist who supported the fascist movement was "hopelessly compromising his poetical genius through his political or, as I prefer to call it, his human behavior."[85] Any artist who embraced fascism, Mann declared, committed "spiritual" suicide.

It was precisely because in fascist Germany a wildly errant philosopher like Nietzsche could no longer put forth a "Superman" doctrine as a mere moral and intellectual exercise that Mann viewed Nietzsche and Wagner as victims, like himself, of Hitler's ignorance and perversion of German moral intellectualism. Any pro-Nazi could be certain that his condemning words could lead to murder or torture, while German intellectuals pontificated about fascism as though it were an abstraction. In rebuke of such cowardice, Mann invoked Goethe, who had counciled that the man of thought "must bear a conscience for the man of action."[86]

Increasingly, as voices of opposition were silenced and German exiled artists and thinkers nervously awaited their future, Mann could not ignore the stark affront which fascism represented to his morality and ideas, and to a lesser extent, his reputation. Hitler's popularity among artists and intellectuals represented to Mann a complete failure of reason in Germany—the loss of the moral "distinction between doing and happening," as he had characterized it in *Young Joseph*—as well as a perversion of the beautiful, natural spirit that Mann held sacred in humankind.[87] The Nazi regime forced Germany to be reckoned as a nation of the world, but it was also a reckoning for all German artists and intellectuals who were the cultural symbols of a nation which long prided itself as Europe's leader in art and thought, and who perceived their own role in almost mythic terms as guardians of this great heritage. Antifascist intellectuals who predicted that their deluded peers would become disillusioned by National Socialism only after putting up "the greatest resistance against recognizing their own folly" were, sadly, only partly right, because it took losing a war for many of them to change their minds. At the Nuremberg trials, defendant General Alfred Jodl, Hitler's Chief of Operations for the High Command, pointed to Hitler's genius at appealing to intellectuals: "The movement would never have gained such impetus if men of repute had not been swept along with it and given the movement some prestige before the German people. That is where propaganda did a terrific job."[88]

Before Mann had left for America in May 1934, he had taken his first notes for a project which he described as a "highly personal and unsparing" work on German affairs.[89] He already referred to the work in specific terms as "the Faust novella," and knew it would be the project to follow the Joseph novels. Yet Mann predicted even at this time that the book's publication "would mean the final breach with Germany," and for this he was not ready.[90] The self-avowed "non public man" always took time to simmer, stew, and brood before bursting forth with a work so bold and brazen that it unsettled all the world about him. In the spring of 1934, Mann felt certain that he faced writing a life-changing book, and this awareness was henceforth to color his actions both as an artist and as a German.

In the summer of 1935, Mann was still at work on *Joseph in Egypt* when he and Katia sailed to America for the second time. He was persona non grata in fascist Germany, but in democratic America he was received like visiting royalty. The trip—another whirlwind affair with tributes and dinners of champagne and caviar—brought Mann to Harvard University, where along with Albert Einstein he received an honorary doctorate and was given a standing ovation by an audience of some five thousand. The highlight of the trip was a private dinner for the Manns with President and Mrs. Roosevelt at the White House on June 30. "When I left the White House after my first visit," Mann later recalled, "I knew Hitler was lost."[91]

This first meeting with Roosevelt spawned Mann's perception of the American president as the haloed antithesis of the demonic Adolf Hitler. To Mann, Franklin Roosevelt was a magisterial commander of a great nation. He was everything Hitler was not, and not a little like himself: educated, refined, humane, munificent, peace-loving, and seemingly a devoted husband and father of a large brood. In fact, the similarities between Mann and Roosevelt were striking. Roosevelt was an aristocrat with an esteemed family heritage and deep sense of loyalty and responsibility to his country, based on love of freedom and culture, Mann believed, not vainglory or thirst for hegemony.[92] Mann identified with Roosevelt as a man who, like himself, stood for what was morally right and had made bitter enemies because of it.

On his visits to America, Mann responded to the atmosphere of intellectual freedom and respect for individual rights as to a refreshing dream compared to the nightmare unfolding in Europe. During the summer of 1935, Premier Benito Mussolini made his first moves against Abyssinia, culminating in his invasion of the small east African country in late October. Mann believed, like most antifascist observers, that Mussolini's trumped-up conflict was a harbinger of imminent invasion, as it turned out to be.

Although Mann found the American public's laissez-faire regard for Hitler and fascism irksome, he came face to face in Washington with powerful symbols of American democracy: the Lincoln Memorial and the Capitol, where he and Katia observed a congressional session in which dictatorship was debated. Before a private tour of the White House conducted by Eleanor Roosevelt, the Manns were driven to Mount Vernon, home of George Washington, whose name carried even more nationalist weight in the United States than did the names of Goethe or Wagner in Germany. Mann, the cosmopolitan guest of Europe's great cities, called Washington "quite the most imposing capital in the world."[93]

At this time Mann could not have imagined expatriation anywhere but in Europe yet his visits to America in 1934 and 1935 were crucial to his awareness that he was as much a German exile now as his friend Hermann Hesse. These visits had a direct impact on Mann's Joseph story and on his growing sense that his destiny, like Jacob's and Joseph's, lay in delivering his people from sin and faithlessness. As such, the entire work—Mann's attempt at "an abbreviated history of mankind"—represents a thrilling instance of an artwork taking on a life of its own, separate from, but having great impact upon, its creator.[94] The Joseph story prepared Mann for his wartime role as spokesman for Germany's exiles. Mann would snuff out falsehood, treachery, and evil. He would single-handedly persuade the democratic powers in Europe and America not to be lulled by Hitler's lies and manipulation. He was a writer in a bond with God, on a mission from God.

After returning from America in the summer of 1935, Mann firmly placed himself in the exiles' camp when a well-meaning American literary critic, Harry Slochower, accused him of failing to oppose fascism more forcefully. Yet, it was not until February 3, 1936, that Mann's long-simmering indecisiveness reached a head. On that damp, snowy winter day, the Zurich newspaper *Neue Zürcher Zeitgang* carried Mann's declared alignment with German exiles, including Jews, in his "Open Letter" to the newspaper, repudiating an article entitled "German Literature in the Exile's Mirror," which had appeared on January 26. Eduard Korrodi, the feature editor, had written that exile German literature was Jewish and, as such, "unrepresentative." Mann's public action was momentous because he had come out to declare that his exile was no longer a temporary sentence, but the test of true German patriotism and artistic virtue.

Mann knew he was risking whatever he had remaining as a German citizen—his passport, his citizenship, and his freedom to be read in Germany, which he considered vitally important to conscientious Germans still in Germany.[95] But he was ready to take the consequences. "The sense that I have struck a body blow against the wretched regime fills me with satisfaction," he wrote in his diary on the day his reply appeared. "It will try to take whatever revenge it can. Let it."[96] On the same day he wrote Alfred Knopf asking advice on obtaining American citizenship.

As Katia Mann had predicted, Mann's public declaration was a defiant act of personal liberation. By accepting the public role of exile, the sixty-one-year-old Mann had thrust himself out of a psychological state rooted in nineteenth-century Germany, as well as his feeling of being "an historical relic, a leftover from a different cultural era which . . . in reality is dead and buried."[97] His new determination to fight Hitler and aid in restoring decency to Germany set him squarely center in the modern, twentieth-century world, even if that world were "a world of debasement," as he felt. Henceforth, Mann's every act became political, and every literary essay—a mainstay of his writing and thinking—became tinged with political activism. He began to call for "militant humanism," in order to bring into power governments of highly moral, intellectual leaders who would be immune to capitalist interests and political persuasion.[98] Even an invitation to take part in a tribute in Vienna on May 8, 1936, to honor Sigmund Freud's eightieth birthday became an opportunity to denounce Hitler's fascism before full houses of rapt Viennese antifascists who shuddered at the thought of a union with Germany.[99]

On December 2, 1936, the German authorities withdrew Mann's German citizenship, as well as his wife's and children's, citing in part his "Open Letter" to Eduard Korrodi. Shortly thereafter, the dean of the philosophical faculty of Frederick-William University of Bonn withdrew Mann's honorary doctorate, citing it as "a consequence of your loss of citizenship."[100] The act was a minor, but symbolic anticlimax to a man who once considered himself "too German" to be an exile. Mann was not a man without a country, however, since on November 19, 1936, through earlier efforts, he had received Czechoslovakian citizenship.

Thomas Mann now embarked upon a period of staggering literary and personal productivity unmatched in his life. His fame as a moral conscience was growing worldwide. In America, he had his biggest sale of his career when in May of 1936 the Book-of-the-Month Club bought sixty thousand copies of *Stories of Three*

Decades, a collection published by Knopf earlier that year. His political correspondence with antifascist Zurich publisher and friend Emil Oprecht was published by Oprecht's Europa Verlag in January 1937 under the title *An Exchange
of Letters* and by Knopf in America shortly thereafter.[101]

On the eve of Mann's third trip to America in April 1937 to deliver five lectures at
the New School for Social Research, an article by Louis Gillet entitled
"Excommunicated" appeared in Paris' *Écho de Paris*, paying tribute to Mann:
"Everyone knows that Monsieur Thomas Mann is the most imposing literary per-
sonage in Europe today. Excepting Paul Claudel or Gabriele d'Annuzio, and perhaps
H. G. Wells and Bernard Shaw, the present-day world holds no artist figure of higher
or more majestic stature."[102] American journalist Dorothy Thompson wrote an even
more gushing encomium, which ran in the *New York Herald Tribune* on April 14.[103]

Hollywood representatives came to New York in April and wooed Mann like a
celebrity to come West and work in the movies. But the allure of Goldwyn, Mayer,
and Warner paled alongside the pantheon of Goethe, Nietszche, and Wagner, and at
the end of April 1937, Mann returned to Zurich, where he became co-editor-in-chief
of a new bimonthly free German journal called *Mass und Wert* (measure and value).
Published out of Zurich by Emil Oprecht and financed by the widow of a
Luxembourg steel magnate, Madame Aline Mayrisch de St. Hubert, the journal's
purpose was to rally the spirits of refugees "during the present German inter-reg-
num," as Mann wryly called this period. (*Mass und Wert* appeared in August 1937,
and ran six times a year until publication ceased in October 1940.)

Mann had finished *Joseph in Egypt* on August 23, 1936. Near the book's cli-
mactic sexual end, Mann created an extraordinary metaphor for German mass hyp-
notism in service to a deified ruler. A New Year's Day Feast, replete with flags,
music, soldiers in military regalia, war chariots, priests, chanting, and processions,
honors not the great leader of the unified Fatherland, Adolf Hitler, but rather the
pharaoh who has unified upper and lower Egypt. Upon the publication of *Joseph
in Egypt* in Vienna in October of that year, Mann told Hermann Hesse, "It was my
way of enduring the last three years, or if you prefer, of playing a trick on them."[104]

In the beginning, Mann had eagerly picked up the story, but in the end, it felt
burdensome. Finishing had required the greatest force of will, since Mann was
plagued by anxiety and sleeplessness brought on by worry over world events.
Afterward, Mann made a conscious decision to turn to a project which would
instill a sense of "serenity." Two fictional works actually resulted before Mann
began the last volume of the Joseph story, *Joseph the Provider*, in the summer of
1940: *The Transposed Heads*, which he termed "a jest," and *Lotte in Weimar* (*The
Beloved Returns*) a "metaphysical work," as he called it, about Goethe and his
youthful muse, Lotte Kestner.

Mann had already completed two chapters of *Lotte in Weimar* when he left for
America again on February 10, 1938, to deliver his most important political lecture thus far, "The Coming Victory of Democracy." At a time when Americans
had little taste for becoming involved in Europe's crisis, Mann exploited their
deeply ingrained idea of moral superiority to make his most direct argument yet
against isolationism. As usual, Mann was filled with self-doubt as he prepared the
lecture. "Democratic idealism. Do I believe in it? Am I only adopting it as an
intellectual role?"[105] Typically as well, visionary thought won out over belea-

guering anxiety to produce a powerful statement, completely assured in its right-ness and unsparing in its point of view. The tour, scheduled to last five months and to cover fifteen U.S. cities, including Denver, Salt Lake City, and Los Angeles, was to be Mann's most extensive and ambitious yet.

"The Coming Victory of Democracy" was a summary of Thomas Mann's Kantian view of the essential goodness and intelligence of man and his inherent sense of justice, truth, and freedom, bound into one "absolute" to render man human. Mann told his audiences—in German as usual—that no matter how deep man descended into "the underworld," this inherent sense of human dignity would eventually pull him up and lead him to do the right thing. Mann told Americans that the political name for this "idea of justice" was democracy, and as such, he said, "America belongs to the cultural territory of the Occident and participates in its inner destiny, in the ups and downs of its spiritual and moral life."[106] A failure to comprehend this fact by maintaining a "laissez-faire, laissez-aller" approach toward fascism threatened the death of democracy.

Mann's tone was grave and firm, but hardly punishing. Privately, Americans' staunch isolationism deeply irritated him, but his respect for America was as prag-matic as it was devout—he knew Hitler could not be defeated without America's help. Mann explained that if Americans were reluctant to join the effort to defeat Hitler, it was only because their moral foundation as democrats prevented them from fathoming his reign of terror and suppression of freedom and truth, because Americans took these principles for granted. "Democracy's danger is the humane illusion, the virtuous belief that compromise with this new creature is possible," he told listeners. He added that any democrat who tried to reason with or cajole the fascists was not only gravely mistaken, but guaranteeing the unfettered growth of their evil power. "In every friendly gesture, in every concession to its demands," Mann warned, "it will only see a sign of weakness, of resignation, and of timely abdication." Mann predicted that Hitler was biding his time, relying on just such a concessionary approach by the democratic nations, so that fascism could "continue its internal and external bluff with greater impugnity, to black-mail the peace-loving democracies and perhaps to achieve its ambitions for power without an actual war."[107] As a result, pacifist politics now were not only immoral but criminal, Mann argued.

Mann's words proved to be startlingly accurate when on March 12, 1938, Hitler's troops seized Austria. Mann's long-held hope that Austria could stave off Hitler was shattered, but worse, the Anschluss stirred in the sixty-three-year-old Mann a horri-fying reminder of the "seizure of power" in Germany five years before. The fall of Austria was a terrific personal blow. His friends in Vienna—intellectuals, Jews, and aristocrats—were among the most susceptible to arrest, torture, and death. Mann's friend Sigmund Freud, who had been until now shielded by his international repu-tation and influential friends, had his passport revoked, his publishing house and apartment searched by Nazi thugs, and his cash and bank account confiscated.[108] An old friend, cabaret performer, and theater critic, Egon Friedell, jumped out a win-dow to his death as the Gestapo climbed the steps to his apartment. The daughter of his friend Bruno Walter, who had been the director of the Vienna State Opera since 1935, was arrested by the Gestapo. The fall of Austria, together with England's unchanged policy of appeasement, a Nazi crackdown in Jewish ghettos in Poland,

and the bombing of Barcelona supported with German planes, convinced Mann that the floodgates of all Europe were opening to Nazi conquest. "The Greater German Reich of a hundred million is being formed by violent means," he mourned. "What a triumph for the majesty of force! What consequences for European thought!"[109]

Fearing that Switzerland could be invaded next, Mann agreed to take an honorary professorship at Princeton University, which he obtained through the help of Agnes E. Meyer, the influential wife of Eugene Meyer, owner of *The Washington Post*, and a leading Washington socialite, Democrat, and political writer. Because Mann had not made the decision to stay in the United States of his own free will, he did not expect the move to be permanent. Nevertheless, America had never seemed more like a safe haven against evil than now, when he and Katia "had the sensation of being cut off, as in 1933."[110] American critics had applauded *Joseph in Egypt*, and the lecture tour, which ended in New York in the third week of May, was a resounding success. He had been received like a messiah before audiences of thousands, raised large sums of money for his Thomas Mann refugee aid funds, and socialized with longtime European friends relocated in Beverly Hills, such as Bruno Frank, Aldous Huxley, and Max Reinhardt. Mann's request for American citizenship was being personally handled by U.S. Secretary of State Cordell Hull, as a favor to Agnes Meyer.[111] Mann felt that at this time he needed above all to live "within the shelter of a society that still loves and honors what I do not so much advocate as represent, and to carry my life's work to its end."[112]

After the tour, the Manns rested at a seaside cottage in Jamestown, Rhode Island. Europe seemed on the brink of ruin, but Rhode Island was the picture of beauty and tranquility, and Mann felt a calming sense of personal safety. His creativity resumed. By the sea which he loved so dearly, he worked on an essay on Schopenhauer and conceived the ending for *Lotte in Weimar*. He and Katia were still in Rhode Island when *The Coming Victory of Democracy*, translated by Agnes E. Meyer, was published in America by Alfred A. Knopf.

When the Munich crisis over Czechoslovakia unfolded in late summer 1938, *The Coming Victory of Democracy* was sounding an alarm for American readers. Whereas in panic-stricken Europe few were reading anything but actual news accounts, in the United States the slim volume sold well, with new editions appearing in July and August.

That summer the Manns returned to Zurich to prepare for their emigration to America. By the time they arrived back in the United States, Hitler's September 21 ultimatum to Czechoslovakia had passed, and when the couple docked in New York, German troops were massed at the Czech border in readiness to invade. Mann was immediately thrust into American-style antiwar fever. On September 25 he addressed a mass rally at Madison Square Garden held by the Committee to Save Czechoslovakia. Nearly thirty thousand filled the arena and spilled outside onto the streets around the Garden.[113] After Czech peasant girls appeared on stage and the Czech national anthem was sung, Mann told the audience, "Hitler must fall!" After his address he felt encouraged by the Czechs' impassioned vow to fight, but he distrusted Hitler and, even more, the posturing, indecisive Allies.

No event in modern times more dramatically illustrates the unpredictable, ephemeral, and at the same time titanic march of history than the Munich crisis, in which Hitler threatened to invade Czechoslovakia unless President Beneš handed the Sudetenland region over to him. On September 28, after weeks of febrile negotations, Hitler, British Prime Minister Chamberlain, and French Premier Edouard Daladier signed the Munich Pact, giving the German dictator Czechoslovakia without his troops having to fire a single shot. Mann characterized the pact to friend Erich Von Kahler as "the realization at last of the filthy play which was being performed all along. . . . The shame, the disgust, the shattering of all hopes."[114]

For two years Mann had sounded the alarm about German fascism, delineating in clear methodical terms its hideousness and proclaiming to the democratic nations of Europe their sacred obligation to safeguard the principles of goodness, truth, and freedom. The ignominious Munich Pact signified the democratic leaders' betrayal of their own sacred trust and the infiltration of fascist ideology in democratic Europe. Mann laid sole blame on the English ruling class, whose mouthpiece, Neville Chamberlain, seemed the worst sinner among a covey of self-protecting evildoers.

In an essay entitled "This Peace" which he wrote in Princeton in the days after Munich, Mann launched the kind of ferocious barrage against England and Chamberlain that he heretofore had aimed against the Third Reich and fascism. The British, he said, had blithely watched as Hitler gathered power, marched into the Rhineland, and annexed Austria. They dismissed murder, torture, and anti-Semitism, treated Hitler as a statesman rather than the monster he was, and failed to take opportunities to stop him—so much so that even Hitler was surprised by their quiescence. Fascism had been "aided, according to a set plan, by the ruling classes of England," Mann wrote, his words flying like steel arrows, and "for all these horrors England, as the protector bears the full responsibility."[115] And then came the "crime"—Munich—the "classic hypocrisy of English statesmanship," which he said did nothing short of "rescuing" fascism.[116] Chamberlain had foisted on a peace-thirsty public the falsehood that Europe's only choice lay between war and peace, and Mann reeled in disgust and loathing at this lie.

"It is hard to imagine the mentality of these British statesmen, conscientious only in the service of their own class and their own interests," wrote Mann, "passing their days in their clubs and their government offices, their week-ends in the country—and wholly undisturbed by thoughts of the thousandfold cases of individual tragedy which were willy-nilly the accompaniment to their astute calculations."[117] Mann's analysis was not clouded by his outrage and disgust; his surfeit of emotion merely added passion to the clarity of his insights. Nearly sixty years after Mann wrote the terse, thirty-page essay and tagged it with its ironic title, "This Peace," the essay remains a remarkably simple and yet sweeping analysis of what millions of war-shattered people came to understand as the "Crime of Munich."

By the time Mann addressed the American Booksellers Association Book and Author Luncheon at New York's Hotel Astor on November 9, 1938, he had reconciled the hideousness of the Munich Pact with a broader human view which furnished the hope he required for the future. He chose to see Munich as the necessary horror that would force the West to see the evil in fascism and Adolf Hitler—and the goodness which must win out if humankind were to survive. This conclusion was in perfect harmony with Mann's moral view of humanity and human history in which events symbolized and presaged still other events in set patterns, and in which evil was required to heighten goodness. (Ironically, this was the same kind of moralization of political duplicity that Mann had used to justify Germany's aggression in World War I.) "[P]aradoxical as it may sound, the spirit has at the same time entered into a new age of morality," Mann proclaimed in his November 9 address. "Yes, once more we are aware, once more we know good and evil. Evil has been revealed to us with such crassness and vulgarity that our eyes are opened to the dignity and simple beauty of the good."[118]

Now that Mann was in America, it was completely natural that he viewed his adoptive home as the rightful leader in this contemporary battle between good and evil. Mann's universal-historical view of mankind always presented the dialectical paradigm, and since he had been mining myths of good and evil (as in Cain and Abel, Jacob and Esau) exclusively since 1926, he easily followed this path of thinking. Nevertheless, in 1938 Mann had no illusions about the American distaste for war for Europe's sake; he understood that isolationist Americans had to be convinced that their nation alone bore the moral authority to save civilization—a lofty mission that Americans refused until the Japanese bombed Pearl Harbor in December 1941. Mann, a practical man as much as a dreamer, was not beneath calculated sycophancy when he addressed his American audiences. Near the dramatic close of his November 9 address to booksellers, Mann gushed:

"[I]ndeed I have often thought that such an epoch of spiritual renewal and simplification might be America's greatest hour. I have said that in this dark age it would be her task to preserve and administer the cultural inheritance of the Western world. What I had in mind was this: her youth, her unexhausted moral freshness; her mental temper, which stands closer to the Biblical and monumental than any in Europe." (Mann used much the same tone five years later in closing *The Tables of the Law*, his novella about Moses, God's scribe.) "In a desolate and morally leaderless world, may America stand the strong and unswerving protectress of the good and godlike in man." In 1945, after the war ended, Mann told Hermann Hesse that, "I wasn't able to speak up, to pour out my heart, until I got to America."[119]

The defeat of Czechoslovakia and growing terror in the rest of Europe created a flood of new refugees, and Mann's work to secure them visas, jobs, and housing increased dramatically. In addition to writing important literary essays on two of his personal icons, Schopenhauer and Goethe, and working on the novel *Lotte in Wiemar*, Mann tirelessly addressed American audiences, including Jewish groups, also eliciting help for the refugees at the highest government levels. After mornings spent writing, his daily routine consisted of fund-raising, hand-shaking, book-signing, and, meeting with college presidents, rabbis, and American theologians like Reinhold Niebuhr and Paul Tillich. He sat for interviews with magazine, newspaper, and radio journalists, and was elected honorary chairman of the League of American Writers.[120]

In the spring of 1939, Mann embarked on yet another coast-to-coast tour to deliver a new lecture, "The Problem of Freedom." Since Mann was used to juggling many balls at one time, his slowness in writing *Lotte in Weimar*, as well as the great pleasure he took in it, is of particular interest, since the book was such a complete artistic failure. Boring, tautological, undramatic, and lifeless (though based on real people in Johann von Goethe's life), *Lotte in Weimar* imagines conversations between Goethe's youthful muse Lotte, now an aging matron, and fans who pay homage to her, but really want only to talk about the great Goethe himself, who also appears.

When he began *Lotte in Weimar* in September 1936, Mann craved a respite from the monumental requirements of the Joseph story, and *Lotte in Weimar* allowed a depleted Mann to moan and groan about the burdens of art and Germanness by merging himself with the persona of an indisputably great German artist, Johann Wolfgang von Goethe.[121]

Mann had identified with Goethe since his youth, seeing in him, as in Nietzsche, another ideal of master artist, a "half-god" who "reigns in an intellectual kingdom of bold and untrammeled freedom."[122] Unlike Nietzsche, however, Goethe was a humanitarian, who, like himself, appreciated man as the sum of good and evil, and God as the sum of the divine and the diabolical. To Mann, Goethe embodied the perfect and rare blend of reason and spirit. In addition to a staggering output of literary writing, Goethe studied alchemy, law, and classical literature, and conducted important experiments in optics, color, plants, and human anatomy. His complete body of work comprised 133 volumes, fourteen of which were related to science. He served the Weimar Court in a variety of administrative positions—a ten-year political sidetrack to his literary work that he later regretted. Pursued by artistic and romantic controversy, Goethe made little secret of his contempt for his literary colleagues, and like Mann, championed art and humanism as foils to Germanic barbarism. In 1925, when fervent German nationalism became the bellwether of patriotism, Mann defended himself by invoking Goethe as his model. Mann wrote that the *Faust* poet could be "the greatest humanist and [could] take the most treasonable stance for 'civilization' and cosmopolitanism, and still be and remain the purest wine of great Germanism."[123] Mann's pronouncement in *Young Joseph* that "the world had arisen by the might of the free and external word" was pure Goethean aesthetic philosophy.

With Mann's ostracism and exile from Germany, the similarities he saw between himself and Goethe intrigued him more than ever. Though Goethe was recognized as the leading German writer of his time, he, too, had been ostracized for his criticism of Germany at a critical juncture in German national history. He had supported Napoleon in his conquest of Prussia in 1806 and had endorsed the Rhenish alliance with France and pan-European unity at a time of emergent radical nationalism in lands which became Bismarck's loose-knit German state in 1871.

Mann praised *Lotte in Weimar* when he finished, calling his portrait of Goethe "intimate, lively, new, not without intimate knowledge of greatness."[124] But his judgment was clouded by his captivation by both Goethe and his own artistic process. In dramatizing Goethe's preparation for his Faust poem, Mann was in the process of conceiving a new, personalized Faust work, but he had not yet moved beyond that point of deep identification with his subject to attain the distance required for the successful artistic whole. And yet Mann's identification with Goethe was just that very complex, intriguing phenomenon which Mann the artist craved now more than ever, and *Lotte in Weimar* reads superficially like the transcription of Mann's late-night sleepless conjurings at a time when everything bedeviled him—from his aching teeth and itchy scalp to the German national character and his self-assumed position as leader of his tribe.

Around this time, another German exile, Heinrich Simon, former publisher of the newspaper *Frankfurter Zeitung*, suggested that it was inevitable that Mann would be the president of Germany after Hitler's fall. Simon's suggestion reflected the fact that Mann was riding a tide which seemed to be carrying him to some position of German leadership. Such a prospect had never been more seductive to Mann. Alluding to Simon's statement, Mann wrote in his diary on April 28, 1939, "Increasingly desirous of influencing the people."[125] Never more than now had Mann faced the challenge of balancing his dual roles as artist and political activist. In *Lotte in Weimar*, Goethe faces the same balancing act, and when Mann found he had to write about it, he couldn't easily. Chapter VII, detailing how Goethe schemed to balance his role as leader and apolitical critic of Germany with the demands of great art, took Mann parts of six months to write and ran to about a hundred pages.

Mann's blind love for metaphysical debate and his canonization of Goethe doomed the work, but for all its flaws, *Lotte in Weimar* is the evolutionary link between the Joseph story and Mann's great wartime novel, *Doctor Faustus*. Many of the ideas Mann etched so dramatically five years later in *Doctor Faustus* are in *Lotte* in fetal form: the barbaric sin of German nationalism and its so-called "intellectual" defenders; the "bargain" the artist must strike with his destiny; and foremost, the burden and blessing of genius. When Mann wrote *Lotte in Weimar*, the destruction of his beloved Germany by allied bombers lay more than five years in the future; his consuming grief in the conviction that the German people had invited their terrible destiny upon themselves, too, lay years in the future—past rage and his arrogant assumption that he could influence history. By 1945, Leipzig, Munich, Mannheim, Darmstadt, Würzburg, Frankfurt, and many other ancient German towns and villages would be reduced to rubble, and a grieving Mann would conclude that the artist could do no more than express man's suffering and plead for salvation from God and his fellow man. In the final years leading up to war, however, Mann still boldly proclaimed the artist's role as leader.

"You make yourself great, make yourself hated, telling the ice-cold truth," Goethe says in *Lotte*, knowing that the master artist is a "ruler of men," "godlike" and endures his burden in a rarified "sphere of art." Mann's Goethe is faithless, selfish, joyless, and self-doubting; yet, he is saved from a tragic destiny because, in that special "sphere of art," the master artist attains the "unity of the All and the Nothing."[126] Through his Goethe persona, Mann concludes that hubris has nothing to do with the master artist's role as leader: "the course of his fate, his work, and his life is effective far beyond the confines of his person, and conditions of character, the culture, and the future of the nation!" It is "laid on one and borne in God's name—enjoy it and forgive, it is there for your pleasure."[127]

While he was writing *Lotte*, however, Thomas Mann, the master artist, was not yet ready to capture the full evil of the German "tragedy," as he saw it. On February 14, 1939, he asked himself how real art could be molded out of so awful a time in humanity, no matter how formidable the artist. "Have reality and art ever before been so utterly incompatible? Art not applicable to 'life.' The deadness of nazism, the paralysis it spreads."[128] For the suffering and greatness of Thomas Mann, there had to be a devastating war of judgment before he could write Germany's tale of sin and woe, and after six years of nihilistic Nazi rule, war finally came.

When Germany invaded Poland on September 1, 1939, Thomas Mann was in Stockholm, scheduled to participate in the international PEN Club Congress. It seems odd that after so many years of avoiding a personal encounter with war Mann should be in Europe at that very time; yet, until war on Germany was declared on September 3, Mann continued to doubt that it might ever come. Though Mann had believed as early as 1934 that Hitler was planning for war, he, like Hitler himself, had long been been certain that the dictator would not have to go to the trouble of waging a war in order to achieve his territorial ambitions. Mann wished for a war to end German's imprisonment by such a demon as Hitler, but nevertheless assumed that the Allies would continue to give Hitler everything he wanted because the dictator was such a genius at deceit and wreaking chaos.

Between the Munich Crisis of September 1938 and June 6, 1939, when the Manns finally embarked on a long-awaited European vacation, Hitler seized Czechoslovakia, made threats on Poland about Danzig, renounced the 1935 naval treaty with Britain, and took control of the Lithuanian city of Memel, where the S.S. had been organizing Germans in the same fashion as in Austria and the Sudetenland. Still, the Allies failed to retaliate. When the French mobilized along the Maginot Line in response to Hitler's ultimatum to Lithuania, Mann had written that the " 'war threat' was as much of a fraud as before Munich."[129]

Mann was right in thinking that the top echelons of the British government rejected an alliance with Russia even at this late date, when Hitler's demands grew increasingly bolder. During the crisis over Memel, Chamberlain called "premature" Russia's plea for an alliance among France, Britain, Poland, Russia, Rumania, and Turkey to stop Hitler.[130] While Mann had no specific knowledge of this latest British obfuscation, he felt certain that Britain's overriding hatred of Russia and bolshevism could be counted on to help Hitler get what he wanted without war. His view was reinforced by events that same month in Spain, where after three years of fighting, Russian-backed Republicans finally succumbed to the more formidable German- and Italian-backed Franco rebels on March 28. For the entire duration of the Spanish Civil War, the governments of both England and France conducted empty diplomatic efforts with Hitler and Mussolini for non-intervention in Spain.

Mann continued to wait for a British military response after Mussolini invaded Albania in April and threatened Greece and Turkey, and after Hitler and Mussolini signed the Pact of Steel on May 22 to create "an invincible bloc of three hundred million people." To Mann's profound disgust and disappointment, the British parliament chose only to "discuss" the pact's ramifications at a special session, and on June 6, 1939—Mann's sixty-fourth birthday—he and Katia, accompanied by their daughter Erika, who served as Mann's translator for audience questions, embarked for Paris, unwilling to wait any longer for the outbreak of war.

The couple vacationed six weeks in Noordwijk, Holland, taking several side-trips to Paris, London, and Zurich to visit friends and family before arriving on August 25 in Stockholm for the PEN conference, which never convened. En route that day Mann confided to his diary, "I do not conceal from myself that I want the war, precisely because its effects are unpredictable and would lead away from the present state of affairs, probably in Germany as well. Above all, it would be so revolting to see Hilter march in once more without meeting any resistance that anything is preferable."[131]

When war was declared on September 3, Mann made hasty arrangements to evacuate Europe. Through Agnes Meyer and the U.S. State Department, the Manns obtained airplane reservations, rendezvoused in Amsterdam with Erika, and then flew on to London.[132] They left most of their luggage behind and made a successful "escape," as Mann called it. Vermouth, sleeping pills, and good food eased his tension during a six-day, "endless" voyage to America, and amidst the calming sea, Mann, like Joseph, decided to "trust in my own destiny." On September 18, 1939, he arrived in America—"my fated berth and refuge, perhaps for the rest of my life."[133]

The war Mann had wished for since 1934 immediately unleashed a torrent of death and destruction when it finally began. In October, Mann sent off the final chapter of *Lotte in Weimar* to his publisher Bermann Fischer, who had moved from Vienna to Stockholm, but communication with Europe was already so unreliable that Mann heard nothing of its receipt. On November 3, he wrote to his son Golo in Zurich, "Nowadays everything is sent into the void, and there are years ahead, I am afraid, in which we'll hardly be able to speak of living in the 'age of communications.' "[134]

Those "years ahead" for Germany and her people were to be what consumed Thomas Mann from the moment war broke out. Mann fully expected America's entry into the war—sooner rather than later—and took Hitler's defeat as a certainty. As a result, the actual fight itself was psychologically only a blip for Mann—an absolute necessity, but hardly the greater struggle which loomed beyond war's end. Far more painful was Mann's fear that a mordant sense of German guilt, coupled with Allied vengefulness, could bury Germany. Henceforth, the crisis which engulfed him turned on the nature of German defeat whenever that welcome event finally occurred.

Assured of his own safe destiny and inhabiting the artist's gracious "unity of the All and the Nothing," Mann immediately began wondering how he could broker a peace between Germans temporarily lost to the Faustian underworld and an allied people who, though they had finally taken a moral stance in waging war, teetered on the brink of that same underworld, simply because they, too, were human. Very early in the war, Mann sensed that when the Allies won, they would sit in judgment like God. But they were not God. The European Allies themselves had not been above reproach; he saw that misguided ideas of state sovereignty had led to bloodshed and power ambition for more than a century. Mann believed that the future of Europe lay in a pan-European association of countries, not separated by state sovereignty, but bound by moral law. In his 1940 essay, "This War," Mann declared that the future of humanity demanded that the Allies separate the German people from "a handful of perverted and bloody-minded men," and he cautioned against the Allied "annihilation" of Germany.[135]

Mann's tenacious sense of mission was tempered by doubts that he would still be alive by the time war ended. Speculation ran that the war might last ten years, and Mann was sixty-four in 1939. Nevertheless, both his determination to secure Germany's future and his brute artistic drive consistently overcame any anxieties concerning age and ill health, and he worked with a blind perseverance.

In December 1939, Mann began research on a new novella inspired by ancient Indian mythology, which he called *The Transposed Heads: A Legend of India.*[136] Hilarious, ironic, simple and yet vastly rich, it carried Mann's infatuation with the dialectic between intellect and nature to an absurd extreme. The story concerns a bride, her smart, but physically weak husband, and his physically robust, but simple-minded best friend. Love and duty make for big trouble for these three naïfs: the friends cut off their own heads out of the pain of knowing they both love her, the bride accidentally transposes them, and after failing in all varieties of living arrangements to accomodate their intellectal and physical longings, they all kill themselves. The work perfectly suited a man who, while physically safe amidst the farmland and erudition of Princeton, New Jersey, was spiritually and intellectually a participant in the strife of war-torn Europe.

Mann, who seemed to be making fun of his own conflicts and obsessions, had a great deal of fun writing *The Transposed Heads*, but the comic relief and easy pleasure he found in writing the novella were to be the last for many years. As Mann brought the work to a close, the war dramatically intensified. Scandinavia, Belgium, and the Netherlands had been plowed over by the Nazis in April and May—a bloody preamble to the fall of France on June 14, 1940, the day German troops paraded through Paris, where Heinrich had been living. Friends were murdered or committed suicide during Hitler's latest sweep, but still more remained under grave threat. (Mann worked tirelessly to arrange escape for these men and women through the International PEN Club and the American Emergency Rescue Committee, which he was instrumental in founding.) Katia's family, once part of Germany's esteemed intelligentsia, were scattered in Switzerland and Belgium, bereft of their former wealth and stature. But above all, Mann's immediate, paramount concern was for his daughter Monika, married to a Hungarian art history professor and living in London; and his son Golo, who in May had volunteered for the International Red Cross against his parents' wishes. Golo was in France at the time of the French occupation, and his whereabouts remained unknown.

As Mann anxiously awaited the expected invasion of England during the summer of 1940, he wrote Erich von Kahler: "The situation is ghastly, a torture to the mind and the emotions. . . . If she [England] falls in one way or another, the gates are thrown open to hell itself everywhere. We must prepare to face total defenselessness and homelessness, with eternity the only refuge. I have always believed that maintaining a kind of personal serenity can bring one safely through the darkest circumstances, and I have trusted to my capacity for adaptation. But these days I often feel hopelessly trapped."[137]

Mann's sense of confinement and fear was based on more than England's fate. Fatherly concern for his six children was evolving into a constant, preoccupying worry for their safety and well-being. His worry was wholly justified, especially given the controversial nature and daring activities of his older children, Klaus,[138] Erika, and Golo, though for Mann's other children, exile and war proved also to be physically as well as psychologically dangerous.[139]

Of all his children, Erika, the eldest child, born in 1905, was the closest to him, and Mann found her risk-taking maddening. A former actress turned polemical journalist, Erika was emotional, strong-willed, and independent.[140] In order to obtain British citizenship and a valid passport, Erika, a lesbian, in June of 1935 married her brother Klaus's friend, the poet W. H. Auden, himself a homosexual, and against her father's wishes enlisted to become an intelligence agent for the British Ministry of Information. In July 1940, as her father cautiously awaited word on the whereabouts of Golo, Heinrich, and Katia's brother Peter Pringsheim, who had disappeared somewhere in Belgium, Erika eagerly counted the days until she could begin her intelligence duties in London. Mann quipped that by her going, he was offering something far more valuable than a destroyer, but his wry humor barely veiled his grim concern.

Fortunately, Mann's trepidations over Erika were mitigated by his ability to help other family members escape the Nazis. Through his influence and work on behalf of the Emergency Rescue Committee, Mann had obtained visas for Monika and her family, and Heinrich and his long-time mistress. In August, the Manns learned that Golo was being detained near Toulon and had not been interned in a camp in Nîmes as they had been told.

Despite this emotional turmoil, Mann felt that the greatest challenge was to continue his writing, and true to his word, in August of 1940 he resumed work on the Joseph story after a four-year hiatus. He displayed his well-worn optimism when he described Joseph in the beginning of *Joseph the Provider*:

Circumstances were powerful; but what Joseph believed in was their plasticity: he felt sure of the preponderant influence of the individual destiny upon the general force of circumstances. When like Gilgamesh he called himself a glad-sorry man, it was in the sense that he knew the happy side of his nature was capable of much suffering, but on the other hand did not believe in suffering so bad and so black that it would prove too dense for his own light, or the light of God in him, to penetrate.[141]

Mann's semblance of calm, however, was to be short-lived. In September, the British evacuation ship *City of Benares*, carrying Monika and her family, was sunk by a German U-boat. She and her daughter were saved after spending many hours in the water clinging to a lifeboat, but her husband, Jeno Lanyi, drowned. For the duration of the war, Monika, along with her daughter, lived with her parents, taking up something of the life of Antonie Buddenbrooks, the temperamental, unlucky widowed daughter in Mann's early family saga. Mann, who had described Monika as "psychologically a frail little thing"[142] even before the rescue, afterward referred to his daughter as "the poor little widow."[143]

Mann felt intensely frustrated that tragedies like his daughter's were ignored by Americans who still failed to comprehend the consequences of Hitler's winning the war. In 1940 no more than one in five Americans wanted direct United States involvement. Even Mann's haloed leader, President Franklin Roosevelt, campaigned for third-term reelection in 1940, promising not to send Americans to fight in foreign lands, "except in case of attack," with America's role instead limited to air and sea support.[144]

Psychologically and emotionally, Mann needed to keep hoping that America was a good country of good, moral, freedom-loving people, and he remained faithful to the idea that Americans, led by their deeply moral president, would not turn their backs on Europe forever. In the meantime, he resolved to be neither bitter nor despondent. He had concluded that endurance was the only marker in a long life. Endurance and work. What else could one hope to control? Mann and his fellow exiles had long since stopped counting the days of Hitler's Reich in anticipation of their return to Europe. "We have learned to recognize an interlude as an era," Mann wrote despondently to Hermann Hesse on January 2, 1941. "I fear—if fear is the right word, that this process is going to roll on and on, and that when the waters recede Europe will have changed beyond recognition, so that one will hardly be able to speak of going home, even if it is physically possible."[145]

In the summer of 1940, Mann decided he needed a change of scenery. His post as humanities lecturer at Princeton had afforded him safe refuge from Hitler, an annual stipend, an adoring university audience, and access to a community of exiled intellectuals which included Albert Einstein, Max Reinhardt, and Bruno Walter. While Mann appreciated his life there, he never loved it. He particularly disliked Princeton's hot humid summers and biting wintry winds. Moreover, he missed the sea.

The Manns took the train west to California, renting a house in the Brentwood district of Los Angeles. Their good friends from Munich, Bruno Frank, a novelist, poet, and dramatist, and his wife, Liesl, were living in Beverly Hills, and the Manns and Franks spent many comfortable evenings together that summer. In 1940 Alfred Doblin, Franz Werfel, Lion Feuchtwanger, and Heinrich Mann all emigrated to southern California, and Mann actually socialized with more German writers in California than he had in Munich. For sun-worshiping German exiles in America, California became during the late 1930s and 1940s what southern France had been to them right after Hitler's seizure of power. The lure of Hollywood, too, was strong for many of Europe's exiled writers, offering high-paying jobs, as well as a safe haven. Mann helped many obtain employment in the big studios.

Mann and his work prospered in the California climate, and the family made the decision to relocate there after setting his affairs in order in Princeton. In mid-March 1941, Mann, his wife, his daughter Monika, and his granddaughter left their large, brick house in Princeton and moved into a small rented house in Santa Monica, about twenty-five minutes from Hollywood. Though the move from Princeton to California was almost as far as from Germany to the United States, Mann was returning to the calm, natural grace, and freedom that he had enjoyed in his favorite seaside retreats in Europe and a state of mind he cherished. Mann had once written that "objectifying and distancing are my normal mode," and within weeks of living in Santa Monica, Mann felt certain he had found an environment well suited to this and other aspects of his nature.[146] The Manns' vacillation over whether to build a permanent home in California evaporated.

Mann's cash flow had been severely limited by the loss of his large European markets and poor American sales of *The Beloved Returns* and *The Transposed Heads*, and Mann took out a federal loan to build a house on land he had bought in Pacific Palisades, overlooking the sea and Catalina Island. His intention to economize in the home's construction was sincere, if somewhat overblown. When on December 1 he was named Consultant in German Literature to the Library of Congress with a $4,800 annual salary,[147] the Manns added refinements which, in addition to wartime labor and supply shortages, delayed completion of the house almost two months, until early February 1942.

The Manns called their new home Seven Palms House, and its building consumed all of Mann's excitement, even blunting the war's impact. Only weeks after the United States declared war on Japan and her Axis partners—Mann's great wish since war broke out in 1939—he boasted, "I shall, Heil Hitler, have the finest study I have ever worked in. . . . We must only hope that this strip of coast will not be evacuated some day, with Seven Palms House becoming the quarters of some American colonel or perhaps later the Mikado!"[148]

The house had a beautiful view of the ocean and a sun-drenched garden with palm, olive, pepper, and eucalyptus trees. Describing his new home to Hermann Hesse, Mann wrote, "the luxuriant flowers, the grass plots. . . . [T]he sky is bright almost all year long and sheds an incomparable, all-beautifying light."[149] Although Mann despaired of ever seeing Europe again, or at least of seeing a Europe remotely resembling the land he knew, his new life in California afforded him a crucial physical ease and spiritual calm. Each day, he and Katia drove ten minutes to the beach, where she swam and he took leisurely walks. Mann had found "the consolations of a sunny world, which make one forget," as Keats had described in "Ode to a Nightingale,"[150] and as he neared the end of *Joseph the Provider*, the final installment of the Joseph story, his work went swiftly and joyously. Mann told a suspenseful, ironic tale of Joseph's humbling before God and his father, Jacob, as he finally fulfills his blessed destiny, saving the Chosen People. In so doing, he becomes isolated from those he loves and loses the blessing. Mann demonstrated once more his mastery of irony: Joseph, "the glad-sorry man," feels not tragic sadness at his long-endured suffering and loss, but great joy because he has learned self-denying love for family and country. Forty years after being exiled in bondage from his home in Canaan, Joseph finds deep satisfaction in knowing that he has been the instrument of God's good will.

If anything tainted Mann's otherwise jubilant housewarming, it was the xenophobia spreading throughout America, which was especially intense on the West Coast and culminated in the internment of Japanese Americans beginning in March. In January 1942, President Roosevelt instituted restrictions on all resident aliens, including even America's most visible anti-Hitler German exile, Thomas Mann. Though he was feted at the White House by Roosevelt himself and now filled a prestigious post at the Library of Congress, Mann was required to request permission to travel each time he toured to lecture, even at the Library of Congress—an irony not lost on him. Before Seven Palms House was ever finished, Mann wondered half-heartedly whether as aliens "we will have to leave our new house and live in a hotel in Kansas City."[151]

This was no small utterance for someone whom history had conditioned to fear sudden danger. Mann deeply appreciated America's warm generosity, but always, as a German, felt it came with conditions. During the German invasion of France, Mann lamented to Bruno Frank, "If Hitler wins, not a single country on the Continent will be accessible to us again, and I would be surprised if America too did not also become impossible to us. What do you think of Peking? It has already been recommended to me several times."[152]

In America, German exiles like Mann felt themselves forced to walk a delicate tightrope, an interesting but difficult balancing act for Mann. Privately, he chastised Germany to his countrymen, but publicly he explained to his American audiences that a parasitic evil had pentrated the otherwise humane German nature, and asked Americans not to judge the Germans too harshly. Mann was always cautious to appear grateful to his benefactors; at the end of 1943, for example, he declined establishing a Free Germany Committee in America out of fear that "as soon as the public hears rumors of such a German group, uneasiness and mistrust arise," explaining to German exile playwright Bertholt Brecht that "our union would be viewed as nothing but a patriotic effort to shield Germany from the consequences of her crimes."[153] Yet, as the fighting wore on, Mann felt a heavy responsibility to see that the German identity he cherished for its querulousness, its curiosity and its creative exuberance not become so blackened by the Allies as to appear fit to be cast into oblivion.

Mann's public persona as the stalwart archetype of the German intellectual bourgeoisie—the image his German enemies called self-righteous and arrogant—gained even more momentum with the American publication in 1942 of two decades of his political essays, *Order of the Day*. Internally, he continued to struggle with self-doubt, and eventually guilt, as a result of living sequestered in the Pacific Palisades, among "those who are still far too well off, considering the nature of the times."[154] But above all, Mann remained resolute and unapologetic both to his German detractors and American supporters. He told Agnes Meyer on August 20, 1942, that America was "a country to which I owe nothing but good, and which the world will one day have to thank for tremendous things. . . . As a German I feel the most profound horror of having the death of America's best young men on my conscience, as it were. But on the other hand, if I had not done my best to prevent all this, I would be in Berlin today supervising the printing of the fourth volume of Joseph."[155]

This particular expression of Mann's infamous "ironic remoteness," as he himself termed his arrogance, no doubt stemmed from his wrenching ambivalence toward his native Germany which was heading for crisis. Not until 1940 had Mann even been able to admit to himself and to the public that the German people were not the unwitting victims of the Nazi scourge. Then he had asked like a mystified child how the German people, with all their tendency toward romanticism and "dark vision," could not have understood that a policy of "force within" could never lead to "peace without."[156] Mann saw that the defeat of Hitler alone would not be enough to eradicate the evil within Germany. Given the uniquely vicious nature of Nazi domination and its contempt for all that humanity supposedly treasured, Mann openly called for the war to be long enough to "cleanse" the German soul of this dark plague. To Mann, renewal was part of human history, an idea he put forth in *Young Joseph*: "the life of mankind cometh to an end several times, and each time cometh the grave and the rebirth, and many times must he be, until at length he finally is."[157] His dilemma lay in the knowledge that German cleansing and renewal carried as high a human cost as German sin.

Mann was winding down his work on *Joseph the Provider* in November 1942 when he made a lecture tour east to Chicago, Washington, and New York. In Washington, he gave an address on the Joseph novels at the Library of Congress as part of his official duties as Consultant in Literature. Introducing Mann to the audience, Librarian of Congress Archibald MacLeish praised his service as consultant "in Germanic literature—a great literature which no evil, no obfuscation, no hatred, no venom can ever destroy."[158] Mann, however, was more impressed by the militarization of the city which he had first visited in 1935. Washington in 1942 was a nation's capital on a war footing. Antiaircraft guns were posted on top of the city's main post office. Temporary navy offices lined both sides of the Reflecting Pool between the Washington Monument and the Lincoln Memorial. Trains passed through Union Station loaded with war materiel, and the population had swelled with those filling positions in the massive war bureaucracy.

On January 4, 1943, after he had returned home to Pacific Palisades, Mann finished the fourth and final installment in his Joseph story. The work had consumed him since 1926—the duration of his exile and more, and when he finished, Mann was thrown into "a state of doubtful weightlessness," a feeling of being adrift. It was not at all a pleasant circumstance, he wrote, for one "who since his early days . . . has lived under multifarious burdens that had to be carried long distances, and who scarcely knows how to live without them."[159]

By happenstance, during the New York leg of the trip, Mann was approached to write the introductory essay to a book to be called *The Ten Commandments: Ten Short Novels of Hitler's War Against the Moral Code*. Ten writers, including Mann's friends Bruno Frank and Franz Werfel, a Jew, who in 1941 published the Utopian novel about a nun, *The Song of Bernadette*, were each to contribute an essay illustrating one of the Ten Commandments breached by Hitler. The book was commissioned by Simon & Schuster and was to be published later that year in several languages, including English. Though Mann had reservations about the assignment when he agreed to it, the project not only produced one of his greatest pieces, but also brought a small blessing to his psyche. Mann was not ready emotionally to leave behind the ancient, mystical world of the Joseph epic, nor was he ready to begin another large work either. The essay ultimately functioned as a bridge between the Joseph story and Mann's future work, over a period of extreme restlessness and disconnectedness which he characterized as "perilous" even before fully appreciating the enormous impact on him of mounting German military losses.

Mann was in desperate need to vent his simmering hatred, frustration, and anger toward his critics when he took up *Das Gesetz (The Commandments)*, and the work seemed to write itself. His assignment to write a short essay rapidly took the shape of a novella in which he depicted Moses as an artist pitted against powerful, damning critics, whom he avenges at the end. Mann later explained, "The curse at the end came from my heart and at least at the end leaves no doubt of the militant intent of this otherwise somewhat frivolous little thing."[160] He completed the work in just two months, and besides its inclusion in Simon & Schuster's 1943 (English) anthology, Bermann-Fischer Verlag published it separately in Germany, the following year, with Alfred Knopf bringing out an English version in 1945 under the title *The Tables of the Law*.

In many ways *The Commandments* was a thematic synopsis of the Joseph books, telling again the story of a man on a mission from God to spread the Word to his people. Chock-full of the moral dialectics Mann loved so well, the Old Testament story of Moses' receipt of the Ten Commandments was ready-made for Mann's brand of moral illumination and instruction. Once again, he used a biblical source to tell a contemporary parable of the German people in moral chaos, and of himself as man, artist, and molder of moral consciousness. The kind of stern, yet loving condemnation of the German people Mann delivered in essays and articles, from the lecture podium, and over the radio resonates in the richly stylized descriptions of Moses's Midianites, a people conscripted by a greedy pharaoh to do work contrary to their natures, and who after generations had lost their spiritual ways, yielding to "spiritual bribery."[161] When Moses receives his mission to deliver the divine word of God and to bring freedom to his people, he feels blessed with "a divine work which in his own very soul he craved to commence."[162] But Moses's sacred ambition is in many ways a curse. He embarks upon his exodus from home "with the weight of the great burden laid on his spirit through the Lord's command." This command sets him apart from others, and his people rebel against him often, accusing him of conceit and arrogance, asking him, "And who made you a prince and a judge over us?" His people take umbrage at Moses' persistent reminders of their sins, but he feels certain that only by ceaseless self-judgment can they attain purity and reverence and find God.

Moses's work is arduous and frustrating. His outward calm hides a simmering rage, and only with the help of his enormous "spiritual vitality" and patience is Moses able to continue. The people are so "lost, bewildered" that they have forgotten the difference between right and wrong. They commit wrongs haplessly— murdering, stealing, dishonoring, defiling, respecting nothing and believing themselves superior to their neighbor. Afterward, they seek justice from Moses, who then must teach simple fairness and decency as though they had never heard the lesson before. "[T]hey heard that in this new idea of right was included the idea of wrong," Mann wrote. "And this the masses for a long time utterly failed to grasp."

Just when Moses seems most likely to fail to bring his people to observe God's divine law, he sets about to bring the collected laws of God down from Mount Sinai. Holding up this biblical story as a simulacrum of contemporary events, Thomas Mann rendered an awesome portrait of Moses as a great wordsmith, cleaving to his personal longing for peace through artistic creation at the same time that he is driven to bring his people closer to God and thus their own humanity. Moses, God's scribe, becomes the writer obsessed with his mission, driven to find through intellect the right words to capture the experience which lay at the essence of human creativity. In Mann's version of the Bible story, Moses is not merely the passive receiver of tablets already filled with the Word, but he is the inventor of a universal moral language which every human being can understand. Through this language, Moses strives to deliver the concepts of goodness, fear, discipline, and reverence—that is, the Judaic concept of one universal God: "He could not invent signs for all the words his people used, nor for the syllables which composed them. . . . So Moses contrived something else—and horns stood forth from his head out of sheer pride of his god-invention. . . . [W]ith them one could set down the whole world in writing: the signs that took up space and those that took none, the derived and the contrived—in short, everything on earth."[163]

The novella closes with a plea for mercy which conveyed Thomas Mann's message to the Allies regarding their treatment of the German people. Just as Moses pleads with God not to destroy the Chosen People for their sins lest the world accuse God of failing to lead them to righteousness, so does Mann beg the Allies to deliver justice and fairness, so German decency can ultimately prevail. When Mann wrote *The Commandments* in the winter of 1942–43, he was still hopeful that he could win the kind of merciful treatment for his people that Moses succeeded in winning for his.

Germany and her people would need all the mercy Mann could muster. In January 1943, President Roosevelt, Prime Minister Winston Churchill, and General Charles de Gaulle, conferring in Casablanca, proclaimed that the only acceptable conclusion to the war was "the unconditional surrender of Germany, Italy, and Japan." Mann's plea that the war be long enough and terrible enough for Germany to be "truly cleansed" seemed likely.[164] Messerschmitts pounded England and France in January of 1943, and German women were mobilized for military service—a sign that the myth of German invincibility had begun to unravel. Starving German forces sustained crushing defeats at the hands of the Russians defending Stalingrad and Leningrad and lost key positions along their lines of defense in the Ukraine and Caucasus. When at the end of January 1943 Allied planes successfully attacked Germany for the first time, a despairing Mann knew it was only a matter of time before Allied troops landed on German soil—"the sacred German soil" that German propaganda had proclaimed to be inviolable. Mann craved German defeat to bring about an end to "the awful impasse into which fate has crowded the German soul."[165] Yet, his devout hope was that Germany—not Hitler's Germany, but his humanistic Germany of Beethoven and Schiller and Goethe, of beautiful cities, spires, and bridges—would escape Allied annihilation. With each passing week, such hope seemed more naive. Horror and despair gripped Mann as he awaited Germany's final collapse, but ambivalence overwhelmed him too. For all his revulsion from German sadism, Mann's deep, mystical belief in God and morality as the fabric of civilization required that even sinners be treated with compassion. He felt utter grief and pity as he awaited the German apocalypse.

Mann's serious doubts at this time as to whether he still had strength for a massive new undertaking paled before the seemingly involuntary growth of ideas for his Faust novel. Although he did not know exactly what he would write, he already had a main character—an artist—and an amorphous idea that the book would be about "some demonic intoxication and its liberating but catastrophic effects."[166]

For centuries the medieval Faustus legend about an old philosopher who sells his soul to the devil in exchange for knowledge and power has pervaded European culture. No version had captivated readers more than Goethe's dramatic poem *Faust*, which the writer began at the end of the Age of Enlightenment in 1774, and finally completed in 1832, after which he promptly died. Enlightenment philosophers, scientists, and statesmen who hailed the triumph of reason over spirit had not put an end to the debate, and readers swept up in the new tide of literary romanticism adored Goethe's exquisite depiction of evil as God's reasoned test for an irreverent mankind. Faust's yearning to experience passionate feeling even at the expense of moral goodness, his terrible suffering, and eventual longing for godly redemption, together with musings on man's relationship to science, theology, politics, and his fellow man, made it an utterly modern work for a modern, emergent Europe.

Mann, too, saw humans in an eternal "Faustian" struggle with themselves and God to be good and loving, and Goethe's *Faust*, Mann wrote, "remained the outstanding model that comes to mind when something extraordinary appears."[167] Everything in Goethe's poem spoke to Mann's ideas about a forgiving God and the struggle by the man of conscience to balance the steely world of intellect and knowledge with the effulgent world of feeling and body. Goethe's "unity of the double," the coexistence of good and evil in man which makes him human, suffused Mann's entire life's work. Man could be pious and virtuous, but he could also use God's gift of free will to commit the most heinous sins imaginable.

For the artist like himself, Mann believed that demonic temptation took on even more complex shadings. The extraordinary vibrant force of his own creativity had long fascinated Mann as a womb of warring contrasts: part arrogance and inhibition, homosexual longing and chastity, piety and paganism, sympathy and mockery, cold intellect and childhood neurosis, vitality and sickness. Mann believed that these conflicts reached a climax shortly before the moment of creativity. Thus, they, too, were another of God's terrible burdens and wondrous blessings. To what lengths, then, would an artist, possessed of an inestimable ambition to create, go to create a masterwork?

For more than forty years Mann had taken notes for a novel about an artist's pact with the devil. He always felt that his Faust would be a work of old age, perhaps even his last, as Goethe's *Faust* had been for him. If Mann had lacked the proper historical or social context earlier in which to set his version, Germany under Adolf Hitler provided the clearest paradigm of a people willing to commit any evil for the promise of a great future. Hitler dwelled, undeniably, in the German underworld like Goethe's Mephistopheles incarnate, whom Goethe had described as a "destroyer," an "annihilator," an "egoist"—all words which aptly characterized Hitler.[168] Goethe's Mephistopheles despises reason and knowledge and is "chaos' odd, fantastic son" whose habitat is the "ocean of untruth." In reading *Faust* today, one may see Goethe's Satan in the chilling light of Hitler and the German tragedy. Satan is a liar who exploits Faust's deepest yearning for freedom from worry and pain by making promises he never keeps, while forever dangling the promise in front of him. The very same fate which awaited Goethe's Faust befell the Germans who cleaved to Hitler's National Socialist golden path: madness, agony, and fear.

Throughout his life, Mann had taken notes for the novel, but it was not until now, when Germany inched closer to collapse, that the work surged forth from the depths of his psyche. In that dark place, Mann linked his artistic essence with that of Germany; he believed both tended to a dark, tragic romanticism, a youthful spirit reaching for the "revolutionary," and a perennial longing for "intoxication." Mann suspected that the dark side of genius veered dangerously close to the devil's realm. He wondered whether in the artist's feeling of triumph and possession and his extremes of joy and despair where reason dissolved into frenzied, irrational emotion, was the artist "the brother of the criminal and the madman?"[169] If the answer were "Yes," did that mean that Mann, who had arrogantly sought to lead his people to righteousness, also shared some demonic essence with Hitler? And if so, did he, too, need to plead for God's mercy at war's end, alongside his terrible, beloved German nation? After all, Mann never felt that he had stopped being a German. Indeed, Mann acknowledged *Doctor Faustus*'s "extremely German coloration," and its composition was to make Mann feel more "German" than ever.[170]

As a result of these many intense personal meanings, from its inception *Doctor Faustus* carried for Mann a sense of danger mixed with terrific yearning, a powerful parallel attraction and repulsion. Fearing that writing the book might kill him, or at the least the book might be his last, in the winter of 1943 Mann decided he was not ready to leap into the project which clearly beckoned him. He briefly considered taking up a novel, *Confessions of Felix Krull, Confidence Man*, which he had left unfinished in 1911 to write *Death in Venice*. Mann had always intended to return to this project, and friends encouraged him to do so now.

But death and catastrophe intruded every day—friends lost to old age and, of course, the war, which droned on. Allied successes against the Afrika Korps in North Africa, RAF bombings of Berlin, the Russian counterattack in the Caucasus, and the well-being of his son Klaus, now a U.S. soldier, and Erika, a war correspondent in Europe, all preoccupied him, and in the end, *Felix Krull*, his "novel about a rogue," lost out to the mystical and vastly gripping Faust story, which by now Mann had decided would center on the life of a music composer. He declined an offer from Sweden to write a book on Germany, and when the U.S. Office of War Information sent a letter thanking him for an article he wrote, Mann could not even recall the article.[171] He was too consumed with the novel, deep in the study of the history and composition of music, medicine, history, religion, linguistics, geography, politics, and sociology, trying to figure out the novel's atmosphere, characters, and symbolism. Mann had always approached his novels like a chemist testing hundreds of vials for his experiments, working from mounds of books, treatises, and documents to give verisimilitude to even the most abstract, dream-filled experience. During the composition of *Doctor Faustus*, Mann's dedication to research reached new heights, because he had never been more fraught with anxiety and fatigue, driven by the need to escape into the purely artistic, while at the same time feeling the burden of depicting moral horror in all its factual reality. *Doctor Faustus* took over his life. "[L]ike no other of my books," Mann later wrote, "this one consumed and took heavy toll of my inner most forces."[172] Mann had made several earlier attempts at portraying the emotional power of music, for example, in *Buddenbrooks*, where the suffering young Johann finds in the realm of music his only comfort. But Mann felt that his earlier attempts were "blundering amateurishness," compared to the musical legerdemain he needed to perform in *Doctor Faustus*, where polyphonic music was to be used to symbolize individual inhumanity and mass evil. Mann felt he could not appear to be fudging or pretending; he had to know enough about the technicalities of musical composition that his artist's music "could be heard."[173]

In his diary, war news blended with intensive Faustus research and planning. He recorded his meetings with composers Arnold Schoenberg, Igor Stravinsky, Bruno Frank, and Alfred Neumann, all of whom had fled Hitler and lived near Mann in California. Completely attuned to the present, he submerged himself in the past as a source of inspiration, creativity, and knowledge, reading the works of Shakespeare, Dickens, Flaubert, Voltaire, Molière, Dostoevsky, Conrad, and Goethe. The mingling of this purely artistic sphere with war news of bombings, air strikes, the French underground—vast, omnipresent mayhem and death—was strange and terrible, and this duality would itself be rendered in the novel, which alternated the narrator's war-torn present with the biographical past of the hero. Nervous and brooding, yet with a vast capacity for joy and ironic humor, Mann did not presume to gain wisdom from history, only pleasure and guidance for his own life and moral code. "Belief in absolute values, illusory as it always is, seems to me a condition of life," Mann avowed early in the novel through the voice of the narrator, echoing his own life credo.[174]

On March 23, 1943, Mann began writing his novel *Doctor Faustus*. In one way the book was not a war novel at all; in another, it was the absolute sum of Mann's view of war as the result of the complete failure of the human moral code. Just seven days before Mann began, the month-long Warsaw Ghetto uprising ended in the annihilation by the German S.S. of some fifty-six thousand Jews from the walled enclave. The stark fear with which the sixty-seven-year-old Mann had faced the project nearly three months earlier yielded to a profound creative eagerness, as well as the sense that it was his destiny to write such a book, a sentiment echoed by his closest friends. While in the past he professed to take neither himself nor his work nearly as seriously as the rest of the world did, he admitted this time to a sense of importance and excitement in undertaking a momentous mission: "This one time I knew what I was setting out to do and what task I was imposing upon myself: to write nothing less than the novel of my era, disguised as the story of an artist's life, a terribly imperiled and sinful artist."[175] This heightened sense of the importance of *Doctor Faustus* exacted a great toll on Mann's physical and emotional health.

The work went slowly. "The thing is difficult, weird, uncanny, sad as life," he explained in June to Agnes Meyer, "in fact, even more so, since idea and art always exceed and exaggerate life."[176] By midsummer 1943 Mann had finished roughly seventy pages, when he put down *Doctor Faustus* for two weeks to write a lecture he was scheduled to deliver at the Library of Congress in the coming autumn. The lecture, entitled "War and the Future," gave voice to Mann's growing concern for the postwar treatment of Germany by the victors. Mann admitted privately that in composing the lecture, he found himself saying "alarmingly 'leftish' things,"[177] specifically referring to his denunciation of the "capitalist democracies" for allowing the unfettered growth of fascism which he attributed to "the bourgeois world's idiotic panic over Communism."[178] He also reiterated his long-held endorsement of a postwar European federation to end the continent's strife permanently.

In substance, the lecture said little that Mann had not been saying openly since the late 1930s, but times had changed. The English, French, and Americans shedding their blood against the Germans were indisputably the world's "good guys," fighting fascism valiantly alongside the Communists, even if they did not really want them as their brothers. The concept of a federated Europe smacked a shade leftist at a time when democratic people despised Germany and wanted her ground into dust. The idea of a defeated Germany participating in Europe's postwar government seemed ludicrous, even if it could make for longstanding peace. Mann himself conceived of this federation beginning only *after* Germany's severe punishment.

On August 17, 1943, the Allies captured Sicily in thirty-eight days of fighting. Despite feeling that "the war is going almost too well at the moment,"[179] Mann and his fellow German exiles had the deep, terrifying premonition that the forced mask of unity between Russia and her allies could peel away at any moment. Stalin was furious over the American and English refusal to invade France, and he had refused to meet with Roosevelt and Churchill in mid-August in Quebec to plan future strategy. Mann wrote wearily in his diary, "Impression that what is going on is scarcely concerned with this war any longer, but with the preparation of the next."[180]

In 1914 Mann had idealized war as a means to German unity and strength. Beginning in the 1930s he began to see war very differently, as the state's way of suppressing its populace and as an "immature escape" from curing internal social problems, which could only be solved during peacetime. Now as Allied successes in Italy, Russia, and the Mediterranean ensured victory, Mann moved even closer to the views of old friends like Hermann Hesse and his brother Heinrich who felt that guilt for war largely rested with the power brokers of all nations.[181] Mann decided to broaden *Doctor Faustus*'s themes, fusing them "in the universalities of the era and of Europe,"[182] and he told large audiences in Washington, Montreal, Chicago, and New York that "it was not Germany or the German people who must be destroyed and sterilized but the guilt-laden power combination of Junkers, army officers, and industrialists, which has been responsible for two world wars."[183]

In truth, Mann's ecumenical vision led him to distrust any one political ideology. Expressing a rare pessimism, he wrote later that winter that humanity would find any number of "pretexts for slaughtering one another," and he presciently observed that only a "uranium atom" would suffice to stop the killing, "for then the game will really be in deadly earnest."[184] Nonetheless, Mann told listeners to his "War and the Future" lecture that he prayed for a Germany cleansed by "revolution, which the victors should not try to prevent, but should instead favor and promote."[185]

Mann was grateful that he could throw himself into *Doctor Faustus*, thereby keeping the disquieting outside world at a distance for a good part of each day. By late winter 1944 the German army was in its prolonged and gruesome death throes. The Russians recaptured the strategically crucial Kerch Peninsula on the Black Sea and drove the Germans out of Odessa and Sevastopol in the oil-rich Crimea. Despite these clear signs of defeat, Hitler redoubled his efforts to defeat his many enemies. He consigned greater numbers to the gas chambers and sent German boys as young as twelve, wearing man-sized helmets too big for their small heads, to fight alongside weary veterans who knew that the war was lost. In March, around-the-clock Allied bombing of Berlin began, leading Mann to write in *Doctor Faustus*: "That the flabby democracies did know after all how to use these frightful tools is a staggering revelation, weaning us daily from the mistaken idea that war is a German prerogative."[186] When Hitler's insane, retaliatory acts continued against Mann's friends still in Europe, he despaired. Upon hearing that the eighty-three-year-old widow of German impressionist painter Max Liebermann had poisoned herself rather than be deported to Poland, Mann felt "suffering, sorrowful, deeply perturbed and weary."[187] He feared for Germany's future, because not only had the Germans shown such submissiveness in the past, but they were unwilling to give up, even now, when it was clear that they had reached a "horrible dead-end street." Mann clung to the hope he cherished of life's vast "possibilities of change and regeneration," but increasingly he feared that "a German revolution, if it comes, will come too late to possess any morally rehabilitating value, but will be a mere sign of utter collapse."[188]

On June 6, 1944—D-Day—Thomas Mann turned sixty-nine. Though he lived for another decade, this birthday marked the beginning of a general decline in his health. Mann had completed just half of *Doctor Faustus* by the end of June, and he had begun to feel the full burden of the task he had set for himself. "[T]he difficulties are mounting," he wrote to his son Klaus, a U.S. sergeant attached to the Fifth Army in Italy. "Did I really have to load something of this sort on myself?"[189]

Mann knew the answer was "yes." Adrian Leverkuhn, the novel's main character, had been particularly inspired by the rabid persona of Friederich Nietzsche. But Mann himself figured everywhere in the book he began referring to as this "biography of mine," "a completely private experiment," and "a radical confessional."[190] His artistic and spiritual torment infused his "God-inflicted" and despairing composer; his rational humanity bloomed in his good-hearted, rather ordinary narrator Zeitblom. He was Leverkuhn in his all-consuming will to create *Doctor Faustus*; he was Zeitblom, mournfully crying "we are lost," like Conrad's Kurtz in the *Heart of Darkness*. And he was Germany, too, before Hitler had twisted her essential nature as Mann saw it—"revolutionary" in spirit, religiously conscious, "the eternal student, the eternal searcher."[191] Though Mann began the book imbued with the sense of righteous leadership which had carried him through the Joseph story, his arrogance had given way to the realization that the writer's only true power lay in what he now termed "expressiveness," the depiction of human agony.

Mind-taxing in ideas and emotional complexity, *Doctor Faustus* merged the dichotomy in Mann's wartime writing between the unbiased presentation of human suffering and the unsparing didacticism of his essays, lectures, and broadcasts. *Doctor Faustus* represented the totality of its creator. It was also relentlessly ponderous, brooding, turgid, and joyless, despite Mann's best efforts to make his readers laugh. No wonder he called it his "book of sorrows."[192] The book is so mournful that the reader can almost hear Mann crying.

Within the book's bleak narrative Mann enfolded a quarter century of evil and suffering: World War I and its confused aftermath—the gruesome crematoria; the "spineless" critics, intellectual "creeps," and morphine addicts seeking emotional escape; the Allied bombings of Germany; the Russian offensive; and German counterattack—culminating in Adrian Leverkuhn's metamorphosis into a loving man and his final plea for humanity in the form of a great choral work, *The Lamentation of Doctor Faustus*. Mann described Adrian's musical composition as monumental, with "echo-like continuations" ending with God's lament on the state of the world, "the most frightful lament ever set up on this earth."[193]

Through his own lament, Mann survived, but barely. While working on the novel's climax, he fell seriously ill in December 1945, and in May, he underwent surgery to remove a malignancy on his lung. For the first time in his career, Mann was forced to stop work for a prolonged period. He believed the work was killing him; yet, when he recovered he felt that it was what had kept him alive.

In writing *Doctor Faustus*, Mann had immersed himself in Germany's human tragedy and found safety in the danger. In that hermetic "special sphere of art," Mann attained his "unity of the All and the Nothing." For, with all its measure of human suffering and guilt from evil, *Doctor Faustus* represented Mann's paean to art as the ultimate life-creating, life-extending force for the artist. Art had become the symbol for everything rich in life: the sensual and the cerebral, the pious and the profane, the beautiful and the ugly. It was protection from hopelessness, boredom, love-sickness, moral bankruptcy, and world chaos. It was salvation to the God-fearing, God-loving artist-man. At the very least, the practice of art constituted a habitual task which filled days otherwise mired in grief. Nothing was more important than art, which for the writer meant the sacrosanct word.

Framing what was to be the writer's salient question for an entire era, Mann wrote in *Doctor Faustus*: "now the question is whether at the present stage of our consciousness, our knowledge, our sense of truth, this little game is still permissible, still intellectually possible, still to be taken seriously; whether the work as such . . . still stands in any legitimate relation to the complete insecurity, problematic conditions, and lack of harmony of our social situation; whether all seeming, even the most beautiful, even precisely the beautiful, has not today become a lie."[194]

Mann's answer lay in the doing. *Doctor Faustus* was forty years in the planning, more than three years in the writing, through war, physical and emotional pain, the death of Roosevelt, the coming of the Red Scare in America, and growing old. No matter how great the evil and suffering which still lay ahead of him, like Adrian Leverkuhn, Thomas Mann would make art until he died.

"[O]nly art could give body to a life which otherwise would bore itself to death with its own facility," Mann wrote of Adrian Leverkuhn in *Doctor Faustus*.[195] This was the scorching, wondrous essence of Leverkuhn's fevered passion, and it was Thomas Mann's essence, too.

Since the beginning of the war Mann had understood that America and the Soviet Union would emerge as the two dominant world forces whose power would dwarf any that the modern world had known. This was a frightening prospect to him and his fellow German exiles, who not only feared the impact of these two powerhouses on Germany, but worried about its potential for inspiring a "future war of annihilation," with even deadlier weapons and more catastrophic human consequences. As Mann faced the devastating end of the war against Germany and Allied plans for Germany's division into four zones of occupation, he attempted to rely on the hope that the Allied nations would embrace a new humanism. But the wisdom and foresight which had protected him from physical danger during the Hitler era was a mixed blessing because it also precluded the more psychologically comforting rose-colored illusion. Twelve years before, Mann had borne witness to the overnight transformation of Germany into a fascist monster, and unfortunately for him, in postwar America he was poised to sense the abrupt change from liberalism to right-wing extremism which overtook his adoptive homeland from the very moment Franklin Roosevelt died and Harry S Truman became president. Mann's worst fears for the future of America, Germany, and the Soviet Union lay just beyond the horizon of Allied victory.

CHAPTER TWO

John Steinbeck

AMERICA AGAINST ITSELF

In his mind a new song had come, the
Song of Evil, the music of the enemy, of
any foe of the family, a savage, secret, dangerous melody, and
underneath, the Song of the Family cried plaintively.

The Pearl, 1945

The year Adolf Hitler came to power in Germany, a quarter of the way around the world in Salinas, California, John Steinbeck was having the worst year of his life. His mother was gravely ill, his father could not take care of her alone, and the thirty-one-year-old Steinbeck and his wife Carol had been conscripted as nurse, cook, and maid to the elderly couple. The four adults crowded into the parents' turreted Victorian house in Salinas, a small town surrounded by cattle ranches and farms, sitting at the top of a long, rugged river valley. A bleak mood of sickness and despair settled over the family. As his mother's health declined, so did his father's. Though the younger Steinbeck saw his father as a victim of his mother's dominance—a silent, unhappy man, defeated by the "swirl of family and money and responsibility"—he understood the kind of warped emotional interdependence they shared, and he feared that his father would not survive his mother's death.[1]

Changing bedpans and soiled sheets was not nearly the worst of it. Steinbeck had published three novels—*Cup of Gold* (1929), *Pastures of Heaven* (1932), and *To a God Unknown* (1933)—but he had toiled in poverty and anonymity. The Depression had turned his situation from terrible to abominable, as publishing companies and magazines went broke and the ones who stayed afloat were reluctant to take on unknowns, especially a new writer whose stories were steeped in magic spells, premonitions, enchanted forests, and powerful symbols of death and destiny.

It had taken all the power Steinbeck could summon to continue writing under the strain of rejection and financial privation; yet, he had persisted, almost superhumanly. Just weeks before moving in with his parents, Steinbeck was so broke that he ripped tar paper off the roof of the shack he and Carol rented to bind a manuscript to send to his agent. Failure had unleashed in him a boundless store of energy and confidence at which even he marveled, and when his future seemed most bleak, he optimistically viewed his troubles as being valuable disciplinary tools which would in the end only make him a better writer.

As Steinbeck nursed his parents, he began to observe their sicknesses following certain predetermined biological rules. Though he appeared to be the quintessential romantic artist, Steinbeck also possessed the coldly probing, questioning mind of a scientist, and his sudden thrust into a sickhouse atmosphere ironically provided the perfect opportunity for him to exercise his longtime interest in biology. In fact, Steinbeck had briefly considered a career in science during his haphazard college years at Stanford University, but his hatred for school and his yearning to be a writer, as well as a dire need for money after his father's feedstore went bankrupt in 1924, killed those aspirations. His interest had lain dormant until 1930, when he met a marine biologist named Edward Ricketts, who shared Steinbeck's intense curiosity about living things, which was inseparable from a deeper search for life's truths. The friends both loved music, art, and literature, and cherished personal freedom, but on a less lofty plane, they reveled in drink and having a good time which for Ricketts, a womanizing divorcé, meant plenty of sex. Through his friendship with Ricketts, who owned a marine laboratory in nearby Monterey, Steinbeck resuscitated his keen fascination in biology. He spent long hours in the laboratory and accompanied Ricketts on specimen-gathering ventures up and down the California coast. They spent countless hours playing mental games, often picking up the other's ideas in a breathless intellectual round-robin. They discoursed on anything—from poetry to car mechanics, Mozart to beer—but in their mutual quest to find universal truths their common subjects were philosophy, evolution, anthropology, and the predetermination of biological characteristics and functions.[2] At the time they met, Steinbeck already held a firm belief in the powerful connection of man to nature.

In 1933, Steinbeck was veritably sequestered in the house with his enfeebled parents, yet he found himself drawing larger, universal conclusions from individual pain and suffering. Added to a mélange of ideas was his observation that the end of a severe, decade-long, cyclical drought in California in 1932 had made indelible impressions on the human psyche. On June 21, 1933, Steinbeck wrote a sprawling, ebullient letter to his college friend Carlton "Dook" Sheffield, explaining his conclusion that when humans, like sick cells, joined together, they formed something completely new and powerful, which behaved in altogether new, often cruel, modes. From this point on, Steinbeck referred to individuals as "human units."

"It is quite easy for the group, acting under stimuli to viciousness, to eliminate the kindly natures of its units," Steinbeck explained. "When acting as a group, men do not partake of their ordinary natures. . . . The fascinating thing to me is the way the group has a soul, a drive, an intent, an end, a method, a reaction and a set of tropisms which in no way resembles the same things possessed by the men who make up the group."[3]

Steinbeck felt he had struck on something monumental; as his ideas blossomed, he merged biology and ancient Greek history with his reading of works by nineteenth-century German philosopher Georg Wilhelm Friedrich Hegel and Swiss psychologist Carl Jung. Hegel's thesis that the human mind is universal (*Weltgeist*) and cannot be identified with any one particular person perfectly fit Steinbeck's ideas about mass psychology, but Carl Jung's work seemed to speak even more directly to his psyche. Since youth, Steinbeck had harbored restless dreams, a fear of darkness, and a belief in symbols, omens, and premonitions, whose perceived power often terrified him.

In the notes and letters he wrote in the brief moments he could steal from his filial duties, Steinbeck began characterizing groups of human beings as a "phalanx," the Greek word for an order of battle, with every action, emotion, and thought stemming from such a group being the unique product of the phalanx. Steinbeck called his theory a "gorgeous thing" that explained so much of mankind's history—mass migrations, plagues, and the willing submission of peoples to murderous dictators such as Genghis Khan, Attila the Hun, and now Adolf Hitler.[4] In the letter to Sheffield, Steinbeck continued: "Think of the lemmings, little gophers who live in holes and who suddenly in their millions become a unit with a single impulse to suicide. Think of the impulse which has suddenly made Germany overlook the natures of its individuals and become what it has. Hitler didn't do it. He merely speaks about it."[5]

Tortilla Flat, published in May 1935, five days after his father's death, was Steinbeck's first novel written under the influence of his new obsession, and it became his first real success. Although he had gradually been moving away from earlier tales of pirates and enchanted forests, delving deeper into the psychological aspects of his characters, placing them in local settings, and questioning the relationship of the individual to the group, *Tortilla Flat* was essentially a literary study of the individual versus the group and represented a major break with his earlier work. Danny and his group of paisanos become a mob that is at once extremely fragile and destructively powerful. Because the group offers the paisanos salvation from depression, loneliness, fear, and economic privation, they will do just about anything to maintain its viability. They commit one transgression after another, even against each other, under the banner of allegiance to the group, whose purity they also believe exonerates them from guilt or shame.

Steinbeck had used the legend of King Arthur and his Knights of the Round Table as a conceptual springboard, but *Tortilla Flat*'s story and characterization were unique, and its surface simplicity constituted nothing less than a literary feat. Steinbeck, who during his long years of struggle performed a variety of tedious, physically grueling jobs that left him too tired to write, had weathered poverty so extreme he had once even gone four days without eating, and endured countless publishers' rejections, depression, and premonitions of death, suddenly was hailed as a new voice in American literature. The book became a national bestseller and garnered the ultimate commercial measure of success: a sale to

Paramount Pictures for $4,000. Since early childhood when his mother had read him fairy tales, Shakespearean plays, adventure stories like *Paul Bunyan*, the Bible, and classical literature, Steinbeck had been obsessed with the mythological past, daydreaming about nymphs, leprechauns, and knights in shining armor. Evidently, the shamans, myths, and philosophers had served John Steinbeck well.

Across the Atlantic in 1935, the new chancellor of Germany, Adolf Hitler, was also realizing the hard-won fruits of his long patience, planning, and contemplation of human nature, also won with the help of mythology, tribal ritual, and psychology. Before long, however, both men would see vivid testimony to their understanding of the human species as a pliable creature ready to die for a purpose when united to his brethren by the right leader.

Had Adolf Hitler not become the murderous leader of the Third Reich, his book *Mein Kampf* (*My Struggle*) would undoubtedly have fallen into oblivion along with countless other racist tracts asserting Germanic superiority. But Hitler did become a towering leader, and *Mein Kampf*, which was published in two parts in 1925 and 1926, set down the principles of his campaign for world domination which would culminate in the Second World War: German expansion east across Russia, known as *Lebensraum*, the quest of the master race for racial purity, and the expulsion of the Jews from Europe.

Hitler wrote in the sweeping language of generalization, spewing hatred against bankers, politicians, Marxists, and especially Jews, as he urged the German people to create a pure "folkish state," based on their primitive ties of blood and soil. But mastery of the German race required the implementation of yet another principle set down in *Mein Kampf*, the *Fuhrerprinzip*, or leadership principle: "absolute responsibility unconditionally combined with absolute authority."[6] A man, Hitler explained in *Mein Kampf*, was "born to be a genius," and his fateful selection to govern millions had nothing to do with choice. The single most crucial mandate for followers of this great leader was to support him and his ideas with "rigid discipline and fanatical faith." Followers were not required to understand these ideas.

Hitler's assumption that he was that chosen leader was a tall dose of absolute megalomania on the part of a poverty-stricken high-school dropout and loner. Prone to histrionic outbursts, tragically unlucky in love, and a devotee of German music, Hitler was especially inspired by the sensational music of Richard Wagner, whose four operas based on ancient Norse mythology spun a dark, insecure world of pagan spirits, heroes, destiny, tragic love, greed, violence, and suicide. Central to the operas was the sin of monetary greed, which the composer called "the tragedy of modern capitalism."

Hitler derived tremendous emotional and polemical strength from these myths, to which he added his own interpretation of the ideas of Nietzsche and Hegel, as well as Charles Darwin's theory of survival of the fittest.[7] Hitler amalgamated these in a philosophy that glorified war, heroes, and the supremacy of the state, in the sense that the state was the embodiment on earth of divine spirit. Hegel, who believed that each man is connected to the greater humanity, forming but one part of the organic whole of the state, described heroes who are fated by a mysterious providence to carry out "the will of the world spirit."[8] While Hegel put forth the doctrine that individual freedom must be sublimated to the will of all, with the state being paramount, Hitler conveniently ignored important aspects of Hegel's concepts—namely, respect for law, justice, and reason—as well as Hegel's thesis that the state's ultimate goal is human freedom and unity.

Propped by such a vast wealth of intellectual support, Hitler's feeling of power grew as though the fates themselves had willed it. He believed that he alone had the power to move whole masses of individuals—human beings bound by their Aryan blood, willing to carry out whatever he asked of them. Hitler, firm in the knowledge he would unite the German people into one supreme Aryan juggernaut, suffered terribly in his relationships with women and may have seen himself as Wagner's tortured lover, Tristam, but he was also King Arthur—the rightful leader of a great Aryan people, eager to bring them the Holy Grail: world supremacy.

When in 1933 the German economy collapsed under a mountain of foreign, mostly American, debt, Hitler channeled the German people's grief into a victorious political endorsement of himself that led to his Nazi swastika hanging all over Germany and his units of gun-toting, robot-like, brown-shirted youths marching through Berlin's streets. Crowds of twenty, thirty, even fifty thousand Germans clamored in the Wilhelmplatz in front of the Chancellory to hear their Fuhrer speak in his magical voice about the supremacy of the Aryan race, as the Badenweiler March played and imperial regalia fluttered in the background.

"We want one leader! Nothing for us! Everything for Germany! Heil Hitler!" Millions followed, wearing symbols of their shared heritage and ambition, bound by racial pride, and a name—Nazi. All for one, and one for all.

As Hitler was consolidating his strategy for world domination in 1938, John Steinbeck was writing his masterpiece of America's own economic depression, *The Grapes of Wrath*. The novel described the desperate plight of the Joads, an "Okie" family, joining the thousands of farm families marching to California, only to be met by hatred, violence, and grinding poverty even worse than they had known in Oklahoma. The book was a scathing indictment of politicians, capitalism, American banks, and the mechanization and consolidation of farms by those banks. Steinbeck portrayed an America transformed into a fascist police state, led by something mysteriously, stubbornly evil like a "Gila monster [that] grabs hold, an' you chop him in two an' his head hangs on. Chop him at the neck an' his head hangs on."[9]

"Units" of men, wearing military-style caps, armed with guns, clubs, gas and searchlights, turn on former neighbors, and the less fortunate are hunted just for eating on land they do not own. Spies and agitators are sent to migrant camps looking for an excuse to murder the innocent. In the novel, America's migrant farmers, like Europe's persecuted refugees, are forced to leave their homes with a few cherished mementos. They fear the discovery of their hiding places and pray that they can pass the border police. All the while, they wonder how they will live away from homes they have known all their lives. "How can we live without our lives? How will we know it's us without our past?" they ask themselves. They also wonder why any one man would need to own one million acres when he can't possibly farm all of it. Steinbeck had dissected in minutest detail a kind of American facsimile of the soon-to-be Nazi war machine controlled by "Gila monster" Adolf Hitler.

Steinbeck loaded *The Grapes of Wrath* with symbols of the Okies' shared suffering and purpose: the jalopy-truck held together with spit and glue and loaded to the sky with meagre possessions; the tattered clothes and shoes with no soles; the withered expressions, worn like anonymous uniforms—badges of hunger, loss, alienation, humiliation, and pleading. And the shared name, too—"Okie"—spoken with hatred by those who saw them as drains on society. Herded into migrant ghetto camps, forced to carry identification papers, denied work, the basics of food, shelter, and hygiene, and even murdered, Steinbeck's American Okies were lacking only a symbol as apparent as the six-pointed yellow star or the pink inverted triangle which the Nazis forced Europe's Jews and homosexuals to wear.

As shockingly realistic as the book was, however, *The Grapes of Wrath* was like a doctrine of hope for bleak Americans whose lives had been ruined by the Depression. While Steinbeck portrayed unrelenting sadness, loss, cruelty, and tragedy, its message was one of eternal hope. The same rules of behavior which he ascribed to associations of the cruel would also work for the righteous, he claimed. The Joads and people like them would survive, Steinbeck promised—as much as warning to those who would quash them—in large part because out of their mass a leader would arise, one man who would rally the disenfranchised and lead the "revolution" that was coming. This leader would take back the land that was rightfully theirs, restore their pride, and give them the respect they deserved.

When Steinbeck began the novel in 1937, he predicted war—not in the larger world, but in America. His research, which had brought him to California's migrant farm camps and cotton fields, had shown him the cruelest side of American capitalism, and when he received death threats, Steinbeck did not underestimate the lengths to which the rich and powerful would go to defend their stake. When the American poor would rally *en masse* to turn their suffering and wrath into combative action, Steinbeck predicted blood, and soon, too. "[I]f you want to run you had better start now because you aren't going to have until the end of 1937," Steinbeck wrote friend George Albee in late 1936, fully convinced that America's poor and disenfranchised were poised for civil war. "I am not speaking of revolution again, but war."[10]

In the autumn of 1938, however, war seemed far likelier in Europe. Hitler had invaded the Rhineland and Austria and was accelerating his principle of *Lebensraum* by also threatening to take the Sudeten territories of Czechoslovakia. Steinbeck had written more than six hundred pages of *The Grapes of Wrath* when the Nazi Party Congress convened at Nuremberg in September 1938. Westerners followed radio and press transmissions of the week-long rally, listened to Hermann Goering call Czechoslovakia "a trifling piece of Europe making life unbearable for mankind," and were thrown into a panic dreading an announcement by Hitler that German forces would invade the tiny country.[11]

From the secluded ranch that Steinbeck and his wife, Carol, had purchased the month before near Los Gatos in northern California, Steinbeck, too, waited expectantly for Hitler's closing speech on the night of September 12, although at this time he doubted war would break out. In his working diary for *The Grapes of Wrath* he wrote that "the whole world is jittery about it [the speech]. All armies mobilized. It might be a shambles by tomorrow. And it might recede for a while. Can't tell."[12]

The speech was another of Hitler's oratorical subterfuges. He condemned Czech injustice against Sudeten Germans, but made no ultimatums, thereby leading the desperate French, British, and Czechs into believing that he still wanted peace. Still, with martial law declared in border areas after riots and strikes by Sudeten Germans and British pressure on the Czechs to give up the Sudetenland, the possibility of war continued to be a distraction that September. The only way Steinbeck could focus singlemindedly on *The Grapes of Wrath* was to "throw out the world," and yet he feared he was "losing this book in the welter of other things. The war about to break."[13]

For Steinbeck, Europe's troubles during the Munich Crisis seemed less important than the battle his emotions were fighting at this time. By day he feverishly described the grueling trials of the Joads, his emotions convulsing along with them, as though he were one of them. (Especially in times of stress, Steinbeck typically described himself as lacking reality, as deriving himself and his emotions from his characters, rather than the other way around.) At night he was gripped by insomnia, nightmares, and premonitions of death. The monumental task that he had set for himself would expose weaknesses in his own nature, he feared, his ineptitude and "overwhelming laziness," among the worst. The task of plotting each section sent him into a frenzied panic, and he anticipated that many middle-class readers would find the book "vulgar" because of its unusually graphic, matter-of-fact depictions of sexuality, religious fervor, pregnancy, and personal hygiene.

Each day that September, as Hitler played his public game of vacillation before the West's cowering leaders, Steinbeck truly vacillated between confident predictions of completion by October and apprehension about his future after *The Grapes of Wrath*. He admitted there was "a kind of safety in keeping in the book that I like."[14]

In October, Steinbeck wrote the book's stunning finish, in which Rose of Sharon Joad, insensible from grief after suffering a stillbirth, gives her breast to save a starving man. Steinbeck's supreme talent at combining stark, often shocking, realism with mystical emotion and symbolism made it one of the most chilling endings in American literature, but its artistic control belied the utterly fractured state of its creator. Steinbeck was a wreck, exhausted both from overwork and lack of sleep, and seized with a "plain terror of ending."[15] At the same time, however, he worried that a nervous collapse might prevent him from finishing.

For all that he diminished his ability, however, Steinbeck sensed he was writing something important, and his ambivalence toward finishing the book stemmed largely from his suspicion that it would change his life forever, which it did. The possibility of huge earnings and even greater celebrity from the book filled him with panic. In his dark and complex view of an impermanent universe, wherever there was good, there was inevitably evil lurking around the corner, just waiting to spring. This belief filled Steinbeck with apprehension of impending doom whenever circumstances were propitious. Bad times were the retribution of "the jealous gods" when one was too happy or healthy, he said. "I'm not a writer. I've been fooling myself and other people," he wrote when he was about half way finished writing the novel. "I wish I were. This success will ruin me as sure as hell. It probably won't last, and that will be alright."[16]

In just four years, John Steinbeck had gone from obscurity and poverty to fame, and if not yet fortune, then at least a measure of monetary comfort. He held firm in the belief that possessions corrupted their owners, and he had worn poverty like a tattered badge of honor, as though he would never be guilty of sacrificing his creativity in the pursuit of money and security, as he believed his father had done. Yet, since the success of *Tortilla Flat*, Steinbeck's life seemed to be moving on an upward course all its own. He and Carol had lived on a mere $400 in 1934, the year before *Tortilla Flat* appeared. By 1936, Steinbeck had sold enough books to reap the bittersweet fruit of success and notoriety, for he was deeply stung by criticism thrown at him for *Tortilla Flat*, a book which dissected the moral and real effects of home ownership and money. When his novel about a labor strike, *In Dubious Battle*, appeared in January 1936, in which he told the downtrodden never to "submit or yield"—the command that became the mantra of *The Grapes of Wrath*—the Left wanted to proclaim a new golden boy, and the Right assumed it had one. But critics and supporters alike who were pursuing a political agenda completely misunderstood the apolitical nature of the writer. When Steinbeck revealed his stubborn independence, he was attacked by the far Left, which felt he was not supportive enough; by the Right, which labeled him a communist or socialist; by literary types; and by California locals, who resented what they perceived as Steinbeck's depiction of Monterey's *Tortilla Flat* denizens as derelicts. Nevertheless, when *Of Mice and Men* appeared next in March of 1937, it became a bestseller and securely established Steinbeck as a literary superstar. Suddenly, it seemed anything with Steinbeck's name was a saleable commodity, even those earliest works he had been unable to sell when he wrote them. When Steinbeck visited migrant camps and met with peace and labor activists in preparation for *The Grapes of Wrath*, he found himself treated like a celebrity, with powerful, mythic qualities ascribed to him by supplicants and enemies alike. Groups wanted him to lend his name to their cause. The poor wanted money—"My boy needs a hundred dollar operation. Please send a hundred dollars," one man requested—and the rich and powerful wanted him dead.[17] Everyone, it seemed, began coming out of the woodwork to claim some piece of him. In 1937, Steinbeck felt so besieged that he forbade his publisher to give out press photos to prevent his being recognized. "It's nibbling me to death," he wrote of the public's demands in the winter of 1938.[18]

Through it all, Steinbeck's reading public multiplied. He was a favorite of Broadway and Hollywood producers and agents—"the dogs of Hollywood," as he called them, and was incredulous at the sums of money he was earning. Fearing his own tendency toward premonition, Steinbeck had early on sensed the sea change that the completion of *The Grapes of Wrath* would mean for him. On July 5, 1938, when he was more than a third of the way into the book, he wrote in his diary, "When this book is finished a goodly part of my life will be finished with it. A part I will never get back to."[19]

The novel was published April 14, 1939, and sold a staggering 428,900 hardcover copies that year. ("The war came but book sales went right on," Steinbeck noted in his diary on October 16, 1939.[20]) Its success owed much to Steinbeck's perfect understanding of America's connection to the land, to the soil itself, the same ideal which Hitler had exploited in *Mein Kampf*, when he wrote about the importance of "volk," a folk state that appealed to a man's pride and love of the

German soil. Steinbeck showed how forced severance from his land wounded a man like an animal ejected from its nest and sent him scurrying to retrieve his identity as a husband, father, brother, son, and man. And he showed the equally powerful struggle of a woman to survive and keep the family together against seemingly impossible odds.[21] Steinbeck's obsession with money's corrupting influence, and his ruminations on the moral responsibility of humans toward each other made him the perfect writer for Depression-era Americans.

By the time *The Grapes of Wrath* won the 1939 Pulitzer Prize in literature, war had come not to America, as Steinbeck had predicted, but once again to Europe's ancient feudal, warring lands. Before long, the carnage would spread west to Charlemagne's France, and Hitler's bayonet-wielding infantry would surge across the same terrain where Steinbeck's beloved medieval knights fought almost a millennium earlier. Those very Americans Steinbeck had envisioned making revolution against their brethren had begun instead to make guns for their allies across the Atlantic. In August 1939, the United States War Department announced an order of $85 million worth of planes and engines, making it the largest peacetime order of military hardware ever. Steinbeck's Rose of Sharon became "Rosie the Riveter," and farm owners became patriotic heroes, providing food for American allies and, later, American soldiers. War, it seemed, was the best antidote for economic woe, unemployment, and agrarian crisis. Though cruel conditions remained for migrants in the immediate years following the novel's publication, the America Steinbeck had observed in 1936, when he began his research for *The Grapes of Wrath*, altered dramatically. By 1942, Depression America virtually ceased to exist. At what cost to humanity, Steinbeck wondered, was this new world taking its place?

On September 1, 1939, Hitler's army invaded Poland, and on September 3, France and England declared war on Germany. Clearly, Adolf Hitler had materialized as the precise embodiment of Steinbeck's theories of a leader of a group of men bound by, among many things, "racial pride."

In the aftermath of the enormous success of his novel, Steinbeck was convinced that his domestic enemies, namely the Associated Farmers, were out to destroy him, although he believed his enormous fame protected him from being murdered. His fears were well-grounded. In June 1939, a sheriff in Santa Clara County, California, who was also a friend, warned him not to stay in a hotel room alone, because "the boys got a rape case set up for you. You get alone in a hotel and a dame will come in, tear her clothes off, scratch her face and scream and you try to talk yourself out of that one."[22] Steinbeck believed that a paternity suit with which he was threatened in the winter of 1937–38 was part of a similar attempt by his enemies to blackmail him.

To retaliate against his perceived pursuers, Steinbeck sent copies of his research to the FBI and the U.S. attorney general. While his wife screened the hundreds of letters a day that Steinbeck received, he restricted his movement in public. As a result, he felt reined in, beseiged, "battered with uncertainties," and had difficulty applying himself to a new work of fiction.[23]

In August, success and the atmosphere of fear and persecution at last openly breached what had long been a combative marriage, despite each partner's dedication to the other, and Carol briefly left her husband. Steinbeck was at a crossroads, and he knew it. A year after finishing a novel of stunningly vivid humanity, he was not only feeling repelled by that same humanity, but downright bored with it—the worst possible danger for a novelist. He tried to write "to bring out something. But nothing of interest is there," he despaired.[24] With war raging in Europe, and his marriage in near-ruin, the kings, heroes, and knights he had seen fit to write about seemed sullied. "Present day kings aren't very inspiring," he declared in the spring of 1939. "The gods are on vacation, and about the only heroes left are the scientists and the poor."[25]

Steinbeck no longer found answers to his ceaseless questions about the nature of mankind. He criticized his work for being "simple" compared to reality.[26] In October, noting the Russian buildup on Europe's western front and the recent German U-boat bombings of two British ships—one a cruise liner, killing a total of more than five hundred people—Steinbeck called the war a "waiting game," and wondered "whether either side knows what it is waiting for."[27]

But Steinbeck's judgment on the war reflected his own malaise and anxiety, for he was now enmeshed in a troubling affair with a twenty-two-year-old singer and aspiring actress named Gwendolyn Conger, whom he had met that June in Hollywood. As the secret affair deepened in intensity, Steinbeck, too, was playing a waiting game, desperately seeking change in his life, yet hoping the affair would end so that he and Carol, who had returned to him, could continue in their marriage. He complained of feeling "changeable and skittish," and the death premonitions and ego submersion which had intermittently plagued him throughout his life returned so forcefully that he burned years of correspondence to prevent the public's invasion of his privacy.[28] At the onset of war, Steinbeck was already emotionally exhausted, and artistically depleted.

Still, his mind was restive to create. He yearned, he wrote in his diary, to "be born again," and as he searched for a source of spiritual rebirth, he landed in the very same place he had mined for his spiritual and literary awakening during his parent's illness—the world of nature.[29]

The world of man seemed to be a world of chaos. If there were any reasons for war, dictators, and wholesale cruelty, Steinbeck believed, they must be found not in man, but in nature, and in our understanding of its laws, devoid of emotionalism, nationalism, propaganda, or moral stricture. Steinbeck had bought a majority interest in Edward Ricketts's financially troubled marine biology laboratory, and he was spending much of his time studying marine creatures from California tide pools. He explained the underlying cause for his interest to Carlton Sheffield in a letter on November 13, 1939:

> The world is sick now. There are things in the tide pools easier to understand than Stalinist, Hitlerite, Democrat, capitalist confusion, and voodoo. So I'm going to those things which are relatively more lasting to find a new basic picture. I have too a conviction that a new world is growing under the old, the way a new fingernail grows under a bruised one. . . . Communist, Fascist, Democrat may find that the real origin of the future lies on the microscope plates of obscure young men, who puzzled with order and disorder in quantum and neutron, build gradually a picture which will seep down until it is the fibre of the future.[30]

In the winter of 1939–40, Steinbeck and Ed Ricketts began planning a six-week, full-scale scientific expedition to study tide-pool life in the Gulf of California around the Baja peninsula. Steinbeck had accompanied Ricketts on many specimen-gathering swings along the California coast during the 1930s, and more recently in the San Francisco Bay area for a high-school marine textbook he planned to write, but this trip was to be a real event. He and Ricketts chartered a 75-foot sardine boat called the *Western Flyer*, and planned the trip for March and April of 1940, when the tumultuous waters of the Sea of Cortez were apt to be calm.

Steinbeck was positively gleeful, like a child on Christmas morning, as they planned the trip. He loved outfitting the boat with scientific equipment for a laboratory, and he was reading everything he could get his hands on pertaining to tide pool marine life. He had abandoned the idea of writing a textbook, but he still intended to write about the trip and wanted to be enough of an authority for scientists to consider him "legitimate." His excitement and anticipation diminished his interest in the planned release of the film versions of *Of Mice and Men* the following week,[31] and *The Grapes Of Wrath* the following month. "I was washed up, and now I'm alive again," he effused.[32]

The *Western Flyer* was turned into a floating laboratory, stocked with scientific equipment and tools for collecting and analyzing specimens, and a library that included volumes such as *Hydroids and Marine Decapod Crustacea of California*. The purpose of the trip was purely scientific. "We had no urge toward adventure," Steinbeck wrote, describing his and Ricketts's effort to convince the Mexican military that they were not spies so that they could obtain the necessary permits.[33] Their arms included a small pistol and an old, partly rusted shotgun, but were primarily harpoons, fish nets, hatchets for chopping off the heads of sea turtles, and saws for cutting through their shells. Binoculars were not for viewing submarines, but starfish. There was plenty of beer for the crew, but the barrels of alcohol aboard would provide no amusement to the specimens preserved in the awful-smelling stuff.

Besides Ricketts and Steinbeck, the crew consisted of three Monterey sailors named Sparky, Tiny, and Tony. Despite the deep cracks in the Steinbeck marriage, Carol, who had earned some desperately needed income as an employee in Ricketts's lab in the early 1930s and had accompanied the two on previous expeditions, was also part of the crew.[34]

As it turned out, Carol's presence was merely a failed measure by Steinbeck to assuage his ever-growing guilt over his affair, but try as he did to bury his feelings about her in biochemistry texts, he could not. In the thirteen years he had been with her, Carol had made enormous sacrifices for him. She had typed his manuscripts after she worked all day to help support them, and had provided careful, perceptive judgment when she saw the slightest hint of falsehood or self-indulgence in his work. She had nursed his ill parents and been thus denied privacy, security, and a home of her own.

Steinbeck clearly recognized her contribution, and for most of their marriage, he was more than thankful. This was the Carol to whom he had once referred as being more "me" than "me." With her intelligence, sarcasm, and outspokenness, she was refreshingly different from the sorority girls of good breeding he had despised during his days at Stanford University, and although they argued vehemently almost from the time they met, her fighting spirit captivated him. This was the Carol without whom he would not want to live, he had once said after dreaming she died. This was the Carol to whom he dedicated *The Grapes of Wrath* not even a year and a half before—"To CAROL, who willed this book." But this was also the Carol who embarrassed him in public and went on drinking binges, whose latent and increasingly open aggression he felt was sucking him dry. Now that the couple seemed to have everything—comfort, economic security, and fame—it was Carol from whom he was hiding with Gwen in Hollywood hotel rooms. In January 1940, he described a "crash within myself. The feeling of finish, the destruction of all form and plan."[35]

The crew left Monterey on March 11, 1940, and the novelist embarked with the intention of completely ignoring the world of man. The Great Depression had brought out man's selfishness and greed, Steinbeck believed, but the war represented his ultimate destruction of himself and his brothers. As the boat traveled south toward Baja, Steinbeck observed the southern California ports, stocked with submarines, protected by airplanes, humming in war mode, and he wondered if the human species was finally on the verge of collapse. He encountered a naval officer who embodied the rigid "Don't think" code that he realized was required of military men (and sufferers like the Joads), and he pondered how different the world might be if soldiers were allowed to consider the excruciating consequences of their actions. The world was better off with nations of "lazy contemplative men," he later concluded. "Wars are the activities of busy-ness."[36]

The *Western Flyer* continued down the west coast of Baja, sailed around the southern tip, then up the east coast of the peninsula and across the Gulf of California over to Guyamas on the Mexican coast, which they reached on April 5, 1940. "Hitler marched into Denmark and into Norway, France had fallen, the Maginot Line was lost—we didn't know it, but we knew the daily catch of every boat within four hundred miles," he wrote unapologetically.[37] There was freedom in nature, and comfort, peace, and security in pure scientific study. To Steinbeck, the tide pool represented cool, eternal nature in all its glory, free from sin, and driven solely by the instinct to reproduce and survive. In light of the overwhelming evil that Hitler and fascism presented, as well as the nearly unbearable burden of his own adultery, the tide-pool waters were like mother's milk to him. Far from the madding crowd, Steinbeck was spared meanness and cruelty, and excruciating visions of human suffering. A starfish floated along the tide pool; barnacles glistened in the sun. The crew had enough spaghetti, canned meat, fruit, and vegetables to last them six weeks. Though tension periodically arose as a result of Carol's presence (and her drinking), Steinbeck could salve his conscience by believing he was making a last-ditch attempt to save the marriage, or at least, postponing its demise.

The contrast between Mexico and the world at war he left behind seemed enormously vast. In Mexico, Steinbeck saw a simpler life untainted by the greed and rampant materialism that he believed characterized America and the nations at war. The Indians of the Gulf owned little more than they needed to survive. There was no bribery among men; no one was indebted or dishonest to each other. They had no need for arms, or war, which he concluded was the folly of neurotic, overdeveloped nations which could not make up their collective minds whether science should be used to develop medicine to save people or bombs to kill them.

"We haven't heard any news of Europe since we left and don't much want to," he wrote March 26, 1940, on board the boat. "And the people we meet on the shore have never heard of Europe and they seem to be the better for it. This whole trip is doing what we had hoped it might, given us a world picture not dominated by Hitler and Moscow but something more vital and surviving than either . . . there is a truer thing than ideologies."[38]

The beauty of nature, the plenitude of life, and the feeling of leisure and conviviality despite the hard work gave Steinbeck a feeling of serenity he had not felt in a very long time, if ever. He reveled in the excitement of learning new things, taking great pleasure in the tasks he set before himself each day. The fear of the outer world left him. Nothing seemed important except his work and pleasure. Life on the boat proceeded at its own pace and according to its own laws, becoming more like that of the Indians they met in the villages. He and the crew "went native," abandoning clothes and shoes. They ate fish they caught and devised a primitive cure for a hangover out of fried fish and "medicinal whiskey." They rid themselves of the contagion of "war and economic uncertainty," as he called it, surmising that the crew had "lost the virus."[39]

The moment Steinbeck stepped foot on home turf, his restlessness within the confines of his marriage and literary status returned. Within weeks after returning on April 20, 1940, he was back in Mexico collaborating on a film entitled *The Forgotten Village* with Herbert Kline, the director who had recently made *Lights Out in Europe*, about the German invasion of Poland. The film offered Steinbeck a means of putting as much distance as he could between himself and oppressive civilization, which over the life of the project also came to mean Carol. In Mexico, however, Steinbeck could not entirely block out events taking place across the Atlantic, since the Nazis were flooding the country with propaganda.[40] He was concerned that if war broke out, the *Forgotten Village* project would be scuttled. Nevertheless, for the time being, Steinbeck was able to separate his deep unhappiness from his work, which continued to carry an optimistic message.

The Forgotten Village, published in book form in early 1941, but not released as a film until 1947 when it won first prize as the best feature documentary at the Brussels World Film Festival, again put forth Steinbeck's view that amidst almost unbearable human suffering, change for the good is coming. When the people of a remote Mexican village begin dying of contaminated well water, only one boy, Juan Diego, believes that more than shaman's eggs and snakeskins are needed to fight the "evil air," and he secretly brings a doctor from the city to treat the water. The village is saved, but not before Juan Diego is disowned by his father for disobedience. As Juan leaves the village to attend school in the city, he is sad, wondering whether he will ever be able to return home to his village and family. The doctor comforts Juan by telling him, "The change will come, is coming."

Despite this message of hope, Steinbeck as usual portrayed an individual estranged from his group. In a way, it was an ironic portrayal, considering Steinbeck's observations concerning the human connection to his brother, and yet one which all of his heroes share. The group largely derives its power from its members' ignorance and submission, and thus, when an individual separates, the group's collective fear, greed, and superstition easily destroy him. Before the end of the war, Steinbeck would give us a hero literally hunted by his fellow villagers in his one great wartime fictional work, *The Pearl*, a novella published in 1945.

Steinbeck's alienation from Carol isolated him further within himself—and increased the lure of Gwen—and he became nervous, his mood angry and dark. He was gripped with a sense of foreboding, and bad dreams bedeviled him. Carol, too, was beset by her own maladies in response to her husband's remoteness and irritability, if not his suspected infidelity. Carol, Steinbeck offered, did not realize that she could "make the tempo of the house," and her despondency and anger heightened his own.[41] He wanted to be with Gwen and free of the marriage, yet he felt he owed it to Carol to remain her husband. The pull was tormenting. Even as he pursued the affair, meeting Gwen in Hollywood when film work brought him there, or in a pine cabin on the beach in Monterey, he wished his marriage would end on its own accord.

As always, Steinbeck found safety in his work. As his marriage tottered toward collapse in April 1941 when he told Carol about the affair, and in the agonizing aftermath of its finish, Steinbeck became a writing whirlwind. In that he was still having difficulty applying himself to a novel, he was concentrating his efforts elsewhere: writing propaganda for the U.S. government, a play which he eventually discarded, a movie version of *The Red Pony*, and the film of *The Forgotten Village*.

Steinbeck was also writing *The Sea of Cortez*, which began as a log of the Baja trip, but developed into a four-hundred-page philosophical treatise on war and man's bent toward self-destruction.[42] He had begun the work before the breakup of his marriage, and wrote it through one of the worst times of his life, as well as during the escalation of World War II. Steinbeck was excited by the project, which he described both as important to his body of work and as a means of "sitting" out the world crisis in order to see it in its proper, historical perspective, but it is impossible to read Steinbeck's words regarding the mess the human species makes of things without hearing the drumbeat of his own inner turmoil and angst. Steinbeck's guilt-ridden consciousness lay beneath his lengthy, deeply felt explanations for Hitler, German efficiency, and the human species' errant ways. The lessons which he proclaimed to have learned from the natural world were as much a way of justifying his own mistakes as the calumny of the warring nations. The world, as well as his own life, really seemed to be coming apart. "The world is crazy. I wonder weather it will ever be sane again. Probably not. Life for me is nearly over any way," he wrote on September 29, 1940.[43]

Steinbeck, an eternally restless man who harbored fear of the future and never ceased to wonder about his true identity, wrote the most profound truth about himself in *The Sea of Cortez*: "[Man] has never become accustomed to the tragic miracle of consciousness. Perhaps his species is not set, has not jelled, but is still in a state of becoming, bound by his physical memories to a past of struggle and survival, limited in his futures by the uneasiness of thought and consciousness."[44]

Even at this late date, the war had not yet made an emotional impact on him, though it had propelled him to escape through his scientific journey to Baja. The *Western Flyer* for Steinbeck was like Charles Darwin's S.S. *Beagle*, and the novelist brought to his conclusions decades of study of philosophy, religion, mythology, biology, and Darwinian theory of the predetermination of the species, which he now believed explained just about every deed committed by man. Steinbeck concluded that the expectation of peace and kindness had no basis whatsoever in man's natural tendencies. Man may talk of war as a terrible horror, he wrote, and yet it is so commonplace, so much an expression of our natures, that periods of peace are actually aberrations and should be viewed as such. Man's basic nature tends toward war, he explained, and to attribute war to externals like economics or territorial claims denies this essential trait. Science did not yet have an explanation for this trait, he wrote, although he suggested tongue-in-cheek that it might have been caused by some "virus, (or) some airborne spore." He called the war in Europe "a zombie war of sleepwalkers which nevertheless goes on out of all control of intelligence," and he wanted *The Sea of Cortez* to be a call for dispassionate analysis, although at the same time he was sure his plea would go unheeded.[45]

Steinbeck looked with a clear eye at the Germans, whom he had been analyzing for years. In his "phalanx theory" of the early 1930s he had codified the biological characteristics that allowed Hitler to harness mobs of Germans for his gain. In the tide pool Steinbeck had confirmed his earlier theories concerning associations of human beings, and he expanded them as he observed millions of fish racing as one in darting schools. He decided that the schools should not be looked at as the sum of individual fish but as a unique animal itself, with its own "nature and drive and ends of its own," all of which had one ultimate aim— survival. Every feature of the unit had survival as its ultimate reason for being, and every act of the whole, no matter how brutal, was justified by that goal. "This commandment decrees the death and destruction of myriads of individuals for the survival of the whole," he wrote. "All the tricks and mechanisms, all the successes and all the failures, are aimed at that end."[46]

To Steinbeck's mind, Hitler was not a unique figure which history had created to lead the German people, as the dictator proclaimed. Rather, like the molecules thrusting an amoeba forward, he saw Hitler as part of the biological determinism of the laws of living beings, in which one emerges through happenstance to find himself at the helm of a great mass moving together in one direction. For this generation it was Hitler; for the next it would be someone else. The German people were not doing anything different from what generations of their human ancestors had done before.

During the period in which Steinbeck wrote *The Sea of Cortez*, Hitler was advancing in Europe. The Netherlands, Belgium, and France fell to his occupying armies in the months after Steinbeck's maritime expedition; the Luftwaffe blitzed London, and the dictator's Afrika Korps under General Erwin Rommel had joined the Italians to drive back the British in Egypt and regain territory in North Africa. Despite these successes, Steinbeck predicted the ultimate destruction of the Wehrmacht, and not from outer enemies, but from the inside. The Germans were doomed to destroy themselves, he wrote incisively, with their obsessive efficiency and perfection. Humans were sloppy in their living and behaviors; all life forms were flawed—Darwin himself had pointed to the wondrous eternal evolution that a species' flaws allowed. Perfection was not meant to be in this world, because the closer a species came to perfection, the more certain its demise, Steinbeck asserted.

Never had the theories of good and evil which had marked his fiction for a decade seemed more personally relevant than now. After a decade in which he had disappointed himself as a writer and especially as a husband, he devised in *The Sea of Cortez* a biological foundation which explained his flaws and mistakes. Though he never attributed his understanding of humanity to his own failures, his seering self-criticism undoubtedly provided him with a deeper insight into the behavior of Hitler and the German people than even his earlier "phalanx theory." If natural laws determined man's self-destructive nature, apologies were not necessary, nor were excuses or even explanations, for that matter. Humans embodied both good and evil, and each emerged at different times in the same man. Perhaps human beings did cut each other down for some predetermined reason. Perhaps war did not signify moral deficiency at all, but functioned to guarantee the survival of the species as a whole. One day we might find the answer, he wrote, but until then, if mankind nearly destroyed itself every few generations, the "why" was irrelevant. Blame was pointless. It was sufficient merely to say: "It's so because it's so . . . . The separate reasons," he wrote, "no matter how valid, are only fragmentary parts of the picture. . . . The whole picture is portrayed by *is*, the deepest word of deep ultimate reality."[47]

Steinbeck continued to espouse the idea that hope for the future was man's best defense, a "shock absorber," as he called it, guarding against the pain of the present, but in truth, while writing the book, Steinbeck saw neither hope nor a way to remove himself from his own suffering. Darwinian theory could not relieve him of the terrific burden of guilt he carried. In the fall of 1940, Steinbeck still wanted to pursue the affair with Gwen; yet, he also believed it would eventually "end, tragically."[48] He was feeling that even if the affair ended, he had ruined what he had had with Carol, and he would die alone.

As 1941 began, Steinbeck was near an emotional collapse. His life was fragmented emotionally, physically, and professionally. Recovering from the flu, he was constantly on the move, from Hollywood, where he was wrapping up *The Forgotten Village*, to Pacific Grove, where he had bought a small house and was working on *The Sea of Cortez*, to Los Gatos, where he was spending guilt-wracked weekends with Carol. In a letter to his editor Pascal Covici on January 1, Steinbeck linked the world condition to his own state of affairs.

And speaking of the happy new year, I wonder if any year ever had less chance of being happy. It's as though the whole race were indulging in a kind of species introversion—as though we looked inward on our neuroses. And the thing we see isn't very pretty. . . . So we go into this happy new year, knowing that our species has learned nothing, can, as a race, learn nothing— that the experience of ten thousand years has made no impression on the instincts of the million years that preceded. Maybe you can find some vague theology that will give you hope. Not that I have lost any hope. All the goodness and the heroisms will rise up again, then be cut down again and rise up. It isn't that the evil thing wins—it never will—but that it doesn't die. I don't know why we should expect it to. It seems fairly obvious that two sides of a mirror are required before one has a mirror, that two forces are necessary in man before he is man.[49]

In January, Steinbeck complained of feeling lost, lonesome and insecure. He despondently noted, "The world we know crumbles slowly and melts away, and the powerful voices of hysteria and terror are in the air."[50] In February, he packed Carol off to Hawaii for a "rest," and when she returned in April, he ended the waiting game he had played for nearly two years, telling Carol about Gwen, with whom he had been living openly in Pacific Grove in Carol's absence. Carol put up a fight—in fact, both women falsely claimed to be pregnant with his child—but after another week of agonizing uncertainty, Steinbeck finally made up his mind which woman he wanted. His marriage's demise gave him the impetus to be free of the Los Gatos ranch, which he had been considering for several months. While he complained to friends after the breakup that Carol had been selfish and emotionally ungiving, in the divorce settlement he gave her the house and most of what he owned, saying that she deserved it. Apparently, divestiture seemed to him the best way to cleanse himself of the moral corruption of materialism.[51]

Still, Steinbeck longed for a home that would give him just the right fit, and his vision of his and Gwen's domestic bliss after the war included a "shabby" house near the ocean in Monterey, with dogs, a horse, and "babies." He yearned for a place of comfort and solace. By August, Steinbeck finished *The Sea of Cortez*. In the year and a half since he began his tide-pool journey, war had been declared and had widely spread, and his long, tumultuous marriage had ended. Beneath the book's discourse on barnacles, Hitler, and man's tendency toward self-destruction, Steinbeck buried the portrait of his private hell. In a sense, the nonfiction book was far more autobiographical than his fiction, which primarily evolved from stories he had not himself experienced, but had acquired by listening to and observing others. In the book's most haunting metaphor of his angst as he feared the end of his marriage, Steinbeck described an Indian custom of erecting a cross on the spot where a fisherman falls and dies, too weak to make it home after a voyage. The crosse Steinbeck wrote, sadly recalls the effort, "from generation to generation, man and woman, . . . struggles always to get home but never makes it."[52] From the time his marriage broke up to the end of the war, Steinbeck became itinerant, much like the Joads. He had lived most of his life within a circle with a mere thirty-mile radius, encompassing Salinas, Monterey, Pacific Grove, and Los Gatos. Within the six months after he left Carol in October 1941, he left Northern California and moved around between New York, Washington, Hollywood, and Mexico. He traveled to Europe in 1943 to cover the war, and then returned to New York, which for a while he deceived himself into thinking was home.

On July 23, 1940, the United States Congress had proposed a Universal Training Act. Steinbeck had wanted to register for military service, but at thirty-eight, he discovered he was too old. Nevertheless, he was eager to use his talents to help his country. In the years since he wrote *In Dubious Battle* and asserted that the controversial, pro-labor book had no political agenda, Steinbeck had come to believe in the underlying principle of propaganda to motivate the public to demand government action when injustice required redress. From its inception, he saw *The Grapes of Wrath* as a book with an important mission, which accounted for part of the intense time-pressure he felt writing it. Even before Pearl Harbor, Steinbeck felt the urgent need for the U.S. government to mount a powerful propaganda mechanism that could surpass Germany's. If we failed to do that, Steinbeck warned during the summer of 1940, Germany "will completely win Central and South America away from the United States."[53] In this regard Steinbeck was far more shrewdly pragmatic than many of his fellow American writers, artists, and intellectuals, who, especially prior to American's entry into the war, were wary of propaganda's power to manipulate public opinion. Whereas Steinbeck saw a model in the operation conducted by Nazi Propaganda Minister Joseph Goebbels, many Americans distrusted propaganda precisely because they associated it with mind-control practiced by the Nazi regime.

Though Steinbeck was ever wary of being an instrument of special interest groups and refused, he said, to be a "front for a mob," he envisioned himself as a key player in the government's wartime propaganda offensive.[54] Beginning during the summer of 1940, Steinbeck met with and wrote a series of letters to President Roosevelt and his senior advisors, to convey his sense of urgency that the allied peoples unite, as well as to outline his ideas for a well-run radio and film office. (Though he vociferously claimed to eschew fame, John Steinbeck expected fully to have direct access to President Roosevelt.) Steinbeck believed his long experience with filmmaking and his connections to many of Hollywood's top producers, directors, and actors, including Charlie Chaplin, Spencer Tracy, and James Cagney, made him the right person to head such an office. Nevertheless, when the Foreign Information Service unit, an early incarnation of the government's Office of War Information, was created during the summer of 1941, Roosevelt bypassed Steinbeck and instead appointed playwright Robert E. Sherwood, one of his speechwriters and a personal friend. Sherwood, a three-time Pulitzer Prize-winner, author of *Abe Lincoln in Illinois*, had a long history of opposing fascism and war, which he once said was not waged by "decent people."

Like Steinbeck, Sherwood believed in the "fundamental conception of the dignity, the essential virtue of the individual man."[55] But Steinbeck's antifascism did not extend to a broader, moralistically shaded ideal shared by many artists like Sherwood and Archibald MacLeish, who became a lead player in the government's propaganda effort, which held that the fight between the Axis and Allied powers constituted a struggle between the forces of good and evil. Eventually, Steinbeck's individualism would get him into trouble in Washington—and everywhere else—and the absence of his name from pertinent government documents indicates he was never considered for a position of authority. Still, when Roosevelt was beginning to mount a propaganda effort in mid-1941, Steinbeck was wanted as a foot soldier. He was offered a job writing propaganda for a new agency, Coordinator of Information—later the Office of Strategic Services—but he turned it down because he didn't want a full-time job.

That autumn, after Steinbeck continued to be courted by the government, he finally agreed to do what he was asked. While he and Gwyn (she changed the spelling of her name in late 1941) were renting the Suffern, New York, farm of friend and actor Burgess Meredith, Steinbeck spent mornings writing overseas broadcasts for the Foreign Nationalities Board, a newly formed unit of the Foreign Information Service. The broadcasts were based on his interviews in Washington and New York with refugees from Norway, Denmark, France, and Czechoslovakia about their suffering under Nazi occupation.

Steinbeck was moved by the testimony of the refugees, and with some of them he achieved the kind of intimacy he had shared with migrant workers who provided information for *The Grapes of Wrath*. Though Steinbeck was working under the confines of an official agency, his imagination began to formulate a fictional story about an occupied American town. "It's about a little town invaded," he explained. "It has no generalities, no ideals, no speeches, it's just about the way the people of a little town would feel if it were invaded."[56] The concept for the play, *The Moon Is Down*, was the perfect embodiment of Steinbeck's brand of propaganda: impartial and realistic, yet packing enough power to mobilize the public. Steinbeck wrote the play quickly that autumn, finishing it just hours after the attack on Pearl Harbor, which he astutely judged would "solidify the country" against the Japanese.[57] (Steinbeck was also prescient in his concern as early as 1940 that growing hysteria against the Japanese in California would lead to a witchhunt. Indeed, internment of the Japanese population of California, including Steinbeck's gardener at his Monterey house, began in March 1942.[58])

Steinbeck was far less astute when it came to his new play, however. He saw no problem with his depiction of Americans as a subjugated people. Rather, he believed he was "doing a good and patriotic thing," by showing Americans that "it could happen here."[59] Clearly, as he was wont, Steinbeck got lost in the purity of his ideas. When the FIS rejected the play on the grounds that it would have a "devasting effect on morale," Steinbeck changed the venue from America to Northern Europe. This was on the advice of his European refugee friends, who believed the story would find a rapt, and appreciative, audience among European resistance fighters. Steinbeck made the conscious decision neither to identify the country, nor even the nationality of the occupiers, to point up the universality of terror, hatred, and suffering. Hitler was referred to as "Leader."

"It isn't any country and there is no dialect and it's about how the invaders feel about it too. It's one of the first sensible things to be written about these things," he boasted.[60] War and occupation presented the perfect backdrop for a novelist assured of the moral obligation of a man to his larger community and of the "holiness" of a group of people working together for a cause. Fascism, collaboration, and resistance—all probed in *The Grapes of Wrath*—were components of this war and easily lent themselves to Steinbeck's new story. The character of Willy Freely, *The Grapes of Wrath*'s pragmatic tractor-driver working for the banker who didn't care that he put his neighbors out of work, was transformed into Cornell, the ambitious, immoral Nazi collaborator. And the character of Tom Joad, the good Okie driven to murder by injustice, was transformed into a soldier's starving widow who kills one of the occupiers with a pair of scissors after he beseeches her to forget about the war and show him some kindness, because a man "dies without love." It was pure Steinbeck. Yes, the Nazis had to be defeated, and Steinbeck wanted to be among their conquerers, but to him, the enemy was no more evil than humans had been thousands of times before and would be thousands of times more in the future. Man *is*. Hitler *is*. Cruelty is a natural part of the human species. The drive of the species to survive could explain everything: the sinister, warped perfection of German thought, the illicit works of the collaborator seeking to save his own skin, and the valiant underground resistance which fought against him.

Steinbeck's portrayal of occupiers as victims, reluctant to do as they are told, and their commanders— one as a thoughtful philosopher just following orders and the others as a marrowless love-beggar driven crazy by the knowledge that his victims hate him—did not comport with the public's image, spread several times a day across the newspaper front page, of the dead at the hands of the Nazi aggressors.

In retrospect, *The Moon Is Down* seems harmlessly absurd. But when it appeared, first as a short novel in March, and then as Broadway play on April 8, 1942, the Axis powers were racking up important victories, and its timing could not have been worse. The day after the play opened, the Bataan peninsula fell to the Japanese after four months of fighting in which 36,000 American and Filipino soldiers died. Less than two weeks later in France, the fascist Hitler-puppet Pierre Laval gained dictatorial powers over the Vichy government. Hitler had declared that his armies would crush the Soviets by summer, and reports of Nazi extermination of Jews in concentration camps were mounting. Reviewing the book, James Thurber, among other critics, intimated that Steinbeck would be responsible if we lost the war. The play was equally reviled by critics and closed after fifty-five performances.[61]

In the end, however, the book and play, which afterward toured out west with a road company, were immensely profitable for Steinbeck, marking his steadily increasing stature and popularity. The book had a first printing of 85,000 and the Book-of-the-Month Club ordered 200,000 copies. Film rights were sold for the most money ever paid by Hollywood for a story. Yet, for Steinbeck, who was lonely and homesick in New York with Gwyn and wrangling with Carol over the divorce settlement, the critics' attacks unnerved him. The "critics have all stopped being critics and have turned propagandists," he complained bitterly.[62]

Steinbeck's rage lashed out in all directions. That same month, he was also furious with the U.S. Navy Department. He and Ed Ricketts had informed the department of the existence of detailed maps of the waters around the Pacific islands drawn up by Japanese marine biologists and available in English to the international scientific community. They had suggested the maps would be helpful to the Navy in planning beach assaults. After six weeks, Steinbeck and Ricketts received a mimeographed form letter, curtly "thanking us for our patriotism."[63] Steinbeck fired off a second letter, this time to the Secretary of the Navy, Frank Knox. Two months later, Ricketts was in his Monterey laboratory when he was visited by a naval intelligence officer. According to Steinbeck, whom Ricketts later told about the visit, the "tight-lipped" officer was impatient when he discovered the men possessed no secret Japanese information about the Pacific islands. He promised the men they would be contacted by the Navy, but they never were. Steinbeck was bitter. "I wondered whether some of the soldiers whose landing craft grounded a quarter of a mile from the beach and who had to wade ashore under fire had the feeling that bottom and tidal range either were not known or ignored," he wrote after the war.[64]

Though he was discouraged by these first encounters with government bureaucracy, Steinbeck was not yet prepared to wash his hands of it. To the contrary, his involvement steadily increased, and throughout 1942 Steinbeck continued to believe—or deceived himself into thinking—that he would be assigned to a full-time intelligence job in Washington for the duration of the war. He saw himself as ideally suited for intelligence work, and whenever he envisioned his future, both personally and professionally, he regarded that future as beginning "after the war."

By May 1942, Steinbeck still had not been invited to assume any post, but he was, however, summoned to the Oval Office for a meeting with President Roosevelt. Steinbeck had been previously asked to write a book for the Air Force on bomber pilots, and he was leaning toward saying no. "Now John, you are going to do what I want you to do—what I want you to do, John," the president told him, according to Steinbeck's own retelling of the incident to a friend. "Then I found myself saying, 'Yes, Mr. President, I am,' and that was it."[65]

In researching the book, *Bombs Away: The Story of a Bomber Team*, Steinbeck and photographer John Swope held to a grueling schedule, visiting twenty Air Force training fields around the country during May and June. The book and film version of *Bombs Away* occupied Steinbeck through the winter of 1943. The experience ended as did nearly all of Steinbeck's war-related commissioned writing jobs, with disappointment and, increasingly, frustration over bureaucratic obstinacy and inertia. First, he was asked to fake the ending of the book, and he refused. Then he and Gwyn moved back to California so he could work on a movie version which the newly formed Office of War Information never made. When he suggested revising *The Moon Is Down* as a film about a small town invaded by the Japanese, the Office of War Information rejected that offer, too.

As his boredom and frustration increased, so did his impatience with obtaining an intelligence commission. Each time he petitioned the government for a change in his status, he was told to wait. Steinbeck, feeling like a pawn, grew angry, weary, and depressed, grumbling that his "desire to help in this war does not include sitting in Hollywood for the duration."[66] Steinbeck was aware he was being investigated by the FBI and was mostly sanguine about it. The Office of War Information screened all candidates, and given that senior Washington officials, even Roosevelt himself, had consulted and courted him since 1940, Steinbeck's continued expectation that he would be hired for a Washington job was not without merit. But government at the highest levels, Steinbeck learned firsthand, often worked at cross purposes. That same May 1942 when President Roosevelt shrewdly appealed to Steinbeck's patriotism, Steinbeck complained to U.S. Attorney General Francis Biddle about the FBI's pursuit of him. "Do you suppose you could ask Edgar's boys to stop stepping on my heels? They think I'm an enemy alien. It's getting tiresome."[67]

Though Steinbeck was not a Communist (he associated Communists with "intellectuals," whom as a group he despised, and distrusted politicians and dogma of any kind), he had been tangentially involved with leftist groups since the mid-1930s, about the time the FBI began keeping a dossier on him. Labor advocates eagerly recruited him, realizing the public relations value in a writer who picked cotton alongside Okies to understand their plight, doled out his own money for food and medicine, and dragged sick and starving migrants out of the mud. Steinbeck spoke out on labor issues and lent his name to such committees as the "Steinbeck Committee to Aid Agricultural Organization." Among various activities, the group was involved in a 1938 cotton strike in Bakersfield, California.

Steinbeck held membership in organizations considered by the FBI as "Communist fronts," such as the National Institute of Arts and Letters and the

League of American Writers, which sought to engage writers to champion the working-class struggle in their work. However, the American Communist leadership actually considered Steinbeck, like Ernest Hemingway and Thomas Wolfe, unreliable—unwilling to subordinate his art to politics. They attacked *In Dubious Battle* because he was more interested in examining mob psychology than in taking a political stand.[68] But the Left's reservations about his loyalty did not convince the FBI that Steinbeck was anything but a "Red," or his writing anything other than "red propaganda." According to Herbert Mitgang, who studied Steinbeck's FBI file for his book *Dangerous Dossiers: Exposing the Secret War Against America's Greatest Authors*, Steinbeck's mail was monitored for Soviet literature until six years before his death in 1968.

Steinbeck endured the army intelligence background check until January 1943, when the slow process finally produced its conclusion: "In view of substantial doubt as to Subject's loyalty and discretion," the Army report read, "it is recommended that Subject not be considered favorably for a commission in the Army of the United States."[69]

After having been strung along by the government for a year, the finality of the decision brought Steinbeck a sense of release. But his casual reaction was also due to the fact that, for the first time in a long time, he was excited about a new project. He and Gwyn had moved to Hollywood where he was writing a script for Twentieth Century Fox at the behest of the U.S. Maritime Commission. Alfred Hitchcock, a director with whom Steinbeck had not previously worked, had been chosen to direct Steinbeck's original idea for a script about a group of survivors of a German submarine attack set adrift in a lifeboat. Though Steinbeck had had the idea as far back as 1941, it coalesced when World War I flying ace Eddie Rickenbacker's plane ran out of fuel six hundred miles north of Samoa in October 1942, and he and five of his six-man crew survived twenty-four days on a rubber raft before being rescued. Rickenbacker, who at the time was the president of Eastern Airlines, was headed for an inspection of American airfields in the Pacific islands at the behest of Secretary of War Henry Stimson when the accident occurred.[70]

Steinbeck's negative experiences on previous government-sponsored film projects had toughened him by now, and he took measures to protect himself if the job did not proceed to his satisfaction. Twentieth Century Fox gave him an unusual amount of freedom, agreeing to let him out of the project if he was unhappy.

The job began so well that Steinbeck felt a renewed sense of creativity and happiness, but in a matter of weeks, the experience turned into an ordeal. Steinbeck was unaware that Hitchcock had wanted Ernest Hemingway to write the script, and when Hemingway had declined, had asked for Thornton Wilder. The film's producer was finally able to persaude Hitchcock to hire Steinbeck.[71] Steinbeck had fought with directors before over creative differences, but he came to despise Hitchcock, whose vision of the story greatly differed from his own. This time, Steinbeck was not simply being asked to alter an ending as he had been asked to do for the Air Force–commissioned film *Bombs Away*. *Lifeboat* was his original idea. Steinbeck had written a realistic story based on his interviews with survivors of sinkings, and he especially objected to Hitchcock's concept for a single, trumped-up set—the lifeboat placed in a tank of water in a Twentieth Century Fox studio.

His experience on *Lifeboat* was the final indignation for Steinbeck as a writer-for-hire for the government. He had gone avidly into war work, expecting that the behemoth American government would be the antithesis of petty, vengeful individuals, of whom he was so sick and tired after *The Grapes of Wrath*, only to find it to be one huge fraternity of such people. He didn't know whether he had been left out or rejected, but one thing of which Steinbeck was sure—he wanted no more of it. Steinbeck began inquiring at newspapers about his chances of getting a correspondent accreditation to cover the war. He wrote to his friend Toby Street, "Everything in the government is so screwed up and complicated and mean that I am going to try private industry. It may not work but neither does the army nor the gov't. I run up against nothing but jealousies, ambitions and red tape in Washington."[72]

Steinbeck's problem with war work turned out to be the same problem he described in his differences with Carol—"a basic disagreement that went even into our cells."[73] He wanted—and tried—to be the good American, the Pulitzer Prize–winner who could bring his reputation and knowledge to bear for the fight. He felt confident that he was offering the government and public something special and of great value because he considered his perspective untainted by emotionalism. But Steinbeck was a lone wolf, a man who had always seen his emotional independence as a key both to his survival as a writer and to the power of his work. Throughout his life, he disdained group-thinking that was so much the subject of his work, and which he believed had led the world into war. In Washington, he was supposed to be part of a group and exploit that same group-thinking through propaganda.

For the two years Steinbeck involved himself with government and bureaucracy, he had held tight to the liberated creed of the artist that demanded the luxury of impartial thinking. In the end, for John Steinbeck, the two worlds of government and art could not meld. The chasm pointed up his naivete, but also illuminated the confused, overburdened, and duplicitous state of government trying to mobilize for war. The right hand saw great advantage in using the country's most talented writers and artists, but the left, most notably in the form of Hoover's FBI, saw danger. The government never could figure out how to deal best with these people since their talent was inextricable from their iconoclasm. In wartime, expediency seemed the only solution, but it came with a cost. Artists like John Steinbeck and Ernest Hemingway became embittered, feeling that the country to which they had devoted their services was not only ungrateful, but antagonistic. Steinbeck's sense that he was being persecuted at a time when America was supposed to stand more than ever for democracy drove him inward and further away from his country. Ultimately, because he was too original a thinker, his nonconformist ideas made him feel like a pariah. The one American writer who perhaps more than any other saw in humans a natural, driving tendency to be joined to others became increasingly the singular individual—isolated, alienated, alone.

Steinbeck's divorce from Carol was finally granted on March 18, 1943, and he and Gwyn married March 29 in the French Quarter of New Orleans. His excitement about leaving for Europe on a journalism assignment was tempered by anxiety about abandoning his new wife so early in their marriage. The divorce had dredged up feelings of guilt, inadequacy, and failure. "It's the first divorce our family ever had and it makes me sad," he had told Toby Street.[74]

Steinbeck had obtained an accreditation from the *International Herald Tribune*, but he was frustrated when several months more of bureaucratic road-blocks delayed his departure. The Allies were taking advantage of their victory over Rommel in Egypt and had begun landings on the North African coast to establish a safe base for future operations against Italy. Steinbeck had correctly predicted a "big push" in the spring, and he wanted to be overseas to see it for himself. When he finally received security clearance in May, he felt a sense of triumph over the "little men with temporary authority who, armed with envy," had made his life "horrible" during the past year and a half.[75]

As a child, Steinbeck had been infatuated by idealized war, where heroes fought gallantly against each other in misty forests, where magic spells changed the course of history, and love was promised for the sake of the realm. World War I did almost nothing to dispell those ideas, since Steinbeck, born in 1902, spent the war years as a high school student; his only war-related experience consisted of picking beans before school as part of a school program to alleviate the farm labor shortage. On June 3, 1943, with the enthusiasm of a wide-eyed child, John Steinbeck departed by troop transport ship from New York. By being close to the fighting, he hoped he might "get some larger picture."[76] But if Steinbeck meant something new in concept, something he had not known before, then he found anything but that in war up close. From the first moment until he returned to New York four months later, Steinbeck saw in war-making confirmation of the very theories he had been espousing since 1933.

Steinbeck saw not individual suffering or bravery when he turned his scientific eye on war, but rather a collective group of anonymous human specimens follow-ing prescribed behaviors. War, with its great masses of men united by purpose, its need for subjugating the individual to the greater needs of the group, the constant fear and possibility of death, and the mechanization of everything from eating and sleeping to shining boots, lent itself ideally to Steinbeck's fascination with the behavior and function of individuals and large groups of men. War and the soldier had replaced the tide pool and the starfish. "Men cannot be treated as individuals," he wrote in his dispatch of June 23, which described life on a troopship. "They are simply units which take up six feet by three feet by two feet, horizontal or verti-cal. They are engines which must be given fuel to keep them from stopping. . . . [T]here is no way of considering them as individuals."[77]

Steinbeck studied fighting men with aloof, clinical observation, as specimens, describing the way they smelled and breathed, and how their feet shuffled across the floor of a troopship. Men were categorized as "sleeping men," or "thousands of men." His dispatch of November 1943, entitled "Symptoms," reads like a medical extract, cataloging the various effects of constant shelling, fear, and sleep depriva-tion on the human body. He recounted little dialogue in his dispatches, and when doing so, usually referred to the speakers as "one of them," and "the other," rather than naming them. His dispatches were nothing like the personalized war corre-spondence of Ernest Hemingway, who wrote about a soldier with such familiarity and sympathy the reader almost got the impression they were old friends. Ironically, Hemingway had not always met the soldiers about whom he wrote.

Perhaps more than any other American writer covering the war, Steinbeck went to Europe with a fully formed, slanted perception of events. Yet, far from being dry and doctrinal, the dispatches gave his *International Herald Tribune* readers an unerringly graphic portrayal of war, filled with the kind of rich description and insight that marked his fiction. He observed that the monotony and tension that fighting men endured before an assault would inevitably erupt into laughter, and described the men's superstitions and need for good luck charms such as amber beads, Indian head pennies, wooden pigs, and an old, beer-guzzling goat prized by a unit of RAF fliers. He wrote about the kind of homesickness that would cause "Sligo" from Brooklyn to risk arrest by disappearing into a group of Italian prisoners being shipped to the States, so he could catch the World Series in New York; and the high-rolling gamblers like "Eddie," who filled his boredom and fear with a different kind of risk. Then there was the recuperating soldier with a maimed hand who worried about his future.

In the days before the landing on Salerno Beach, Steinbeck traveled with a secret forces naval commando unit, led by the actor Douglas Fairbanks Jr., whose primary mission was to divert the Germans north along the coast in preparation for the allied attack.[78] Steinbeck left his PT boat and joined the land forces on the beach several days after the invasion on September 9. With the landing on Salerno, Steinbeck saw front-line battle for the first time, and he was terrified. A large part of the German force in southern Italy had retreated north since the fall of Mussolini in July and the allied victory on Sicily in August, but what remained of it was lying in wait for the Americans. The waters were heavily mined, machine guns were buried in the sand and there were 88s on the hills above the beach. After four days of intense fighting, the Allies finally advanced with the help of troop reinforcements and heavy shelling from support ships. Steinbeck spent most of the time on his belly on the dusty beach as shells flew above his head, but his worst wounds came when he was hit by shrapnel from fifty-gallon oil drums bombed by the Germans. He remained in the hospital a week and thought he was going to die.

Steinbeck returned to Fairbanks's commando unit and took part in raids on small islands off the Italian coast. In the days after the invasion, he seemed to marvel at the fact that he had survived. He was scratched up, had twisted his ankle during a jump onto the beach from a landing craft, and was having trouble hearing—a souvenir of battle that would afflict him for many months after the war—but that was the extent of his wounds. "I've had a charmed life these last three weeks or someone had me in his prayers," he wrote Gwyn on September 22 shortly before returning to London.[79] His sister's husband, Bill Dekker, a lieutenant colonel who was with troops landing on Sicily, had been missing since July 17 and was by now presumed dead.

Now that he had seen battle in the raw, Steinbeck adamantly believed that the truth about war was conveyed in the small, subtle quirks of the human response to fear, pain, and grief. *His* truths about the invasion of Italy echoed from the "willies" that gripped a captain entering a deserted Palermo, or the frustration of a soldier, renowned as an ace souvenir hunter, who dragged an enormous carved mirror through every battle only to have it break the first moment he hung it. When Steinbeck described the successful effort by American officers and a bartender to retrieve the man's daughter from a tiny island threatened by imminent Nazi attack just before she is about to give birth, he was writing his brand of battlefield propaganda—the revelation of good deeds by entirely unexceptional members of the human species. Steinbeck had always relied heavily on firsthand observations and actual detail which he researched scrupulously for his fiction, but rather than reducing reality into succinct, neatly wrapped phrases, he sought to expand it, finding deeper, often hidden meanings in those details. *The Grapes of Wrath*, for example, had begun with his series of newspaper articles published in October 1936 in the *San Francisco News*, entitled "The Harvest Gypsies." Steinbeck had depended on the rigorously detailed material concerning migrants and camp conditions which had been compiled by the government camps' director, Tom Collins, who documented everything from the migrants' speech patterns, to the songs they sang, to the prayers they invoked. His direct use of this rich material, as well as anecdotes provided by Collins, who guided Steinbeck on tours of farms and camps, had given the book its extraordinary authenticity, but *The Grapes of Wrath* reads like anything but a muckraker's account. It took him nearly two years to digest the material he accumulated in his research before he could begin writing the novel, and when he did, Steinbeck took the "facts" of a people's plight, and wrote a tale of suffering, goodness, evil, and heroism of biblical proportion. The necessity for the journalist to strictly adhere to "facts" always constrained John Steinbeck's sensibility and imagination.

"I have never had much ability for nor faith nor belief in realism. It is just a form of fantasy as nearly as I could figure," Steinbeck wrote to a friend in 1933 in defense of *The Red Pony*.[80] A quarter of a century later, as he reviewed the journalism pieces he had written during World War II, he held their reflection of truth in extremely low regard. "[I]n light of everything that has happened since, perhaps the whole body of work [is] untrue and warped and one-sided. . . . They are as real as the wicked witch and the good fairy, as true and tested and edited as any other myth."[81]

As hard as Steinbeck was on himself, however, he was merciless on his peers, whom he disdained for their statistic-laden war reports. In his opinion, their emphasis on guns and tactics and their ingratiating themselves with officers to get the inside scoop on strategy decisions failed entirely to give the reader the true sense of war. He felt that many war correspondents embodied the same pettiness, arrogance, self-aggrandizement, and biased thinking that marked Washington bureaucrats. That he felt the brunt of the same jealousy and resentment he had perceived in Washington only inflamed his low regard for his colleagues. "I arrived as a Johnny-come-lately, a sacred cow, a kind of tourist. I think they felt I was muscling in on their hard-gained territory," Steinbeck wrote after the war, noting that more than one had told him his "stuff stinks."[82] But Steinbeck was not about to let them get away with this, and he exposed them in print as liars who blatantly ignored the truth. In a vivid, scathing critique which appeared in the *International Herald Tribune* datelined October 6, 1943, Steinbeck wrote of his fellow correspondents: " 'The 5th Army advanced two kilometers,' he will write, while the lines of trucks churn the road to deep dust and truck drivers hunch over their wheels. And off to the right the burial squads are scooping slits in the sandy earth." After going on to describe the grotesque sights the correspondent would really see, such as the soldier crying over a "twitching body," and the little girl "with her stomach blown out," Steinbeck wrote acidly: "These are the things he sees while he writes of tactics and strategy and names generals and in print decorates heroes." It was the effective equivalent of a cop going public with police corruption charges. It was no wonder that Steinbeck again found himself on the outside.

In September 1943, several weeks before he left the battle to return to London, Steinbeck experienced several harrowing, near-death experiences while attached to Fairbanks's unit. These included the narrow escape at night by his torpedo boat when a German convoy somehow failed to recognize it in the darkness, and the seemingly impossible capture by the Allies of a German radar station on the island of Ventotene in the Tyrrhenian Sea led by a tiny band of five brave American soldiers in a whaleboat. It is difficult to imagine a reporter brave enough or crazy enough to accompany five commandos on a small boat in the Mediterranean as they set out to conquer a German force, yet Fairbanks let him go, and Steinbeck's Ventotene dispatches were the most vivid and compelling he wrote of the war. Looking back on his skirmishes with death, Steinbeck was later to describe his definite intention to get himself killed as a way of offering himself as a sacrifice, because it seemed to him that to die for one's country in a great war was "an active creative death." With his usual wry humility Steinbeck wrote, "I took really miraculous chances, with every kind of weapon and warfare and outside of getting smacked with a gasoline can I couldn't even get scratched."[83]

In London, Steinbeck was bored, homesick, and miserable, and he left in October, more than a month before his contract was up. He came away from Europe more assured than ever that the soldier on a mission was like any other man, the sum of his courage and fear, goodness, and evil. The last words he wrote for the *International Herald Tribune* concerned the jittery Americans' lack of sleep as they awaited the transfer of their Nazi captives from Ventotene. For Steinbeck, plagued by horrifying nightmares since youth, sleep was ever the secret purse for man's sins. While he had gone to war hoping to gain a deeper understanding of man's greatest moral, spiritual, and intellectual dilemmas, the terrifying reality of war would instead rocket him into nightmare hell.

Steinbeck was chomping at the bit to get back to writing fiction now that the war was behind him, and he and Gwyn were reestablished in New York. He had taken notes for a novel while covering the war, and though he had lost them in November when his English torpedo boat was fired on off the coast of Genoa, Italy, Steinbeck was able to move forward with the purposely nonwar *Cannery Row*, a story of the bedraggled denizens of Monterey, California. By mid-January of 1944 he was back in Mexico working on yet another project, *The Pearl*, which he planned also to make as a film there. After such a long creative lull, Steinbeck's mind was bursting; yet, once again he found himself feeling nervous, plagued by insomnia and nightmares, and homesick for California. Some pleasure came from his work on *Cannery Row*, a "silly, fun" book, he called it, about Monterey's underclass of prostitutes and drunks, led in a magical way by Ed Ricketts's fictional incarnation, Doc. But back in New York and awaiting the birth of his and Gwyn's first child, his war-induced hearing loss persisted, and in April doctors diagnosed his problem as two burst eardrums. He was also having blackouts, temporary memory loss, and was so exhausted he began taking vitamin injections.

Looking back on his time in Europe, Steinbeck expressed regret that he had gone at all. There was nothing mythic about war, and certainly nothing heroic, he had decided. Sin and "racial pride" were everywhere. Writing to his longtime friend Carlton Sheffield in the fall of 1944, Steinbeck wrote, "modern war is the most dishonest thing imaginable."[84] He hated himself for having written about it in a way he believed had glorified it. The pieces were rubbish, and "had a profoundly nauseating effect on me," he later wrote, confessing that newspaper work was "not natural to me."[85]

In July, he and Gwyn celebrated the birth of their first child, a son, whom they named Thomas. Steinbeck continued work on *Cannery Row*, which he considered a way to "mark time" while the ideas for a big book, first conceived in 1941, stirred in his consciousness. Though Steinbeck called the book "silly," *Cannery Row*'s veneer of wanton gaiety masked a new, foreboding view of humanity's power to love and survive, and the book marked a subtle, yet at the same time radical change in Steinbeck's thinking.

As recently as 1941, Steinbeck was insisting that no matter how grave the threat, the human species would survive with just two remaining individuals to share their pain and suffering. Steinbeck was so transfixed by this concept that for him it had marked the essence of a man's hope for the future. When Rose-of-Sharon Joad gave her breast to a starving man at the end of *The Grapes of Wrath*, human life prevailed. In *Cannery Row*, however, the "gift of survival" is not given to man, but to ordinary animals: the coyote, the common brown rat, the English sparrow, the housefly, and the moth. If there was a God, he was "Our Father who art in nature." Men and women no longer unite against pain but use it to lacerate each other out of habit. And hope, man's "shock absorber," as he had called it in *The Sea of Cortez*, became in *Cannery Row* the warped product of a kind of poverty and disappointment-induced insanity. In his earlier fiction, Steinbeck might have created an eccentric like Mrs. Tom Talbot, who cuts out a magazine picture of baked ham and serves it on a platter, and who gives tea parties for the neighborhood cats because she can't afford real parties. But in *Cannery Row*, Mary Talbot is bereft of the dignity, the didactic social warping, or more plainly, the fun of Steinbeck's earlier eccentrics. She merely seems daft, stricken by a life of wishing and deprivation.[86]

Most powerfully, before the war Steinbeck perhaps would not have created *Cannery Row*'s most enduring image—the mass execution of frogs by hunters using a "new method." Though the scene had a core of personal truth in a frog-collecting trip Steinbeck had made in the summer of 1923 while a zoology student at the Hopkins Marine Station in Pacific Grove, Hitler's Final Solution to rid Europe of its Jews appears to have found its most imaginative metaphor:

But how could they have anticipated Mack's new method? How could they have foreseen the horror that followed? The sudden flashing of lights, the shouting and squealing of men, the rush of feet. Every frog leaped, plopped into the pool, and swam frantically to the bottom. Then into the pool plunged the line of men, stamping, churning, moving in a crazy line up the pool, flinging their feet about. Hysterically the frogs displaced from their placid spots swam ahead of the crazy thrashing feet and the feet came on. Frogs are good swimmers but they haven't much endurance. Down the pool they went until finally they were bunched and crowded against the end. And the feet and wildly plunging bodies followed them. A few frogs lost their heads and floundered among the feet and got through and these were saved. But the majority decided to leave this pool forever, to find a new home in a new country where this kind of thing didn't happen. A wave of frantic, frustrated frogs, big ones, little ones, brown ones, green ones, men frogs and women frogs, a wave of them broke over the bank, crawled, leaped, scrambled. They clambered up the grass, and they clutched at each other, little ones rode on big ones. And then—horror on horror—the flashlights found them. Two men gathered them like berries. The line came out of the water and closed in on their rear and gathered them like potatoes. Tens and fifties of them were flung into the gunny sacks, and the sacks filled with tired, frightened, and disillusioned frogs, with dripping, whimpering frogs. Some got away, of course, and some had been saved in the pool. But never in frog history had such an execution taken place.[87]

In many ways *Cannery Row* was a repackaging of *Tortilla Flat*, but it lacked the complex simplicity of that earlier work, and is one of Steinbeck's least successful novels if judged purely by its ability to present characters and circumstances which move the reader. Yet, Steinbeck seemed pleased with the book when he completed it late in the summer of 1944. Like all his books, *Cannery Row* was the outlet for Steinbeck's brewing philosophies, in this case, a deepening belief that man was an animal occupying a natural world, and that life was best spent mining creative, spiritual impulses rather than conforming to societal restraints. But possibly Steinbeck's satisfaction with the novel reflected an unconscious appreciation for its value as postwar mental therapy. Gwyn later recalled Steinbeck's mood during the entire year after he returned from the war—the period during which he wrote *Cannery Row*—"one solid year after he came back from the war he had no sense of humor at all. He had a chip on his shoulder the whole time. He was mean, he was sadistic, he was masochistic, he resented everything."[88] When he discussed the novel with Carlton Sheffield, Steinbeck noted, as though it were a badge of honor, that *Cannery Row* "never mentions the war—not once." Curiously, in the next breath, he wondered whether in times past, humans were "sounder then. Certainly we were thinking more universally."[89] His world vision, despite the life force of new fatherhood, was narrowing.

By late summer 1944, Steinbeck could no longer stand his homesickness for California, and he and Gwyn made plans to permanently return to Monterey in October. Though he was excited, he also worried that something would happen to ruin the homecoming, and indeed, the couple's return proved to be disastrous. Steinbeck did not understand that the Monterey which he so lovingly missed and wrote about in *Cannery Row* was the underside its more respectable residents least wanted exposed. Many locals already resented him for his earlier portrayals, and when he came home he immediately found himself persona non grata. When he tried to rent an office, he was told by the landlord, "we don't want people like [writers]. We want professional people like doctors and dentists and insurance."[90]

When *Cannery Row* appeared in January of 1945, locals, even old friends, ostracized their most famous son, and Steinbeck saw conspiracy when town fathers approved numerous building permits, while denying his repeated requests to reno-vate the historic landmark house he and Gwyn had bought. He complained, "60 homes are being built for rent and we can't get a plank to replace a rotten board in the kitchen."[91] Critics, who gave the book scathing reviews and judged Steinbeck's choice of subject matter to have been in poor taste, were "gunning for him to whit-tle him down,"[92] and he accused them of completely misunderstanding *Cannery Row*'s meaning and subtlety.

Steinbeck tried to put a good face on the criticism, saying it put him into a fight-ing spirit to write, but he felt harassed and abandoned. He couldn't wait to leave for Mexico, and was giving serious thought about moving there permanently. He wrote to Pascal Covici a few days before leaving, "I hate a feeling of persecution but I am just not welcome here. . . . This isn't my country anymore. And it won't be until I am dead. It makes me very sad."[93]

World War II ended while John Steinbeck was in Mexico suffering from dysen-tery and finishing the movie script of *The Pearl*.[94] On the surface, his retelling of an ancient Indian parable of a poor fisherman and the beautiful pearl he finds had nothing to do with war, yet *The Pearl was* John Steinbeck's war novel—a dark, harrowing story of pursuit and death. In *The Pearl*, a "song of evil" stinks the air, hope is the absurd product of ignorance, and familial love is defenseless against an evil enemy. Steinbeck had taken all the fear, frustration, feelings of abandon-ment, and persecution he had felt during the past five years and woven them into Kino's desperate attempt to keep the pearl from being stolen so he can pay for his poisoned son's cure. He feels "alone and unprotected," afraid of everyone, as he and his family are forced to flee their village and are hunted by old friends. Kino turns into a murderer, then into a stealthy animal in order to save his family, flee-ing high into the dark, shadowy clefts of the mountains to guard his family. Still, he cannot prevent the hunters from killing his infant son before he kills them. Kino and his wife return to their village, broken with grief, and Kino throws the pearl back into the water. Rejoined with nature from which it was greedily taken, the pearl's evil power immediately evaporates. The whole riveting series of night-marish events ends just as abruptly as it began, but as a result, Kino has lost his manhood, his soul, his son, and his home. In the simple declaration that Kino "had lost one world and not gained another," Steinbeck exquisitely sets forth the essence of the brutal tragedy.

In the winter of 1946, Steinbeck sold the Monterey house, and he and his bud-ding family—Gwyn was pregnant with the couple's second child—moved back to New York. Only the previous autumn he had rejected the city, but after the trouble in California, he welcomed the kind of anonymous life that New York offered. It was a city, he said, where "Littleness gets swallowed up."[95] On June 13, 1946, another son, named John, was born.

The vision Steinbeck had held in 1942 for his future after the war seemed partly to have come true. He had the wife and the babies; two adjoining houses with a small garden on East Seventy-eighth Street were a far cry from his dream of own-ing ten acres on the California coast; yet, Steinbeck threw himself into his work in New York and tried not to look back. But the man who anticipated that the "jeal-ous gods" would deliver a smashing blow whenever life was too kind got exactly what he expected. His marriage, which had never matched his sunny ideal of it, quickly disintegrated in the mire of diapers, sleepless nights, and pent-up resentments. When Gwyn asked John for a divorce in August 1948, Steinbeck told friends the marriage had been bitterly unhappy for more than four years. Steinbeck had exaggerated Gwyn's domesticity, complimenting the former actress on her lemon pies and her lack of complaints. But his effusive praise masked the fissure which had grown between them, probably from the time when he left for Europe right after they were married, worsening with Gwyn's very difficult second pregnancy. Gwyn came to resent his moods, independence, travel, and long hours working downstairs while she and a nurse cared for the children upstairs. Steinbeck made his own list of grievances and wondered whether she was making up the list of illnesses of which she complained, which among many repercussions brought sexual intimacy to a grinding halt. The couple began drinking heavily, Gwyn took to her bed, and Steinbeck descended into a deep depression which spilled out on every page of his next novel, *The Wayward Bus*.

The America which John Steinbeck repeatedly fled, mostly for Mexico, during the war years made him feel mean-spirited, guilty, and bitter. This America reminded him of his failed first marriage, of the public's clawing, bottomless demand for him, and the critics' hardness toward him, which he believed was founded above all on jealousy. The America that he had once loved for its endless beauty and possibility and quirky spontaneity—even if foul darkness lay just beyond a river valley or wood—had in his eyes become forever more the overly developed, neurotic nation he characterized in *The Sea of Cortez*, cluttered by mass production, gross consumerism, and dishonesty—a cheap, Kewpie-doll-hawking society. Not even his native California, which had provided him so much creative inspiration, had escaped what he saw as the country's transformation during the war, from a sweeping, fertile panorama of hope and ingenuity to a bleak, highway-skewered fiefdom ruled by huge corporations. It was a country where businessmen took credit for winning the war and veterans were unwelcome burdens. Only a "vet" like Ernest, the quick-talking novelties salesman of *The Wayward Bus*, who returned from Europe and jumped on the consumer bandwagon, could fend off the scorn of the newly rich.

In 1937, Steinbeck had hoped—and believed—that America was on the verge of a revolution. He thought all the victims of injustice were going to rally and rebel against the rich and powerful. But if Steinbeck's nineteenth-century America lingered into the early 1930s, the America of the Joads and good people like them seemed to have died with the war. In Steinbeck's view, America had come into a spineless twentieth century, and the only revolutions in his first postwar novel were those made by the revolving lunch-counter pie-shelf in Juan Chicoy's bus stop. In *The Wayward Bus*'s portrayal of phoney, postwar America, not even Mother Mahoney's "homemade pies" are really homemade. A flush toilet, which in *The Grapes of Wrath* represented America's elusive wealth and progress, became a twelve-inch novelty in *The Wayward Bus*—a whiskey glass with a pull chain that dispensed the whiskey into the "toilet bowl."[96] To a gravely disappointed Steinbeck, the salesman-on-the-make came to represent the war's strongest legacy. In *The Wayward Bus* there is neither hope nor nobility. Men and women, who used to prop each other up in Steinbeck's world, are now tearing each others' eyes out in all-out war. Lies, secrets, and hurtful games are played endlessly and the players can't seem to stop, no matter what the cost. Hollywood's phony celluloid picture of happiness, wealth, and beauty steers their disappointment, and they escape despair with pills, alcohol, and empty sex. Steinbeck's signature ragtag collection of individuals rides his "cosmic" bus, but they lack any strong moral purpose or spiritual ideal which connects them to one another. Each individual pulls his own way, smack against the other: daughters against parents, wives against husbands, husbands against wives, employees against employers—all lost, aching, fighting souls—disconnected from the land and each other. Worst of all, even when people try to change, they just revert to their old habits. They make tiny stabs at rebellion, engaging in an illicit affair, telling off a dominating husband, but these are the merest blips of self-assertion and have absolutely no result. Fear wins, as in the end the people are more afraid of change than of what they know.

Since the early 1930s, Steinbeck's rich fictional world was populated by flawed humans who are motivated by astonishingly convoluted, illogical thinking. One warped premise begets another and yet another in an endless stream of human violations until a moment of rampant disaster ensues. Reality is a constantly fluctuating creation, and the highest moral intentions are invoked when crimes like murder, suicide, theft, adultery, and public mayhem are committed. But always in these earlier works, Steinbeck's charity toward his messy charges allowed them the promise of a leader they not only wanted, but deserved, because of their self-reliance, pride, and inherent goodness. Now, a decade after *The Grapes of Wrath*, Steinbeck told readers that people were too selfish to deserve a true leader. And if they were undeserving, Steinbeck asked, did they have any right to ask for help? Juan Chicoy, the wayward bus's driver, is provisionally responsible for his riders, but with his own tattered marriage, adultery, and dreams of fleeing his alcoholic wife for a simpler place like Mexico, Juan is no different from anyone else. When the bus reaches a flooded bridge and a decision must be made whether to try to cross it, turn back, or take a detour via an old road, Juan is told to make a decision for the group, but he doesn't want to be anyone's leader, and he resents their demands on him.

"He had been trying to push this carload of cattle bodily about their business in which he had no interest. There was almost a feeling of malice in him now," Steinbeck wrote.[97] Juan wonders whether he can later be exonerated from blame if he acts only at the insistence of his followers. The passengers finally unite to hoist their entrapped bus out of mud, but once embarking on the detour, they return to their old deceits. They forgive each other for their sins, but only because it is the only way to go on living. In postwar Los Angeles, as the bus heads for its destination, the lights were "lost, lonely in the night, remote and cold and winking." The people, led for so long, have forgotten how to take care of themselves.

For years after John Steinbeck returned from Europe, he refused to talk or think about the war. It had unnerved him so deeply that he tried to suppress all memory of it—"a screaming hysteria to me—a thing of nightmare and madness," he called it in 1950 in a rare admission.[98] When his discipline faltered and his mind admitted the war during those first years after he returned, he found he could not discern the "pattern" of its meaning, attributing his failure to the war's recentness. As the years passed and understanding continued to elude him, Steinbeck settled for making generalized commentary on soldiering, military conditioning, and military leaders and Washington bureaucrats, as he did in his 1952 novel *East of Eden*, whose time frame spanned the period from 1862 to the end of the First World War. When Steinbeck dared to think of what World War II had meant, all thought disintegrated into the blind, confusing, wartime fear of one pitch-black night when he had to leave his destroyer and go ashore, and his penis retreated into his abdomen so that he could not urinate. Heroics were fine in a romanticized version of ancient, feudal knight errantry, but this kind of raw fear which he could not put into intelligent thought, spoken word, or prose was the true, terrible, lingering aftertaste of war, which held him in its grip like a monster. On a war destroyer somewhere off the coast of Italy in 1943, John Steinbeck fell into a habit of fear from which he could never again break loose, no matter how hard he tried. The fear spread over him like a gooey grit which would not wash off, eventually penetrating deep into his pores, and giving rise to an often paralyzing fear of death and aging, but even more harrowing, a terror that he could no longer write. When his character Cyrus Trask, the military impostor in *East of Eden*, says, "nearly all men are afraid, they don't know what causes their fear—shadows, perplexities, dangers without names or numbers, fear of a faceless death," Steinbeck put his finger on the fear, as well as his lack of understanding, without directly linking it to the war from which he had returned.[99]

When Steinbeck finished *East of Eden*, his volcanic interpretation of the biblical Cain and Abel story, in 1952, he permanently closed the door on California and his former life in the Salinas Valley. As always when he was working on a big novel, Steinbeck described it as the hardest thing he ever attempted, and he regarded this one as the sum of thirty-five years of living, learning, and suffering. Unquestionably his greatest novel after *The Grapes of Wrath*, *East of Eden* could never have been written had Steinbeck not attained the emotional distance from California brought about by a new and deeply satisfying marriage in 1949 to Elaine Scott, a former stage actress and ex-wife of movie star Zachary Scott, as well as his recognition that California had become too synonymous with pain and rejection to be his home ever again. (*East of Eden*'s premise is that human evil stems from the basic act of rejection by one human being of another who craves his love.) But the happiness he found when he fell in love again had not come without a price: in 1948 Steinbeck had suffered a nearly total nervous breakdown when his friend Ed Ricketts was accidentally run over by a car and killed and Gwyn had left him shortly thereafter.

Steinbeck was deeply shaken. Overeating, drinking, whoring, and working like an automaton, he described having felt closer then to death than he ever had in Italy during the war when he tried to get killed. The end of his marriage had churned up a sickening indifference to life and death, a hellish condition he later described as "a rusting, corroding waste away."[100] Typically, when he arose from the depths of his despair and found he could love and work again, he used his own emotional despair to shape his explanation for postwar, atomic-era, human experience, which he characterized as cowardly and small-minded, and wallowing in a pervasive restlessness, nervousness, and fear—"Weltschmerz" or "world sadness," as he called it in *East of Eden*. But never had this supremely social, caring man cared less for mass humanity or its fluctuating and natural process of decay and birth than now. Absolutely terrorized by his brush with spiritual and creative death, and alarmed by widespread Soviet repression of artists, Steinbeck now cared only for the salvation of the individual human creative impulse. He wrote to the novelist John O'Hara on June 8, 1949:

> I think I believe one thing powerfully—that the only creative thing our species has is the individual lonely mind. Two people can create a child but I know of no other thing created by a group. The group ungoverned by individual thinking is a horrible destructive principle. The great change in the last 2,000 years was the Christian idea that the individual soul was very precious. Unless we can preserve and foster the principle of the preciousness of the individual mind, the world of men will either disintegrate into a screaming chaos or will go into a grey slavery.[101]

This concept would find direct translation in *East of Eden*, which bestowed the same kind of creative, world-changing power on an individual as *The Grapes of Wrath* had bestowed upon the group. At the ripe old age of forty-eight, the writer who could dissect human motive with the clarity of a scientist and the emotional depth of a poet, and who before World War II was willing to take on America's rich and powerful to better the lives of common people, now had no such grand ambitions. "I cannot be God," he wrote in 1950. "My work is very important to me because I am an animal conditioned to this kind of work but it is not very important in the world."[102]

Ironically, this wisdom, or maturity, or whatever this newfound concept of the supremacy of the individual and the creative spirit could be called, utterly and sadly failed John Steinbeck. Excluding the intensely creative period right after he returned from the war in Europe, which was largely an attempt to drown the demons of war and a second failing marriage, and the two-year period during which he worked on the truly extraordinary *East of Eden*, Steinbeck suffered from the agonizing despair of writer's block, which relentlessly pursued him until his early death in 1968 at the age of sixty-six. Though his unique brand of this artistic disease permitted him to publish a respectable body of work after *East of Eden* and only intermittently brought his writing to a halt, these works were agonizingly forced out to satisfy his desperate need to prove to himself that he was not used up. Stories and novels were begun but not finished, plays failed, and concepts never left the development stages. His youthful and passionate sense of right and wrong and black and white was overwhelmed by the tide of fear and sadness that came of living through war and seeing what the world had become in the Kewpie-doll, Red Scare era, whose texture of evil and violence seemed to him to have started the moment World War II ended, if not before. A man whose imagination was fired by childhood fantasies and dreams, but more profoundly, the hope that man would take God's gift of free choice and use it in the virtuous search for perfection, could not bear the knowledge that heroes were a thing of the past, that in "kneeling down to atoms," men had become "atom-sized in their souls," as he had written in *East of Eden*. He spent the postwar years subsumed by the wrenching feeling that men had lost all dignity and stature, but worse for him personally, the fear that he had joined the ranks of other American writers in being caught in the past no matter how hard he wanted to move forward into the present and onward to the future.

"It is almost as though we wanted to define a past which probably never did exist. The stories of childhood, the stories of the frontier, the novels of one's old aunts, etc. This is fine but there can be enough of it," he complained to his agent in 1954 describing his inability to finish some stories. "It has occurred to me that we may be so confused about the present that we avoid it because it is not clear to us. But why should that be a deterrent? If this is a time of confusion, then that should be the subject of a good writer if he is to set down his time."[103]

The harder Steinbeck tried and failed to shed the old stories and formats and to find some new form, "some clean approach," the more horrified he became at his own impotence.[104] Though he wanted to believe that even after tragic sorrow, "every man in every generation is refired," as he had optimistically proclaimed in *East of Eden*, Steinbeck seemed to be unable to find his own igniter. Steadfastly refusing to dwell in the past, he could not move into the future, and thus he became stuck in a no-man's-land, a creative limbo, a morass of fear and anxiety. By 1954, he felt that his old style had become a "straightjacket," dictating not only style, but the very subject matter itself.[105] And though he did not want to return to the hard times of the old days, it seemed to Steinbeck that his artistic difficulty coincided with true marital happiness and financial security. The more money he made, the more he worried about losing it. Steinbeck became obsessed by bleak thoughts of death and aging, certain that he had a dwindling number of earning years left to him, although in 1954 he was only fifty-two.

In this desperate, ceaseless struggle to find the means to express himself, his characteristic restlessness and nervousness led him to become a world traveler, even prompting him to take up residence for a time in Paris and in the gentle landscape of England's Somerset near Glastonbury Cathedral. In this beautiful part of ancient England which he loved more than any place he had ever lived, Steinbeck tried desperately to adapt his favorite story since the age of nine, Thomas Malory's fifteenth-century *Le Morte D'Arthur*, in what became a Sisyphian struggle emblematic of his entire postwar biography. In this late age of the atom bomb, political corruption, broken families, and television scandals, Steinbeck had come to see the twentieth century as a mirror of the fifteenth, his own people as "unconsciously savage and as realistically self-seeking as the people of the Middle Ages," but he had also come to see Malory as the archetypal writer, and the ill-fated quest for the Holy Grail as a metaphor for the novelist's dismal failure to attain his goals.[106] "For a novelist is a rearranger of nature so that it makes an understandable pattern, and a novelist is also a teacher, but a novelist is primarily a man and subject to all of a man's faults and virtues, fears and braveries," he wrote in April 1957 from Rome, where he had gone in yet another futile search for the answers in his frustrating quest to merge the past of Malory's tale, the present, and the future into the story of mankind.[107] Haunted by a subject he humbly felt was "so much bigger than I am. It frightens me," Steinbeck threw out three hundred pages at a time, believing he failed to find the right "symbols of form" to adapt the ancient morality tale so that men of his own day might learn how to retrieve a humanity toward each other which had been lost in war and atomic devastation, as well as the less overt but equally destructive greed, laziness, and material plenty of the present.[108] He worked on the book intermittently from 1956 on and never finished it. Perhaps bearing out his own convictions about greed, his widow published *The Acts of King Arthur and His Noble Knights* in 1976, based on the work that he had deemed unsatisfactory and certainly unfinished, together with excerpts of Steinbeck's letters concerning the work. The book garnered rave reviews for the dead author and became a *New York Times* best-seller.

In the end, it was as though the very day Steinbeck set foot in Europe during the war, he was catapulted against his will out of the comforting mists of a violent imagination softened by hues of play, fancy, and hope into the stark terror of pure, unforgiving objectivity. Reality and dreams, which he always insisted merged, broke apart like Humpty Dumpty and he could not put them back together again. After the nightmare of war, his hope for America yielded to a sense of "haunting decay," for when he looked around, there was no morality, no dignity, and worse, no prophets to lead the way.[109] When he won the Nobel Prize for literature in 1962 during the Cuban Missile Crisis, Steinbeck, who had suffered several bouts of ill health prior to that time, had come ironically to a particularly aching halt in his writing and feared he would never write again. The prize and ensuing worldwide reverence only made him more despairing, for he felt such a prize rang a death-knell, signifying that the best of his life lay far behind.

For a time in the early 1960s it seemed that his old passion was refired in America's latest war—race war—and he was an early opponent of the Vietnam war, although like *East of Eden's* Cyrus Trask, he eventually sent both his sons off to be soldiers in that war, seemingly proud that they were going to be tested as men. In early 1967, he traveled to Southeast Asia to cover the Vietnam war for *Newsday*. After his return, he met at the White House with President Lyndon Johnson, Secretary of Defense Robert McNamara, Secretary of State Dean Rusk, and Vice President Hubert Humphrey, and offered criticism of America's Vietnam strategy he hoped would be helpful. In a reprise of his experience with Washington during World War II, Steinbeck was left feeling that his most impor-tant suggestions were rejected. Years before America finally pulled out of Vietnam in ignominy, he knew America could not win the war, and he felt those running it were out of control. Nevertheless, as in so many other instances during the postwar years, Steinbeck could not put his ideas into writing. What for others represented his crystal-clear insight, to him seemed only muddled and confused. He had grown weary of yearning to feel a connection with something no longer there, either in himself or his country. On December 20, 1968, John Steinbeck died of heart failure.

In his last novel, *The Winter of Our Discontent*, published in 1961, as well as in his nonfiction account of a 1960 tour of America, *Travels with Charley*, which appeared in 1962, Steinbeck insisted that he did not mourn the old days like one of those old-timers who harp on the "good ol' days." He was enough of a realist not to romanticize the vast numbers of deaths by disease, starvation, and child-birth—the hardscrabble life of the remote farm and ranch which modern life had thankfully vanquished. But whereas Lewis and Clark bravely ventured west for two years, confronting privation, danger, and hardship, Americans in the 1960s complained like babies if the milk delivery was late or there was an elevator strike. Though he intended his tour around America on the eve of the presidential election to rekindle his appreciation for the land and its people, it only confirmed his worst feelings about a nation in which men had lost their principles and opinions, and where caution reigned. He asserted that Soviet Russia—no prize either, in his view—had become the scapegoat for America's boredom, lack of opinions, and gripes, and though he had launched the trip expecting to learn about the heart of America, he learned more about his poodle Charley, who had clear motives and principles and whose needs were basic and guileless.

"What was I doing wrong?" Steinbeck pleaded in *Travels with Charley* in sadness and frustration over his inability to draw deep and uplifting truths about his country. He felt "muddled," he told his readers. Before he embarked, Steinbeck had privately called the trip "a frantic last attempt to save my life and the integrity of my creative impulse." Thus, his comments about being a ghost and a dead memory in Salinas with old friends take what is often a charming work, marked by Steinbeck's winsome ability to observe human foibles without contempt, and transform it into a chilling memoir of a great writer who has lost his way.[110]

In his last novel, *The Winter of Our Discontent*, Ethan Hawley, the morally tormented hero and World War II veteran, comes upon his son play-acting with his old Knight Templar sword. "You make a symbolic picture, my son," Hawley tells his son. "Call it 'Youth, War and Learning.' "[111] In what was otherwise a throwaway line, John Steinbeck had written the whole sorry story of his war-begotten illness. The writer with the imagination of an errant boy and the seeing power of a veteran reporter had simply learned too much.

CHAPTER THREE

Virginia Woolf

THE OUTSIDER'S LAMENT

Roger Fry cherished as a guilty secret a profound skepticism about all political activity and even about progress itself and had begun to think of art as somehow his only possible job.

Roger Fry: A Biography, 1940

On May 13, 1940, Virginia Woolf brought the corrected proofs of her latest book, *Roger Fry: A Biography*, to the printer. She was pleased with the book, which had proved difficult to write, but her happiness was tempered by Adolf Hitler's devastating invasion two days before of Holland and Belgium. She had an intense feeling about the book, she wrote in her diary, but given the war, wondered if there was any "importance in that feeling." Venting the kind of ambivalence that would haunt her to her death less than a year later, Virginia Woolf then asked herself, "Or is there more importance than ever?"[1]

Several days later, Woolf's husband, Leonard, informed her that he had volunteered to join a lay battalion on guard against German parachutists over the gentle downs and marshes around their Sussex, England, country home, Monk's House. Leonard Woolf was a fierce antifascist Labour Party member with a long-standing history promoting pacifism and disarmament, and Virginia was surprised and peeved at his sudden leap to the militaristic. It seemed to her that "gun and uniform to [Leonard were] slightly ridiculous."[2] Indeed, Leonard Woolf hardly looked the part of soldier. He was a small man with a large, spade-shaped nose and soft eyes, who might have been mistaken for an East End tailor, were it not for his tweed jacket and pipe and the perennial books and papers he carried about with him from meeting to meeting.

When her ire subsided, Virginia and Leonard returned to a subject they discussed with increasing frequency: England's—and their—future, were Hitler to win. Although Virginia had tried to kill herself twice during manic-depressive episodes, the couple's joint suicide pact was a calmly and rationally conceived plan in the event of a German invasion. Leonard, a Jew, was already keeping gasoline in the garage if such a day were to come. This spring day, however, newly released from the rigors of her Roger Fry biography and nearly finished with her next book, a novel provisionally entitled *Pointz Hall*, Virginia rejected suicide for herself. Yes, the world was coming apart, but the war could not last, she believed then. What if she killed herself, and the war ended, and Hitler didn't win? "Why am I optimistic?" she wrote in her diary. "Or rather not either way? Because it's all bombast, the war. One old lady pinning on her cap has more reality."[3]

Virginia Woolf had given war considerable thought before Hitler ever took his first prize, the Rhineland, in 1936. Her 1929 essay, "A Room of One's Own", had blamed women's historical lack of literary success on their subjugation by men, and Woolf's 1938 pacifist manifesto, *Three Guineas*, was an extension on a feminist theme, but with worldly ramifications. Woolf was a devout pacifist, and war, she contended, was yet another contest illustrating men's insatiable need for power and glory. War-making was not an urge of human nature, she argued, even if it had become instinctual, but rather the result of "law and practice." Male bastions of British higher education, such as Oxford, Cambridge, and Eton, groomed men of wealth and means to be hawks, while women, who perceived war in more human terms of death and destruction, were barred from these schools. The ownership of magnificent homes, which promoted intimacy among a small group of men of rank and wealth, and colorful military ceremonies, with gilded and feathered uniforms, all enforced in men the idea that war brought glory to the morally and physically superior. These men of influence, who viewed war as a profession and source of excitement, were the "insiders" who directed the nation's course, she wrote. The primarily self-educated daughters of these men were the ineffectual, impotent "outsiders."

Virginia Woolf's vision of war as a dialectic between the sexes was consistent with her general viewpoint and fascination with gender roles. Throughout her personal and literary life Woolf had been preoccupied by the differences between the sexes and how these differences applied to history, culture, sexuality, and even Christianity. She read voluminously on the subject of gender, including such books as *The Autobiography of Christopher Kirkland*, a three-volume fictionalized autobiography of a woman who changed her sex in order to tell her story, and in 1940, while she was researching the expulsion of women musicians from the Bournemouth Municipal Orchestra for her novel *Pointz Hall*, she was reading Havelock Ellis's *Studies in the Psychology of Sex*, and also *Pain, Sex and Time: A New Hypothesis of Evolution* by Gerald Heard, a friend of her friend Aldous Huxley.

Woolf heralded the legal right of upper-class British women to earn a living, which was won after World War I, as the key to the educated woman's ability to bend society toward her will. The salient question Woolf asked in *Three Guineas* was, now that woman had changed the rules of the game, "how can she use this new weapon to help . . . prevent war?"[4]

When Woolf began writing the work in 1936, shortly before the outbreak of the Spanish Civil War—before Hitler carved up Europe, before her beloved nephew Julian Bell was killed driving an ambulance for the Spanish Loyalists, and before the ensuing war would confirm her worst assessment of the human race and convince her of the incontrovertibility of the "manliness of war," she was still hopeful that there was an answer to the burning question she posed. In many ways, this physically fragile woman esteemed learning above action, but the awesome power and courage of Virginia Woolf's intellect had the dynamic force of action, and her prescription outlined in *Three Guineas* represented no less than a call to social extortion. Women must be willing to use their newfound earnings, she wrote, to wield power just as men always had, but they must exercise it for the good of society:

> If the working women of the country were to say: 'If you go to war, we will refuse to make munitions or to help in the production of goods,' the difficulty of war-making would be seriously increased. But if all the daughters of educated men were to down tools tomorrow, nothing essential either to the life or to the war-making of the community would be embarrassed.[5]

Woolf further asserted that women's independent wealth could buy the election of political candidates with an antiwar platform, and could bring about other necessary changes in men's education and way of thinking, not just about war, but also about women's physical and intellectual inferiority. Only after men were thus sensitized to the truths women had always held sacred could the sexes unite in a common bond of humanity. "For now at last we are looking at the same picture," she wrote, describing her ideal world of gender equality. "We are seeing with you the same dead bodies, the same ruined houses."[6]

A mere twenty years had passed since World War I, the "war to end all wars," and indeed the dead bodies and ruined houses of that war were still fresh in the mind of any European who was old enough to remember. More than ten million were killed in World War I, twenty-one million were wounded, and nearly 125 million had been left impoverished. Nineteen thousand British alone were killed in one day in the battle of the Somme, and when the war was over, the 745,000 dead represented nearly nine percent of all British men under the age of forty-five.

Woolf and her Bloomsbury circle of illustrious philosophers, economists, artists, writers, and politicians whose leanings were primarily left or left-of-center had witnessed the rise of fascism in Europe through the 1920s and mid-1930s with a peculiar mixture of intellectualized repugnance and terror, and in 1936, most of Britain's influential men of the type Woolf characterized as "insiders" espoused the position that a big war could be averted through traditional diplomatic means.

Under the cloak of this philosophy, England mastered the art of appeasement. In June 1936, the British government reneged on its threat to punish Italy for Mussolini's unprovoked war on Abyssinia, the east African nation lodged between British Somaliland to the northeast and the British colony of Kenya to the south, thereby abandoning the strategy adopted by its less powerful League of Nations partners. When the Spanish Civil War broke out in July of that same year, England, like the United States, remained neutral, her leaders believing it would be a terrible mistake for Britain to get involved. Although some nervous Britons feared the spread of civil war to France, where the new French leader, Leon Blum, was a Socialist, and the powerful extreme French right preferred Hitler to Stalin, the British leadership had determined that the best way to deal with dictators was to mollify them quietly. British rightists, however, felt no qualms about being loud and obnoxious. In 1933 Sir Oswald Mosley founded his British Union of Fascists and, protected by his own cadre of Black Shirts at London's Olympia Auditorium in June 1934, rallied fifteen thousand, most of whom agreed that he should be made dictator of Britain. Subsequent rallies by Mosley in the years leading up to the war erupted in violent confrontations between his followers and British anti-Fascists and Communists, but British official policy toward Europe's Fascists gave Mosley no real cause to worry that his movement would be quashed by the authorities.

As war came perilously nearer, Virginia Woolf did not join pacifists like her brother-in-law, Clive Bell, who asserted that war would be worse than any fate Hitler might present to England. (Leonard Woolf was so offended by Bell's 1938 pamphlet, *Warmongerers*, sponsored by the Peace Pledge Union, which contended that a "Nazi Europe would be, to my mind, heaven on earth compared with Europe at war," that he could not read it.) Virginia Woolf had shared the prevailing expectation among the British that Adolf Hitler would curtail his aggressions. As late as mid-July 1939, she still believed there would be peace, even though her friend Harold Nicholson, a Member of Parliament for West Leicester since 1935, predicted that war would break out in a matter of weeks.

"I cant [*sic*]* help letting hope break in,—the other prospect is too mad," she wrote just five days before war was declared.[7] Despite her renowned outspokenness and the lending of her name to some antifascist petitions, Woolf claimed to find politics inscrutable and often useless. In her 1937 novel, *The Years*, Woolf's character North, a war veteran and farmer, terms political groups and societies with their leaders and megaphones, "poppy-cock," and he concludes that the world would be much better off if each individual began "inwardly, and let the devil take the outer form."[8]

If Woolf wanted to escape politics before World War II, however, she could not. Leonard was secretary of the Labour Party's Advisory Committee on Imperial and International Affairs; a founder of the ill-fated League of Nations; member of the Whitley Council, which settled wage disputes among civil servants; and member of the Fabian Society, a group of British intellectuals founded in 1884 to reorient the government's emphasis from individual interests to those of society as a unified collective. (In its fledgling days, the British Labour Party took many members from the Fabians, but not all Fabians were Socialists.) Additionally, Leonard was the author of numerous books and pamphlets on sociology and government and served as senior editor of several political publications, including the Fabian organ, *New Statesmen*. Leonard despised fascism, as well as British imperialism, the effects of which he had seen on the poor when he

*Virginia Woolf customarily omitted apostrophes for contractions in her writing.

was a diplomat in Ceylon in the early 1900s. Earlier, he had advocated an isolationist policy for Britain, but after the German invasion of Austria in March 1938, Leonard Woolf supported Winston Churchill's strong stand against Hitler and henceforth worked tirelessly to direct the British government toward a more active role in fighting fascism. "Leonard is in the thick of meetings; the telephone never stops ringing; agitated editors arrive with articles intended to prevent war," Virginia wrote in late winter 1938, "though I can do nothing, and scarcely now understand, my mind is all a ruffle and a confusion."[9]

From the 1920s on, the Woolf household was restive with political activities, in addition to Virginia's regular literary and intellectual lunches, teas, and dinners. Leonard shared his party's mistrust of the policies of appeasement practiced by Prime Ministers Baldwin and Chamberlain. He and longtime friend H. G. Wells were among protesters of the French and British proposition of September 18, 1938, that offered to turn German-speaking areas of Czechoslovakia over to Hitler. But Leonard despised Stalinist communism as much as he did fascism, and therefore worried about far more than merely containing the maniacal German leader. Tenacious as Leonard was in his efforts to change the immediate course of history, he was not hopeful for mankind. As war's threat grew ever larger, there was an underlying anxiety in the Woolf household over the future of humanity in the larger sense.

The Woolfs' dim view of the future had grown over the two decades since German philosopher Oswald Spengler wrote in his massive *Decline of the West* that every culture was destined to decay, and that Western civilization was in its twilight. While Spengler's prediction that "the Weimar Constitution is already doomed" had bolstered Adolf Hitler's ambitions to dictatorship in Germany, pacifists reeling from World War I felt that Spengler had written a blueprint of terrible things to come.

For British pacifists like Virginia and Leonard Woolf, World War I was the seminal event which separated the civilized past from the barbaric future, and it forced its way into Woolf's fiction like an iron spike driven into a plank of wood. Reality belonged either to a tranquil, orderly time before the war "when you could buy almost perfect gloves," as she had written in her 1925 novel, *Mrs. Dalloway*,[10] or after, when "the world's experience had bred in them all, all men and women, a well of tears."[11] Those Britons who had put a good face on that war as it was being fought, hoping it would herald a new world of spiritual adventure, emotional freedom—an "expansion of the soul," as Woolf characterized the hope in *The Years*—were sorely disappointed. Not only did the devastating war take an incalculable psychological toll on the British nation, but it also wrought enormous changes in the social, economic, and political structures of the class-conscious empire. Families were not just dislocated; the nature of the British family was permanently altered. The removal of such a significant number of potential fathers from the population, in addition to the wider dissemination of birth control which accompanied women's rights, reduced the average family size. Yet, this was but one of the many factors which raised living standards and blurred differences between the middle and working classes, as British workers increased their wages, and labor unions and the Labour Party gained strength. Men like Leonard Woolf, whose mother was left nearly penniless with nine children when his father, a lawyer, died, were able to play a role in government only because of the weakened social and political power of the landed class after World War I. The huge financial cost of that war and ensuing high taxation made it impossible for any of the upper class except the richest to live as extravagantly as they had in prewar times. Changes in laws forced the selling of millions of acres of land which had been held since feudal times by only one class. There was even a decline in the number of servants.[12]

While liberals of the postwar era optimistically looked to a more egalitarian future, members of the aristocracy and people just beneath their class, like Woolf, who prided themselves on having created a rarefied world of good taste and breeding, sensed that the coming political changes signified a deep, permanent challenge to that world. Power and money were not the only things at stake; those who treasured long hours spent listening to Wagner and reading Chaucer, gardening and attending formal dinners at country houses, sensed that the new, brusque world would not accommodate their leisured pace. "In 1914 in the background of one's life and one's mind there were light and hope," Leonard Woolf wrote in his autobiography,

[B]y 1918 one had unconsciously accepted a perpetual public menace and darkness and had admitted into the privacy of one's mind or soul an iron fatalistic acquiescence in insecurity and barbarism. There was nothing to be done about it, and so, as I recorded, Virginia and I celebrated the end of a civilization and the beginning of peace by sitting in the lovely, paneled room in Hogarth House, Richmond, which had been built almost exactly 200 years before as the country house of Lord Suffield, and eating, almost sacramentally, some small bars of chocolate cream.[13]

As war clouds grew heavy in the late 1930s, members of the British ruling class could not hide from one cold, hard truth, no matter how much they might have wanted to: another big war would force them to share real power with the lower classes. The closer war came, the more deeply Woolf and her circle mourned the coming of a new, more "democratic" world of lower-class philistinism and mediocrity.[14]

Virginia Woolf was not "upper class" in the strict sense of the word. She traced her roots back to Aberdeen serfs, but she had been born in 1882 into a family of education and status, with strong connections to both the British aristocracy and the English world of arts and letters. Her father, Leslie Stephen, was an eminent author, critic, and essayist, and the son of a knighted under-secretary of the colonies. His first wife was a daughter of William Makepeace Thackeray. Her great great-grandfather was a reputed lover of Marie Antoinette. Woolf's social circle was a veritable Who's Who of British society. The aristocratic inhabitants of England's great ancestral homes, like Penshurst Place and Sissinghurst Castle, for example, were among their friends, as were many of the country's leading thinkers and policy makers—sociologists, philosophers, career politicians, poets, and writers of international renown, such as W. H. Auden, Aldous Huxley, W. B. Yeats, Stephen Spender, Lytton Strachey, and T. S. Eliot.

Woolf identified with many of the values of the leisure class; yet, in truth, she had earned her own living since she was a young woman. Her novels, particularly those written after 1924—*Mrs. Dalloway* (1925), *To the Lighthouse* (1927), *Orlando*

(1928), *The Waves* (1931), and *The Years* (1937)—sold respectably in England and America, though prior to the Second World War, she depended primarily on her income as a journalist, book reviewer, and publisher. The Woolfs' publishing company, Hogarth Press, founded in 1917 and mostly financed by Virginia's royalties, published a small, but prestigious list of writers, including T. S. Eliot, Christopher Isherwood, Bertrand Russell, Katherine Mansfield, E. M. Forster, and Sigmund Freud, in addition to their own books, and employed seven people by 1938. Virginia Woolf may have worried about finances when the war initially dampened book sales but Hogarth Press was the couple's labor of love, and was neither intended nor required by Leonard and Virginia as a major source of income. By the late 1930s, Virginia Woolf was not only recognized as an important novelist, but had achieved a large international readership, and when World War II began, the Woolfs were at the height of their earnings. They leased their London homes, but owned outright Monk's House, whose property included two cottages where house guests and servants were accommodated. When rationing began in the winter of 1940–41, Virginia Woolf suffered a reduction in her freedom, but little in the way of her comfort was disturbed. Mabel, the couple's cook, asked to leave when air battles over Rodmell became too much for her, but the Woolfs still had a maid, Louie, and a gardener. In fact, despite Virginia's worry that they were headed for the poorhouse, the Woolfs gave Louie a small pay increase in the fall of 1940.

To the Woolfs, artists like Beethoven and Shakespeare could make life sublime, but art and gentility were not in themselves the essence of civilization. Civilization required a combination of ethics and aesthetics, or truth and beauty, with all its responsibilities to moral rectitude and justice. For them, war was horrific, but peace without civilization was scarcely better. If the Woolfs believed the First World War was the beginning of the end of civilization, a second world war would certainly be its death-knell. "[W]ith a solid block of unbaked barbarians in Germany, what's the good of our being comparatively civilized?" Virginia Woolf wondered.[15]

The reaction to *Three Guineas* when it appeared on June 2, 1938, was swift, strident, mostly negative, and highly personal. The book prompted a veritable fire storm of controversy which barely subsided in the year that followed. Political theorist and Labour Party leader Harold Laski hailed it as the "greatest book since Mill," referring to the nineteenth-century philosopher John Stuart Mill's *The Subjugation of Women*, but the message of *Three Guineas* was not usually so warmly received.[16] The book antagonized most male reviewers; one anonymous critic labeled it "[i]ndecent, almost obscene,"[17] and in some cases female reviewers were no less offended—one called Virginia Woolf a "social parasite."[18] The book inspired a flood of high-pitched reaction among the reading public as well. "[E]very day I get a packet of abuse or ecstasy," Woolf noted. "Letters, I mean, from that hysterical and illiterate ass the Public."[19]

Woolf was pleased by the vitality of the controversy, but it also unnerved her to the end of her life, because, ironically, the outspoken Woolf was so sensitive to criticism that depression usually followed the completion of a new work. At a time when governments and most of their citizens believed it unconscionable not to rally 'round the flag, *Three Guineas* seemed ceaselessly to call into question her patriotism. Woolf considered patriotism "English," but advised against being swayed by blinding emotional fervor. Patriotism was inextricable with male ego, she steadfastly believed, and when leaders talked about patriotism, they failed to stress the resulting death and destruction.

"[O]f course I'm 'patriotic': that is English, the language, farms, dogs, people," she wrote to friend Ethel Smyth, the first week of June of 1938, "only we must enlarge the imaginative, and take stock of the emotion. And I'm sure I can; because I'm an outsider partly; and can get outside the vested interest better than Leonard even—tho' a Jew."[20] As the war progressed, Woolf would feel an ever-increasing emotional burden from being an outsider, with the word's literal implication of alienation and isolation, but in the meantime, like other wives of Britain's politicians, Virginia Woolf was an "inside" outsider, witnessing history in the making, up close.

In the summer of 1938, a state-of-siege mentality was fulminating in London where the Woolfs had lived since 1924. Children were being shepherded out of the city to the countryside. People died testing their gas masks on exhaust pipes; workers were buried alive digging trenches. Hitler had taken Austria that March, and London was "waiting for what Hitler may do next," Woolf wrote at the end of July. "People are tired of talking about war; but all the same we do nothing but buy arms. The air is full of aeroplanes at the moment."[21] The Woolfs prepared for the possibility of German attack by fortifying their stone-lined storeroom at 52 Tavistock Square with books and mattresses.

By September, Hitler threatened to occupy Czechoslovakia on the pretext that the Sudeten Germans on its western borders were being oppressed. On September 15, Prime Minister Neville Chamberlain arrived in Munich and agreed in principle to a concession to Hitler. A week later, Hitler increased the stakes by asking for all of Czechoslovakia. He demanded that the Czechs begin evacuating on September 26 and be out by 2 P.M. on September 28. German troops were to move in during the two days to "restore order." The French army and British navy were partially mobilized, although in London, Chamberlain quashed a communiqué drafted by Winston Churchill and the Foreign Office promising support by France, Britain, and Russia if Hitler invaded Czechoslovakia. Instead, Chamberlain put the onus on Czechoslovakia: accept Hitler's demands or forget about western support.

As the days passed, Europeans feared that war was a certainty. Few doubted Hitler's sincerity, especially after the dictator delivered a crazed speech attacking the Czech president on the night of September 26. The next day, Chamberlain delivered his own speech to the British people, comparing the crisis to a "quarrel in a faraway country between people of whom we know nothing." Still, war seemed inevitable and on Wednesday, September 28, the prime minister asked Mussolini to intervene. Chamberlain again went to Hitler, and returned on September 30 with a declaration signed by himself, French Premier Edouard Daladier, Hitler, and Mussolini, which in essence gave the Sudetenland to Germany. The agreement called for all Czechs to vacate the disputed territory. The four leaders pledged their nations would never go to war against each other again, and Hitler vowed the Sudetenland to be his last territorial claim, just as he had said about the Rhineland in 1936. Chamberlain assured England he had brought back "peace with honor."

On Tuesday, September 27, while Leonard was preoccupied with politics, Virginia sat in the basement of the London Library reading the *Times* from the year 1910 for her book on Roger Fry. An old man who was dusting books told her that everyone had been ordered to put their gas masks on and informed her that the library had stocked sandbags in the event of a bomb attack. If that happened, "there wouldnt be many books left over," the man noted ironically as he dutifully continued to dust. Perhaps believing it was the last time she might see the world's great artworks, at least for a while, Virginia Woolf walked through the tumultuous, crowded streets of London to the National Gallery of Art.

Her beloved city was revving for war at fever pitch. Most stores were closed. People were fleeing to the countryside and some even to America. Those who remained stood in long lines to be fitted with gas masks; loudspeakers were blasting warnings; men were digging trenches and piling sandbags. At the art museum she was again ordered to wear her gas mask. The museum was full and a crowd was listening to a lecture on eighteenth-century French painter Antoine Watteau. "I suppose they were all having a last look," she wrote.

By the afternoon, the government ordered anyone who could leave London to do so, and as the Woolfs gathered a few belongings, Virginia wondered what they would do if "marooned in Rodmell, without petrol, or bicycles?"[22] The couple joined the throngs of citizens leaving London that night and retreated to Monk's House, where they were fitted with more gas masks and told to expect the arrival of two East End children the next day. "The nightmare feeling was becoming more nightmarish; more and more absurd," she wrote, "for no one knew what was happening, and yet everyone was behaving as if the war had begun."[23]

In a letter to her sister, Vanessa Bell, who was in France at the time, Virginia Woolf provided one of the most vivid, behind-the-scenes descriptions of the frightening Munich Crisis:

L. came back [from the offices of *New Statesman* magazine] and said Kingsley was in despair; they had talked for two hours; everybody came into the N.S office and talked; telephones rang incessantly. They all said war was certain; also that there would be no war. Kingsley came to dinner. He had smudges of black charcoal round his eyes and was more melodramatic and histrionic than ever. Hitler was going to make his speech at 8. We had no wireless, but he said he would ring up the BBC after it was over and find out the truth. Then we sat and discussed the inevitable end of civilization. He strode up and down the room, hinting that he meant to kill himself. He said the war would last our lifetime; also we should very likely be beaten. Anyhow Hitler meant to bombard London, probably with no warning; the plan was to drop bombs on London with twenty-minute intervals for forty-eight hours. Also he meant to destroy all roads and railways; therefore Rodmell would be about as dangerous as Bloomsbury. Then he broke off; rang up Clark, the news man at The BBC; "Ah—so its hopeless . . ." Then to us, "Hitler is bawling; the crowds howling like wild beasts." More conversation of a lugubrious kind. Now I think I'll ring up Clark again . . . Ah so it couldnt be worse . . . To us. No Hitler is more mad than ever . . . Have some Whiskey Kingsley, said L. Well, it dont much matter either way, said K. At last he went. What are you going to do? I asked. Walk the streets. Its no good—I cant sleep. So we clasped our hands, as I understood for the last time.[24]

The Woolfs were at Sissinghurst Castle, the home of Harold Nicholson, Member of Parliament, and his wife, writer Vita Sackville-West, on Thursday, September 29, 1938, when they heard that the stalemate had been broken. The Italian king had threatened to abdicate if war broke out. Leonard predicted peace without honor for six months, but his prognosis did not hold true even for a week. Hitler took the Sudetenland on October 5, with no interference from France, despite her treaty with Czechoslovakia guaranteeing protection of that border region. Later that fall and winter, a series of nonaggression pacts were signed with Germany by many of the countries Hitler would soon conquer: France, Denmark, and Hungary. Then, almost a year to the day after one hundred thousand of Hitler's troops marched into Vienna unopposed to take Austria, Hitler took Czechoslovakia on March 15, 1939.

Still, Adolf Hitler was far from Britain's only worry that spring. Days after forty thousand Spanish Loyalist troops surrendered to Franco at the end of March, Mussolini invaded Albania in early April, and the British fleet on the Mediterranean sailed to protect Greece and Turkey against possible aggression by the very same Italian leader who had signed a pact with Britain the year before.

All this paled in comparison to the reality of a million and a half German troops crossing Poland's borders on September 1, 1939, after the country refused to surrender Danzig. After two years of hoping Hitler would be appeased with less, there was no turning back for the Allies, and two days later, on September 3, Britain and France declared war on Germany. Directing pitifully inadequate British air, sea, and land forces was Neville Chamberlain, king of appeasement, more than ever out of his league.

A sense of defeatism took hold in leftist and pacifist circles in London, where the bleak expectation prevailed that Hitler would taunt the British throughout the winter by attacking their shipping and then launch a massive offensive on May 1. If Italy and Spain collaborated, defeat could come as early as July. The British had never wanted war, but now that it was here, how was Hitler to be defeated? In these early days of war the big question at breakfast, lunch, and dinner, and on the streets outside Whitehall was "Can we win?" In France, too, some government ministers recognized that by their inertia they might be handing Hitler victory; yet, if defeat were almost a certainty, should they deplete their treasuries and expose their men to mass annihilation? Leading British pacifists like the philosopher Cyril Joad were not so uncertain over what path his nation should take; Joad pronounced it preferable to submit to Hitler and surrender liberty rather than to sacrifice the blood of beloved sons and husbands.[25]

British leaders debated and then dropped aggressive plans to fight the Germans. On September 29, 1939, Churchill made his suggestion to mine Norwegian waters to impede the flow of Swedish iron ore to Germany, and although the British and French did endorse the plan in April 1940, by then it was too late to prevent Hitler's invasion of Scandinavia. The strategy Britain followed instead was based on defense. In Woolf's London, zeppelin-shaped barrage balloons, intended as an impediment to low-flying bombers, floated overhead, anchored in parks and other open spaces, while prefabricated air-raid shelters were sunk into city gardens. Shop windows were taped and each night citizens prepared for the blackout ritual. Virginia Woolf's beloved London, which she had equated with life and a love of life in her novels, was again darkened by war, just as in 1914. The Woolfs contemplated a time in the near future when they might be forced to move Hogarth Press, which operated from their basement, out of London, or shut it down altogether. But there was more than a physical threat to the press— "nobody is reading anything but politics," Virginia Woolf noted that April.[26]

Worried that the war would distract the public from buying books, Virginia began writing articles, some for publication in America, where she had won a significant readership with her unique unmasking of characters' innermost thoughts and feelings. Writing articles was something she did not like doing, and to allow herself and Leonard more time for writing books, they had sold a half interest in Hogarth Press in April 1938, though Virginia continued to play an active role in deciding what books the company would publish. In September 1939, the press brought out *After the Deluge*, the second volume of Leonard Woolf's study in communal psychology, after much discussion of whether to bring it out at all at a time when war was keeping residents off the streets and out of bookstores.

At this time, Virginia Woolf's Fry biography had become her own private war, with grave personal consequences. She found writing it the most difficult challenge of her life, and throughout the project she feared that she had taken on something beyond her abilities. She complained, "I think I've mounted a barren nightmare in this book."[27]

Roger Fry, who died in 1934, was one of the twentieth century's greatest art critics, as powerful as John Ruskin had been in England in the nineteenth century. Fry mounted the scandalous first postimpressionist exhibition in London in 1910, where critics and the viewing public stood before paintings by Cezanne, Derain, Matisse, Van Gogh, and Gauguin and either laughed or sneered at what they considered pornographic "works of idleness and impotent stupidity," as the critic Wilfrid Blunt called them. Nevertheless, Fry's lectures and articles not only changed the way critics and the public saw modern art, but influenced a generation of young British artists, including Clive Bell and his wife, Vanessa, Virginia Woolf's sister.

Virginia Woolf saw Fry's early identification of Cezanne's genius, when others thought the painter's work was "rubbish," as just one of an infinite number of noble battles Fry fought throughout his life in a self-sacrificing defense of art purely for art's sake. He brooked no falsehood, modesty, self-censorship, sycophantism, snobbery, or class-consciousness. Like herself, Fry engaged in a life-long tug-of-war with professional critics and the critical British public, whom he accused of refusing to accept new ways of seeing and wanting to "harness all art to moral problems."[28] He detested the Cambridge brand of political activity, male arrogance, and cronyism all as impediments to truth and vision, called the political man "a monster," and nationalism, which led to war, "the most monstrous and most cruel" of "all the religions that have afflicted man."[29] When, near the end of his life, Fry became interested in art of the primitive, nonwestern world—"the art of the uncivilized races," as Woolf characterized it—he demanded the "complete collapse of Anglo-Saxondom" since its hegemony in art, thought, and action had led, he wrote, to herd societies of "social insects like bees and ants." But above all, Fry, who was also a painter, fought for the artist's right to live detached from the outside world in order to cultivate his vision, and therein Woolf found affirmation of her own artistic tendencies, which she was convinced had rendered her a whipping boy for critics, who appreciated neither her detachment nor her vision.

Rather than finding gleeful relish in Fry's bold retaliation against his critics, however, Virginia Woolf was finding the task of interpreting the great volume of Fry's letters and personal papers overwhelming. Biography was her favorite reading material, but she "didn't like shoddy history," and while writing *Roger Fry*, Woolf complained of feeling "often crushed under the myriad of details." She groped to present Fry accurately, fully, and interestingly, without intruding herself. "I feel now and then the tug of vision, but resist it," she had written in her diary, and Leonard believed that therein lay her difficulty with the book.[30] By suppressing herself and becoming preoccupied with an orderly presentation of the facts, Virginia was writing "against the grain," he believed.[31] This had been a danger to her psyche in the past. Woolf had suffered a mental breakdown in 1936 after the completion of her "novel of fact," *The Years*, with which she was not happy, despite extensive editing before its publication, and which Leonard believed she had conceived as an answer to critics who said her books did not portray reality.

In truth, a more significant source of her difficulty lay in the fact that much of Fry's emotional and intellectual biography fit Woolf snugly as though her own, and her real problem was not so much to suppress her vision of him as to keep from feeling as though she were writing about herself—an act both personally dangerous and artistically wrong. Like herself, Fry suffered acute despondency— "the sin of gloominess," he called it—and a sense of failure at not being a painter on the level of those he hailed. Fry's woeful admission to his parents that "to fail in art is much more complete a failure and leaves one a more useless encumbrance on the world than to fail in almost anything else," now more than ever before echoed Woolf's sentiment.[32] Woolf was also well-equipped to write about Fry's suffering in his marriage to a woman whose mental illness led to her first confinement shortly after their honeymoon and eventually resulted in permanent confinement. Virginia Woolf felt a keen mixture of loving gratitude for her own husband's patience with her mental illness and guilt over being a burden to him.

The period during which she labored on the Fry book was intensely disruptive and unsettling. During the summer of 1939 the Woolfs undertook a move from their house at 52 Tavistock Square in Bloomsbury because a nearby foundling hospital was being torn down, and their house was threatened with demolition. The specter of war loomed over the move—when the furniture mover, an ex-soldier, got his call-up notice, he abruptly informed them, "I shan't be here tomorrow, Sir."

While their new home at 37 Mecklenburgh Square was being renovated, Virginia and Leonard stayed in Monk's House in Rodmell, Sussex. There Virginia Woolf treasured what illusory insulation from events they had. "Its so hot and sunny on our little island—L. gardening, playing bowls, cooking our dinner: and outside such a waste of gloom," she wrote Vita Sackville-West on August 29, 1939, just three days before the invasion of Poland. "Of course I'm not in the least patriotic, which may be a help, and not afraid, I mean for my own body."[33]

She and Leonard remained at Monk's House until mid-October 1939, but when they returned to London, even the new home was not safe. The chaos of moving was heightened by the declaration of war. London was astir in war panic. Ambulance sirens screamed; people hurried through the streets on their business, expecting Hitler to bomb them any minute. "No one ever sits down," Woolf reported. Irish laborers were digging trenches in the square around her new home. The Woolfs decided to return to Rodmell, where they thought it was safer, and they remained primarily there until her death.

Not even in the quiet Sussex countryside could denizens escape the fact that the world was a far noisier place after September 1939 than it had been two decades before. Radio had come to the English countryside in 1920, when a fifteen-kilowatt station began transmitting two half-hour daily programs of news and music in Chelmsford, north of London near the east coast. Powerful interests—including the military, which did not foresee the crucial role radio would play during World War II—considered the Chelmsford broadcasts "frivolous" and forced their temporary end. Nevertheless, popular mass culture had arrived in the bucolic English countryside.[34]

In 1939, the film *Gone with the Wind*, banned in Germany until after the war, fired the passion of the European masses with its message of native pride and stalwart resistance during wartime. Starring British stage actress Vivien Leigh, the movie played at the Ritz Theatre in London for nearly the duration of World War II. Nevertheless, the British upper classes were still reluctant to embrace such popular "mass" culture, and, especially in the countryside, people like Virginia Woolf had maintained their quiet Victorian lifestyle of reading, writing, gardening, lawn bowling, and daily socializing—even through bombing raids—as though this genteel lifestyle might stave off the inevitable end of civilization as they knew it.

With interruptions from air raids, evacuees, friends, and Hogarth Press employees fleeing London, Woolf tried to keep calm by working and reading. "It is very difficult to go on working under such uncertainty," she had written April 17, 1939, "but I myself feel it is the only possible relief from perpetual strain."[35] Yet, Woolf could not continue as before, and writing began to become a supreme effort. Less than a week after war was declared, she expressed the feeling of being "completely cut off. Not in the body. That is, there's an incessant bother of small arrangements—2 Hogarth Press clerks to put up; mattresses to buy, curtains to make; the village swarming with pregnant women and cottages without a chair or table to furnish out of scraps from the attic. So why does one feel inert, oppressed with solitude? Partly I suppose that one cant work. At least today I wrote ten sentences of Roger, but each word was like carrying a coal scuttle to the top of the house."[36]

Woolf had spoken of that cherished "other world" of imagination before, and of the state of concentration required to get there. Once war began, many believed it would rage for years—if Britain weren't immediately defeated—and a year and a half before her suicide, Woolf expressed doubt that she might never again achieve that precious and vital state. When Vita Sackville-West's cousin complimented her on her novel *The Waves*, Woolf replied on October 25, 1939: "It was nice of you to write to me about the *Waves*. Its the only one of my books that I can sometimes read with pleasure. Not that I wrote it with pleasure, but in a kind of trance into which I suppose I shall never sink again."[37]

As the war progressed, reading books rather than writing became Woolf's anesthetizing shield. Books, "the treasured lifeblood of immortal spirits,"[38] as she called them in her new novel *Pointz Hall*, were not just her passion, but a way of life, an anchor to time and place, and apart from Leonard, books were her most valuable friend. Reading, writing, and book reviewing had formed the basis of many of her most sustaining friendships, and during wartime, when separation from those friends caused her acute despondency, books afforded crucial serenity, confirmation, comfort, and protection.

"I'm not going to tell you all the bothers: the expectant mothers, curtain making, entertaining refugees—for the less we talk of these things and the more we talk of Plato and Shakespeare the better," she wrote to a friend in September 1939.[39] In the fall of 1940, as London endured its third month of devastating aerial bombing by the Nazis, Woolf declared, "I take the unfashionable view that Kilvery—oh and Augustus Hare—whose six volumes gave me acute pleasure— are more real than war."[40] Almost daily, Woolf reported to friends what she was reading. That fall of 1939, she wrote that if she were still alive, she planned to read Tolstoy's *War and Peace*, and the next winter, *Anna Karenina*. (She preferred Tolstoy's romantic, sweeping depiction of war to Aldous Huxley's prescient *Brave New World*, with its cold, scientific horror: "[a]ll that seems to be a bore."[41]) Her interests were wide, including all the European literatures, science, philosophy, history, human sexuality, and biography. "I read myself into a state of immunity," she admitted.[42]

That books posed a credible, powerful alternative to reality explains in part Virginia Woolf's evident distance in the early years of the war from human suffering—the more astonishing in that she inhabited such a highly charged political and humanitarian sphere. Labour Party meetings were held in their London living room. Harold Nicolson was doing regular BBC broadcasts on current political affairs; W. H. Auden and Christopher Isherwood had been to China to write on that country's war with Japan in 1938 and published their beautiful (and blatantly leftist) book, *Journey to a War*, in 1939. Whereas other Londoners talked over the Munich Pact with shopkeepers or the milkman, Virginia Woolf discussed the situation with eminent economist John Maynard Keynes, who had predicted the tragic fallout from the Versailles treaty in his 1919 book, *The Economic Consequences of Peace*, and who came to tea a few days after the pact was signed. Her good friend T. S. Eliot came to dine after he was turned back by Italy, where he was scheduled to deliver a poetry lecture carrying an entreaty to Mussolini that Italy remain neutral.

In spite of her proximity to all this, Woolf's vision of war's mass-scale destructiveness and futility inured her to feelings of sympathy for human beings on an individual basis. This might have seemed an ironic fact, given the microscopically detailed temporal worlds of her fictional characters, in which a single day in a life could be cogitated upon, dissected, and unraveled, bit by bit, hint by hint, inflection by inflection, until the reader understands precisely that when Big Ben strikes the hour and Mrs. Dalloway crosses a London street, she is thinking about grave, wounding things and not the flowers she is on her way to buy for a party later that day; or when Mr. Ramsey looks at urns filled with red geraniums in *To the Lighthouse*, he is contemplating the whole nature of human civilization. But Woolf's characters, introspective to the point of near madness, are themselves cut off from the world and even those closest to them, always posturing for protection against pain and regret, endlessly belaboring mankind's largest and most persistent philosophical questions, "Who am I?" and "What is the meaning of life?" in a slow gloppy mire of existentialist gloom and misery that becomes all the more troubling when they discover that there are no answers. In Woolf's fictionalized world, absent of the comfort of answers, women particularly must be satisfied with fleeting feelings, images, and moments. Inanimate things, such as rain, wallpaper, and flowers, acquire sensibility and depth of meaning lacking in humans. Memory almost always takes the place of action; ephemeral things fill up the deep, lonely places between her characters who are stuck in a tortured, cut-off place, antiseptically wondering, "Am I wrong to think too much?" Occasionally, when a character feels too suffocated by another's crushing will, the clear stream of his overintellectualized impressions is temporarily transformed—poisoned by a rage shockingly potent so as to make the character think of "dynamite" or "murder"—"taking a knife and striking his father through the heart," as James Ramsey fantasizes doing in *To the Lighthouse*, Woolf's stunning, devastating portrait of her own father's domination. But such secrets let out are as quickly withdrawn as a bullwhip. Inner feeling invariably succumbs to outward sobriety: men escape through books, intellectuality, and prestige; women through trifling repetitive household tasks, children, and parties. Making art was the preserve for only those most cut off and most fortified to resist domination. A war between the sexes was always being fought between the covers of Woolf's books, as well as a war between excessive introspection and aloofness about the external world that she fought moment to moment, like her characters.

As a result, Woolf reported war casualties with less emotion than if she were describing a new chair, skirting the subject with the merest wisp of a mention: "Then there's the war—black outs: a man shot in the river where I walk; and the Labour party meeting here."[43] Scenes of individual human tragedy paled by comparison to the destruction by bombing a year later of her favorite haunts in London, which, with their deep literary and nostalgic associations, caused her to grieve deeply: "to see London all blasted, that too raked my heart."[44] When on October 30, 1939, the British government published a white paper on Nazi atrocities against Jews, Virginia Woolf made no mention of the report, nor for that matter did she ever remark upon the plight of European Jews in the whole of her wartime correspondence, despite the fact that Leonard was Jewish. Later, after rationing was implemented throughout Britain, a lump of precious butter threw Virginia Woolf into paroxysms of joy such as she almost never expressed over people.

For a writer who now more than ever needed the protection of books, it was no mere coincidence, then, that one of Woolf's last projects called for her to reread many of the books she had treasured in her youth. While picking blackberries for dinner one night in September 1940, she returned to the idea of doing a book on the effect of social history on literature. Woolf never finished the book, but in preparation for it, she wrapped herself luxuriously in Chaucer, Shakespeare, and

Dickens. As 1939 came to a close, however, escape became increasingly difficult for Virginia Woolf.

By the end of September 1939, the first month of war, two and a quarter million, or five percent of the total British population, had left their homes. Although many eventually returned, the urban poor, the middle class, and the more prosperous country dwellers were thrown together in three major evacuations from the cities. The first one, on September 1, 1939, was well documented by the childless Virginia Woolf, who uncharitably referred to these unwanted urbanites—women and children primarily—who shattered her Sussex countryside calm and serenity as "refugees." "[T]hough I've no cause to complain," she groused to Ethel Smyth on September 26, "since we escaped 3 East end children, visitors fritter one's day to shreds. The last went this morning. So until raids begin we shall be alone—save for raids from our neighbors."[45]

As much as Virginia Woolf championed women's rights, she addressed herself almost exclusively to women of talent, education—genius, even—women like herself and her friends, and she did not really concern herself with women of the "working class" with whom she felt no affinity. Ironically, Leonard was as democratic as Virginia was elitist, and many of her confrontations with the working class during the war were the result of Leonard's sympathy for those very people she most wished to avoid. The war prompted Virginia to suffer through countless evenings when strangers of lower social strata came to her house for his meetings and lectures. "Now I must put on our dinner—To do this I must crash through a meeting of farm laborers which Leonard is holding in the hall," she would complain to her friend Ethel Smyth in November 1940. "They are going to grow cooperative potatoes; each man his strip. Why am I so much shyer of the laborer than of the gentry?" she asked.[46]

The question, which had consumed her for years, had suddenly jumped out, almost before any other. Woolf bore complex emotions concerning her aloofness to the plight of the less fortunate—which implied less cultured—and her fiction is replete with examples of lower-class women who despise their upper-class counterparts for their bookish insouciance, wealth, and grooming, while at the same time these lower-class women lack any shred of grace or culture as they concern themselves solely with their economic survival. Conflict between Woolf's female characters often turns precisely on this socio-economic-psychological footing. Bitter, hostile, and steeped in Virginia Woolf's self-consciousness and guilt, it was never more succinctly demonstrated than in her 1925 novel, *Mrs. Dalloway.* Like Leonard Woolf, Clarissa Dalloway's husband, Richard, is a humanitarian politician, and like Virginia Woolf herself, Clarissa is cold to the needs of her husband's downtrodden beneficiaries. In an interior monologue which uncannily foreshadows Woolf's own thoughts during World War II, Woolf presented Clarissa's reflections: "And people would say, 'Clarissa Dalloway is spoilt.' She cared much more for her roses than for the Armenians. Hunted out of existence, maimed, frozen, the victims of cruelty and injustice (she had heard Richard say so over and over again)—no, she could feel nothing for the Albanians, or was it the Armenians? but she loved her roses (didn't that help the Armenians?)."[47]

One might be inclined to believe Woolf was satirizing an emotion she had clinically observed among her aristocratic friends (and perhaps she was) had she not privately, repeatedly, expressed the same feelings. In *Mrs. Dalloway*, Clarissa defends herself against the "snob" charge (as Woolf herself did in her essay "Am I a Snob?") by declaring that her behavior only reflects a great love of life. As World War II increasingly forced Woolf to confront these same feelings in herself, like Clarissa Dalloway, she felt troubled by them, but never apologetic. When, for instance, she expressed rare sympathy for the "masses" during the London Blitz, it was to mourn that they had not read Shakespeare or been to Italy. At other times she let her elitism show more blatantly. "A Private in the air force comes to play chess with Leonard," she wrote from Monk's House. "His name is Ken (Sheppard). He is in love with a dairy maid. He is very beautiful, but proletarian."[48]

Woolf might have hailed the virtues of the working class which she was beginning to know for the first time, as well as the benefit of a newfound intimacy with charwomen and plumbers, but in reality she much preferred the company of brilliant thinkers like John Maynard Keynes and Sigmund Freud, who had been published by Hogarth Press in translation since 1924 and had moved to London after the Nazis invaded Austria. It was not until later in the war that her self-consciousness of being an elitist turned to biting self-criticism. Then, overwelmed by the suffering and common sacrifice of common English men and women, Woolf suffered the devastating feeling that her elitism had made her an inadequate member of humanity. But for now, her mourning over the daily bombardment to a way of life she had always known left little room for the troubles of common people.

During the winter of 1939–1940, the Woolfs remained exclusively at Monk's House while Virginia finished *Roger Fry*. It was one of the severest winters on record—a "medieval winter," Woolf called it. Cold, gloomy rain fell day after day. Trains were late, mails were delayed, services were cut off, electricity failed, pipes froze—in addition to the casualties of war. Woolf had recently described similar such details in her Fry book, only then she had been describing the First World War. The past was vivid as she held Fry's letters and essays in her hands; also vivid was the tragedy of human history repeating itself. She explained how Fry endured World War I, by keeping the different "rhythms" of art and life distinct. For Fry, no matter how tumultuous, chaotic, and painful the outer world became during that war, "there was always art."[49]

Woolf's voice resonated in the work, as though by drumming Fry's wisdom into herself she might better endure this latest war. "To live fully, to live gaily, to live without falling into the great sin of Accidia which is punished by fog, darkness and mud, could only be done by asking nothing for oneself," she wrote. "It was difficult to put that teaching into practice. Yet in his private life he had during those difficult years forced himself to learn that lesson. . . . Whatever the theory, whatever the connection between the rhythms of life and of art, there could be no doubt about the sensation—he had survived the war."[50]

Now as then, the British carried on with their lives, always wondering whether they would be alive to realize plans. Holidays would be spent with loved ones only if someone's house were still standing, and if and only if the trains were still running to take one there. In the autumn of 1939, the normally one-hour train trip from London to Monk's House took up to four hours, with a four-mile walk from the station, because no buses or taxis could be gotten so late. Woolf's invitations began: "If life continues in the autumn," or "if Hitler allows," won't you please come to dinner?

Nevertheless, under threat of invasion, with rattling windows, the sound of bombs, and the sky overhead filled with the black smoke of downed airplanes, Woolf remained almost merry in her correspondence. Occasionally, she mentioned the possibility of being killed, but more often she expressed the opposite sentiment, as though the bombs could not touch her. "We shan't I suppose be killed," she wrote May 17, 1940, although at that very moment the low countries were being ravaged by the Germans, and the tense atmosphere in the Woolf house gave rise to "memories of unremitting defeat" from the First World War and a "premonition of disaster."[51] In Rodmell, Virginia Woolf tried to make the best of being separated from her intellectual friends by taking part in "village plays," as she called them, written by the wives of a gardener and a chauffeur, and enacted by other villagers in an air-raid shelter. No doubt these amateur productions were a far cry from the brittle, literate, fictional pageant play being performed by villagers in her new novel, *Pointz Hall*, which would be her last finished work, and proved to be tediously wooden and colorless. Woolf's attempt to satirize British history and show the miserable human continuum throughout the millennia was ill-suited to her particular talents, especially at a time when the rush of outward stimuli prevented her from connecting with any of her characters. All are miserably unhappy, "truants," alienated from each other, "neither one nor the other; neither Victorians nor themselves. They were suspended, without being, in limbo."[52] But given Woolf's own frustrations at the time, it is no wonder that the only character whose emotions we can touch is the pageant play's writer, as she battles audience prejudice and ignorance, and feels that she has failed to portray reality. "Panic seized her. Blood seemed to pour from her shoes. This is death, death, death, she noted in the margin of her mind; when illusion fails."[53]

In April 1940, shortly before the Germans invaded Norway, Woolf had finished the final typescript of *Roger Fry* and began to ready it for a July publication. Despite her criticisms of the book, and her belief it would only be of interest to her subject's friends, it received good reviews after its publication in late July and sold well until the London Blitz brought sales to a halt.

The war inched closer to Virginia Woolf all that spring and summer. In April, German forces routed the Allies in their first direct military confrontation in Scandinavia, where the British action was woefully late and pitifully weak. The Germans quickly overwhelmed the small British forces defending Norway's port cities of Narvik and Trondheim and retreated to England on May 2 and 3, prompting the collapse of the Chamberlain government at last. Although as recently as winter 1939 Winston Churchill had been seen as too "belligerent" by pacifists who despised Chamberlain and wanted him replaced, Churchill was now seen as Britain's only hope.[54]

The floodgates were flung wide open. On May 10, 1940, the same day Churchill made his first official appearance as prime minister, the Nazis invaded the low countries. Rotterdam fell quickly after a massive Luftwaffe attack, and the Dutch government and Queen Wilhelmina fled to London. Belgium, supported by heavy French artillery, put up a stronger fight on the ancient craggy cliffs of the Meuse River, but the Allies could not overcome the better equipped, better organized German tank and airplane divisions. By the afternoon of Monday, May 13, "Nazi rubber boats reached the far shore unmolested. . . . [T]he outcome, to use a word that was on everyone's lips that week," wrote historian William Manchester, "was *une debacle*."[55] The Nazis stampeded across the river into France, rampaged through French forces which lacked adequate radio communication and in many cases weapons, and were cut off from the main French forces in the south. On June 4, nearly 350,000 British, French, and Belgian troops, led by the Royal British Navy, evacuated Dunkirk to escape annihilation by a staggeringly victorious Nazi air, tank, and artillery onslaught. Ten days later, Hitler's storm troopers marched up the Champs-Élysées.

In England on June 18, the new prime minister with the staunch English-bulldog face delivered his famous speech promising that Britain would continue the fight alone if necessary: "Let us therefore brace ourselves to our duties, and so bear ourselves that if the British Empire and its Commonwealth last for a thousand years, Men will say: 'THIS was their finest hour.' " In truth, the British defeat in Scandinavia had been a cold shock of reality to a country whose people assumed Britain's long-standing naval superiority could overwhelm German land and air power, but even this was nothing, compared to the fall of France. Hitler's victory was like the advance on Gaul by Attila the Hun in 451 A.D. Now, only the English Channel separated the Nazis from their own doorsteps. With the fall of France, the Woolfs' emotional friend, *Nation* editor Kingsley Martin, predicted that the British government would soon be moving to Canada, with Hitler taking over the country. As a Jew, Leonard's fate seemed sealed, and the specter of suicide was raised again.

Over Monk's House, air battles increased. "[F]ive raiders almost crashed into the living room. Then they machine gunned the next village," Virginia Woolf reported in August.[56] The Germans stalked over the marshes nearby, and English troops training in south England camped in their fields, with their officers resting slightly more comfortably in the cottages at Monk's House. Woolf continued working on *Pointz Hall*, now retitled *Between the Acts*, as best she could, and invited friends to visit even as sandbags were carried down to the river and guns were set up on the banks. She reported to a friend on September 3, 1940, that "we are humming with Germans here—as we were playing bowls one came down low, and we took it for English till they started firing."[57]

Despite Hitler's success in France, the British Royal Air Force had scored heavily against German mine-laying and sweeping, and on September 4, 1940, Hitler announced an all-out war on British cities in retaliation. The Germans had been amassing barges in the French Channel ports and on September 7, after more than a month of night bombings over Britain, the first main daylight aerial attack on London took place. For fifty-seven nights from then on, an average of two hundred German bombers flew over London. Each night, the sky over London glowed with pyrotechnical shows as search lights and fire tracer bullets caught German planes. Nerves of Londoners were shattered by the relentless, round-the-clock drone of planes, whistles of bombs, blare of British guns in Hyde Park, and wails of air-raid sirens. Many people stayed up all night in shelters. A red fog of dust shrouded smouldering ruins, and the air was filled with the smell of cordite. People had nightmares about being blown up and buried alive under masonry. When the guns died down in the distance, Londoners knew they would start up again in fifteen minutes. Walking anywhere was hazardous, lest an attack suddenly begin. Train service was disrupted; people were stranded. As citizens listened to the drill-like sound of the planes and watched them circle above their heads, they knew bombs were dropping, and wondered where they were going to land—what ancient church, or statue honoring a former hero or family-member would be obliterated? On September 13, 1940, Buckingham Palace was struck thirty yards from the king, and was hit again on September 15, when the contest between the RAF and Luftwaffe became the most intense of any day, resulting in the loss of fifty-six German and twenty-six British planes.

Hitler's ambition to break British morale in anticipation of possible German invasion seemed to be working. Londoners' nerves were stretched to the breaking point, and they were easy targets for Communists who visited air-raid shelters soliciting signatures for peace petitions to submit to Churchill.[58] In the countryside, where the atmosphere was just slightly less oppressive, residents kept track of how many German parachutists were taken prisoner, and strollers after a raid made a hobby out of picking up machine-gun bullets. The sight of dogfights over a sunlit garden or shimmering stream never failed to impress sensitive English observers.

The Woolfs remained in the country during the London Blitz of September and October 1940, but they hardly felt safe. Air battles raged over Monk's House, and when the planes disappeared, it meant they had flown on to attack London. In the second week of September, the Woolfs defied danger and went to London to pack up Hogarth Press and move it out of the city. Woolf saw the smoking ruins of the house across the street from 37 Mecklenburgh Square—"All killed, I suppose."[59] Little more than a week later a bomb which had landed in a Mecklenburgh Square flower bed several days before finally exploded, leaving her own house in ruins. London, Woolf recorded, "was like a dead city."[60]

During the Blitz one particular event occurred which impressed both Woolfs, so much so that Leonard still recalled it thirty years later in his autobiography. When they weren't despairing, Leonard and Virginia expressed an almost comical defiance of the bombings. They disliked air-raid shelters and refused to go into them. Even the democratic Leonard found the closeness to so many disparate human beings unpleasant, and he preferred, he said, to die "a solitary death above ground and in the open air."[61] Nevertheless, one day as the couple was motoring from the country to London, they drove head-on into a bombing in Wimbledon and were forced to take shelter in a gun emplacement, or "pillbox" as they were called. Inside huddled a homeless East End family. The Woolfs' unexpected encounter with London's hoi polloi gave rise to an honesty on her part that was as appallingly smug as it was innocent and well-intentioned. Virginia marveled at the good humor with which the family endured its tribulations. Though they had been in the pillbox for three nights, with only a kettle and a spirit lamp and wind blowing through the gun holes, they were "cheerful as grigs," she reported afterward.[62]

The Woolfs moved Hogarth Press to Letchworth in Herefordshire to the offices of a printer with whom they had done business. The press continued to operate in Letchworth for the rest of the war, with Leonard occasionally making the arduous, day-long round-trip train visit to the press from Monk's House. The war continued to affect operations in Letchworth, however, as paper rationing limited publication, and it became difficult to obtain the work of continental writers like Bertolt Brecht and Jean-Paul Sartre from abroad.

Virginia and Leonard Woolf retreated to Monk's House with whatever they were able to salvage from the London house, including her dust-covered writing paper. On September 11, 1940, Churchill had warned that Hitler was planning an all-out invasion of Britain, and if nature had cooperated, it would likely have brought German troops past the front gate of Monk's House, since Rodmell was three miles from Newhaven, where the Germans had intended to land.[63] High winds and rough seas prevented operation "Sea Lion," as the invasion was dubbed, but everyone, including Virginia Woolf, assumed it would come that spring. At the time, they did not know that RAF strength during the Battle of Britain had pursuaded Hitler to forsake England and launch his doomed invasion of the Soviet Union.

The Woolfs' home at 37 Mecklenburgh Square was repaired, but the couple felt that London was still too dangerous a place to live. Yet, from Rodmell, which lay just west of the corridor, Nazi bombers flew on their way from the sea to London, and Virginia Woolf despaired of the destruction to her beloved England. "I dont like sitting of an evening and thinking the drone which is weaving its web above me is about to drop," she wrote on October 12, 1940. "The bombs don't fall upon us—only on the convent at Newhaven, or some field."[64] Still, Woolf was confident of their survival because life was still worth living. She repeatedly told Leonard she wanted to live another ten years, in part because she had so many ideas for books[65]—or, as she put it to her friend Ethel Smyth, "so many Surinam toads (thats Coleridge) [are] breeding in my head."[66] Cut off from friends and London, "book inventing," as she called it, was an antidote to boredom.

There were other small diversions, other ways that the fighting piqued her senses. Sometimes when bombs fell, Woolf felt fascination, a "great delight of seeing the smoke and being within an inch of Heaven."[67] In mid-November, German planes attempting to hit a nearby cement works missed and instead bombed the bank of the River Ouse. The combination of a strong wind and high tide forced the bombed section of the bank to give way, flooding the Ouse valley all the way to the bottom of the Woolfs' garden. The artist in Woolf had the facility for partitioning the purely visual from its underlying horror, and in the flood and ensuing destruction, she saw a scene to praise rather than decry. "[T]o my infinite delight, they bombed our river," she wrote on November 14 to Ethel Smyth. "Cascades of water roared over the marsh—All the gulls came and rode the waves at the end of the field. It was, and still is, an island sea, of such indescribable beauty, almost always changing, day and night, sun and rain, that I cant take my eyes off it. . . . The road to the Bridge was 3 foot in water, and this meant a 2 mile round; but oh dear, how I love this savage medieval water moved, all floating tree trunks and flocks of birds and a man in an old punt, and myself so eliminated of human feature you might take me for a stake walking."[68]

By the autumn of 1940, shipping—on which the island of Great Britain was dependent—was reduced to essential cargo, and in November the first of a series of rationings began. Their effect on Virginia Woolf was to be catastrophic. Train travel had been difficult since the start of war, but Woolf could still travel by car to London to visit friends and favorite haunts like London Tower, Oxford Street, and Picadilly. With the institution in early November of gasoline rationing,

London, which she called "the passion of my life," became painfully remote, and Monk's House, a virtual prison.[69]

Virginia Woolf loved the countryside of Rodmell. Its quietude and calmness had enchanted her and helped her work, but it was also a mere hour from the social flurry of London she craved so dearly. Friendships were not just a pleasant diversion to her, they were a conduit to life. She treasured dirty gossip as much as lofty ideas, and derived material from both for her novels. But more importantly, the whirl of teas, lunches, dinners, and parties provided security and equilibrium. Her need to be with people whom she liked was so strong that even during the Blitz, before Mecklenburgh was destroyed, the Woolfs visited the city every two weeks for days of frenzied politicking and socializing, although many in their circle, including W. H. Auden and Christopher Isherwood, had left England for America.

As far back as September 1939, Woolf complained of feeling "completely cut off." It was a state of powerlessness she abhorred, for it gave rise to stinging childhood memories of emotional domination by her narcissistic father ("children coerced, their spirits subdued," she wrote in *To the Lighthouse*), and sexual domination by two older stepbrothers. Woolf had spent her entire adult life fighting against powerlessness only now to find it foisted upon her with no possibility of recourse. On December 1, 1940, Woolf complained to Vita Sackville-West's cousin, Edward, "Sometimes a country is so heavenly and reading and writing become so absorbing I've been very happy; then all at sea. Its like living on an island. . . . I've not seen a clever person this six months, save the family over the way [at Charleston]. I daresay its good for one; but oh lord—how bare and barren in many ways."[70]

Woolf began to wear down from so many pressing daily practical concerns. Despite Leonard's insistence that they had plenty of money to endure the war, Virginia's worries over money became persistent. According to Leonard, her anxiety stemmed not at all from the reality, but rather from a deep, irrational financial insecurity inculcated in childhood by her father, who, though a highly successful author, editor, and property-owner with a "virtually impregnable" bank account, nevertheless "lived in perpetual fear of bankruptcy, convinced every Monday morning that he was being ruined."[71] Although Virginia Woolf managed most of her life to sidestep paralyzing money worry, this became impossible for her in the wartime atmosphere of privation, hardship, and general ominousness and tension. "We're devilish poor," she wrote on Christmas Eve 1940. "Lord, what a bill for rent and removal and no money coming in, and the taxes! I shall have to write and write— till I die—just as we thought we'd saved enough to live, unwriting, till we died!"[72]

Woolf professed at first to be pleased after the cook quit, but her praise for the calming effects of cooking was empty talk for a woman who, albeit an arch feminist, had been raised in comfort with servants and food aplenty. "I spent 2 hours carpet beating, and still the flakes of our bombed ceiling flock, and drown the books just dusted. I'd no notion, having always a servant, of the horror of dirt," she wrote with exasperation on March 10, 1941, about two weeks before she killed herself.[73]

She and Leonard were faring better than many Europeans; yet, her world had been torn apart no less than if she had been wounded by a Nazi bullet. Woolf's fragile psyche needed to be wrapped in the protective mantle of imagination and intellect, and thus, the challenge of household duties during wartime became too much. At a time when her psychological mettle was tested by the hardships of daily life, her deep, unsteadying discomfort in the more pedestrian role of common woman largely proved her undoing. Leaking ceilings in the cold, the futile searching for hay, hosting Leonard's plebeian guests, and cooking on meager rations in a cottage overcrowded with heaps of furniture and piles of books from her evacuated London houses all drove her to a level of distress with which she could not cope: "This hand doesn't shake from book hugging, but from rage. Louie being gone to a funeral, I cooked lunch: and the rice floored me," she reported in January 1941. "That's why I rage. . . . I'm too rice-infested to make any sense."[74] With gaping holes torn in her "safety curtain," Woolf began to succumb to a dismal sense of futility. By the winter of 1940–41, she turned from cool and aloof, someone who could see beauty in a bomb-induced flood, to despondent, hopeless, and suicidal.[75]

Virginia Woolf had been plagued by numerous bouts of manic-depression since her first mental breakdown at the age of thirteen. She had succumbed to complete nervous breakdowns, or periods of "madness" as she called them, three times—the first in 1895 after the death of her beloved mother; in 1904 after the death of her father; and in 1913–1915, coinciding with the onset of World War I. Twice she had tried to kill herself. In 1904 she jumped out of a window and in 1913 she took an overdose of the barbiturate Veronal.

The symptoms varied little despite the huge gaps of time between illnesses. They began with a headache near the lower back of her head, and insomnia. This was invariably followed by a manic stage of excitedness, racing thoughts, emotions, and speech. During this manic stage she became delusional and heard voices. From this apex of giddiness, she fell into a nadir of despair. She became uncommunicative and would not eat. In 1913, after months of depression, she fell into a coma for two days after taking too many barbiturates.

Woolf's acute sensitivity, narcissism, and emotional distancing served her well as an artist, but it was also her undoing. Much of the time, she seemed remarkably able among a group of remarkable individuals. In her lifetime, she authored ten novels, two biographies, six works of literary and social criticism, and countless articles and book reviews. The publishing company she founded with her husband published a prestigious list of books, many by authors whom the Woolfs discovered. Her intellect was keen and provocative, and she approached her writing utterly professionally. She did not shrink from judging others. Her acerbic tongue could be rapier-sharp against those she disliked.

Woolf could go along for months with no apparent symptoms—working, socializing, traveling—but she required tranquil, orderly living in order to be well, according to her husband, and if she underwent even a day of severe emotional or mental strain, she might have to take to her bed for a week. If she neglected herself or was careless in her diet and sleep, she might require weeks of rest in a dark room and constant attention before resuming her normal routine. Always, the complete collapses were precipitated by periods of extreme physical or emotional strain.

Virginia Woolf's completion of any new book was always viewed by her family as a mixed blessing. Perfectionism caused her to suffer menacing feelings of incompetence. Moreover, she wrote controversial treatises and nonconformist novels, which by definition open an author to harsh review, and criticism unnerved her so deeply that she fell victim to a kind of artistic "torture" the moment she finished a first draft.[76] Woolf's doctors could only guess at a treatment for her depression; yet, their prescription for immediate and total bed rest in a darkened room, drinking large quantities of milk, eating considerably and well, seemed to work, and she would usually return to normal within two weeks. In 1941, however, there could be no return to normal.

The beginning of a new year brought increasing anxiety in England that Hitler was going to attack as soon as the weather improved. In North Africa and British Somaliland, British forces were reversing Axis victories, but in London, a lull in the bombing was interpreted as evidence that Hitler was saving planes and gas for the invasion. As the grip of war tightened, food rationing of essentials began, with gradual cuts in allotments occurring throughout the war. In mid-1941, for example, the weekly ration of food was just half a pound of meat, one ounce of cheese, four ounces of bacon or ham, eight ounces of sugar, two ounces of tea, and eight ounces of fats (including not more than two ounces of butter). Compared to a prewar English home of the Woolfs' economic status, the weekly ration was about equal to one good meal—"about the size of my thumbnail," she complained.[77]

During what was to be the last winter of her life, Virginia Woolf lamented the shortage of butter and went into paroxysms of joy when she received gifts of cream, milk, and butter from friends Octavia Wilberforce and Vita Sackville-West. After she spent an hour shaking a bottle of milk in an attempt to produce butter, only to have the single yellow lump be eaten off the table by the cat, the sudden arrival of the mailman with butter from Sackville-West in February 1941 was "like the voice of God in answer to our prayers." Her overexuberance over a period of months regarding these gifts hints at what she herself described in her diary less than a month before her death as food having become "an obsession."[78] "I grudge giving away a spice bun," she admitted. "Curious—age, or the war?" she wondered.[79]

Human beings often crave most what they cannot have, and for the entire European population, food became a source of worry and frustration during the war, but Virginia Woolf's hypersensitive concern with food was not new to wartime and was an indicator of another deeply troubling psychic trauma. Woolf herself admitted that she and her sister had been repeatedly sexually abused as children by their older stepbrothers, Gerald and George Duckworth, and fifty years later she still rememembered the humiliation. "I still shiver with shame at the memory of my half-brother, standing me on a ledge, aged about 6, and so exploring my private parts," she wrote just two months before her death.[80] As a married woman, she remained disinterested in heterosexual sex and deeply uncomfortable with her own body. Her expressed feelings of guilt, shame, and inadequacy, and her dissociation and hostility, which also define her fictional characters, as well as her conflicts about food and weight, are all characteristic of sexual abuse victims. She complained especially during bouts of depression about being fat, when photographs taken of her show otherwise.

Virginia Woolf's obsession with food underlay destructive psychological forces, and the level of her preoccupation was an important indicator of her mental health. During periods of psychological breakdown, Woolf would stop eating, and after a period of depression or mental strain she made a point of keeping friends and family abreast of her diet and weight as proof of her recovery. But even during periods of equanimity, when she was reporting to friends the minutiae of her diet, she often had to be goaded into eating, and her husband recalled that getting her to eat was "a perpetual, and only partially successful, struggle; our quarrels and arguments were rare and almost always about eating or resting."[81]

Leonard's experience came long before the recent medical understanding linking food disorders such as anorexia and bulimia, which primarily afflict highly intelligent woman driven to perfectionism, self-loathing, and guilt, with sexual abuse, and Leonard was astute in his supposition that beneath Virginia's resistance lay "some strange, irrational sense of guilt."[82] In fact, when Woolf was at her most manic she was unwilling to accept her symptoms as being caused by illness, but rather attributed them to her own "laziness, inanition, gluttony."[83]

Given the precarious state of Virginia Woolf's mental and physical health, the shortage and limited variety of food, including the dairy products which Woolf required to maintain her well-being, was no mere inconvenience. That winter of 1941, it was as though she were a diabetic, and the war had cut off her supply of insulin. Although milk does contain the sleep-inducing amino acid tryptophan, her doctors were groping in the dark by prescribing it, and psychiatrists today discount its effectiveness on manic depression. Nevertheless, there is much evidence to support the power of suggestive thinking on patients' mental states. While it is unlikely that being deprived of dairy products had any significant clinical effect upon Virginia Woolf, her belief that it did could have been enough to destabilize her.[84]

In the winter of 1941, Virginia entered what she described in her diary on January 25, her fifty-ninth birthday, as a "trough of despair."[85] Nearing completion of *Pointz Hall*, she despaired to Ethel Smyth that despite working hard, "what's the good of what I write, I havent the glimpse of an idea."[86] She had complained of her difficulty concentrating and working, almost from the moment Hitler invaded Czechoslovakia in 1938, although in a testament to her strength and will, she continued working. She finished *Pointz Hall* (*Between the Acts*) around February 26, and continued to work on her social and literary history which she had titled *Anon*. As always, she was contemplating numerous other book ideas, presumably some of the twenty books "sizzling in my head" she had told a friend about in the fall of 1940, but in the last weeks of her life, the challenge of concentrating evolved into an uphill battle she could not win.[87] In a letter Woolf wrote February 1, 1941, she complained how difficult her research had become: "I read and read like a donkey going round and round a well; pray to God, some idea will flash. I leave it to nature. I can no longer control my brain."[88]

Depression began to darken her view of her recent work. She was unhappy with *Pointz Hall*, and despite favorable readings of it, she had withdrawn it from publication at the time of her death. Leonard published the book in 1941 with a note telling readers that she had not "fully revised" the manuscript at the time of her death. Describing to Ethel Smyth the immense task she was undertaking with *Anon*, she wrote, invoking Keats' "Ode to a Nightingale," "By the time I've reached Shakespeare the bombs will be falling. So I've arranged a very nice last scene: reading Shakespeare, having forgotten my gas mask, I shall fade far away, and quite forget."[89]

For Leonard, too, the war had become inextricably tied to the spiral of their life and work. Looking back on the final two weeks of his wife's life, "the most terrible and agonizing days of my life,"[90] Leonard wondered whether Virginia had attempted and then changed her mind about suicide about ten days before her March 28 death, remembering that she returned from a walk in the rain, "soaking wet, looking ill and shaken."[91] Her explanation was that she had accidentally fallen into a dike.

In the days before her death, Woolf spoke of seeing no future, mourning that the war was no different from the last, of being disconnected—the price that writers pay, she said, for being gifted with "that rare detachment" which she had so pleasurably enjoyed in better days. For a long time the author of *Three Guineas* weathered the war with aloofness, the armor of the intellectual. War was made by men and fought for their own glory and prestige. The horror could have been avoided. Words. In the end, the words succumbed to bombs and despondence.

During the first winter of fighting, Woolf had viewed the war as a setback to the mission she summoned women to assume in *Three Guineas*, but she was still filled with hope. Men could change, and the sexes could come to an understanding which would effectively eradicate war. In the last months of her life, however, the experience of war had finally disillusioned her and left her feeling hopeless. *Three Guineas* had roused a few thinking individuals but, alas, it had accomplished nothing. Events moved forward—war came again. The sexes would never come to an understanding, she now saw, but would merely procreate ad infinitum as they had in the past. This was to be the final, somewhat ambivalent message of the bleak *Pointz Hall*. Woolf had become resigned to humanity's base animalism, symbolized in black birds massed upon a tree—"a quivering cacophony, a whizz and vibrant rapture, branches, leaves, birds syllabling discordantly life, life, life, without measure." Life, Woolf finally concluded, represents an indomitable essential continuity with all its torments and troubles.[92] *Pointz Hall's* raging, frustrated playwright recovers her instinctive urge to write, and an unhappily married couple make up, and "[f]rom their embrace another life might be born."[93] Yet, the couple still hates each other, and the writer still hates her audience in that paralyzing moment when the curtain rises and she feels it is her enemy.

"It seems a little futile to boil with rage as I do about twice a week—in these marshes," Virginia Woolf wrote to a woman friend. "This morning it was the soldiers saying women were turning them out of their jobs. The human race seems to repeat itself insufferably. . . . No, I dont see whats [to] be done about war. It's manliness; and manliness breeds womanliness—both so hateful. I tried to put this to our local labour party: but was scowled at like a prostitute. They said if women had as much money as men, they'd enjoy themselves: and then what about the children? So they have more children; more wars; and so on."[94]

Two weeks later, Woolf painted her sad picture of futility and stasis with the kind of impressionistic brush that marks her fiction: "Clive is digging a trench; Nessa feeding fowls; Duncan painting Christ; Quentin driving a tractor—all as it was in 1917. . . . But one cant lift a fringe on the future. Thats whats so odd—the blank space in front."[95] There was nothing more to say.

Near the end of her life, Woolf made several references to her age, and her letters hint at a recognition that beyond this bout of depression, she no longer had her whole life ahead of her. Had the Second World War not occurred, Virginia Woolf would probably have endured her usual despondency after finishing a work, and she would have emerged to continue living and working. But the press of events was too powerful. Civilization was at an end. Were sanity to prevail, the war might still kill her. Her fate was beyond her control. "Two nights ago they dropped incendiaries, in a row, like street lamps, all along the downs," she wrote March 13. "Two haystacks caught and made a lovely illumination—but no flesh was hurt. . . . Its difficult, I find, to write. No audience. No private stimulus, only this outer roar."[96]

Virginia Woolf's sense of frustration, impotence, and uselessness, both as a woman and a writer, were strong enough to precipitate her final bout of depression, but she was confronted with yet another war-related ignominy in the final weeks of her life. In February of 1941, reviewing a published poetry lecture entitled "The Leaning Tower," which Virginia had delivered to the Workers' Educational Association, her old friend Desmond MacCarthy, writing in the February 2 issue of *The Sunday Times*, criticized her for using the pronoun "we" when she addressed a group of "working men."

"I assure you my tower was a mere toadstool, about six inches high," she defended herself to MacCarthy. "And when you say 'She herself as a writer owes everything to having seen the world from a tower which did not lean' you make me gnash my teeth."[97]

Woolf had borne the brunt of such criticism for years. Just a year before, she had been referred to as an "Ivory Tower Dweller" along with Marcel Proust and James Joyce by the editor of *Horizon* magazine, Cyril Connolly, and an otherwise favorable review of Woolf's *Roger Fry* by *Spectator* magazine's Herbert Read pilloried Fry himself for "the pettiness and the protectiveness of the Ivory Tower, against the benevolence of the Liberal outlook. . . ."[98] In the past, she could slough off the accusation as competitive jealousy, but during war, the charge of being an "Ivory Tower" writer was more powerful, because it implied that the ivory tower intellectual was unpatriotic, useless, and morally bankrupt.

With *Three Guineas*, Woolf had found herself defending an intellectual thesis; with *Roger Fry*, she had felt forced to defend the very character of her biographical subject, and in doing so, felt coerced into defending her own passive resistance. Woolf had explained that she chose to write about Fry, who had been a close friend, because she admired and respected him more than anyone, but on a deeper level, in Fry's pacifism, hatred of nationalism, and self-sacrificing defense of the artist—"a new kind of saint . . . who leads his laborious life 'indifferent to the world's praise or blame'; who must be poor in spirit, humble, and doggedly true to his own convictions"—Woolf had found self-justification, and rebukes to him were like piercing arrows to one so sensitive to personal criticism as she.

But the Connolly, Read, and MacCarthy assaults opened a festering and particularly painful wound Woolf had sustained the prior summer from Vita Sackville-West and Harold Nicolson's son, Ben, an art critic and writer who was then serving as a lance-bombardier in an anti-aircraft battery in Kent. In August, Woolf and the young Nicolson became embroiled in an emotional debate in which the latter accused Fry of doing nothing to combat Nazism. Although Virginia had in the past stated that as an outsider she owed society little if anything, the young

Nicolson laid out his concept of the artist's social responsibility in such dogmatic and righteous terms that disagreement almost necessarily made one appear shamefully callous and inhumane. As a result, the debate with Nicolson distilled Virginia's quandary regarding her obligation to society while bringing deep feelings of guilt and impotence to the fore.

Woolf responded in part by attacking Nicolson's own privileged background and life within an exclusive world of the very same "sensitive and intelligent" people with whom Nicolson had accused Fry of consorting. Writing during a bomb attack on nearby Chatham, she launched her own counteroffensive, asking Nicholson pointedly: "Why didn't [you] chuck it all and go into politics?"[99] As an outsider, this choice did not apply to her—politics was not an option for women—nevertheless Woolf could not escape asking herself where her own responsibility lay. After defending Fry's life and work, Woolf offered an explanation which reflected her own heartfelt bewilderment on the subject:

> I loathe sitting here waiting for a bomb to fall; when I want to be writing. If it doesn't kill me its killing someone else. Where can I lay the blame? On the Sackvilles. On the Dufferins? On Eton and Oxford? They did precious little it seems to me to check Nazism. People like Roger and Goldie Dickinson did an immense deal it seems to me. Well, we differ in our choice of scapegoats.
>
> But what I'd like to know is, suppose we both survive this war, what ought we to do to prevent another? I shall be too old to do anything but write. But will you throw up your job as an art critic and take to politics? And if you stick to art criticism, how will you make it more public and less private than Roger did?[100]

When Woolf was forced to consider the artist's real ability to change society— as her debate with Nicolson prompted—she concluded that even the greatest artists of the nineteenth century, such as Keats, Shelley, Wordsworth, and Coleridge, ultimately had no influence, and thus could do nothing to alter the factors which had precipitated the First World War. She explained to Nicolson that it had been her goal to educate the public to the wonders of great literature and feeling, but in the end, she had concluded that if poets ventured into politics, it was more likely that they would write "worse poetry" than effect any change. Woolf had concluded that "it was hopeless for me to tell people who had been taken away from school at the age of 14 that they must read Shakespeare."[101] Educating the great masses was best left to the politicians—that is, to career politicians and not artists-cum-politicians.

In the last months of her life, Woolf's sense of the artist's impotence within society evolved from this staunchly positive argument for insularity and self-absorption within the artistic realm to a doleful plaint over her own self-perceived uselessness. By late winter 1941, she felt there was no place for her kind of writing. Trying unsuccessfully to write an article for the *Common Reader*, Woolf lamented on March 1, "I am stuck in Elizabethan plays. I cant move back or forwards. I've read too much, but not enough. Thats why I cant break into politics."[102]

Two weeks before her death she expressed the feeling that "politics at the moment seem more pressing than autobiography."[103] The following week, this feeling of disconnectedness and conflict between her own literary essence and the outer world at war became lacerating. Political works like Leonard's just-published *The War for Peace* "seemed . . . the only thing worth writing now," she told her friend Lady Cecil. "Do you find you can read the novelists? I cant."[104] Together, these were riveting statements for someone who disdained politics and derived sustenance from literature.

The war had caught the painfully self-critical, guilt-ridden Virginia Woolf in a web perhaps more dangerous than self-loathing—a sense of negligibility and purposelessness. Woolf was a novelist at heart, for whom "the only reality" was intense friendship and the trancelike state of the imagination. Her fiction *was* blatantly self-absorbed; she did not tell "stories" so much as to place a mirror before her mind as it went through its intricately fine-tuned thought processes. Woolf knew she could not be something other than she was, for all that imagined stories did not suffice when pitted against orphan children, widowed mothers, and shell-shocked fathers. The fact that she mentioned her inability "to break into politics" reflected the critical awareness she evidenced at the war's beginning. "I'm reading *Little Dorrit*; I'm reading Erasmus; I'm reading Plato; I'm reading Gide; I'm reading William Rotherstein's memoirs," she wrote a friend in November of 1939. "So there—Does that make you think the worse or better of me, for that's the real question I want answered, my appetite for compliments being undiminished. And of course it may not be a compliment."[105] Exacerbating her feelings of inadequacy, guilt, and alienation was her marriage to Leonard, who, like her, saw civilization as in its death throes, but nevertheless refused to allow pessimism to deter him from working tirelessly for change. Gentle, humane, and generous, Leonard was a ceaseless reminder to Woolf of her own solipsism.

"I was saying to Leonard, we have no future," she wrote to Ethel Smyth on March 1, 1941. "He says thats what gives him hope. He says the necessity of some catastrophe pricks him up. What I feel is the suspense when nothing actually happens. But I'm cross and irritable from the friction of village life. Isn't it foolish? But no sooner have I bound myself to my book, and brewed that very rare detachment, than some old lady taps at the door. How is she to grow potatoes or tomatoes?"[106]

In a letter Woolf wrote (and never mailed) possibly a week before her suicide, she explained to a recently widowed friend of her father's that partly because of the woman's war activities, she had "a great deal more than most of us to look forward to." In the letter of condolence on the woman's recent loss, Virginia briefly described her life with Leonard in the country, calling it a "vegetable existence here, surrounded by the melancholy relics of our half destroyed furniture." In this melancholy gloom, looking back over her life, feeling like little had changed since the First World War, she spent all that afternoon "trying to arrange some of my father's old books"—leather-bound classics from a more civilized time saved from Mecklenburgh Square and heaped in dusty piles on the floor of their Monk's House sitting room.[107]

In the last weeks of her life, the encroachment of the outer world of war and privation had made Virginia Woolf's life impossible. London, city of "Chaucer, Shakespeare, Dickens" was "all rubble and white dust," she grieved.[108] In the country, Vita Sackville-West's cows, which had provided her with precious butter, were starving. Even Vita's pet birds had died from a shortage of birdseed.

Beginning in January her allusions to the difficulty of writing took on a more desperate, despairing tone. "It's a washout," she wrote on January 25 to her friend and doctor, Octavia Wilberforce.

In this state of mind, Virginia Woolf awaited the invasion of the Germans just miles away from her home. "I can't help wishing the invasion would come," she wrote a week before her suicide. "Its this standing about in a dentist's waiting room that I hate."[109]

Her mental state took a turn for the worse. She wavered between rational thoughts and manic behavior. She was hearing voices and having trouble concentrating and working, and yet to the end she maintained a quirky grasp on reality which may have contributed to her decision to kill herself.

Her sister Vanessa Bell had written on March 20 with heartfelt concern, trying to shake Virginia out of her depression, by appealing to her guilt. Bell taunted, "What shall we do when we're invaded if you are a helpless invalid. . . ."[110] But Bell miscalculated fatefully. The last thing Woolf wanted was to be a burden to her family, if and when the German invasion came. The strategy backfired.

The possibility that Virginia Woolf might kill herself always lurked beneath the couple's most placid days, because of her previous suicide attempts and the ease with which she slipped into depression. In March 1941, Leonard had the strong fear she would take her own life, but he was wary about confronting her too pointedly about her behavior, for fear it would send her over the brink instead of restraining her. He was finally able to convince her, however, to see her doctor, Octavia Wilberforce, in Brighton, and on March 27, 1941, they paid her a visit. Though Leonard had engaged nurses to watch Virginia during previous severe depressions, it was decided that this time constant surveillance would do more harm than good. The consultation seemed to Leonard to have improved his wife's mood, and the Woolfs were to return for another consultation the next day or the day after. Doctor Wilberforce never saw Virginia Woolf again.

Woolf was well aware how much attention she required. She had already written that there was no place in the world for the novelist, and now she believed there was no place in this world for the overly sensitive, outsider wife of an insider husband whose work was so important to society. Responding to her sister's plea to pull herself together, Woolf wrote, "I feel he has so much to do that he will go on, better without me, and you will help him."[111]

On March 28, 1941, Virginia Woolf slipped out of the house while Leonard was in the garden and threw herself into the River Ouse. When he came in for lunch he found one of three suicide notes she left. Not finding her anywhere in the house and suspecting the worst, Leonard ran down to the river, where he found her walking stick lying on the river bank. Nearly a month later, on April 18, Virginia Woolf's body was found by children downstream. Her family speculated that since she could swim, she put on heavy gum boots, which would have weighted her down once they filled with water. They were puzzled that the hat she was wearing had not risen to the surface, and her sister Vanessa surmised that it remained on her head with an elastic band.[112]

Virginia Woolf had defied the Luftwaffe, playing lawn bowls during bombing raids in her Monk's House garden. She had watched pilots parachute over her beloved fields and marshes and the cascade of light coming from bomb bursts in the sky, and had found an odd kind of pleasure in the sight. From a garden knoll high above those very fields and marshes stood two great elms whose boughs entwined and which the Woolfs had named Leonard and Virginia. Virginia Woolf's ashes were buried at the foot of one of those great elms.

Three months after her suicide, on June 30, 1941, Adolf Hitler launched a massive offensive in Russia from the Arctic to the Baltic Sea. The Germans never invaded England.

CHAPTER FOUR

Colette
THE SURVIVOR

That there is merit in enhancing beauty,
in accentuating it in a hundred ways, and
that to adorn it, in however barbarian a setting, is to await and
already to honor peace. . . .

From My Window, 1942

C olette was sixty-seven when the Nazi juggernaut swept into a deserted
Paris on June 14, 1940, and set up their comfortable Gestapo office on the
elegant, tree-lined Avenue Foch, not far from her home in the Palais-
Royal. For decades before World War II, Colette's sexually tense stories of well-
kept courtesans, spurned and desperate lovers, suicide, and financial ruin made
her France's most popular and celebrated woman writer. She had lived a life of
extremes few women could claim, and was a quick study in the suffering of
women at the hands of their men.

Her output had been amazingly prodigious since she first took up a pen and
recorded the jaunty tumultuous life and loves of a girl coming of age in the isolated Burgundy countryside of the late nineteenth century. *Claudine at School*
sold fifty thousand copies when it appeared in 1900, and three more Claudine
novels followed. After that, often working twelve hours a day, she never stopped
writing. Within days of finishing one novel, she was writing the next. Many were
still being written when their first chapters were serialized in magazines. By 1940,
Colette had published more than forty books, countless newspaper and magazine
articles, columns, reviews, film scripts and theatrical adaptations of her books.

But Colette's celebrity was entwined with two difficult marriages singed by cruelty, domination, and infidelity. Her first husband, Henri Gauthier-Villars, made her a writing slave and stole her money. Rapacious and money-obsessed, he took credit for writing the Claudine novels and gave away her rights to all future income from them. Her second husband, Henri de Jouvenal, was more polished in the same obsession with money. The renowned editor of the newspaper *Le Matin* and later a politician, Jouvenal was just as ambitious, and worse, a remorseless adulterer who eventually left Colette for a wealthy, politically connected woman. The couple's taste for good houses, fine food, and clothing that far exceeded their means—and caused Colette to squander what she earned—fueled their unhappiness. "Money's short"—the words her first husband used to persuade Colette to take up writing—became the "daily leitmotif" of her entire life and work.[1] That and the silent desperation as she waited for her men to return.

When the marriages dissolved, Colette, like her characters, was forced by financial necessity to rely on her ingenuity and indomitability to scrape out a living, each time, reinventing herself. A prosperous, anticlerical Paris had opened its sexual floodgates about the time her first marriage broke up in 1906, and Colette dove in. She threw off all convention, traded in the bustle for the feather pasty and loin cloth, and joined a pantomime troupe that traveled around France, performing in stylized pieces like "The Gypsy," "Love, Desire and the Chimera," "Pan, Birds of Night," and "The Egyptian Dream." She paraded in Roman sandals and occasionally played the love scenes bare-breasted, titillating a young fellow performer named Maurice Chevalier, who nearly fifty years later appeared in the film version of Colette's 1942 novella, *Gigi*.

Colette's wit, spontaneity, and *joie de vivre* became her signatures, but in reality, they masked fear and dread that some catastrophe might at any moment come crashing down on her and ruin her life. "We are an innumerable lot of women, all tormented by the thought of tomorrow," she wrote in her wartime memoir *Evening Star*, expressing what was her unrelenting sense of doom.[2] Yet, as early as 1901, a twenty-nine-year-old Colette had already written an amazingly accurate description of the operative mood of her life as it was to remain. In *Claudine in Paris*, she wrote: "My mood isn't easy to define clearly. . . . It's the mood of someone who expects that, at any moment, a chimney may fall on their head. I live with my nerves strung up, waiting for this inevitable fall. And when I open the door of a cupboard, or when I turn the corner of a street, or when the post comes in the morning . . . my heart gives a slight jump. 'Is it going to happen this time?' "[3]

It was the perfect description of the Damoclean sword which hung over Colette's head from the time she was sixteen and her family overnight lost their home and all their possessions. Only the largesse of her older stepbrother, a doctor, saved the family from the street. Her apparently halcyon world instantly exploded, revealing itself to have been a sham perpetrated by a possessive mother who disparaged men to her daughter and a distant father and husband whose mismanagement of his wife's huge inheritance—the estate of her first husband, an alcoholic wife-beater known about town as "the Savage"—left the family penniless and confirmed Colette's mother's worst judgments about men.[4]

Within three years of this cataclysmic assault on her family's well-being, Colette was married off to Henri Gauthier-Villars, a man deemed suitable largely because her parents believed he had money. But he perpetrated a sham, too, and the only real money he would have would come from his wife's labors. It was Gauthier-Villars, a packager of third-rate books and sometime-writer, who, ever looking to capitalize on popular taste, contracted his wife's birth name, Gabrielle Sidonie Colette, into her pen name, "Colette"—simplified, more alluring, a name to sell books. Then he tired of her. As much as Colette despised her life with Gauthier-Villars and long considered fleeing "the freebooter," as she called him in her 1936 memoir, *My Apprenticeships (Mes Apprentissages)*, she was devastated when he fell in love with another woman and suggested they separate. Aside from the habit of her servitude, Colette doubted she could support herself from her writing, since she had published works either exclusively under her husband's pseudonym, "Willy," or toward the end of their marriage, as "Colette Willy."

Colette became convinced that the "twin deities—love and money" were inextricably linked, and she pursued them with equal assiduousness, while at the same time believing that they were destined to cause a woman great suffering.[5] When her second husband left in December 1924 for a rich woman, her wealth made the pain doubly searing. And though Jouvenal had made no secret of his extramarital affairs, his sudden, cowardly abdication from the marriage while Colette was away on a lecture tour seemed all the more cruel. Once more, Colette was devastated. Recalling later the wounding of his departure, she wrote, "It seems to me it must be a big consolation to lose a man only because he's dead."[6] Colette would look back on her two early marriages and remember having felt more alone *during* them than in those in-between periods when work and her own self-reliance propped her up. Waiting for wandering husbands to return home left a deep shame as well as bitterness at their neglect. Later, writing in the autobiographical *Places (Trois . . . Six . . . Neuf . . .)* during World War II, Colette complained that during those unhappy years of her first marriage she did nothing *but* wait for her husband to return to her.

Fortunately for her readers, Colette's emotional pain and insecurity fortified her imagination. In her books, tender, placid moments could instantly turn into a maelstrom of jealousy or financial disaster. Love that seemed pure and infinite could be destroyed by the sudden discovery of love letters to another, an unexpected offer from a rich suitor, or a flippant joke that pains a lover to the core. Her entire literary world turned on her constant dread of catastrophe, and readers flocked to Colette's portrayal of traumatized women with too little to eat and stockings that require constant darning, who love so passionately that the streets they walk echo with the name of their lover. Colette's women may marry to escape poverty, but they are no gold diggers. Rather, they are frightened, reluctant women, timid to ask for too much, lest their men will drop them instantly. Her women powder their skin, dye their hair, truss their stomachs—anything to stave off the ravages of aging that might make them less appealing to the opposite sex. They do anything to survive.

In real life, Colette developed an exceptionally gritty stoicism to match her remarkable self-sufficiency. She prided herself on not showing emotion, maintaining the "code of silence," as she repeatedly called it, to conceal the shame she felt at her own perceived weakness.[7] She believed that silence was essential to dignity, secrecy was preferable to emotion, and cowardice was a sin far more evil than any adultery which might have spawned it. In her 1932 book, *The Pure and the Impure* (*Le pur et l'impure*), Colette characterized the code as part of the "etiquette of survivors," and later wrote in her 1939 novel *The Divan* (*Le Toutonier*): "a woman is ashamed only of what she lets others see, not of what she feels."[8]

Although Colette believed a woman always risked alienating her man if she seemed too strong, her stoicism sustained her at the most difficult times of her life and became the hallmark of her strong heroines as well. In Colette's 1920 novella, *Cheri*, the handsome young gadfly of the title throws over the aging Lea despite his love for her, in order to marry a rich and well-connected young woman. Lea grieves; she cries if no one is looking. She worries inwardly about the loss of love, youth, beauty, money—everything, in fact, but shows none of it. ("Weakness [was] ill-suited to her face," Colette wrote of another of her abandoned survivors.) Lea chooses instead to show indifference and arrogance. Her pain at losing Cheri is kept private. Her grief is suffered alone. She relies only on herself. She survives.

Throughout the tumultuous 1930s, when books sold poorly and the Depression reduced Colette's longtime lover, Maurice Goudaket, to selling "bargain cheap washing machines and a charming utensil for cleaning water pipes and toilets," Colette maintained a feverish pace of writing and international lecture tours despite recurring bouts of bronchitis, shingles, leg pain, and the grippe.[9] The couple had been so short of money that they had even tried launching a beauty-products business, with the indefatigable Colette demonstrating makeup to women shoppers at the Printemps department store. Travels abroad hawking her beauty products only slightly slowed Colette's writing output, but the business eventually failed anyway. She was sixty years old. "I have also reduced the Claridge to the lowest possible rent, and we forge ahead," she wrote to a friend at the time.[10]

During the 1930s and early 1940s, Colette's novels turned uncharacteristically dark and brooding as she fell victim to the economic crisis ensnaring Europe, and polemical fascism gave way to ironclad reality in the regimes of Hitler, Mussolini, and Franco. In Colette's fictional world, disaster loomed closer than ever. Lovers were not merely going to end an affair and casually move on to the next; they were going to die if things didn't work out. Colette's women were no longer young and in love, like Claudine and La Vagabonde. They had grown up, but not necessarily gone on to better lives, nor stopped yearning for love. The women of her 1930s novels were widows, desperate spinsters, wives separated from their husbands, or mistresses kept at a wrenching distance from their married paramours, believing that if only their men would take them off to Mexico or Monte Carlo, everything would be all right. And always, because they would not compromise themselves and marry for money, the specter of poverty loomed before them. Colette was Alice of the 1934 novel *Duo*, but she was also the sisters Colombe and Hermine of the 1939 *Le Toutonier*, driven to excessive yearning for a man, then crazed with fear that he would abandon them and leave them penniless.

By 1940, Colette's sixty-seven-year-old, once-strong body on which she had relied like a mooring was failing. The brown bell-shaped tresses had long since erupted like a willowy seaspore into the famous Colette coif; the triangular-shaped face and eyes, "elongated like leaves," had become puffy, the nose hooked; the body she had flaunted so freely on the music hall stage had grown ample with maturity, good food and wine, and the effects of motherhood at the age of forty, which cut short her pantomime career. Since her thirties, she had been afflicted with painful arthritis.

Her solace was a man named Maurice Godaket, whom she married in 1935. Her marriage to Godaket defied her own deepest expectations about love. Her third marriage was the first based on mutual respect, friendship, and complete devotion. She referred to Godaket as her "best friend" and "perfect companion." He was also a Jew.

Colette had been nearly inseparable from Maurice since the two first met over the Easter holidays in the spring of 1925 at the house of a mutual friend at Cap d'Ail on the French Riviera. Colette, whose male characters could be conniving, secretive, narcissistic, boring, and pretentious—at the expense of their women— had found in the reticent, bookish, and completely devoted Goudaket, sixteen years her junior, the ideal love for which she had always hoped but believed impossible.

The two could not have been less alike in manner, religion, birth, and work, yet Colette and Maurice immediately found common ground. They both recalled suffocating childhoods reared by parents with inescapable obsessions with money, who kept them isolated from other children because they thought them superior. In Colette's case, her mother, Adele Sidonie, nicknamed Sido, kept her out of school altogether. Maurice's unhappy father had instructed him that women were out to take men for all they were worth, while Colette's mother taught that men were out to destroy women through love, marriage, and motherhood. When Colette considered marrying de Jouvenal, her mother tried to discourage her. "Anything would be better than marriage," she implored Colette. Men, she told her daughter, take the "most precious gifts" of a woman in love.

In the early days of their relationship, Colette referred to Maurice lightly as "the kid Maurice," or jokingly as "Satan," because he seemed to her impossibly kind. She treasured his reticence, which had caused him to feel cowardly and inadequate since youth, and they talked for hours at a time. Maurice, she felt, was one of the "few males who, without changing their tone or raising their voice, can say . . . what needs to be said."[11] Slender and quiet, a Noel Coward look-alike, Maurice was warm and serene—an antidote to Colette's frenzy and intensity. He was "the tamer of his wife's wild beasts and of the enchanting wild beast that she was herself," wrote the couple's close friend, Jean Cocteau.[12] Colette fell head over heels in love with him. He was a "skunk," she said, for making her do that.

Almost instantly after they met, Colette found even the shortest separations from Maurice difficult to endure. With him as her guide, she had fallen in love with the south of France and traded a house in Brittany for one on the bay of Saint Tropez in 1926. The house was called "Tamaris-les-Pins," but Colette made it thoroughly her own, planting one of her famous herb and flower gardens and renaming it "La Treille Muscate" (The Grape Trellis). She reveled in the Provençal sun and pine trees, and until the Second World War, when she was forced to sell the house, she spent summers there, and sometimes Christmas. Whenever Maurice left La Treille Muscate to return to work in Paris, Colette wrote volumes of letters, keeping him abreast of the minutiae concerning the house, the weather, neighbors, and her adored menagerie of animals, including her household pets, Chatte, her cat, and Souci, her bulldog. The author of such books as *Dialogue of Beasts, Creatures Great and Small, The Cat,* and *Terrestrial Paradise,* Colette was known for ascribing human qualities to animals and spoke to the spiders and flowers that provided her with amiable company when she was alone. But always there was an irrepressible longing for Goudaket, though she tried to be strong to endure his absence. "I must possess my soul in patience, and possess it without you. . . . This country ceases to be entirely comprehensible when you are not here with me," she wrote to him in 1926.[13]

Colette was fifty-two when she and Maurice met, and she was wildly skeptical that a man and a woman could make a workable relationship based on neither money nor sex. With two failed marriages of her own, and having been witness to her parents' dismal relationship, Colette thought her and Maurice's love was too good to be true. She expected he would leave her for a wealthier woman, just as Jouvenal had left her. Colette believed, like the motherly Lea of her novel *Cheri,* that Maurice was the "great love that comes only once!" This made her all the more fearful of the relationship's demise. Like Lea, Colette believed that the deeper the love, the greater the chance for emotional ruin.

Not surprisingly, Goudaket harbored the same anxious feelings that the relationship had no future. Meeting Colette for the first time, he felt "suddenly brought face to face with [my] destiny," and was conscious of having found the "maternal wing" his soul was seeking, though he wondered why so brilliant and illustrious a woman as she would love a man without pedigree or money.[14] His anxiety was heightened because his parents had also endured a bitterly contentious marriage, and although he had been nervous and ill at ease with women in the past, Colette represented everything he wanted in a woman. She was bold, witty, spontaneous, and insatiably curious, with a natural ease that put him in awe. At her urging that he pursue his deepest longings in art and literature which he had submerged as a youth under parental pressure, Maurice found happiness he had never known. He later explained, "She gave me back a world of taste, smell, and natural shapes, a world that I had let drift away from me."[15] He expected that eventually she would tire of him.

As a result of their mutual faint-heartedness, Colette and Maurice walked gingerly on a domestic tightrope for ten years before they married. They shared a home only in Saint Tropez, and there, only for days or weeks at a time; in Paris they maintained separate apartments altogether. Their hesitancy to admit to the permanence of their union was somewhat comical, for, over the years as their relationship deepened, they moved geographically closer to each other in a series of relocations, eventually renting adjoining apartments. Still, they could not take the step of living in the same apartment until the spring of 1935, when the Depression's strain on their finances and American conventionality pushed them to marry before leaving for the "prudish United States" on a journalism assignment.

In the spring of 1938, the dense atmosphere of war was thickening over Paris's crystalline blue skies. Touring the site of the 1937 Paris Exhibition, whose buildings were then being demolished, Colette's good friend, Jean Cocteau, wrote, "Paris looked like a city of ruins."[16] Cocteau's premonition spurred him in 1938 to write *La Fin du Potomak* about "the Dictator Adolf" playing chess in the Berchtesgaden, "moving the pieces with a soft hand and smiling, under his moustache, at the terror of his adversaries," but Colette, uninterested in war clouds, was more concerned with the real weather. She was writing articles for *Paris-Soir* magazine and spending time at her vacation house on the Riviera. "The state of the weather has always had a large place in my life," she explained at the time.[17]

In the last days of peace before Hitler's invasion of Poland, Colette observed that the weather in Paris was "almost as lovely as it was in 1914."[18] By then, war was expected to erupt any day. Maurice urged Colette to leave Paris, but she refused, insisting that the city was no more dangerous than the rest of the country. But less than two weeks after the French declared war on Germany on September 3, dogfights over Paris were so intense, and money, jobs, and supplies were so scarce that only one other resident besides her and Maurice remained in their multistory building. The war was not a month old when Colette discovered that her concierge was starving. Colette and her husband waited out air alerts in the subbasement of the adjacent Hotel Beaujolais, but the stifling glut of humanity so repelled her that the couple waited out future air raids in their apartment. For the next eight months, Colette and Maurice walked or drove at night from their apartment to Radio Paris-Mondial, the radio station where she transmitted to France and America a daily essay on life in France during war. Maurice introduced French plays in English and a translator read Colette's script after she introduced it. Her essays comprised a kind of women's survival kit on how to be pretty, domestically frugal, and clever when war challenged a women's ingenuity. At the time, Colette was also at work on her novella *Duo*, about a husband who commits suicide after discovering his wife's shameless adultery.

On May 10, 1940, the Germans demonstrated the efficient destructive force of blitzkrieg, or "lightning war," when they invaded Holland, Belgium, and Luxembourg with a barrage of predawn air bombings. The French army was in retreat from its defensive positions along the Meuse Valley, and within a week German tanks were scouring the eastern French countryside. General Philippe Pétain, aged hero of Verdun, was brought in as vice-premier and chief military advisor by the new premier Paul Reynaud, an arch-antifascist who had consistently throughout the 1930s protested French and English appeasement of Hitler. When later in the month the Belgian and Dutch governments surrendered to the Nazis, the French government condemned their acquiescence, especially since Parisians were terrified they would be next.

At the end of May, Colette and Maurice moved into a three and a half room house they had bought the previous spring in Mère, a small town in the Paris suburb of Montfort-l'Amaury. The couple finally sold their cherished house in Saint-Tropez in the summer of 1939, "for a pittance, thanks to Mussolini," when war threatened, and the south of France suddenly seemed unsafe.[19] Maurice commuted daily between Montfort and Paris, where he was working as an editor for *Paris-Match* and *Marie Claire* magazines, and for *Paris-Soir* newspaper. As a decorated, though disillusioned, World War I veteran, Maurice at this time still expected to be conscripted into the army.[20]

Renovation of their Montfort house had been slow and intermittent, since the workmen were often compelled to put down their hammers and take up guns. Moroccan soldiers billeted in the unfinished house in the winter of 1939–40, and Colette eventually bribed the local minister of public works to get them out. By late May when Colette and Maurice moved in to what they had originally thought would be a safe haven, Hitler's planes were bombing close to Paris. The hill from their new house provided "box seats" from which to view the air attacks.

In Paris, citizens grew daily more afraid of a German attack. Food shortages were strangling the city. A scientist with the Academy of Sciences advised Parisians in the magazine *Le Petit Parisien* that they could safely eat the leaves of elm, linden, and ash trees to stave off starvation.[21] By June 8, 1940, the Germans had taken the lower Seine Valley. Two days later, on June 10, the same day Mussolini's soldiers attacked French divisions across the Alps, the French government fled from Paris to Tours and then to Bordeaux, where pro-German ministers were plotting control.

When Maurice arrived in Paris on June 11 for his regular biweekly visits on business, he was alarmed to find the city braced for tragedy. Grim silence, but at the same time a sense of feverish haste, pervaded the city, as Parisians hurriedly packed their cars to flee in advance of the Germans. Government workers were burning documents, and at the offices of *Paris-Soir* newspaper, Maurice encountered employees clearing out their desks.

Maurice returned to Montfort and tried to convince Colette that they, too, should abandon their cottage and head south, but she refused. Confident that she would change her mind once she saw the hoards of new refugees crowding the roads south with their ox carts, wheelbarrows, and cars laden with mattresses, Maurice told Colette, "Very well, then let's go for a ride." In the car, Colette said, "When do we leave?"[22]

As the couple left Montfort at four in the morning on June 12, 1940, with a good supply of gasoline, Colette lamented history's cruel repetitiveness, recalling her mother's stories of German occupation of Burgundy during the Franco-Prussian War.[23] She and Maurice were accompanied on their flight south by Colette's servant, Pauline. Colette took few possessions, but among them was a small, loaded revolver. They joined Colette's daughter, Colette de Jouvenal, nicknamed Bel-Gazou, in the "habitable part of a ruined castle" in Curemonte, Corrèze, south of Limoges, where the Jouvenal family had its estate and where Bel-Gazou was already living.[24]

Over the next three days, the awful predictions of a German invasion of Paris came true. On June 14, the Nazi legions marched up the Champs-Élysées. From hundreds of buildings all over Paris—hotels, ministries, apartment buildings, even from the top of the Eiffel Tower—the black, white, and red swastika was hung. "Deutschland siegt auf allen Fronten"—"Germany conquers on all fronts"—Nazi posters read. Premier Reynaud resigned on June 16, unwilling to sign an armistice, and Marshall Pétain became head of a new government, installed in the spa town of Vichy. With the rich, pro-German Pierre Laval as Pétain's right hand man, the Vichy government signed an armistice with the Germans on June 22, giving legal occupation of the northern half of France and the Atlantic coast to Germany.

Even when the threat to Paris mounted in late May, Colette had continued to believe Paris was no more dangerous than the countryside, and when she and Maurice found themselves completely cut off in Curemonte, she was sorry she had agreed to leave. Provisions in Curemonte were scarce. "The butcher comes when he comes and only has veal," she complained. "Come autumn, all this greenery around us will disburse pears and apples, walnuts and chestnuts. Until then, no fruit."[25] For a month, they had no access to gasoline, newspapers, telegraph, or mail. Colette did not even know the status of *Paris-Soir*, the newspaper for which she, too, had been writing. To her, an occupied Paris was preferable to a miserable existence in Curemonte. "When security means total isolation, it's nauseating, and I don't want it," she wrote to her Jewish friend Misz Marchand on July 12, 1940, a month after being at the castle.[26]

Despite her troubles, Colette continued writing at Curemonte as though circumstances were normal. Not even "disaster or an exodus involving a whole nation" could keep her from working, she later wrote, recalling this sad, nervous time, but in truth, work, or the habit of work, was her protection as it had always been—a bulwark against fear and the realities of otherwise insurmountable circumstances.[27] With the onset of occupation, Colette determined that the danger of refugee life in German-occupied France was not any worse than the alternative of disintegrating from lack of work, boredom, and grinding loneliness. For Colette, the war had come down to just this: one had no other reason to arise in the morning, clean oneself, and make one's bed, than the "persistence of an obtuse dignity, the need for a routine, however simple."[28] In writing yet another book of autobiographical recollections, *Looking Backwards* (*Journal à rebours*), Colette advised those who had been driven to the countryside to throw themselves into any simple exercise, be it weeding a garden or drawing water from a well, and these tasks, she felt, must be repeated endlessly, talked about endlessly, no matter how inane the chatter. For herself, however, only the task of writing could keep her from lapsing into crippling fear and physical decay, and so she disregarded the castle's inhospitable conditions, constructed a writing table, and finished her novella *The Rainy Moon* (*La Lune de pluie*), about two sisters in love with the same man. "Every sight I see provokes me to the same duty . . . to write, to depict," Colette explained.[29]

The trial of her confinement was exacerbated by the very first letter that reached her, informing her that one of her German translators, Erna Redtenbacher, had committed suicide along with her female lover. By early August Colette's angst was such that she could stand Corrèze no longer. The debilitating isolation was only part of her motivation to return to Paris. Maurice's and her money was fast evaporating and what reserves they had were in Paris, along with any possibility for work.

On their attempt to reach Paris, she and Maurice were turned back at a crossing into the Occupied Zone. As Maurice stood by, the guard mistook first Colette, then Pauline, for Jews. "You're utterly mistaken," Maurice told the guard in German. "I alone here am of Jewish birth." Maurice was risking danger when he volunteered himself as the sole Jew in the group, but the discovery that someone was lying or had falsified identification papers was equally dangerous. Years later in his memoir, *Close to Colette*, Maurice partly attributed his honesty at that moment to "stupid pride." Colette, who traveled with her loaded revolver concealed inside her glove, was "airily swinging in front of her this empty glove, one finger of which . . . remained stiff and pointed."[30] Colette later relinquished the gun in Paris, since the Nazis forbade gun ownership at the price of death.

Forced to turn back at the crossing and unable to reach Paris, the trio traveled to Lyons, where they knew the city's longtime ex-mayor, Edouard Herriot, president of the Chamber of Deputies since 1936. Herriot was a moderate reformer, fierce patriot, arts connoisseur, and intellectual. The people of Lyons were so loyal to him that the new pro-Nazi French government, which had considered Lyons first as the site of its new home, rejected the city and chose Vichy instead.

While Colette, Maurice, and Pauline awaited a letter from the Swedish Consulate that would enable them to get back to Paris, they lived for three weeks in Lyons in a mouse-infested hotel where the animal-lover Colette fed morsels of bread to a mouse. There, Colette finished her latest memoir, *Journal à rebours*, which was already being serialized. She had begun the book years earlier, and had never anticipated that it was to become the powerful, minutely detailed record of her flight from Montfort and her trial of endurance in Corrèze. With the help of Herriot, who shortly thereafter was arrested and taken to Germany, where he was imprisoned until the end of the war, the couple finally obtained gasoline, and on September 3, 1940, Colette and Maurice reached a deserted Paris.

In the months following her return, Colette examined the effects of German occupation, particularly on women, which included the hardships of putting children to bed in a cold house, doing without adequate food and hygiene, and taking care to keep oneself from gossiping in hallways. *From My Window* (*De Ma Fenetre*), published in book form in 1942, was the kind of beautifully written, subtly observed woman's advice sheet at which Colette was a genius. Just as her radio broadcasts of 1939 had offered listeners tips on how to survive the dim, prewar days with ingenuity and style, Colette now told readers suffering the harsh effects of war how the chestnut, always plentiful when other foods were scarce, could be boiled and spread with jam and served as a "complete desert," and how haricot beans could be cooked in red wine and served on square biscuits as a more than serviceable replacement for good pastry.[31] By the time *From My Window* appeared in 1942, Colette would long for the days when cake and a good bath figured anywhere in the picture of what she herself yearned for.

With the Germans in occupation and aided by a multitude of Pétain's Vichy commissions and the French fascist party, Parti Populaire Français (PPF), anti-Semitism was being disseminated in Paris daily in newspapers like *Je Suis Partout*, magazines, the radio, and in such films as *The Jewish Peril*. French people were advised to "learn from now on to recognize in them the eternal Jew—the exotic outsider who will never belong." Propaganda spread the monstrous notion that Jews were France's enemy, "aliens," a lazy, but rapacious people whose ulterior motive was to destroy the country and its people. Warnings against the harboring of Jews at the price of death were pasted on walls all over the city and published in newspapers that either had been right-wing before the war or had been commandeered by the pro-German forces. French book publishers suffered the same fate under the Nazis as their magazine and newspaper counterparts, and many Jewish publishers, like Colette's own at Ferenczi, fled the city. Calmann-Levy, the Jewish-founded publisher, was placed under the control of an avowed anti-Semite who changed the name of the firm to Aux Armes de France.

Like any French citizen over the age of fifty, Colette had seen the stark face of French anti-Semitism before. A surge in Jewish immigration at the end of the nineteenth century, mostly from Russia, had fanned a long period of vicious French anti-Semitism which began in 1871 when France lost its war with Prussia and used Jews as the convenient scapegoat for the collapse of the Second Empire. Sensational anti-Semitic books like Edouard Drumont's 1886 *Jewish France* (*La France juive*) and his newspaper *La Libre Parole* helped create the blistering atmosphere that led to the false conviction in 1894 of Captain Alfred Dreyfus, a wealthy Jew who was accused of selling military secrets to Germany. Eventually, incriminating documents were found to have been forged, but the Dreyfus affair ensued for more than a decade until his release in 1906, after bold evidence emerged that he had been the victim of a military conspiracy. The case disclosed the power and passion of the rightist army, supported by the Catholic church, in concert with fervent anti-Semitic nationalists. It divided the country between Left and Right; anti-Semite and philo-Semite; pro-monarchist and pro-republican, and became an international cause célèbre, with writers like Marcel Proust and Émile Zola coming to Dreyfus's defense. Although the Republic won in its defense of Dreyfus, who was even promoted to the rank of lieutenant-colonel during World War I, anti-Semitic fervor thereafter became an established feature of the sizeable right-wing, church-backed constituency which opposed universal equality, wanted a return to monarchy, and favored fascism. Throughout the decades prior to World War II, right-wing publications in France disseminated vicious anti-Semitism, employing some of the country's most brilliant journalists, such as Robert Braissilach, editor of *Je Suis Partout*. The period saw the growth of influence of fanatical ideas, such as extermination of enemies, spread by writers like the poet Charles Maurras, who in 1905 founded the militant, xenophobic, anti-Semitic Ligue de l'Action (Action Francaise) movement and three years later established his notorious newspaper *L'Action Française*. In 1927, the publication *The Jewish Invasion* (*L'Invasion juive*) described Jews as "oriental lepers and the real vermin of the world," and warned the French to look out for "hooked noses, fleshy lips, crinkly hairstyles, the owners of which jargonise in their native Yiddish."[32]

Colette was living in Paris during the Dreyfus affair, married to the anti-Semite Henri Gauthier-Villars, churning out her first books for his "literary factory," as Colette called his firm, and participating against her will in his literary salon, which included André Gide, Jean Cocteau, and Paul Valéry. Although the couple's wide social circle included the pro-Dreyfus—and Jewish—Marcel Proust, Gauthier-Villars was one of those who was absolutely convinced of Dreyfus's guilt. When he refused to sign a petition in support of Dreyfus, one of his former writers declared, "It's the first time that he hasn't wanted to sign something he didn't write."[33]

The direction Colette's life took after Gauthier-Villars—her marriage to Maurice and her close friendships with Jews—raises the likelihood that the unflattering comments about Jews in the Claudine books were inserted by Gauthier-Villars. In the subsequent battle for just attribution of authorship of these works, Colette would say that his contribution was limited to "some puns, some obscenities, and nasty stories designed to satisfy his personal grudges."[34] Phrases like "a Jewish dealer in precious stones," or "in Paris, all the milliners are Jewesses," are not characteristic of Colette's subsequent work. Not until late in the war did

Colette evince any religious fervor which might have predisposed her to intolerance of other religions. At best, she had a casual relationship with her Catholicism; surely her devotion lacked the passion which colored the French nationalist, anti-Semitic rhetoric.[35] During World War II, when Colette tried unsuccessfully to have Maurice convert to Catholicism, it was survival, not faith, that was the driving force. Colette was too iconoclastic, too unsynchronized with the rhythms of convention and conventional prejudice, to have been swept up in mass French hatred. To her core, Collette was a Burgundian, not a Frenchwoman, and Burgundy was historically France's militant hotbed of rebellion.

It was the Burgundians in alliance with the English against the French during the Hundred Years War who captured a seventeen-year-old Lorraine farmer's daughter at Compiegne in 1430. When they sold the girl to the English who burned her at the stake, they made Joan of Arc a French Catholic martyr.

Burgundy came under French control in 1482, but the area remained a center of antimonarchical dissent, for which Colette's own family history bore deep scars. Her maternal grandfather and his brothers belonged to a "secret society" opposed to King Louis Philippe, who represented rich bankers and large landowners. In 1832, her mother's brothers, both journalists, were suspected of plotting to kidnap the king, and they went into hiding to escape imprisonment or deportation. Louis Philippe was eventually toppled by bloody insurrections in 1848, but not before Colette's uncles fled to Belgium after writing attacks on the same king their father despised. Now, nearly a century later, economic inequality and ethnic and religious hatred again blended in Europe to spread terror to anyone outside the mighty power structure. Colette's uncles were long ago dead in Belgium, but their niece now looked with similar fear to her future.

The winter of 1940–41 was one of the coldest on record in France, and Paris was cruelly gripped by Germans and below-freezing temperatures alike. Life became one long quest for food, coal, and wood. What food there was in Paris could be bought only at exorbitant prices. On New Year's Day 1941, Colette described Paris as being "reduced to a skeleton."[36] Fortunately, she had had the foresight to arrange for shipments of food from friends in the countryside and had stocked up on coal in 1939. She and Maurice had heat, but Colette was stricken with bronchitis and grippe. Her brother Leo's death that winter at the age of seventy-three contributed to her ill health.

During the weeks she was confined by war, illness, and the cold, Colette began a new novel, *Julie de Carneilhan*, the story of a countess divorced from her husband, a prominent politician, whom she still loves. Unlike in the past, when Colette wrote happily and at lightning pace, the work went slowly and was difficult. Nevertheless, she was prodded by their financial straits; the couple was experiencing a return, she wrote, to the hard times of the early 1930s. "It had to be done," she explained.[37]

As World War II ground on, Colette found herself in poverty and loneliness painfully similar to that she had experienced during the First World War. In 1914, she had remained in Paris to continue writing for the city's newspapers and magazines, sending her eight-month-old daughter off to a seaside resort on the Brittany coast. Her separation for two months from Henri de Jouvenal, then a lieutenant, was an unbearable strain that eventually drove her to Verdun just to be near him.[38] More than anything, what burned in Colette's memory of the First World War was her fear of going broke. Food shortages, waste matter dropped from dirigibles, and bombs exploding like "white bouquets" had been tolerable compared to her fear that the war would prevent her from earning a living.[39] Jouvenal had warned her that as the Germans got closer to Paris, newspapers would stop printing and be replaced by official government bulletins. "I'd never have believed the human species would come to this again," Colette confessed in a letter to a friend just after World War II broke out in 1939.[40]

In April 1941 the Nazi vise on France squeezed tighter when the Reich established tough new measures governing French Jews. A Commission for Jewish Affairs issued its definition of Jew, as well as restrictions on work that Jews could perform. Journalism, Maurice's profession since 1935, was among the work prohibited to Jews. No matter how badly he and Colette needed the money, defiance of the order was not an option. Movements of Jews were monitored by the Police for Jewish Affairs, a special agency created in April of 1941 to mete out "justice" to Jews who disobeyed the rules. Jews had to be wary of several French police forces operating under a panoply of brutal commanders: the gendarmes, the mobile guards, and the judiciary police. Jews also had to be on the lookout for bands of hate-intoxicated teenagers, members of the fascist Parti Populaire Français, wearing dark blue shirts, leather belts, and PPF armbands.

Needing to do anything to earn money, Maurice began selling out-of-print books, and an appalled, but resigned Colette limited her magazine work to what was "safe." In the past, she had written articles covering everything from life in Italy during World War I to the last public beheading in France in 1939, but her articles during the occupation were limited to fashion, gardening, and how to survive on less food. Her ability to separate the fiendishness of Nazi aggression from her own economic need allowed her to write for the pro-Nazi *La Gerbe* and *Petit Parisien* newspapers, the latter of which had been commandeered by Nazi collaborators. While Maurice's I.D. card was stamped with a yellow star and the label "JEW," Colette used her press card stamped with the swastika of the German Propaganda-Staffel to make the money they needed to eat. As usual, Colette was too pragmatic, too concerned with the basics of life, for hatred of the Germans or political ideology to be of any use to her. France had been gripped by economic depression, financial scandal, political upheaval, and labor strikes since the early 1930s, but what always mattered most to her was that as a result of the chaos, "Books are selling so badly."[41] In 1937, at work on a collection of short stories, *Tender Shoot (Bella-Vista)*, during a transport workers' strike, Colette asked, "I'm working, but what will become of writers?"[42]

Throughout the four-year occupation, fellow French writers like Jean-Paul Sartre, the avowed Communist Louis Aragon, and her friend André Gide took unpopular, even dangerous, political stands, while many others, including her own daughter, used their writing to fight the Nazis directly. They established underground Resistance newspapers like *Notre Voix*, *Franc-Tireur*, and *Fraternité* to reveal Nazi atrocities and serve as a practical warning to Jews, as well as a moral outcry. Marguerite Duras, whose husband was imprisoned by Nazis, established a network to obtain information regarding prisoners and deportees. Unlike these colleagues, Colette consciously shunned involvement with the Resistance. Above all, she wanted her Jewish husband safe, and was not prepared to do anything that might put the two of them—with their delicate "marital situation" as she called it—at additional risk. "I am among those who did nothing but wait," she admitted in her memoir of the era, *Evening Star*, fully aware that she used Nazis and their French collaborators when she needed them, and never did anything to defeat the tormentors of her husband and friends.[43]

But Colette's neutrality, superficially so blithe as to be almost baffling if one did not understand her essential self-protective nature, also had much to do with her underlying views on war and her aversion to politics, which had been framed in her earliest memories of a remote father, bored with his profession, who aspired but failed at being a local politician. Later, her marriage to Jouvenal and stints as drama and literary editor of *Le Matin* during World War I confirmed her view that politics and war were games played by ambitious men holding a grudge. When, years later, she recalled the exhilarating atmosphere of *Le Matin*'s editorial offices, populated by brilliant men with glittering personalities, Colette recalled that she was treated with condescension and was not invited to participate in political discussions conducted by the offices' male journalists. "I was shown an indulgence, a kindness, that could not have been bettered for the villiage idiot," she wrote in *Evening Star*, noting how as soon as she appeared in a room where they were assembled, the general bonhomie died, as though a foreign invader had penetrated their territory. Part of it, she attributed to shame over their sexual dalliances—the "public man's exploits." These men clothed their vanity in gentlemanliness and suavity, and Colette was highly impressed by the nonchalant way the editors fraternized with government leaders at "one of those masculine lunches" where expensive French wine, rich food, and cigars quickened their conspiracy.[44]

The differences between the sexes became grossly apparent to her. Her entire perception of who she was in relation to these men of power was shaped by their game of gentle arrogance and cultivated superiority—"a mixture of affected cynicism and literary paradox by which, round 1900, intelligent, bitter, frustrated men maintained their self-esteem," she would write in her 1943 story, "Le Kepi." Though Colette had traveled the world, written successful books, held a position of seeming authority as an editor on a prestigious newspaper, these powerful, politically connected men planted in her a feeling of separateness, impotence, and inferiority. She called men "dear enemies."

Her considerable experience with men like the debonair Henri de Jouvenal, who once challenged a rival editor to a duel with revolvers over "editorial" differences (both men would live to proudly show their wounds), taught her that wars were made by this kind of "public man." Describing his nature, she referred to the public man as a "wild animal," who "plays and roughly handles its offspring at will," and balances a "weight of paternal pride and despotism."[45] She believed the public man makes war and lives to write and talk about it.

"Men are talking about war," she had written to her friend Renée Hamon on February 25, 1938. "But an old woman like myself, to whom yet another war would only mean sitting tight and at best dying without fuss, takes less interest in such matters."[46] Colette believed that war only made more dire the terrible fate of a woman to wait for her man, and she bluntly described that fate during

World War I: "The deep thought, the only thought, that of all women in war: waiting."

That terrible, inevitable fate—inevitable given that her husband was a Jew in Nazi-occupied France—fell on December 12, 1941. That day began what Colette later described as a "classical nightmare of absence."[47] In the early morning hours of that December day, 743 "intellectuals"—Jews of French citizenship—were rounded up in Paris by the Gestapo. Since prior arrests and killing of Jews and Communists in occupied Paris had been intermittent and carried out under the guise of military security, the December 12 roundup represented a brutal and decisive escalation in the Third Reich's aim to exterminate the Jews of Europe. Throughout the City of Light that morning, two hundred Gestapo and three hundred sixty Wehrmacht police simultaneously swooped down on the homes of lawyers, doctors, teachers, and scientists—many of them decorated World War I veterans. As wives stood by terrified, helpless, and confused, the men were told to get dressed quickly and take only a few possessions. Consistent with the Reich's obsession with quotas, about three hundred foreign-born Jews were added from Drancy, a camp just three miles out of Paris, which the Germans had created out of an unfinished low-income housing project. The "criminals" were taken to a German-controlled prison camp about fifty miles north of Paris in Compiegne, a small village set inside the huge Compiegne forest and dominated by the palace of Napoleon III. Although Pétain had promised—and Colette had believed—that Jewish war veterans, especially those wounded and decorated like Maurice, would receive special treatment, a German directive the day after the roundup announced there would be no special treatment for any Jews.

For months the Germans had been preparing for the mass killing of Jews, building all over Poland prison camps equipped with gas chambers. On December 14, 1941, two days after Maurice's abduction, the first announcement in France appeared in the newspaper that "a large number of criminal Judeo-bolshevik elements" were to be deported to prison labor camps in the East.[48] All but a few of those taken to Compiegne on December 12 were deported to the Auschwitz concentration camp on March 27, 1942, in what was the first trainload of Jews to leave France. The delay in the prisoners' transfer to the camp was a result of the perverse grace demonstrated by the Nazis toward their own: all available French trains were used to bring home their boys for Christmas holiday. Of the 1,112 Jews shipped to Auschwitz on March 27, only twenty-two survived the war.[49]

Maurice was among the rare few who were allowed to return home in the weeks after the December 12 roundup. His unfortunate label as an "intellectual" was ironic, considering he had only turned to journalism in the 1930s, as a second career, after his pearl and gem business failed under the weight of the Depression and the rise of the Japanese pearl trade. As a young man, Maurice had dreamed of becoming a writer, but at seventeen his dream was quashed when his father informed him that not only would he not support Maurice in the endeavor, but that the family was nearly penniless, and Maurice would have to get a job. His father's ultimatum summarily snapped Maurice out of his flirtation with art, and he reluctantly followed the career of his father, a diamond and gem dealer.

Maurice Goudaket embraced the sense of freedom that journalism brought him, but he could not have taken the step without Colette's help. Colette gave Maurice confidence in himself when he floundered, and convinced him that writing was not an unattainable dream, but a practical means of earning an income. Her strength and encouragement became the rock of Maurice's renewal as a man. When he was arrested by the Nazis, her strength and influence saved his very life.

Even during the first few weeks of his absence, when Colette did not know if he was dead or alive, she did not allow herself the "luxury of being very tired."[50] She waited by the telephone for news, and it became a conduit of terror. In Paris, rumors abounded about conditions at the camps, that prisoners were beaten, tortured, starved. The sick and dying lay beside the healthy in filthy, unsanitary conditions. Brutal guards stripped prisoners of jewelry and money, and a black market for food, cigarettes, and smuggled letters thrived among prison guards.

The first communication from Maurice came in the form of a tiny torn square of notepaper. Subsequent communications consisted of requests for food, alcohol, and spices to make the harsh prison food more palatable. The winter was bitterly cold; it was fourteen degrees below zero in Compiegne where ancient cobblestones dripped with historical associations of hate, hysteria, and retribution. As recently as June 21, 1940, Hitler had symbolically exacted Germany's revenge on France by dancing a jig in the very forest clearing where Marshall Foch and German Secretary of State Matthias Erzberger signed the Armistice ending World War I. But Compiegne, too, was where Joan of Arc had been put to death. Colette surely wanted no martyr made of Maurice here or anywhere else.

Once again a beloved was gone. It was what Colette had dreaded each time she had fallen in love, and what she had written about so often and so precisely with such eerie premonition. Just months before Maurice's abduction, Colette had completed her novel *Julie de Carneilhan*. Against the setting of a nation on the verge of war, Julie hopes her ex-husband, whom she still loves, will ask her to come back to him. When she realizes that her hope is in vain, she returns to her family's country estate and the dependable men of her youth—her brother and father. *Julie de Carneilhan* is a melancholy story of strength and resignation about a woman "ready for any drama, provided they were dramas of love . . . capable of triumph, subtlety, kindness, ferocity or stoicism, if these were the by-products of love."[51]

When fiction came unsettlingly close to reality and Colette was unsure whether Maurice would return to her, she insisted, "We must keep a firm grip on ourselves. Tenderness is very dangerous at that time. Affectionate words and warm, tumultuous tears are just what we must refuse ourselves for the moment."[52] During the entire eight weeks while Maurice was gone, Colette observed to the letter the "individual code [that] forbade the display of emotion," as she had described it in *The Divan*. Crying would not bring Maurice back, just as it would not bring Cheri back to Lea, Espivant back to Julie, Michel back to Alice, or any of Colette's irretrievable men back to the women who yearn for them. "You don't weep for a man who's dead; you forget him, or you replace him, if you don't die yourself from his absence!" Alice tells herself.[53] This was a lesson Colette had learned during her long years of marital unhappiness. Ironically, these marriages groomed her now to bear the grueling wait for Maurice.

Even as the Nazis took Maurice away, Colette stoically bid him adieu with a kiss, the words "Off you go," and a "friendly tap on [his] shoulder." Eventually, however, confinement and isolation from friends who might have alleviated her suffering had they not retreated to the country to escape the Nazis made her despairing. She no longer had even the companionship of her beloved cat and dog, both of whom died in 1939, and she wished she could be near the ocean she loved, so that she could "breathe a tidal wind."[54] All alone in her apartment, Colette survived Maurice's absence in part by staring at a gilded porcelain horse for hours at a time, forcing herself into a state of hypnosis that might help her endure the suffering. "I yearned, like everyone else, for the return of a time, before the war, that we used to find just bearable before having experienced what was to follow," Colette wrote in *Evening Star*. "Among other earthly blessings I longed for the freedom it would grant me to relish my sadness. 'Oh, when everything's all right again, I'll let myself go, I'll cry in buckets.' "[55]

Celebrity had been a bane to Colette in the 1930s when flocks of gawkers descended on La Treille Muscate to catch a peek at its famous owner, but during wartime, it was proving to be highly useful to her. In Montfort in 1939, she had bought off a government bureaucrat to get soldiers out of her house; and in Lyons in 1940, friends in high places allowed her and Maurice to return to Paris. As it turned out, had Colette not been in Paris when Maurice was arrested, it is more than likely that he would have died in Auschwitz along with most of the prisoners rounded up in the December 12 sweep.

When Maurice did not immediately come home from Compiegne, Colette exerted the full weight of her celebrity to obtain his release. Although it is not clear exactly who was responsible for his release, evidence points to the direct involvement of Ambassador Otto Abetz, the highest ranking civilian Nazi representative in Paris. Abetz, an anti-Semite and francophile, was an old friend of Henri de Jouvenal's son, Bertrand, with whom Colette had had an affair which ended when she met Maurice. Abetz had studied art in Paris, spoke French, and as ambassador in the 1930s had promoted strong ties between Germany and France. When the Nazis took over France, Abetz, who had developed wide support among French right-wing, anticlerical intellectuals, wasted no time drawing up lists of pro-German, anti-Semitic writers, journalists, and publications which could further the Nazi cause. An intimate of Laval's, Abetz convinced the French premier that France would incur Hitler's favor if the government instituted anti-Jewish measures, and it was Abetz who on December 7, 1941, made the case for attributing murders of Germans to "Jews and their agents in the pay of Anglo-Saxon and Soviet secret services," a suggestion put into action on December 14 when announcements were posted in Paris that the murderers would be shot.[56]

Several warm letters from Abetz's French wife, Suzanne, to Colette shortly after Maurice's release express gratitude for favors rendered. One thanks Colette, whom Suzanne later referred to as "my dear protégée," for her gift of flowers and says, "I'm pleased at your happiness." Suzanne Abetz's invitation to Colette to take tea with her at the German embassy was accompanied by a note expressing the hope that Maurice would "be in Paris" on the appointed date.[57] (Three years later Suzanne Abetz would have her own problems when Otto fled France with his mistress and a cache of stolen art treasures.)

On February 6, 1941, Maurice was set free, eight weeks after his arrest. He took the train from Compiegne and the metro to the couple's apartment in the Palais-

Royal, a handsome quadrant of nineteenth-century buildings encompassing the Théâtre du Français and the Comédie-Français. When an emaciated Maurice appeared, Colette was shocked by his appearance. "I had never before seen in a man such non-human colouring, the greenish-white of cheeks and forehead, the orange of the edges of the eyelids, the grey of the lips."[58]

Maurice's reluctance to discuss his imprisonment made the experience all the worse for Colette, whose exhaustive memory of the events of her own life and whose vicarious nature required that she know exactly what had happened to her husband. Colette had already written the story of a married couple ruined by their inability to communicate. "I'm beginning to think that a man and a woman can do everything together without any trouble, except make conversation," she wrote in *Duo* in 1934. The man "listens politely as if he were deaf, or else replies from a hundred miles away, from heaven knows where, from a reef where he makes signals, lost and solitary."[59] Maurice's telling of the friendships forged among the prisoners at Compiegne, who "shared a bar of chocolate or a blanket," rankled too.[60] In a small way, she became jealous and envious of the bond between these men in grave danger that somehow seemed to her deeper than that between a husband and wife.

Now that Maurice was home, Colette's health, which had held up during the eight weeks of fear, separation, and waiting, suddenly and dramatically declined. In 1940, despite her arthritis, Colette could still be seen talking to neighbors and walking across the garden of the Palais-Royal, "with her cane, her silken cravat, her flat felt hat, her fine eyes, her bare feet, her sandals," as Jean Cocteau had observed her.[61] From the time Maurice returned, however, her arthritis worsened exponentially. By the spring of 1942, the pain was so excruciating that Colette could barely walk. She began "modern miracle" therapies, as she called them— acupuncture, doses of "thermal water," and painful X-rays which burned her thighs and midriff and forced her to lie motionless on her back afterward for seven hours at a time.

While Maurice Godaket spent the remainder of the war dodging the Nazis, the crippled Colette became a virtual prisoner of her apartment, and of her fear that he would be murdered, and of the knawing memory of the fear itself, endlessly relived in her memory of the "ring at the bell, the hobnailed boots, . . . the coarse whispering voices."[62] Her bed and red divan, "the divan-raft on which I've floated for so many years," became her favorite places of work in an apartment that, as the war continued, increasingly provided her emotional protection.[63]

The first-floor room in the Palais-Royal building where she and Maurice moved in January 1938 and where she spent the war and the years beyond was little different from the room where Maurice first visited her in her home in Auteuil in 1925. Like her fictional music hall performers who tow their baggage from one seaside casino town to the next to eke out a living, Colette had moved from town to town, house to house, each time fashioning nearly the identical writing room for herself. It was her way of creating a minute world of stability out of the chaos and uncertainty of her life.

She treasured her window view of the Palais garden, the "sealed-off world" of the verdant, colonnaded square. She had actually lived in the same building once before, from 1927 to 1931, and thus she knew many of the local residents, merchants, and restaurateurs, who were exceedingly generous, bringing her sumptuous dishes, gifts, and gossip. When she grew lame, friends carried her to her chair at the nearby Grand Vefour restaurant, where she and Jean Cocteau were such regulars that bronze plaques marked their special spot. The familiarity of the neighborhood gave her the feeling of security that she needed now more than ever.

Colette had defied danger during World War I by riding her bicycle to a deserted Bois de Bologne to eat lunch; now she was too crippled by arthritis to take the metro, and she had no car. But with her bed pulled up to the floor-length window ("it follows me like the shell of a snail"), it was as if she could "sleep outside" during spring and summer, as though neither wall nor infirmity separated her from the rich world of the garden below. "Alicia is no angel," Gigi's grandmother says of her reclusive sister in Colette's 1942 novella, *Gigi*. "But I must confess that she is long-sighted. And that without ever leaving her room."[64] From her window during the war, Colette saw "Paris sink into suffering, darken with grief and humiliation," but she could also observe the first buds of spring, the pink flowers of the nearby chestnut tree.[65] The Palais-Royal garden gave her a sense of promise and renewal at a time when she and Maurice needed a good dose of luck more than anything to remain alive, because over the next three years, as Colette gradually became sequestered in her apartment, her beloved "perfect companion" lived the life of a hunted man.

On January 20, 1942, while Maurice was at the Compiegne prison camp, the so-called Wannsee conference in Berlin formally decreed the extermination of all European Jews. The "Final Solution," as it was called at Wannsee, would result in the death of eleven million people, including eight million Jews. Adolf Eichmann, who was in charge of the plan of extermination, put the number of Jews in France at 165,000 in the Occupied Zone, and 700,000 in unoccupied France. Five months of ensuing preparation for the roundups revised the figures: in France, 180,000 in the Occupied Zone; 260,000–280,000 Jews in the unoccupied zone. Eichmann's aim simply was "to rid France of its Jews."[66]

The planning was carried out with smooth precision with the cooperation of Pierre Laval, president of the Vichy government, who surprised even the Germans with his offer to turn over Jewish children under age sixteen for deportation from the Free Zone. The Compiegne camp where Maurice had been imprisoned was only one of dozens built in France by the summer of 1942, when the massive roundups of Jews began. During the war, about four hundred thousand French Jews were imprisoned in camps such as Orléans, Beugency, Vendôme, Pithiviers, Beaune-la-Rolande, Drancy, Le Vernet, Argelès, Rivesaltes, Gurs, Châteaubriant, Noe, Saint-Sulpice, and Recebedou. Guarded by French police, these camps served as transport centers for deportees on their way east to German camps like Auschwitz, Dachau, and Buchenwald, for extermination. Prisoners were told they were simply being transported to Germany to work.

The long, hot days of the summer of 1942 brought heightened terror to the Palais-Royal and to the rest of Europe. Beginning in July, foreign-born Jews all over western Europe, Holland, and Belgium, were arrested and taken to concentration camps. In France, the day it began, July 16, 1942, was called Black Thursday. In Paris, about twenty-seven thousand Jews of foreign nationality were rounded up in a two-day period, taken by bus to the Vélodrome d'Hiver, a cycle-racing track arena in Paris, and later transported to Auschwitz. Arrests were carried out by nine thousand French police, because the Germans shrewdly determined that their victims could be more easily lured by their own kind. The Paris public transport system (Compagnie des Transports en Commun de la Région Parisienne, or TCRP) supplied the buses that conveyed prisoners from the police trucks to the detention camps.

At the time Maurice was detained in December 1941, only adult males were arrested. Black Thursday signified the Reich's grim new policy of total Jewish extermination: more than four thousand children of foreign-born parents were arrested on July 16, along with pregnant women, the elderly, the sick, and the dying.

Colette later remembered hearing the screams of Jewish babies being taken from the Palais-Royal in the middle of the night. Marguerite Duras described in her shocking book *The War* the manner of death for these infants: the French police gave the babies to women who killed them by pressing on their carotid arteries until they died. That summer as the Germans were making big advances in Russia and North Africa, French police teams all over Paris made simultaneous sweeps before daybreak, like nocturnal predators out on the hunt. First they blocked off streets and surrounded city zones to prevent escape. Then they began on the first floor, knocking at doors and shouting "open up," and continued upwards to the top floors. Sometimes, if there was no answer, the police would break down the door. Suicides were common, especially by mothers; people threw themselves out the window at the sound of the knock at the door. The hunted knew that capture meant death, since escape from holding centers set up in schools, police stations, and gymnasiums was nearly impossible.

Colette's friend, Misz Marchand, the Jewish wife of her collaborator on stage adaptations of *Cheri* and *La Vagabond*, committed suicide that July, despondent over the disappearance of her family in Poland and anticipating her own arrest in roundups of foreign-born citizens. Certain that Maurice would be safer out of Paris, Colette pondered what to do. Like her heroines, she was ready-made for this kind of critical problem solving. "Let him do the sleeping; it's for me to do the thinking. I'll contrive our flight with perfect tact and discretion," Colette had written nearly twenty years earlier, describing Lea's plans to hide her affair with Cheri in the south of France. Now, after giving the matter considerable thought, Colette decided to send Maurice into the Free Zone, to Saint-Tropez, where he stayed with old neighbors from their La Treille Muscate days.

Colette and Maurice wrote to each other every day of the three months he was away. The separation was not excruciating the way it was when he was imprisoned in Compiegne, but over time the loneliness took its toll on her. "Physically and morally I am without oxygen . . . so many days are passing and I feel so old," she wrote to a friend on November 6.[67] The memory of Maurice's abduction continued to haunt her. Since the moment the Gestapo came to their door and for years after, the ringing of the doorbell so unnerved her that it prompted an involuntary twitch. The sound of boots and strangers' voices filled her with terror. "I'm too old to get over it," she would write three years later.[68]

Eventually, Colette and Maurice realized that Jews weren't safe in the Free Zone, either. Germans occupied most of southern France, and on November 11, 1942, the Allies under General Dwight Eisenhower's command landed on French North

Africa, across the Mediterranean from Saint Tropez. Pétain had agreed to turn over Jews from the Free Zone, and roundups were being planned. Commissioners of police all over southern France agreed to comply, the head of police in the Nice region going so far as to say that "he would be grateful for the removal of all Jews from his area."[69] Camps were set up throughout the south of France to handle the prisoners, who were transported by freight trains bearing the Third Reich's transport motto: "Our wheels are rolling to Victory." Freight cars were used since all available passenger trains were transporting soldiers to the Russian Front.

Maurice felt that he was in grave danger and left Saint Tropez November 11, 1942, the very day the Allies landed on North Africa. Back in Paris after a harrowing journey that included his feigning to be a passing peasant's country lawyer, the only way Maurice could avoid a roundup was to be in hiding when the police came knocking. His was no easy task, but the hunted received a measure of help from resistance fighters who printed fliers which members slipped under front doors warning of impending roundups, and a friend on the inside could also put one on alert. But as a Jew, Maurice was always at risk, and he spent the remainder of the war hiding each night in a small room under the roof of their building. Maurice later described his hiding place as "hardly more than a garret lit by a narrow fanlight."[70] He made Colette promise never to watch the bombings from the window while he was in hiding.

By this time, many Palais-Royal residents had fled to the countryside or had been abducted in roundups, but the remainder of their tight-knit community banded together and staunchly defended itself. Black marketeers provided sustenance; neighbors shared keys to hiding places and information that might save a life, such as on how to climb down a knotted rope. At the nearby Comédie-Française, actors turned the classical theater into a hospital, used vintage costumes for nursing gowns, and protected themselves with a stash of guns—antique props—which they hid in the boiler room.

Each night at midnight Maurice left the apartment for the attic and each morning about nine he returned when passage seemed safest. Yet, no matter how careful he and Colette were, they knew that Maurice was never really safe. Trains carrying prisoners east were slow and inefficient, and the Germans insisted that cars be full beyond capacity to speed the extermination process. To that end, they listed goals for numbers of prisoners to be taken in a given roundup, and the French took great pains to observe them. The police often made several return visits to the same address in one day, reluctant to let anyone slip away from them.

Despite the many burdens of war during the summer of 1942, it was while Maurice was in Saint Tropez that Colette began working on the novella which would become *Gigi*, a lighthearted, optimistic novella about a teen-age girl who falls in love with an older, sophisticated gentleman. She wrote it quickly, and it was serialized beginning in October in the magazine *Présent*, a weekly, which like many during the war had moved out of Paris to Lyons at a time when the French thought it would remain part of the unoccupied zone.

Gaston Lachaille, handsome heir to a sugar fortune, is reeling from a very public jilting by his unfaithful mistress when he realizes his love for the fifteen-year-old Gigi, a vivacious innocent of scant means, who is a longtime family friend. Her Grandmama Alvarez and rigid Aunt Alicia are grooming Gigi to marry a man like

Gaston, drumming into her her family obligation: "we sink or swim together." Nevertheless, Gigi is a reluctant student. She balks at society's expectations for young girls, preferring gifts of a music case and licorice to silk stockings and jewels, and card-playing to waltzing at tea time. Gigi sees Gaston's sudden romantic interest in her as the ruin of their cherished friendship, and it is only when he convinces her that his love is genuine and pure that Gigi agrees to marry him.

In many ways, *Gigi* was the same story Colette had written dozens of times, set against the same background of music hall performers, professional mistresses, and intensely proud women of faded elegance, whose lives are steeped in worry over money and nostalgia for past lovers. With *Gigi*, though, Colette *had* written something new. The love between Gaston and Gigi is pure, devoid of ulterior motives like sex or money. The book is infused with Gigi's vitality and idealism, and the ending is storybook perfect. Since happy endings were absurdly implausible, with France occupied by the Nazis and Colette burdened by the constant fear that Maurice would be killed, Colette removed her story from the dark present and placed it in the year 1899, a time when Paris was not a vanquished city of death and terror, but a magic world of coy smiles, lace corsets, high hats, and Mistinguett.[71]

Manufacture of the great French automobile, the Renault, began in 1899, the year Gigi took Gaston Lachaille's "four-seater de-Dion-Bouton-with-the-collapsible-hood" for a gleeful spin. In 1942 in real-life Paris, huge Renaults and Citroens used for ferrying prisoners at daybreak to the next stage on their way to death camps were among the few cars left on Paris's streets. These automotive symbols of French industrial might were commandeered by the Nazis for prison deportee movements when convoys of TCRP buses and police vehicles proved insufficient to carry prisoners.

The Paris that Colette recreated in *Gigi* harkened back to a time when wealthy bachelors in top hats and with walking sticks strolled carelessly along the Champs-Élysées at all hours of the night, and beautiful women wearing "eau-de-nil Persephone corset[s], with rococo roses embroidered on the garter[s]" paraded as though up for sale. It was a frivolous time when people seemed not to want to go home. Now, a Nazi-imposed eleven P.M. curfew cleared Paris's streets for death squads of soldiers wearing heavy wool uniforms and tall, shining boots not for dancing, but breaking bones. In neighborhoods at night, the worry in 1942 was not over the scandal of "dipped pearls" or adultery discovered and reported in the tabloid newspapers as it was in Gigi's day, but of being caught in a roundup or by the stray bullet of a rooftop sniper. And now, the juicy tabloids were dormant, and newspapers carried stories of people being burned alive.

Like Gaston Lachaille, Maurice Godaket strolled the Champs-Élysées during the war, but out of boredom and curiosity. Strolling was one of the few activities left for Jews. Parks, swimming pools, sports stadiums, gymnasiums, museums, libraries, theaters, and cinemas were all barred to Jews, as were cafés and restaurants. With little to do, Maurice had plenty of free time, though once his strolling nearly cost him his life.

The Allies had landed in Normandy in June of 1944 and as fighting raged that summer in the countryside, Parisians expected liberation any moment. Germans had begun fleeing Paris, and the French police had begun retaliating against those remaining. On August 24, Maurice's curiosity led him outside to see what was happening, and in front of the Place de la Concorde, he got caught in machine-gun fire during a confrontation between German occupying forces and French police. For two nights he was trapped in a ditch in the Tuileries Gardens near his home. He shared his safe haven with a gardener who "snored like a trumpeter," and supplied them with tomatoes to eat during the ordeal.[72] On the third day, Maurice was finally able to escape when the Swedish Embassy arranged a cease-fire. When he returned, cold and starving, Colette was so angry that he had put himself in danger that she received him with a "volley of abuse."[73]

In the meantime, Colette was fortunate that friends like Renée Harmon were supplementing the couple's meager rations with potatoes, garlic, onions, fruits, and vegetables shipped in crates from the countryside. Shopping became impossible for the crippled Colette, and Jews were only allowed to shop between three and four in the afternoon, when most stores were closed. "[W]hat a treasure trove you have sent me," a delighted Colette wrote on one occasion, thanking her friend, whom she nicknamed "pirate." "And the reddish-brown onions! And the princely apples. You are a love of a little pirate—and to cap it all, the herbs!"[74]

Colette savored good food—"pessimists have good appetites," she explained in *Gigi*—and food played an important element in that work, as in all her fiction. Detailed descriptions offered subtle indications of the inextricable states of love and finances. In crucial times of love-induced nervous excitement, rivers of coffee wash down meals consisting of dozens of cigarettes. When the catastrophe momentarily passed, thoughts again turned to food. "For a woman, attention to the lower parts is the first law of self-respect," Gigi's grandmother declares. But there was something especially poignant in 1942 about the wealthy Gaston eating a fillet of sole with mussels, a saddle of lamb with truffles, and chocolate cream at one of Paris's best restaurants, as Gigi and her grandmother eat leftover French peasant fare. At the time *Gigi* appeared, French restaurants reserved the best cuisine for the Nazi occupiers, while a ration card would buy a French citizen half a pound of noodles and half a pound of vegetables for a week.

When Colette wrote *Gigi*, the days of the Belle Époque's "women worship" were long gone. Colette had been among those writers who celebrated and mythified prostitutes as smart, gay, beautiful women who wore expensive clothes and prepared eligible bachelors for marriage. When she sat down to write *Gigi*, Colette drew a thick, rose-colored blind over wartime reality, called her prostitutes "great professional women," and described creamy complexions and sinewy bodies when she well knew otherwise.[75] Before the war Colette used to speak to a self-confident young prostitute by the gate of the garden of the Palais-Royal. Then Renée disappeared in 1942. She was not pretty, but she was "exceptionally healthy looking," according to Colette, with particularly attractive legs. One day in 1943, Renée suddenly reappeared. Her fingers were gnarled, and she walked with a painful limp. She told Colette how she had been taken to Germany for slave labor, made to carry burning hot pots with bare hands, and later imprisoned. After that day, Colette never saw the woman again.

Gigi presented an innocent world of girlish modesty and playful sexual games, readying a guileless virgin for a suitable man. Colette was twenty-seven in 1899, newly married, living in Paris, and already miserable. Setting *Gigi* in 1899 was a way of reinventing her own entry into womanhood and marriage, while obliterating the pain of the present. For, like the young Gigi, Colette had found the perfect mate, but Maurice was nothing like the wealthy, gregarious womanizer Gaston. The Great Depression had reduced Maurice to selling washing machines, and the war had made him a frightened nomad. In 1942 only a Gaston Lachaille with the word "Aryan" stamped on his I.D. card could expect a happy ending.

On January 28, 1943, Gabrielle Sidonie Colette turned seventy. "I feel terribly old," Colette wrote later that summer. "Is it because I have not left Paris in the past four years, or because I have passed the seventy-year mark?"[76] She was at work on another story, "Le Kepi," which became the title story for a collection published that year, and was not among Colette's better works.

"Le Kepi" dramatized the complete transformation of a poverty-stricken, middle-aged woman, a writer-for-hire, by sudden wealth and a love affair with a young army lieutenant. "Voracious, unhoped for love" changes a spare, hard-working bohemian into a fat, lazy bourgeoise. But she finds herself loveless once again, after she makes the fatal mistake of innocently mocking her soldier with a little ditty and a taunting gesture. She loses him and stops eating from grief. Her slender figure returns, but even better, her writing fee is doubled from "one sous a line" to two. The story shares *Gigi*'s flight into optimistic fantasy, but in "Le Kepi" the flight seems jaded, even perverse. A sense of insecurity and unhappiness suffuses the story.

That summer of 1943 Colette was afflicted with intestinal parasitic poisoning which persisted through autumn. For ten weeks, she was unable to leave the house. Her dear friend Renée Hamon, who had suffered greatly from uterine cancer, finally died on October 16, 1943, at the age of forty-four. It was a severe blow to Colette. "If I become mute and savage when I am not happy, it is because I find my strength in silence and unsociability," she wrote two weeks later.[77]

In the spring of 1944, rumors abounded that the Allies were planning an all-out invasion for the middle to latter part of June. When the Normandy invasion did finally take place on June 6, Paris was cut off from a major source of food supplies, and shortages became worse than at any other time in the war. What food there was could only be obtained at exorbitant prices. Paris was struck every few hours by intensified air bombardments. There was no hot water, and electricity was cut off for hours at a time. Bombardments were so close and powerful that they jostled Colette's apartment, where she remained with her faithful servant Pauline rather than join others in the shelters.

As Paris reeled from the effects of the Normandy invasion, Colette was writing her memoir of occupation and, soon, liberation, *Evening Star* (*L'Etoile Vesper*). She had written a shelf of memoirs; it seemed as though Colette remembered every moment of her life—loves and losses, of both humans and animals, the dresses she had worn on specific occasions, the food she had eaten, the homes she had lived in, and all the grand emotions she had experienced in between. Colette had a staggering memory and facility to describe, and what always came through the detail was her humor, her tendency towards deadly truth, her fierce loyalty to friends, her unapologetic emotionalism, and her strength. When Colette wrote *Evening Star*, memory was not merely a tensile instrument of an adventurous woman's pleasure and financial need, as it had been many times in the past. It was an absolute necessity, because she could no longer carry the burden of silence and optimism in the face of terror. *Evening Star* reads like the life preserver it was.

Colette herself explained that she wrote the memoir in an effort to reconcile the years of fear that Maurice would be killed with the joy of life itself, a life which, though difficult, she savored and sadly felt ebbing. More than anything, the book was an act of defiance, a way of staving off death and the clouding of a vibrant, uncompromising memory on which she had relied for strength and creativity. Defiance worked; Colette finished *Evening Star* in the summer of 1945 after the war ended, and she lived nearly another ten years.

She would work for a few hours, then pain might overtake her and she would stare out her window or look through her possessions and fall into a reverie of remembrance. Sometimes she spent whole nights when pain kept her awake and Maurice was in hiding just trying to remember some dim sliver of the past, but then abruptly the sounds and smells would fade, or a distant voice would be silenced in what she surmised was the approach of death. She pondered: "A life slips by, work finishes and begins anew, an estate is mortgaged, crumbles to dust—a war, a love-affair, are born, come to nothing, another war—what's that, another war? Yes, one more. So I ask you, where is one to take one's stand, to find security?"[78]

After work or when her memory failed, when the pain was less great, she fixed her "fringe" of hair, applied makeup, and welcomed an array of guests, mostly writers and artists who had braved airplane attacks in ditches on the way to her house. Occasionally, she was visited by young awestruck journalists intent on eliciting her philosophy on life and work. Colette suppressed her mild contempt for their ambition and ignorance, laughed behind a well-rehearsed mask, and gave answers that she knew would play better in an article than the truth. Work had been a habit, an obsession, a way to protect herself from the "dangers of idleness," and a way of "winning people over." There was nothing philisophical or ideological about it. She boasted far more affinity with a couple of young black marke-teers who, like herself, lived on the edge and flouted danger. Their youth and energy were bittersweet reminders of her old age and infirmity, which sometimes sent her into a tirade as she dreamed of places she could go and activities she could perform, if she weren't crippled. Lying in bed, gazing at the sky as it rained bombs down on the black marketeers rushing to sell their pirated goods, Colette did not begrudge them the astronomical prices of eggs or rabbit which took into account "the water in the ditch . . . the burst tyre, the peril that throbbed in the air."[79] Colette saw herself in the black marketeers, a thrashing swimmer in a swirling eddy, doing what one needed to do to survive. As she looked back upon her long and tumultuous life, Colette recalled those days when as a young jour-nalist during the First World War she saw how men engaged in a "duel of female versus male" to achieve superiority. She realized that men misunderstood a woman's inherent power because it was neither political nor territorial. The fem-inine zeal to prevail, Colette concluded, was a desire for something more basic— "The will to survive, . . . and the lust for physical victory."[80] This ferocious lust far exceeded any ambition of men, including warmongering, which men pursued, she noted, despite being war's "cruel and arbitrary victim."

In April 1945, the Russians were on the outskirts of Berlin, and there were inaccurate reports of Hitler's suicide days before he actually killed himself on April 30. After five years of occupation, restaurants in Paris were full of people counting the days until the war ended and yearning to have something to celebrate. Still, the imminence of Allied victory also brought a withering sense of nervous expectation, and as the war entered its waning weeks in the early spring of 1945, Colette continued to feel its "arbitrary" cruelty.

For Jews and their families and friends waiting for word on the Allied liberation of concentration camps, emotions were a complex mixture of hope and fearful expectation.[81] As the Germans fled, they were killing prisoners *en masse*, and French newspapers were showing the gruesome photographs of the liberated camps at Dachau and Buchenwald, where Colette's daughter had friends among the prisoners. It was a bizarre sight when the released prisoners, drained of life, and crippled by beating and starvation, were met at Paris's train stations by an exuberant band playing the "Marseillaise" or "It's a road that goes on and on and never ends." More than 140,000 prisoners of war were repatriated by the spring of 1945, and in front of a café in the Palais-Royal, Colette saw women whose legs bore the savage scars of mauling by Nazi prison camp dogs.

Amidst this winding-down of monumental human disaster, another of Colette's closest friends, ravaged by age and confinement, committed suicide. The Marquise de Belboeuf, nicknamed "Missy," was the niece of Napoleon III, the daughter and ex-wife of dukes. Abundant in size, thin-lipped, and given to wearing men's clothing, Missy had been seeking excitement in the déclassé musical hall theater when she and Colette met in 1906. The two shared an intensive, lifelong friendship and fended off accusations that they were lesbian lovers for years after Missy, dressed as a man, kissed Colette on stage in their opening night performance of "Egyptian Dream" at the Moulin Rouge in 1907. During that far more innocent time, before World War I left ten million dead, and World War II left fifty-five million dead, the incident caused a scandal in Paris, and the piece was removed from the show after one performance. As she had grieved the loss of other friends who had died since the war began, Colette mourned Missy's passing, which left a huge void. Throughout her life, she had leaned heavily on friends for companionship and support, especially through divorce and illness, but recent deaths were also an intimation of her own.

On May 7, 1945, the Nazis officially surrendered in a school in Reims, France, where throughout the war escapees of the Nazis hid in twelve miles of damp, underground tunnels alongside bottles of aging Mumm champagne. France's cities and farms lay in ruins. Her population, like the rest of Europe, was decimated, including most of her Jews.

Hitler's Final Solution was a terrifying bookend to a life guided by dread, but always ruled by indomitability. By war's end, Colette had written dozens of magazine articles, short stories, memoirs, essays, and radio broadcasts. The seventy-two-year-old writer, barely slowed by physical suffering and agonizing terror, had also completed the full-length novel *Julie de Carneilhan* and the novella which brought her international fame, *Gigi*. "Agitated or not, I have had to work," she explained before Liberation.[82]

In the years after World War II, Colette became deaf and the arthritis spread throughout her body, eventually crippling her hands so that she could barely grip a pencil. Yet, she wrote nearly to the end, scribbling in her notebook shortly before her eightieth birthday, "Do I have a skill for suffering?"[83] Accolades accumulated, it seemed, by the month, beginning with her election to the prestigious Académie Goncourt on May 2, 1945—the second woman to be elected among a group of ten male novelists. (She received the chair of a member who was expelled as an alleged Nazi collaborator.) Her fame grew worldwide, especially when the musical version of *Gigi* opened on Broadway in 1953, followed by the film version in 1958, starring Leslie Caron and Colette's former admirer, Maurice Chevalier.[84]

In the weeks before her death, Colette was on an invalid's diet that included milk diluted with water, but on the day before she died in her sleep on August 3, 1954, she drank champagne.

Ernest Hemingway

WAR AS AN APHRODISIAC

Cowardice, as distinguished
from panic, is almost always
simply a lack of ability to
suspend the functioning of the
imagination. Learning to suspend
your imagination and live completely
in the very second of the present minute
with no before and no after is the greatest gift a soldier can acquire.
It, naturally, is the opposite of all those gifts a writer should have.

Men at War, 1942

In 1936, Ernest Hemingway was heading into one of the roughly ten-year, tor-nado-like spirals in which his life seemed to swirl. At once vicious and rap-turous, these spirals sucked in wives, children, friends, and work, before the protean Hemingway saved himself by spinning off in a new direction.

From the first moment Hemingway became widely recognized as a significant literary figure with the publication of his second novel in 1929, *A Farewell to Arms*, he had grown increasingly disgusted by the "business" of writing—chasing a sale to drum up a dollar, pleasing an editor, standing up to critics offended by his absorption in death and muscle-man escapades like boxing, hunting, and bull-fighting, and fending off personal attacks from former confidants like Gertrude Stein, who had once been so close to him that Hemingway had named her god-mother to his first child. By 1933 the closeness with writers such as Stein and Sherwood Anderson was a thing of the past. In Stein's memoir that year, *The Autobiography of Alice B. Toklas*, she called him "yellow . . . just like the flat-boat men on the Mississippi river as described by Mark Twain," and took credit, along with Anderson, for "making him."[1]

None of this, however, rankled and embittered Hemingway as much as the politicization of writers and editors in the tumultuous 1930s. Hemingway despised those who he believed had adopted the political, patriotic cloak as an expedient to popularity and self-importance, and he vehemently believed that both he and his recent books, *Death in the Afternoon* (1932), *Winner Take Nothing* (1934), and *Green Hills of Africa* (1935), which he deemed his best writing to date, were all victims of an anti-art mood cultivated by literary types on both sides of the political spectrum. He was particularly infuriated by the American reviewer Edmund Wilson. When Wilson wrote in the December 1935 issue of *The New Republic* a scathing attack on Hemingway's popularity among Russian readers, referring to Hemingway's recent *Esquire* magazine pieces as "rubbishy," Hemingway charged that people like Wilson were trying to kill his career because they refused to separate good writing from their own political agenda.

"I would like to take the tommy gun and open up at 21 or in the N.R. (*New Republic*) offices or any place you name and give shitdom a few martyrs," Hemingway ranted to his close friend, leftist novelist John Dos Passos.[2] When Dos Passos sent the infamous Wilson article to Hemingway at his home in Key West, Florida, so he could read it himself, a seething Hemingway only felt more certain that the New York critics refused to judge art solely on artistic merits as they should, and only "like you or your writing for what you or it are."[3]

But the real problem for Hemingway at this time was hardly the critics' desire to peg him this way or that in a political popularity contest in which he was sure to fail. Hemingway had traveled to Africa on safari in late 1933 and returned three months later to prosaic homelife, with the "smell of death" in his nostrils and a longing for physical indomitability and pure, carefree adventure in the wide open, where he felt "animally happy"—a state almost equal to the ecstasy he felt when he was writing well.[4] Hemingway did not for a moment doubt his will or talent to write, but the combination of critics' fire, dampened sales, money worries, and personal attacks—more accurately described as retaliations by old allies for Hemingway's sadistic meanness against them—hit harder than they might otherwise, because they came at a time when Hemingway himself was barely sure who he was or was not.

Hemingway's contradictions defined him as they tore at him. He was a drunk who hated "rummies," an inveterate liar who demanded truth from others—especially in writing—and a man who needed to fill the strict role of responsible family man, providing for his "dependents," as he called his family, yet who felt suffocated by too much domesticity. He was not a communist, but he deeply mistrusted the American government, which he equated with a "Big-Brother" Internal Revenue Service, money-corruption, and arrogance. As the Midwestern son of a Bible-toting mother who castigated his lavish spending, "loafing and pleasure seeking and . . . neglecting God and your savior," and an equally God-fearing physician-father who lectured his son on sexually transmitted diseases, cigarettes, and the righteous might of "the Great Creator," Hemingway despised the drunken rich.[5] Yet, as an expatriate American, he hobnobbed with them at the horse races in Auteuil, at the bullfights in Pamplona, on the ski slopes of Schruns, in Paris cafés, and on the Riviera. He married one of them in 1927 after leaving his first wife, Hadley, whom he still deeply loved, in a sad breakup that marked a significant loss of innocence for the writer, an eternal scar of how hurtful he could be to someone he deeply loved.

With his new wife, Pauline Pfeiffer, a Southerner of gale-force will who stole her best friend's husband, Hemingway left Paris; moved to Key West, Florida, which was as far from Main Street, U.S.A, as the Champs-Élysées had been, and in a grand house bought by Pauline's uncle, a cosmetics magnate and land baron; began a cockeyed marriage in which he worried about selling a story for $500 to stay out of debt at the same time the couple's *bon-vivant* lifestyle, which included two maids, a child-nurse, a gardener, and a yard man, was subsidized by gifts of stocks and bonds from his wealthy father-in-law. Hemingway constantly tried to keep pace with his debts while feeling superstitious that writers who made too much money, like his friend F. Scott Fitzgerald, ruined themselves and their talent. It was a marriage which produced two sons, appeared happy on the surface, and by 1936 threatened to swallow him altogether. With the great success of his novel about World War I, *A Farewell to Arms*, seven years in the past, Hemingway felt disillusioned and defeated, professionally and financially.

That year Hemingway finished two of his greatest stories, "The Short Happy Life of Francis Macomber" and "The Snows of Kilimanjaro," as well as his novel *To Have and Have Not*. Into them he poured his sense of defeat and self-pity, guilt over lying, contempt for the wanton rich, and mistrust of the American government. Quintessential works of Hemingway, the two stories ache for their dishonest slobs who face death consumed by fear and cowardice and beseiged by the torment they have lived a lie, either in their work or with their women. In "The Snows of Kilimanjaro," a dying writer recognizes that lying has become a way of life—the very substance of his marriage to his rich, bored wife, and the foundation for his writing. *To Have and Have Not*, a story about an unlucky fisherman who runs contraband between Key West and Cuba, would have been simply a Grade B "shoot 'em up," were it not for the richness of Hemingway's psychology, enfolded in the leanest prose, propounding the idea that suicide may be the best way out of defeat, humiliation, and guilt. Any method would do to put an end to one's misery, but Hemingway singled out the "native tradition of the Colt or Smith and Wesson" as best "designed to end the American dream when it becomes a nightmare, their only drawback the mess they leave for relatives to clean up."[6]

Suicide and a Smith and Wesson had been irrevocably linked in Hemingway's subconscious since he was six, when, from across a foul sickroom, Ernest witnessed the horror of his grandfather Anson's misery and helplessness. He witnessed as well his father's unforgiving, consummate power, as Ed Hemingway prevented the aged Anson from taking his old Civil War gun and killing himself to put an end to his suffering. It was a moment that etched itself in Ernest Hemingway's being as the tragic duel between the selfish living and the dignified dying, in which the latter become victims of the former's ruthless will. Hemingway began to believe that death was to be welcomed, even if it were feared, and that to help end the suffering of another was a generous act of sympathy and brotherhood. Hemingway's fiction is replete with characters like Harry Morgan of *To Have and Have Not*, who kill out of love, respect, or responsibility toward others. Hemingway believed that his father had denied his grandfather an inalienable human right to peace and freedom from pain, and he never forgave him. When Ed Hemingway shot himself on December 6, 1928, to escape debt and illness when his son was twenty-nine and on the very brink of fame, Ernest not only found a bond with his taskmaster father who had taught him, as his father had before him, to be deft with a hunter's shotgun, but also felt a sense of shame at his father's cowardice and submissiveness to a hysterical and domineering wife. Most profoundly, Hemingway came away with the fear that he, too, would some-day kill himself.

In 1925, before the fear, Hemingway was a young, hopeful writer at work on his first novel, *The Sun Also Rises*, and still fresh enough from World War I ser-vice as a Red Cross ambulance driver in Italy to praise the literary usefulness of war to F. Scott Fitzgerald, who rued missing it. War, the twenty-six-year-old Hemingway instructed like a seasoned veteran of the writing game, was "the best subject of all" to write about, better than love or money. "It groups the maximum of material and speeds up the action and brings out all sorts of stuff that normally you have to wait a lifetime to get."[7] A decade of life and disappointment later, it was to be war in the flesh and machine-gun rat-tat-tat, where each moment of bat-tle was a canvas of pain and suffering, and where a man faced death as a hero or as a "chicken-shit," that Ernest Hemingway was to see the purest test of one's humanity and courage. Suicide would ever loom as the permanent escape from defeat, but it was to be in war, brutal and terrible, where Ernest Hemingway felt the deepest repose from his relentless sense of fear and loneliness, and where he felt most at home.

The Spanish Civil War was eight months old when Ernest Hemingway arrived in Spain in March 1937 to collaborate with renowned Dutch filmmaker Joris Ivens on the film *Spanish Earth*. Commissioned to make the film by his longtime friend Archibald MacLeish, the three were members of Contemporary Historians, a group of leftist writers whose purpose was to promote and raise money for the Loyalist cause. Proceeds from the film were to be used to buy ambulances.[8]

When it came to Spain, Hemingway put aside his disillusionment with political causes and their trumpet-bearers. Whereas the conflict was undoubtedly a fight between political sides, Hemingway focused on the monumental human suffering engulfing a beautiful, rugged land that he had called "the best country in Europe" in 1923, after he began trout fishing in Galicia and making annual summer pil-grimages to watch the bullfights in Pamplona.[9] Throughout the 1920s Hemingway had closely observed Spain's plight as it began to be fought over by leftist antimonarchist revolutionaries and promonarchist fascists backed by the Catholic church and rich landowners. In 1931, Spain's King Alfonso XIII was forced to flee, and the country became a republic, but with Hitler and Mussolini entering a cagey complicity after Hitler's election as chancellor of Germany in 1933, Spain became the object of their fascist ambitions. A mere nine months after Hitler's election, Hemingway predicted that the dictator was aiming for war,[10] and in a piece he wrote for *Esquire* in July 1935 called "Notes on the Next War: A Serious Letter," he set 1937 or 1938 as the likely time for a second world war, which, he contended, "is now being prepared and brought closer each day with all the premeditation of a long-planned murder."[11] Though Hemingway harbored no love for the "Reds," who backed the Republican side against the Franco-led fascist rebels, he despised fascism with a boiling ferocity. "There is only one form of government that cannot produce good writers, and that system is fascism," he wrote in 1937. "For fascism is a lie told by bullies. A writer who will not lie cannot live and work under fascism."[12] Hemingway was certain that a fascist victory in Spain would guarantee that "Hitler and Mussolini can come in and take the minerals they need to make a European war."[13]

Hemingway headed for Spain filled with vigor and hope, certain the anti-Franco Republicans would win, confident the world would agree with the righteousness of their cause and see the imperative of quashing fascism in Europe. When he arrived to film with Ivens behind Loyalist lines, at times in the direct line of fire, Hemingway was fiercely protective of and paternalistic toward the country and her Republican fighters. With Ivens shooting the footage and Hemingway writing an overlay script which he would narrate in the final product, the men recorded some of the most stirring images of war ever put on film: panic-stricken villagers after a bomb explodes, women running for safety in a train station, new refugees sobbing at the destruction of their home, and pitiful-looking bands of men going off to fight, crossing the very same fields they had cultivated before the war began.

After his work on *Spanish Earth* was completed, Hemingway made four trips to Spain between March 1937 and May 1938, covering the war for the North American Newspaper Alliance (NANA). Though his intention had been to go to Spain to write "antiwar" pieces, to convince the United States to stay out of an inevitable and imminent second world war, after returning to New York on May 18, 1937, Hemingway delivered his only political speech, an impassioned address, to the Second American Writers' Congress meeting at Carnegie Hall, in which he called the Spanish cause "the mission of the writer in our time."[14] He demanded direct military intervention by the United States and France on the Republican side.

Hemingway emphatically believed the fascists would not attack elsewhere until they won in Spain; therefore he viewed Spain as the singular test of the West's commitment to defeat fascism. Because of his stature as a novelist, his well-known sympathies, and the fact that *A Farewell to Arms*, his World War I novel, was a favorite book of Soviet Army General Paul Lucasz, commander of the Twelfth International Brigade to which Hemingway primarily attached himself in Spain, Hemingway was granted special access to high officers of the Soviet and European communist-backed military.[15] His bravery was legitimate: he was almost killed several times getting a close look at battle, especially when he and three other journalists were surveying the Brunete front, and their car was mistaken for an enemy staff car. Yet, in hotel corridors and bars after a day's work, Hemingway passed himself off as much more than a high-paid celebrity journalist thrown the choicest morsels of the war. Hemingway purported to have fought alongside the Loyalists and to have conducted intelligence work for the Republicans. He claimed to have murdered a truck driver while helping to transport art from the Prado Museum for safekeeping in Switzerland. One incredible boast he made to fellow correspondents was that he had the power to obtain an

American warship to rescue American brigade members about to be captured. And he claimed to have been made a liaison between the British and Republican generals before they surrendered to Franco in the spring of 1939.[16]

Most of Hemingway's claims of action were disputed by fellow journalists and members of the International Brigade, the voluntary bands of fighters from Europe and America. Allowing that his special status did not endear him with his fellow journalists who were jealous of his stature and connections and saw him as a ridiculous poser, Hemingway's claims to action were still laughably absurd for a journalist covering a war. His boast about being a liaison between British and Republican generals was patently impossible—Hemingway was already back in Key West at the time he purported to be in Spain.

Whether Hemingway taught Spanish youths how to use a gun or took part in the murder of suspected fascists at a garbage dump, or whether he just play-acted the part of soldier, quick with a tall story to prop his ego, is uncertain. What is clear, however, is that with his binoculars, compass, and custom-designed canteens that held a quart of whiskey each, Hemingway acted the part of a non-commissioned officer. He studied battles afterward, going over them with officers, as though "he even thought of himself as a tactician, and sometimes even a strategist," noted one observer who was with him in Spain.[17] No wonder that among newspapermen, Hemingway was sarcastically called "the best-equipped soldier in Spain."[18]

For the most part, Hemingway was untroubled by his colleagues' mockery, although the affronts sometimes erupted into fistfights, especially after drinking. He was accustomed to "jealous" critics, "who really seem to hate me very much, and would like to put me out of business," and in Spain, Hemingway was in his glory.[19] He was highly paid for his NANA assignments, finished *To Have and Have Not*, which became a national best-seller when Scribner's published it in October 1937—the same month he was featured in a *Time* magazine cover story—and a new novel about the war in Spain took root.[20] His film, *Spanish Earth*, which appeared in September 1937, was hailed as a masterpiece, despite heavy government censorship of "horror" shots and references to German and Italian intervention. Reviewing the film for London's *World Film News* in December 1937, Basil Wright wrote, "those who complain that Hemingway's work is falling off had better prepare to eat their hats, for he has written the best commentary in the history of sound film."[21] In all, the comaraderie, the danger, the inspiration, and the creative burst prompted Hemingway later to call that "period of struggle, when we thought the Republic would win, . . . the happiest of our lives."[22]

Beyond the danger and the glory and the knowledge he was taking part in an important cause, Hemingway derived more intimate satisfactions which accounted for his divine happiness. Hemingway's ten-year marriage to Pauline Pfeiffer was essentially over when he left Key West, Florida, and headed for Spain in 1937, although Pfeiffer did not know it at the time. Her family wealth had finally made him feel resentful and out of place, recognizing that "my sympathies are always for the exploited working people against absentee landlords," as he had brashly confided to a writer-friend, "even if I drink around with the landlords and shoot pigeons with them. I would as soon shoot them as the pigeons."[23]

Hemingway's resentment of the rich had its roots in his mother's stubborn insistence that the family move from a modest home they shared with her father into a three-story home with a thirty-foot music room big enough to accommodate her new Steinway. The move wrought chaos and tragedy. Financial pressure, coupled with weariness of battling a wife of iron determination who aspired to grandeur beyond her husband's means, had driven Hemingway's father to kill himself with Anson Hemingway's Smith and Wesson .32 revolver. Thus, when Hemingway left for Spain eager to be rid of a wife whom he feared would ruin him with her money, it was no less an escape than World War I had been from the stranglehold of his parents' domination. Just as that war had provided the kind of sexual freedom he craved at nineteen, the marriage-weary, thirty-eight-year-old writer renewed his manhood amidst the dust and rubble of Spain's Civil War.

Hemingway was ready and willing to be drawn to the striking, blond-haired, blue-eyed, and opinionated twenty-eight-year-old Martha Gellhorn when he met her in December 1936 in Key West, where she and her family were on vacation from St. Louis.[24] Gellhorn had already published a novel and several short stories, and her attraction to the celebrity writer was equally spontaneous, although accounts of their early relationship paint Gellhorn as a kind of literary groupie. Soon after they met, Gellhorn obtained an assignment to cover the war for *Collier's* magazine, and in Spain, as well as during hiatuses in Paris and New York, they carried on a passionate and open love affair.

For a dynamic man who had grown up in suburban Oak Park, Illinois, in a buttoned-down, religious, Protestant home, where liquor was forbidden, sex was said to be dirty and to cause horrible, disfiguring diseases, and Hemingway, like his fictional characters, felt forced to lie and conceal, the freedom he found in Spain during war was an emotional and sexual bonanza. He was only too glad to be out of the house he shared with Pauline, who let her boyishly short hair grow long in a pitiful attempt to compete with Martha, about whom she learned more than she probably wanted to know. After returning to Key West from his final trip to Spain in late January 1939, where he saw the last vestiges of the defeated International Brigades before their evacuation, Hemingway remained in Key West only intermittently during the next year, fleeing at first to a fifth-floor corner room in the Hotel Ambos Mundos in Old Havana, Cuba, and later, to a hilltop hacienda that Martha found for them to rent. Nine blocks from his favorite bar, the Floridita, the Hotel Ambos overlooked the sea and the harbor, and was a place whose tranquility Hemingway had discovered in 1932, when he began using Cuba as the base of his Gulf Stream fishing expeditions. Though he complained of going broke writing the novel, in this hotel-room sanctuary with no telephone, Hemingway and his new paramour, Martha or "Marty," as he called her, were blissfully enfolded together like Robert Jordan and Maria under their blanket in the snow, the characters whose rapturous, self-denying wartime love story he was then writing.[25] His writing was going "as good as the best it ever went in my life," and he brimmed with excitement, pride, and the wonder of intense creativity.[26] "[W]orking the way I do now I feel as happy and as good as when I was going good on *A Farewell to Arms*," he wrote to his editor Maxwell Perkins on March 25, 1939.[27]

Hemingway had begun writing *For Whom the Bell Tolls* in October 1938 on his way to Spain for the fourth time, still filled with excitement about the Republican cause, and still believing it would win. The novel told the story of an American Loyalist, Robert Jordan, who has been commanded by a Soviet officer to blow up a bridge behind fascist lines in time for an imminent Republican offensive. But while the book is essentially a portrait of the heroic efforts of an idealistic hero, Jordan's idealism is overshadowed by a thick veil of cynicism and pessimism. He rages at Spain and its crazy, jealous, ambitious military commanders—even at his Spanish guerrilla-fighting comrades—but most of all, at himself, certain that his mission is doomed from the outset, yet driven by the need to win, even if it costs him his life.

Like Jordan's, idealism, Hemingway's faith in the rightness of his position was blunted by the bitter realities of the Spanish Civil War. Once the lofty rhetoric about "good" Stalin-backed Republicans versus "evil" Hitler-backed Franco rebels was put aside, not even the Republicans could be seen to have clean hands. Hemingway had been a firsthand witness to (and perhaps a participant in) a massacre committed by Republicans at a garbage dump, and he depicted in the novel a fervid, cold-blooded massacre of Catholic priests by drunken Republicans who taunt them in an ecstatic haze, before killing them with clubs and sickles and throwing them over a cliff.

For Hemingway, brutal scenes like this were a fact of war. And while his depiction of communists in the novel inspired the wrath of American communist writers like Michael Gold, who charged in the *Daily Worker* that Hemingway's "class egotism" and "poverty of mind" prevented him from grasping the truth about Spain, no atrocities committed by the Republicans or their communist allies enraged him as did the failure of France, America, and especially Britain to come to Spain's aid in fighting Franco.[28] Like other Loyalist sympathizers, Hemingway did not fully anticipate the breadth of Adolf Hitler's military and financial support for Franco, nor did he appreciate just how adamant America and its allies were about remaining neutral. As evidence of Soviet atrocities in Spain mounted, disillusioning and dividing left-leaning intellectuals in Europe and America, Hemingway loyally stuck by the communist leadership in Spain, emphatic that the fascists must be defeated no matter how distasteful the Soviet-backed Republicans were to England, France, and America.[29]

"If you have a war you have to win it," Hemingway told Maxwell Perkins in December 1939, outlining mistakes in Spain to be avoided in the Allies' four-month-old war against Hitler. "If you lose you lose everything and your ideology won't save you."[30] This was Hemingway's pared-down political ideology that blended the teachings of nineteenth-century German war philosopher Carl von Clausewitz with his own tough pragmatism, intolerance for equivocation, and blind hatred for fascism, and it was expressed to perfection through the voice of Mujer, Hemingway's hard-bitten Republican fighter in *For Whom the Bell Tolls*, as she recalls the horrible massacre of priests by her drunken fellow-fighters. The massacre "was the worst day of my life," she says, "until . . . [t]hree days later when the fascists took the town."[31]

In January 1939 Spain finally fell to Franco's rebels after two and a half years of civil war. Two months later Hitler seized Czechoslovakia, and war in Europe broke out in September 1939 almost exactly when Hemingway had predicted a year earlier, reducing the bloody Spanish Civil War almost to a footnote in twentieth-century history.[32] Hemingway's mournful sense of disillusionment was quickly subordinated to his longtime hatred for authority and, hence, politicians, whom he accused of being too blind to see the fascist danger which had been clearly evident. Hemingway bitterly charged that Franco's victory, as well as the larger spreading conflict, was the result of a lack of "decency from democratic countries in acknowledging merely in supplies the fight against fascism or egoism, such as Mussolini's or Hitler's egoism."[33] He lashed out especially at the British, "a degenerate people," he sneered, noting, "They gave us the worst bitching anybody ever did in Spain where we fought both Hitler and Mussolini for them for nothing and could have kept them tied up there indefinitely (exactly as the Peninsular war beat Napoleon) if they had only given any aid at all—any at all."[34] When the British failed to protect Norway's seaports when they came under massive German land and air assault in April 1940, Hemingway devised a term which he believed aptly summed up a decade of British foreign policy: "Coitus Britannicus . . . translates: F—cked from the back with withdrawal."[35]

Hitler's aggression only intensified Hemingway's long-standing conviction that fascism must be eradicated at any cost, but his innocent faith that the West would act morally was gone. The Allies' one-sided perspective on the Spanish Civil War, especially by the rabidly anticommunist British government, as a fight between the "evil" Spanish "communists" and the "humane" Franco left him feeling "betrayed and sold out a dozen different ways."[36] Hemingway himself recognized a loss of innocence: "That sort of lying kills things inside you," he explained, and in the void left behind grew a strict and punishing conviction that wars were made by politicians with an eye only to the ballot box and a blithe disregard for the human life they sacrificed.[37] On June 10, 1940, the day Mussolini declared war on France and England, Hemingway wrote in his yacht's log: "current not as strong as other days—water paler blue—breeze fresh ENE. Today Italy declared war—24 years since last time—still same vile jackal politics."[38]

Four days later, German troops occupied Paris. France fell to the Nazis on June 22, and Britain began bracing for an all-out German invasion. Yet, for Hemingway, in Cuba, the war in Europe was like a dimly playing record. As he wrote the final pages of *For Whom the Bell Tolls*, "the smell of death," cognac, and battle in Spain were strong in his dreams,[39] though the people and country he loved were now almost forgotten by the world in Hitler's blitzkrieg on Europe. Hemingway was experiencing what for him had long been the spectacular symbiosis between a war he knew firsthand, the written word, and his essence as a writer, and the lure was more powerful than anything else he cared about, except a woman. Perhaps the politicians had adulterated the pure contest between men on two sides of an idea, but the Spanish Civil War remained alive in his senses as a separate, cherished world unto itself, fresh and real without taint of "carnival treachery and rotten-ness."[40] Hemingway had called *For Whom the Bell Tolls* "the most important thing I've ever done," and the exhilaration he felt in depicting the shocking and offensive truth about the war as he saw it—lepers, drunks, whores, and all—made the war in Europe seem uninteresting and untantalizing in comparison.[41]

For Whom the Bell Tolls took America by storm when it was published in October 1940. Within a month, demand forced Scribner's to publish an additional

160,000 copies over the 100,000 first printing, and the Book-of-the-Month Club purchased 200,000. Paramount Pictures bought the film rights for $100,000, the highest price ever to that date for a novel.

In the glow of his runaway success, on November 21, 1940, Hemingway wed Martha Gellhorn in Cheyenne, Wyoming. Gellhorn was awaiting leave on assignment in Europe for *Collier's*, and she had already been to the Finnish front to cover the Russian invasion in the winter of 1939–40. In an interview for the *Kansas City Times* five days after their marriage, she declared, "Right now I'm the war correspondent in the family."[42] Like her new husband, Martha had also published a novel in 1940, *A Stricken Field*, which blended firsthand journalistic accounts of fascist oppression with passages describing the couple's actual love affair.[43] Hemingway was still smarting over Pauline—"the rich bitch," as he called her during bitter divorce negotiations—and his separation from their two children, and he professed openly how proud he was to be in love with a strong, fearless, globe-trotting woman who earned her own income. His apparent delight in her career had not prevented him, however, from suggesting before their marriage that her byline be changed to "Martha Hemingway," a suggestion she staunchly refused.[44]

With the rescue of his finances after a long dry spell, and the kind of critical praise he had felt was imperative to turn around his flagging sales and reputation, Hemingway rested by playing hard in Sun Valley, Idaho, doing what he loved best next to writing: fishing, hunting, and horseback riding. Though he did no actual work on it, he decided he wanted to write a "story of the Gulf Stream." This nebulous concept was separate from an idea which had already resulted in his 1936 story "On the Blue Water," about an old fisherman alone on the sea who battles a swordfish for four days and finally gets it alongside his boat only to have it eaten by sharks. Hemingway, who had been fishing in the Gulf Stream since the late 1920s, first off the Florida Keys, and then off Cuba, did not foresee at the time the novella-length *The Old Man and the Sea*, which evolved more than a decade later. (Hemingway's other land-sea-air book was never finished, although it was published posthumously in 1970 under the title *Islands in the Stream*.) In an interview with the *Kansas City Times* in November 1940, Hemingway said he conceived of a factual work which would do for fishing what *Death in the Afternoon* had done for bullfighting.[45]

Hemingway felt confident about the future, but reminders surfaced now and then that he was no longer the young gadabout he had been in Italy during World War I or in Paris in the early 1920s, when tutelage by the expatriate literary icon, Ezra Pound, made him feel he had a boundless literary future. A week after *For Whom the Bell Tolls* appeared in October, F. Scott Fitzgerald died of alcoholism at the age of forty-four, after failing as a hack Hollywood scriptwriter. The two writers had met in Paris in 1925 after the publication of *The Great Gatsby*, and became like brothers. Then came a falling out of operatic proportions, the bitter sniping, the dirty meanness. Although in recent years the two men had achieved a cautious rapprochement, this probably never would have happened had Fitzgerald's fortunes not waned as Hemingway's star rose. Fitzgerald was ill and his creative powers dried up when in 1939 Hemingway reread his last completed novel, *Tender Is the Night*, and found much of it "amazing," although at the time the novel was published in 1934 Hemingway had criticized it for being forced and contrived.[46] Hemingway was just forty-one at the time of his old friend's death, yet it was a painful reminder of the passage of time. Thomas Wolfe, who during the 1920s had completed the trio of trend-setting wunderkinder edited by Max Perkins for Scribner's, was also dead, from alcoholism and tuberculosis. One year younger than Hemingway, Wolfe died in 1938 at age thirty-eight. Then, on March 8, 1941, another old friend and mentor from his early struggling years, Sherwood Anderson, died at the age of sixty-five.[47]

Hemingway quipped, "Writers are certainly dying like flies. . . . I suppose finally no one will be left alive but the Sitwells," referring to the aristocratic British literary siblings, Edith, Osbert, and Sacheverell Sitwell.[48] But the sudden run of death was really too close to be funny. In "The Snows of Kilimanjaro," Hemingway had written one of the most plaintive laments of a man who feared boredom, death, and loneliness. "When everything you do, you do too long, and do too late, you can't expect to find the people still there. The people are all gone. The party's over and you are with your hostess now." Now, seemingly in the blink of an eye, a quarter of a century had passed since *his* world war; contemporaries were dying, and the Hemingway eligible for war this time around was his eldest son, John, nicknamed "Bumby," who at seventeen was almost the same age he had been when he volunteered for Red Cross service in World War I.

Though Hemingway could hardly ignore the pull of war, at forty-one he felt too old to play the kind of active role he had performed even a few years earlier in Spain. (He was nearly blind in his left eye from birth, a defect which kept him from induction as a soldier in World War I.) Part of him did not want to be left behind when so many others, including his new wife, were racing to be near the action, but from the beginning of the war Hemingway wrestled with his intense ambivalence over how much direct involvement he should seek. He wanted to help defeat the fascists, but he was angry with America and her allies for their myopia about Spain. He despised propaganda, which he considered dishonest and less potent than good writing from the battlefield, and he categorically refused to be used as an instrument of the American government. "There is so much panic and hysteria and shit going around now. I don't feel like writing any flagwaving stuff," Hemingway had told Perkins in July 1940. "I will fight but I don't want to write that syndicated patriotism."[49]

Hemingway had strong feelings about America, and none of them were good. A small-town Midwestern Protestant upbringing that was rule-filled, proper, and given to petty neighborly gossip and competition left a bitter aftertaste which often overshadowed the freer, more imaginative fun and games at Walloon Lake in Upper Michigan where the family spent its summers. Hemingway viewed America's social atmosphere as primly repressive, its keenness on deal-making and materialism contemptible, and its government bureaucratically titanic and intrusive. Now that the United States had begun mounting an effort to help the Europeans defeat Hitler, Hemingway recognized his value to the propaganda campaign, but he also realized that his work during the Spanish Civil War, his residence in Cuba, and his left-wing affiliations made him unpredictable, if not suspect.[50]

Hemingway's original leftist sympathies stretched back to the 1920s when, like many American and European writers, he was attracted by the social, moral, and economic renewal that communism seemed to offer. As he matured, Hemingway's sympathy for the "common man" never wavered, but by the mid-1930s he had concluded that all institutional systems of government, once they became big enough, were inherently antihuman and unjust, including communism. "[T]he state I care nothing for," he explained to a Russian friend in 1935. "All the state has ever meant to me is unjust taxation."[51] Hemingway emphatically believed that "patriotism" and "class consciousness" made for bad writing. He decreed that the artist must neither show allegiance to any type of government whose "hand will always be against him," nor to revolutionary causes—a position he clearly set forth in 1934 in *Green Hills of Africa*.[52] While Hemingway knew or was friendly with many of the party's leading American writers and publishers, including John Dos Passos, Max Eastman, and Joseph Freedman (most of whom he was subsequently to fall out with after personal squabbles), until the Spanish Civil War, he remained primarily a fringe player to the American communist movement, signing the occasional petition and attending some meetings in New York. He loved making trouble too much to shower unqualified praise on anyone or anything, and even went so far as to distance himself from his Communist friends in Spain by writing in *For Whom the Bell Tolls* that their ideology suited an army, but was "incompatible with human fallibility."[53] His hero, Robert Jordan, denies being a "real Marxist," insisting rather that he is an "anti-fascist," a remark which perfectly reflected the fact that Hemingway's loyalty to the left during the 1930s largely grew out his perception of the growing threat of fascism in Europe and not his allegiance to the ideology itself. Two years earlier, in *To Have and Have Not*, Harry Morgan's explanation of his philosophy went even more to the core of Hemingway's system of belief. "I ain't no radical," he said. "I'm sore. I been sore a long time."[54]

Nevertheless, there was much in communism with which Hemingway agreed, especially since the Russian Revolution and its romantic portrayal came at the same time World War I had left him mourning the moral decadence of the West. When in 1918 American communist Floyd Dell wrote, "Not only did the public need truth and candor in a world of lies; it was also more interesting to talk truth than to create beauty," he was writing the credo Hemingway relentlessly pursued as an artist until his death.[55] But Hemingway set no ideological standard for judging what other writers did or did not do, as opposed to proselytizing idealists like Dell, who loudly chastised the "writer who seeks refuge in cave or garret or 'ivory tower.' "[56] Beyond the essential kinetic appeal of communist ideology, Hemingway had little patience for rhetoric about the writers' responsibility "to regard literature as only a weapon, an instrument, in the service of something larger than itself," as the deceased poet Walt Whitman was alleged in 1917 to have once said.[57] Whitman's artistic purism made him a favorite of both Communist and Socialist writers, but the doer in Hemingway scorned philosophers and ideologues. In "The Snows of Kilimanjaro" he satirized Tristan Tzara, France's Dada art movement leader, as "a Roumanian . . . who always wore a monocle and had a headache." While Hemingway could talk politics as well as the next, it was action, raw action—the kind that filled up every iota of loneliness and anxiety and tested cowardice—that best suited him. "No pleasure in anything if you mouth it up too much," says Wilson, the white hunter in "The Short Happy Life of Francis Macomber."

In early February 1941, after a brief trip to Hollywood to consult on the casting of Paramount's film version of *For Whom the Bell Tolls*, Hemingway sailed to Asia accompanied by Martha, whose idea of a honeymoon was to observe the Burma Road with her new husband.[58] Unaccustomed to being the passive touring companion and unwilling to forgo the chance of good pay, Hemingway obtained an assignment from *PM*, a New York daily newspaper, to write a series of dispatches assessing the likelihood of war between the United States and Japan.[59] The trip gave Hemingway the opportunity to write nonpropagandistic journalism while still feeling like he was part of the war, as he had told Maxwell Perkins he wanted to do. His agreement with editor Ralph Ingersoll specified that if war broke out, he would remain in Asia to cover it. Martha had her own magazine assignments and toured with him much of the time, until splitting off to go to Jakarta in May.

Hitler's manipulation of Japan was yet another example of the dictator's far-seeing global strategy. Since 1936, the German dictator had been encouraging Japanese aggression in the Pacific with the intent of diverting Allied ships and planes from Europe. Japan, wrote William Shirer, "was the key to Hitler's efforts to keep America out of the war until Germany was ready to take her on."[60] In July 1937 Japan had attacked China in a major offensive and immediately established control over a narrow swath from Tientsin on the Gulf of Chihli north one hundred miles to Peking. Despite the unification of Chiang Kai-shek's Nationalist military forces with his enemy Mao Tse-tung's Communist Chinese fighters, the Japanese moving south quickly overran Shanghai and Nanking and by December 1937 had established a provisional government in Peking.

China's vulnerability had dramatically worsened since the spring of 1938, when British writers W. H. Auden and Christopher Isherwood traveled throughout the Chinese war zones, collecting information for their book, *Journey to a War*.[61] At that time, foreign consuls and *bon-vivant* expatriates living within the International Zone in occupied Shanghai carried on a lavish, lazy lifestyle, while thousands of Chinese refugees lived a shadowy existence, waiting to return to their homes. The British ambassador practiced his putting in the garden of his borrowed villa and at dinner parties listened attentively as Japanese generals assured the British that the mass bombing of Canton was "more humane" than military occupation, and that the Japanese were really on the side of the Chinese, because they wanted to drive the "Red menace" from China.[62] In September 1938 Japan offered to support the Reich and Italy with military force, and true to their word, in the weeks before Hitler invaded Poland—and the Japanese launched a major offensive against the Chinese—the Japanese intensified attacks on British shipping along China's overseas trade routes. In August 1940 the British, under siege from massive German air attack, finally pulled out of Shanghai, and, when Germany, Italy, and Japan signed the Tripartite Pact on September 27, the Japanese threat to China loomed ever more ominous.

In the months before Hemingway left for Asia, German pressure on Japan to enter the war by seizing British possessions in Asia intensified. German ambassador Joachim von Ribbentrop, meeting with the Japanese ambassador General Hiroshi Oshima on February 23, 1941, reportedly urged Japan to make a move "as soon as possible in its own interest," assuring the Japanese ambassador that a "surprise intervention by Japan was bound to keep America out of the war." Ribbentrop suggested that "America, which at present is not armed and would hesitate to expose her Navy to any risks west of Hawaii, could do this even less in such a case."[63] With the Japanese already in possession of lands which included Canton in the far south, it was likely to be just a matter of time before Japan made its move beyond the Chinese border south into Burma, Indochina, Malaysia, and the Philippines.

Writing from Rangoon, Hong Kong, and Manila, Hemingway's job was to explain the strategic and economic importance of the region, assess the impact of China's war with Japan, and make Americans understand why it was so important to keep Japan's hands off the region. This was no easy task. Thousands of miles even from Hawaii, the cluster of countries fringing the South China Sea, including Indochina, the Philippines, and Malaysia—then called Malaya—were virtually unknown to the West. Yet, most of the world's rubber supply, and raw materials such as tin, hemp, oil, and iron—all vitally necessary if England fell and the United States were forced to wage war against Hitler—came from the area. Americans understood what war in Europe meant. War in Asia was another story. Americans "mistook Singapore for Shanghai and thought it was a Chinese city," wrote William Manchester in his 1979 book, *Goodbye, Darkness: A Memoir of the Pacific War*. "To this day," Manchester noted, "few GIs and Marines have the remotest idea of where they fought." What Americans knew of the lush region, according to Manchester, was what they had seen in Hollywood movies and Broadway plays, which depicted an "exotic world where hustlers like Sadie Thompson seduced missionaries . . . wild men danced on Borneo . . . and lovely native girls dived for pearls wearing fitted sarongs, like Dorothy Lamour."[64]

In Asia, Hemingway was once again placed in a country at war as the celebrity American writer who understood military strategy and war politics better than anyone. He observed Chiang Kai-shek's arsenals and the military academy at Chengtu, established by the same German General Alexander Von Faulkenhausen who vouchsafed Germany's good intentions toward Britain to Auden and Isherwood right after the German seizure of Austria in 1938. He visited the army at its northern front against Japan, interviewed Chiang Kai-shek, and observed supply efforts along the Burma Road and Chinese Communist guerrilla movements across Japanese lines. Known as the "Red Spears," these guerrillas were comprised of farmers and peasants who had developed a highly organized intelligence network which cooperated with the Chinese military leadership. When regular forces were driven out by the Japanese, the "Red Spears" continued to menace the Japanese, blowing up bridges and vehicles.

Once again, Hemingway was rubbing shoulders with the kinds of men he idolized as he did no other: courageous men fighting for a cause and fearless of death. Sounding like his own character Robert Jordan marveling at the bravery of the Spanish guerrillas who help him blow the bridge in *For Whom the Bell Tolls*, Hemingway wrote with reverence for the Chinese guerrillas who succeeded in getting trucks through the Japanese lines by "dismantling them—into the smallest possible pieces—and carrying them by hand."[65]

No matter how tough the Chinese guerrilla fighters were, however, they ultimately posed insubstantial resistance to the Japanese, who took revenge by burning villages and executing women and children. Hemingway's piece, "Russo-Japanese Pact," reflected how much Chiang Kai-shek's Kuomintang army had come to depend on Soviet military aid, less than three years after Isherwood and Auden found the entire subject of Soviet military aid to China "so taboo as to seem almost indecent."[66] Hemingway reported the sober luncheon he and Martha Gellhorn enjoyed in Chungking with Madame Chiang Kai-shek the day the Russo-Japanese neutrality pact, signed on April 13, was announced. According to Hemingway, he assured Madame Chiang that the pact, whose aim was to free Japan and Russia to wage war against foreign nations without fear of mutual reprisal, did not imply a withdrawal of Soviet aid. Hemingway wrote: " 'If they are going to withdraw aid,' I told her, remembering how it had happened in Spain, 'the first move will be to withdraw the military advisors, the instructors and the staff officers. As long as they stay on, it means the aid will continue.' "[67] One can only take Hemingway at his word that, pen and pad in hand, wearing battle vest, khakis, and the iron-rimmed Chinese Army Issue glasses he would wear for the rest of his life, he comforted the Dragon Lady of China over lunch concerning Soviet military intentions. In a dim reprise of the special-status luxury he had enjoyed in Spain, in nationalist China under Japanese attack Hemingway was again enjoying the benefits of being a celebrity journalist. In his Russian-numbered room in the officers' club in Northern Szechwan Province, Hemingway praised the "various delicacies . . . including cocoa and tinned butter come by way of Vladivostock and Chita."[68]

As the scenario unfolded, however, Hemingway was as mistakenly optimistic about China as he had been about Spain. Without knowledge of the secret conniving between Japan and Germany, Hemingway had believed if the Allies slowly, rather than abruptly, reduced oil supplies to the dependent Japanese, they could buy time to build up military strength in the region, while simultaneously maintaining Japan's dependence and forcing her to use up her meagre less-than-one-year supply. He also believed that the bellicose Japan would remain occupied by her war with China, and that it would take the fall of Britain to the Germans to give her the confidence to reach south across the glistening China Sea and grab what she wanted. Writing in the June 18 PM article "China's Air Needs" that "Japan will not risk war with England and America until she sees a possibility of England and the U.S.A. being so occupied that they cannot oppose her adequately,"[69] his conclusion was reminiscent of his miscalculation four years earlier that "Franco is out of luck."[70]

In late June 1941, Hitler effectively removed the Russians as an impediment to Japanese ambitions by battering them in a massive offensive, and only a few short weeks after Hemingway's visit ended, the Japanese invaded Indochina, including Vietnam, on July 24, 1941. Immediately, the Americans, followed by the British, and finally the Dutch colonial government in Jakarta, cut off oil supplies to Japan. For the remainder of the summer and into the autumn of 1941, the Americans and Japanese wrangled with each other, submitting ultimatum after ultimatum in a kind of unrehearsed, yet stock prewar dance. The United States would not agree to cease arming the Chinese or fortifying in the region; the Japanese would not agree to withdraw from China and Indochina or sign a nonaggression pact. Then on December 7, 1941, a Japanese armada of warships and three hundred sixty warplanes attacked an unprepared Pearl Harbor, killing or wounding more than 3,500 Americans, sinking eighteen ships, and destroying about one hundred seventy airplanes. President Roosevelt immediately declared war on Japan.

Hemingway had just finished hunting and fishing in Sun Valley, Idaho, and was enjoying a leisurely automobile trip south, en route to the Gulf coast through "the Indian country," when the Pearl Harbor attack came.[71] Immediately, he was thrust out of his traveler's serenity and into a paroxysm of rage and frustration. Pearl Harbor confirmed everything that Hemingway hated about political and military leaders, whom he believed had abandoned American servicemen to die. Hemingway revered soldiers at the battlefront, who put their lives and the lives of others on the line, and he despised those "power-hungry leaders" whom he accused of cavalierly putting their careers before the safety of their men, and of acting brave and smart when they were neither. To Hemingway, there was a right way and a wrong way of doing everything, whether it was hunting, fishing, writing, loving, or waging war. His fictional heros are precise and expert at their chosen craft, and often it is the mercilessness of bad luck which dooms them to defeat—the advent of snow in *For Whom the Bell Tolls*, the crippling cramps in Santiago's hand in *The Old Man and the Sea*. Against these mighty outer forces, the heroes hunker down, summon all of their mental and emotional strength, and fight, which makes their efforts all the more tragic. They tell themselves not to think, not to get tired, but only to endure. If they die, let them die with dignity after a brave fight. The dead sailors of the U.S.S. *Arizona* personified Hemingway's bitterest condemnation.

In the days following the attack, Hemingway joined the loud chorus of critics blasting American naval leaders, calling them "incompetents" and "week-end admirals." Although throughout his life Hemingway assigned a ferocious brand of blame—on parents, wives, ex-friends, politicians, the IRS, and most tragically, himself—those responsible for protecting American servicemen were an easy target because of the number of American casualties and seeming surprise of the attack, when rumors had swirled for weeks. A constant alert had not been issued; men had been given their regular Saturday night leave; only a quarter of the anti-aircraft guns were manned and aircraft were left on airstrips, like sitting ducks in a shooting gallery.[72] Whether Washington had foreknowledge of the Pearl Harbor attack remains controversial to this day; nevertheless, Hemingway placed full blame for the attack on military and political higher-ups, especially the Secretary of the Navy, Frank Knox. Hemingway fumed that Knox was not fired from his post within twenty-four hours of the attack, adding that he wanted to see "those responsible at Oahu for that disaster shot."[73] Knox, a Rough Rider in the Spanish-American War, a former newspaperman, and a Republican vice-presidential candidate in 1936, remained secretary of the Navy until his death in 1944.

On December 12, the day after the United States declared war on Germany and Italy, Hemingway was gloomy, pessimistic, and still seething, when he confided to his publisher, Charles Scribner, his view that as a result of American "laziness, criminal carelessness, and blind arrogance we are fucked in this war as of the first day and we are going to have Christ's own bitter time to win it if, when and ever. . . . No matter how many countries you see fucked and bitched and ruined you never get to take it easily. Having to watch all the steps and know them all so well."[74]

Indeed, Hemingway had been railing against military inertia and politics for years, and now Pearl Harbor had materialized as the quintessential, textbook instance of the "sin" of military unpreparedness. In 1938 Hemingway had cast his judgment on that kind of "sin" in a prescient, scathingly tongue-in-cheek magazine article entitled "A Program for U.S. Realism," which he wrote after returning from his third trip to Spain. Commenting on the likelihood of war in Europe, Hemingway quoted generously from Carl von Clausewitz, "the old Einstein of battles," and Count von der Goltz, Otto von Bismarck's ambassador to Paris during Prussia's war with Austria. " 'The Statesman, who, knowing his instrument to be ready, and seeing war inevitable, hesitates to strike first,' " Hemingway quoted von der Goltz, " 'is guilty of a crime against his country.' "[75] Later in the war, Hemingway became fixated on a capricious American marine sergeant whose brutal act he had seen in an unedited copy of the film series about World War II naval operations, *Victory at Sea*, which he obtained from the American embassy in Havana. Hemingway was enthralled by the twenty-segment film, which he watched repeatedly in his living room, memorizing many of its scenes. The particular scene which most captivated him showed an American marine sergeant capturing a group of Japanese prisoners who had offered no resistance. Hemingway had the projectionist freeze the film at the scene where the sergeant burned his victims alive, occasionally smiling at the camera as he commits his hideous act. Unable to remain a mere observer of any action, Hemingway told his friends to memorize the sergant's face so that they could kill him someday.[76]

This image of soldiers dying at the hands of a "chicken-shit" officer became etched in Hemingway's mind as indelibly as images of the hounded husband tormented by his wife's merciless criticism and sexual taunts, the scorned son ordered to conform, or the writer lascerated by the critic who had not the slightest idea what it was like to strive to write something good and honest. In Hemingway's view, America's commanders were traitorous scum, and as he and the country reeled from the shock of Pearl Harbor and the United States' entry into the war, Hemingway predicted that these "week-end admirals" had condemned the country to war "for the next ten years."[77] He did not want to go to Europe to cover a war he believed could have been avoided, but should he change his mind, Hemingway felt he had plenty of time.[78]

It wasn't every day that one picked up and left paradise for hell, even if that hell had attractions for one as enamored of rogue excitement as Ernest Hemingway. Far away from the shell-shocked castles of Spain and the Burma Road, Hemingway was living in Cuba like a king with a retinue, and he adored it. His home since late 1939 was a large, sun-drenched sanctum with whitewashed walls called La Finca Vigia, on a hill overlooking the town of San Francisco de Paula. Because of the hill's strategic position as one of the region's highest points and only about eight miles southeast of Havana, around the turn of the century, Spanish soldiers had built a small fort, including a wooden watchtower, on the spot where the house was later built. The name of the house came from the Spanish word for watchtower, *vigia*. La Finca Vigia came with twenty-one lush tropical acres and included a working dairy, which Hemingway subleased, a tennis court, and stable. Holstein cattle grazed on sections of land not teeming with mamey, tamarind, mango, and almond trees, and after 1942, when Hemingway began a cockfighting and gambling operation, the squawking of gamecocks sizzled through the dense tropical air.

Hemingway desperately needed people surrounding him, although he roundly asserted his need for tranquility to work, and La Finca Vigia had immediately become a gathering place for his vast and eclectic entourage of friends and hangers-on, including gambling cronies, Cuban political dissidents, fishermen, boxers, baseball players, Hollywood movie stars like Gary Cooper and Barbara Stanwyck, and writer friends from Europe and the United States. But in the swirl of war and hectic lives, the home that began as an exquisite love nest for Hemingway and Gellhorn increasingly became for him a painful symbol of separation and loneliness. Martha's boastful jest right after she and Hemingway were married about *her* being the war correspondent in the family came to haunt her jealous, insecure husband, who fell into deep despair when alone. Hemingway had deluded himself during the couple's 1941 Asia trip that Martha "wants to chuck correspondent's work now and stay home," out of his desire for her to be someone she neither could be nor wanted to be.[79] By mid-1942, Gellhorn's absences while covering the war had become the standard state of affairs in the couple's marriage, and Hemingway roamed La Finca Vigia's rooms and grounds at night with a .22-caliber pistol stuck in his belt, like a sentinel guarding Windsor Palace while the queen is at Balmoral. Even when Martha was home, she was occupied writing her own articles, and in 1941 she had published a new novel, *The Heart of Another*. That year her more famous husband had barely done any fiction-writing. Still replenishing his energy after *For Whom the Bell Tolls*, no new novel gripped him. Yet his name had launched a veritable literary factory by 1941, and when he was not hunting, fishing, or entertaining houseguests, he busied himself in trivial details concerning the repackaging of old work into a multitude of new editions and collections, tracking sales and royalty statements, and criticizing the film script of *For Whom the Bell Tolls*, which was still being rewritten and cast. Hemingway had become the very kind of "professional writer" whom he had always held in contempt, who immerses himself in the business of his writing and deludes himself into believing he can still write from deep within his subconscious.

For such a high-flying adventurer and hard-liver, who tended to morbidity, sullenness, and pugnacity when not the center of attention, being married to a tough, independent wife who could fight and swear as hard as he did was a turnabout to which Hemingway was unaccustomed and which he definitely did not like, once the novelty wore off. Far worse, however, were the dreaded loneliness and deep anger that Hemingway felt as the result of Martha's absences. It was a potent one-two punch which sent him into a vicious spiral of self-loathing and drunkenness. The obsequious journalists who were impressed by Hemingway's disciplined work schedule at La Finca Vigia—rising at seven, working until noon, more work after an afternoon nap—failed to appreciate the gargantuan consumption of alcohol that punctuated each part of his day, beginning in the morning in the swimming pool. Wine accompanied lunch, then more drinking after the afternoon nap, more wine at dinner, then still more while he read until bedtime. When he went to La Floridita, he carried a thermos in the event he could not finish the last of the ten or more frozen daiquiris he ordered in an afternoon.

In 1935 Hemingway explained to a friend that he drank to ward off the "mechanical oppression" of contemporary life, not unlike Robert Jordan in *For Whom the Bell Tolls*, who calls absinthe the "medicine . . . [that] kills the worm that haunts us."[80] But Hemingway had also used liquor as a means to mask his loneliness and to be top dog among those who shared his same need for rollicking camaraderie. On journalism assignments, his well-stocked hotel rooms were magnets for fellow journalists—even in Madrid during the Spanish Civil War, when his hotel stood dangerously near a heavily bombed electric power station. To friends and bar-mates he bragged that he had a drinking capacity ten times that of other men, and deluded himself into believing he could "boil out" liquor from his system through intense physical exertion, especially boxing. But on the blank page where he confronted the truth, he exposed his alchoholism for what it really was—a protection against thinking of things that caused him pain. "If you don't think about it, it doesn't exist," he wrote time and again.

Hemingway paid a painful emotional penance for the pleasures of drinking, or what his teetotaling parents called the "sin of intemperance." He professed to hate drunks and littered his fiction with a scurrilous cadre of "damned rummies," whom he described as cowards, which was the worst epithet he could attach to someone. In 1936 he had written in "The Snows of Kilimanjaro" that Harry, his lying, dying writer, "had destroyed his talent by . . . drinking so much that he had blunted the edge of his perceptions." By the 1940s, Hemingway had begun sadly to look more and more like another creation, his aging boxer in the 1925 story, "Fifty Grand," suffering from insomnia, worrying about everything, and finally falling asleep after getting drunk.

In 1941, Samuel Feijoo, a Cuban artist, encountered a lonely, despondent, and drunk Hemingway while painting in a solitary spot up the Cojimar River. "We talked about solitude," said Feijoo. "I explained that I went there to paint in search of solitude. He told me that he did the same, that he needed solitude because he was bored with the world around him, and that people made him mad. He said that he was misunderstood, and that he had no friends and that those around him were there because he was a famous writer. They were really friends of his fame." Feijoo, who did not know who Hemingway was at the time, noticed liquor bottles in his rowboat. The two men spent three or four hours talking, during which time a drunken Hemingway repeatedly said he and the artist were "failures unto death." He told Feijoo he left America because life there was terrible, and in Cuba, "at least people smile at you."[81]

Several months later, an inebriated Hemingway took out his frustrations in a far less subdued manner. He was entertaining Brooklyn Dodger baseball players Hugh Casey, Kirby Higbe, and Billy Herman with a day of pigeon-shooting at his gun club, the Club de Cazadores del Cerro. It was March 1942, and the Japanese were overwhelming the Pacific, capturing Singapore, which had been considered impregnable, in February, and then Java, New Guinea, and the Philippines. After some war talk about the Japanese, the evening followed a course of heavy drinking. By the time Martha went to bed, according to Billy Herman, "Hemingway was really loaded." The evening ended with Hemingway, a die-hard baseball fan who loved being around athletes, challenging the husky Dodger pitcher to a boxing match. The fight between two drunken giants was messy, with lamps, furniture, and glass flying. Hemingway was losing to Casey when he suddenly sucker-kicked him in the groin, just as Hemingway's fictional character Jack Brennan had sucker-punched Jimmy Walcott in his story "Fifty Grand." Afterwards, Hemingway told Casey, "Hey look, spend the night with me. You got the best of me. You beat the hell out of me. I was real drunk, but tomorrow morning we'll both be sober, and we'll duel." Hemingway offered a selection of knives, swords, and guns, and the ballplayers fled. The next morning at the ballpark, Herman remembered, a contrite, embarrassed, sober Hemingway was "apologizing all over the place, almost in tears."[82]

Lonely and bored, Hemingway directed his wrath against the war, its leadership, and the U.S. government, which sent him an IRS bill of $103,000 in 1942. Barely a year and a half had passed since Hemingway had received his whopping check from Paramount, waved it over his head, and gleefully announced, "Our old age is secure."[83] With La Finca Vigia costing nearly $4,000 a month in upkeep, three children in private school and college, alimony to Pauline, a yacht, a running liquor tab at La Floridita, a menagerie of cats and dogs, and a generous propensity to pay for free-loading friends, Hemingway was forced to borrow $12,000 from his publisher, Scribner's, to pay Uncle Sam.

"At present my principal war problem is financial," he wrote to his first wife, Hadley Mowrer, on July 23, 1942, expressing bitterness that the United States had taken his hard-earned money to drive its war machine.[84] Now that he was in debt with no immediate sign of the kind of grand relief he had enjoyed in 1941, Hemingway calculated that if the war lasted as long as he predicted, he'd be broke in five years. To Hadley he lamented having "made a fortune at a time when whatever you make is confiscated by the govt," and complained that his young wife spent money as though it would never stop flowing. "[S]he doesn't know that when you get older you have to have a steady something to live on between books—books get further apart as you get older if you write only good books."[85]

Despite feeling financially strapped, Hemingway turned down a $150,000 offer in early 1942 to write a script for a "March of Time" program on the crack volunteer squadron known as the "Flying Tigers," claiming that it smacked too much of "syndicated patriotism."[86] Hemingway set about to find other ways more to his liking to supplement his income, and to that end, he and his gardener bought twenty fighting cocks, built a cockpit on the grounds of his home, and launched a cockfighting operation.

One bid to write about the war did come along in 1942 which suited Hemingway's credo of honesty and his desire to stay free of government influence. He accepted an assignment to compile an anthology of writings about war written over the centuries for Crown Publishers, and then he set about making it a vehicle to express his disgust for the American leadership running the war.

Men at War, published in 1942, included Hemingway's selections on decisive battles in history like Thermopylae, Hastings, Waterloo, and Shiloh. The compilation included only two of Hemingway's pieces, "The Retreat from Caporetto," an excerpt from *A Farewell to Arms* about the 1918 battle between Austrian and Italian forces, and "The Fight on the Hilltop," an excerpt from *For Whom the Bell Tolls* about the defeat of a tiny band of Republican fighters holding a hill against the fascists. Nevertheless, in his passionate introduction and series of brief section

preambles Hemingway plainly set forth the personal philosophies which characterized his fictional opus and which, now, during a war, rang out stridently as
antagonistic, objectionable, and even anti-American. Hemingway was hardly trying to make friends in the FBI when he decried national politics as "the womb in
which War is developed in which its outlines lie hidden in a rudimentary state,
like the qualities of living creatures in their embryos."[87]

His writing was crisp and moving, and the result was a powerful expression of
the brutality of war, as well as its futile repetition throughout the ages. Using historical precedent to illustrate his views, Hemingway reiterated his views on the
need to win a war once it has started, the failure of leadership, the courage of
fighting men, the extent to which chance plays a part in whether one lives or dies,
and the inevitability of death. He worked on the book as the Germans under
General Rommel advanced on North Africa, and *Men at War* had a persuasive
immediacy, despite being an anthology of old and, in many cases, ancient pieces.

Men at War also included Hemingway's denunciation of propaganda, as
though he meant it as a one-time explanation to the public for his repeated refusals
to write what he called "syndicated patriotism." Propaganda was inherently dishonest and impotent, he wrote, and he compared the act of writing well to waging
a war. Both were bitterly difficult, requiring honesty, good judgment, careful
planning, resolution, and courage. "Everything is simple in War, but the simplest
thing is difficult." Hemingway had drawn a similar, though less direct, parallel in
For Whom the Bell Tolls, when Jordan, mulling over all the killing he has done
since coming to Spain, decides he must not lie to himself about it to assuage guilt
feelings. "You have no right to shut your eyes to any of it nor any right to forget
any of it nor to soften it nor to change it."[88]

As Hemingway neared completion of *Men at War*, he told Evan Shipman, a good
friend who was journalist, poet, and novelist, that he doubted the introduction was
any good, because he wrote badly when he had "nobody to show it to," since Martha
was off covering German submarine activity in the Caribbean for *Collier's*.[89] But if
Hemingway was feeling darkly self-critical, nowhere was it evident in his writing.
He ended his introduction to *Men at War* with a nervy challenge—and a warning—
to American leaders: "It is very easy to fool the people at the start of a war and run
it on a confidential basis," he wrote. "But later the wounded start coming back and
the actual news spreads. . . . I am sure that as the war progresses, our government
will realize the necessity of telling the people the truth . . . because times are coming in this war when the government will need the complete and absolute confidence of all citizens if this country is to endure."[90]

With little confidence of his own in the American government, no burning
desire to leave Cuba, and longings to be a hunter, fisherman, and renegade stirring
his blood, Hemingway began playing the part of soldier-sailor-spy in a venture
that rivaled the antics of Don Quixote. In 1942 German submarines were sinking
Allied ships in the Caribbean. On the Atlantic side, too, there were sightings of
German subs hunting Cuban ships, and rumors abounded that Nazi spies had infil-
trated Cuba. Beginning in the spring of 1942, Hemingway recruited twenty-six
informants from among Loyalist refugees he knew in Cuba, many of them
Basques, and began operating an intelligence network for the purpose of spying
on pro-Franco Spaniards in Cuba who were likely to be Nazi sympathizers. Far

from the battlefields of Europe, in his mango-studded sanctuary high above the sea, Ernest Hemingway at last fulfilled his wish to become a commander in charge of a battalion. La Finca Vigia became the clearinghouse for all intelligence gathered by his "agents," and two or three times a week he reported the findings to his liaison at the American Embassy in Havana.

Always taken with nicknames, Hemingway called his intelligence network the "Crook Factory," named for the Crooked Islands off the north central coast above Camagüey. His battalion included four full-time "spies" and fourteen bartenders and waiters who worked part-time. Presumably he thought it a good bet that drunken spies would open up to career listeners.

Hemingway was not content to let his friends have all the fun, however, and in the summer of 1942 when German submarines began sinking Cuban freighters in the Atlantic, the burly writer began searching for German U-boats in the blue waters off the Cuban coast aboard his thirty-eight-foot, two-engine, customized cabin cruiser, the *Pilar*. He called this venture "Friendless," after one of his many cats, and financed it himself and with backing from his good friend, millionaire polo player and *bon-vivant* Winston Guest, a nephew of Winston Churchill. Guest and Hemingway had met in 1933 in Kenya while on safari, and the two immediately became good friends, based on their mutual love of wicked fun, adventure, food and drink, and, not least important, Guest's readiness to play "the ideal subaltern," as Hemingway himself defined his submissive friend.[91] But Guest also had a sensitive side, according to Hemingway, as evidenced by his reading of Renan's *Life of Jesus* during the war, "due to his thinking he ought to have some spiritual influence in his life in these grave times."[92] In addition to Guest, Hemingway's hodgepodge of comrades on *Pilar* surveillance excursions included Cuban fishermen, ex-soldiers, Spaniards living in Cuba whom he knew from the Spanish Civil War, the cabin cruiser's cook, and a well-known jai-alai player. "Half-saints and desperate men" was how Hemingway termed the men of his crew years later in his unfinished fictional account of "Friendless" activities in *Islands in the Stream.*[93]

Hemingway was thrilled by the hunt, which took on the character of a full-fledged paramilitary action, with Hemingway as its El Jefe. Amazingly, through the United States embassy in Cuba, Hemingway managed to obtain the FBI's blessing and U.S. government sponsorship. After September 1942, the group came loosely under the aegis of the American ambassador to Cuba, Spruille Braden, who supplied Hemingway with fuel and a thousand dollars a month to pay informants. The FBI first had to be mollified that a remark Hemingway had made in 1940 concerning an FBI agent active in Cuba was a joke. Introducing the agent, Raymond G. Leddy, to a friend at a jai-alai match, Hemingway had jested that Leddy was "a member of the Gestapo."[94]

Now that he was receiving the benefits of being in league with the U.S. government, Hemingway no longer had to settle for merely standing on the *Pilar*'s prow and shaking his fist at a U-boat if he saw one; he could fire at one with .50-caliber machine guns, bazookas, and grenades provided by the Navy. But what actually made Hemingway's Crook Factory a wildly bizarre operation, however, was not so much its literary chieftain and his eclectic band of friends, but the fact that despite receiving the FBI's blessing, J. Edgar Hoover simultaneously was monitoring him as a subversive and leftist. Raymond Leddy, the legal attaché inside the U.S. embassy in Havana, had compiled a dossier which painted him as a "Communist sympathizer," and a drunk whose judgment was "questionable."[95]

Hemingway knew he was being spied on, but he hardly cared. He took precautions in his personal correspondence, telling Evan Shipman, "anybody who thinks indiscreetly or criticizes in time of war adds to whatever dossiers of photostated letters he has accumulated in a lifetime," but he carried on unintimidated, uninhibited, and even slightly bemused.[96] One day, while sitting at La Floridita with a friend, he nodded to a group of three strangers. They were not the Floridita's usual clientele of Cuban politicos, prostitutes, journalists, and sugar and rice planters, or American movie stars like Errol Flynn and Ava Gardner, who were regulars. Hemingway told his companions that they were intelligence agents tailing him. Years later, Hemingway took his amused revenge, when he described in *Islands in the Stream* "the inescapable FBI men, pleasant and all trying to look so average, clean-cut-young-American that they stood out as clearly as though they had worn a bureau shoulder patch on their white linen or seersucker suits."[97]

Undoubtedly, the intrigue contributed to the great fun Hemingway was having, and no amount of FBI intrusion could diminish it. Under their Navy cover, he and his friends were allegedly specimen-fishing for the American Museum of Natural History, and the *Pilar* bore a wooden sign reading "American Museum of Natural History." The ragtag group joked about their masquerade and said that all their paraphernalia, including the hanging leather wine bags and wide straw hats of the kind Bahamian spongers wore, was "scientific."[98] In the deeper sense, however, the venture allowed Hemingway to play soldier as he had been doing since his boyhood days on Walloon Lake. He "delights in shooting imaginery wolves, bears, lions, buffalo, etc. Also likes to pretend he is a 'solser,' " Grace Hemingway once wrote to a friend, describing her young son's antics. "When asked what he is afraid of," she went on, "he shouts out 'fraid a nothing' with great gusto."[99] The only difference between then and now was that now Hemingway could tell himself his mission had a legitimate national purpose.

Indeed, Martha Gellhorn found her husband's maritime escapade juvenile and ridiculous, and she watched in disgust as Hemingway became consumed by what she deemed an inflated excuse to obtain rationed gasoline and go marlin fishing. Martha, who had teased Hemingway about his military pretensions as far back as the Spanish Civil War, calling him "Scrooby" or "The Pig," was repulsed by her husband's dissolute friends and his filthy, smelly appearance when he returned from *Pilar* excursions, which were essentially alcoholic bacchanals involving obsequious acolytes willing, unlike her, to feed Hemingway's growing ego.[100] The Crook Factory became a source of intense fighting between the couple. Martha, who at this time was writing her novel *Liana* between magazine assignments, urged her husband to fight the war with his pen at the front lines, not from the bow of a fishing boat, but eventually, her objections became moot. By December 1942, the FBI was having strong second thoughts about Hemingway's covert mission for the U.S. government. While it bothered the Bureau that as recently as 1940 he had signed a petition condemning the FBI for action it took against Loyalist supporters, the FBI had also become suspicious of Hemingway's benefactor, Ambassador Braden, whom they described as "a very impulsive individual." They worried that Braden would use Hemingway to implement his own anticorruption agenda against Cuba's dictator, Fulgencio Batista. On December 17, 1942, FBI agent D. M. Ladd wrote in his memo that Raymond Leddy, the U.S. embassy's legal attaché in Havana, "stated that he has become quite concerned with respect to Hemingway's activities and that they are undoubtedly going to be very embarrassing unless something is done to stop them." The memo concluded that "Hemingway is going further than just an informant; he is actually branching out into an investigative organization of his own which is not subject to any control whatsoever." Ladd reaffirmed Leddy's fears that the vigilante impulses of Ambassador Braden and Ernest Hemingway would be responsible for causing Batista to throw the FBI out of Cuba altogether. On December 19, 1942, J. Edgar Hoover responded definitively. "Hemingway is the last man, in my estimation, to be used in any such capacity."[101]

In April 1943 the duties of Hemingway's Crook Factory were taken over by seasoned American intelligence agents dispatched to Cuba. Thereafter, Hemingway became disgruntled with the limited way in which the U.S. government was using him, and he decided against offering his services in the future. He continued unsanctioned patrols in Cuban waters on the *Pilar*, complaining about the ineffectiveness of propaganda written by writers unfamiliar with war, the kind of men who had to be shown "which end of a battlefield was which."

In all, the Friendless operation sighted one German submarine two or three miles in the distance. Except for Hemingway's practice drills, during which grenades were tossed at flotsam floating in the distance and fuel drums on which the crew had painted faces of Hitler, no machine guns were ever discharged and no grenades were thrown. When Hemingway fictionalized the operation in 1952, his shoot-em-up, marine spy-fantasy showed mission leader Thomas Hudson getting fatally shot by German infiltrators in a blaze of gunfire replete with .50-caliber machine guns, grenades, and tracers.

As U.S. and British troops squeezed the Axis toward surrender in North Africa in the spring of 1943, Hemingway toyed with the idea of going to Asia—perhaps China—where he believed fighting would continue for at least another five years. He was bored, restless, lonely, and drinking heavily, and, even in a drunken haze, he often couldn't sleep. Awake, he could only dream of writing fiction—the work which gave him a degree of equilibrium and staved off the boredom of daily life.

Still, he made no formal moves to go abroad. In a sprawling, somewhat confused and guilt-laden letter which Hemingway wrote in May 1943 in response to Archibald MacLeish's inquiry on his war plans, Hemingway feigned cheerfulness, telling his old friend not to worry about him, protesting that he was working hard, was "never happier," and had no desire to volunteer for military duty when it only meant he would have to write propaganda.[102] MacLeish, who shared Hemingway's rigid code of honesty in writing and took a dim view of propaganda, had nevertheless adapted his idealism to the practical challenge of winning the war. In the spring of 1943, MacLeish was Librarian of Congress, but he had already served as director of the short-lived Office of Facts and Figures and as assistant director of the Office of War Information when it replaced the former in June 1942. Washington bureaucracy, speeches, endless obligations became the stuff of the writer's life, and although MacLeish resigned from the Office of War Information in June 1943 in part over policy differences, he nevertheless endured his many grievances because he saw himself fulfilling a valuable role. There was something sad, even pitiful about Hemingway's entreaty to MacLeish that he take a break from Washington and come and visit him. At La Finca Vigia Hemingway had what every writer dreams of—free time and free choice—and a beautiful place to work; yet, in spite of all this, Hemingway found himself apologizing before his noble, self-sacrificing friend, offering MacLeish testimony that he had become "good, non-righteous, non-bragging, non-boasting, almost non-chicken-shit," but since he was estranged from his old friends, he was "liable to die and nobody will ever register it."[103] There was personal history behind Hemingway's plea for MacLeish's sympathy and forgiveness. Back in the spring of 1934, MacLeish had distanced himself from their friendship when he began to be repelled by Hemingway's intensifying egomania, and Hemingway reacted by accusing MacLeish of being too political. Though the men had remained nominal friends and collaborated to aid the Republicans during the Spanish Civil War, MacLeish remained wary of Hemingway and the two never recovered the easy closeness they had once shared.[104]

Despite Hemingway's indecision about his immediate future, he knew he wanted to write another big novel. He told MacLeish he had "found out two or three more things and usually only had one each new to a book."[105] Yet even in this he felt self-doubt. Imaginary or not, like his father, Hemingway had become haunted by money worries which he wrongly attributed to the war and alimony payments to a woman whose father "owns 76,000 acres of land and whose uncle is worth, say 40,000,000."[106] He envisioned writing the big novel around 1945, but since he expected the war would still be on then—if not "for the rest of our lives"—he feared he would be too broke to write it. Hemingway's parents' bitter arguments over money had cut a deep gash in his psyche, and ironically, his fear about being left destitute came at a time when *For Whom the Bell Tolls* had sold close to 700,000 copies, the most for a novel since *Gone with the Wind*. Hemingway asked MacLeish tongue-in-cheek, "Do you think the Library will be able to give me a grant to write a novel in that year? Or will writers be abolished by then?" Hemingway closed his letter with the wish that his old friend could be with him to alleviate his cynicism and gloom. "Maybe it is because it is the broken bones you think with and the barometer is wrong but there are alot of things that don't taste good any more that used to taste all right," he lamented.[107]

Over the next months, Hemingway struggled with writer's block while his wife was at work on a new novel, unburdened by any of her husband's anxieties. Since Hemingway "had gotten rid of many things by writing them," like many of his fictional heroes, he felt his entire being swelling with anxiety and frustration.[108] In August 1943, he finally admitted to MacLeish he hadn't "written a line now for just over a year," and for the first time since moving to Cuba in 1938, Hemingway expressed the desire to leave the tropics for a few months so he could write. His ambivalence over whether he should go to the war to write about it was reaching a head. He proclaimed his "great joy" at discovering in the past year the "vice of anonymity which is a fine good snotty vice,"[109] but at the same time he tested the waters with MacLeish for an accredited correspondenceship for the Library of Congress: "Is there any chance that we might send guys to the war not to write govt. publications or propaganda but so as to have something good written afterwards? Do you think I have enough category to get any such assignment after finish work here? The British are useing (cq) both writers and painters that way. If we don't want such people maybe I could get a job with the British."[110]

In the autumn of 1943 Ernest Hemingway was still undramatically ensconced in Cuba, spending his days fishing, duck hunting, betting on his fighting cocks, watching the heavy summer weather give way to "air clean washed and wonderful"—and drinking—when Martha Gellhorn left for London on October 25, 1943, to cover the war in Europe for *Collier's.*[111] In an odd reversal of the scenario with Pauline six years earlier, Hemingway did not recognize that his wife's leaving signified the end of their marriage. At the time Martha pursued the assignment, Hemingway thought he, too, would be away for three months scouring the Caribbean with his male troop aboard the *Pilar.* In a letter he wrote on August 31 but never mailed, he gave evidence of none of the marital discord which had marked the previous two years: "She is lovelier than ever and we love each other very much but I cannot go with her to the sector of the war that they send her to anymore. Once, when we had only one war at a time, it was easy and we could have a nice GHQ in the Hotel Florida. But now there is such expansion that husbands and wives cannot make the same shows anymore together without somebody being unfaithful to something."[112]

Martha's parting words just weeks after rang with no such tenderness for her husband. As she walked off down La Finca Vigia's path, she encountered the couple's friend and doctor, Dr. Sotolongo, whom they had met in Spain in 1937 when Gellhorn was writing a magazine article on the doctor's Twelfth Brigade. "I'm saying goodbye to you, Doctor," she announced. "I'm leaving for Europe and I won't come back to the beast."[113]

Hemingway went into an emotional tailspin. "It is lonesomer than Limbo here," he wrote on October 30, 1943, to his son Patrick, who was a student at a Connecticut boarding school. "Only the cotsies [cats] for company." Hemingway described to his son the doings of the cat menagerie in extraordinarily minute detail, then closed to his son with his grand plans for the day. "Must go in town now to meet the lower element for lunch at the Floridita. . . . Today is Sat. Always a big day at the Floridita."[114]

In the weeks that followed, Hemingway's loneliness "in the big empty house" grew into a deep depression facilitated by hours of steady drinking and insomnia which even his customary two Seconals at bedtime could not conquer.[115] (Hemingway began taking them when he was writing *A Farewell to Arms* as a means to prevent awakening before daylight to think about the next day's writing.) Restless and unable to focus, he found it difficult to perform even simple obligations, finding that after he drank with his cats he fell asleep on the floor with the record player still on. He longed desperately for Martha and his children, but John, his eldest, had left Dartmouth College and was incommunicado in England, leading a platoon of military police, and Patrick and Gregory were both away at school. His sole companions in the house, besides five dogs, became his cats— eleven of them, with names like "Tester," "Thruster," "Dillinger," "Furhouse," "Fats," "Friendless," "Uncle Wolfer," "Blindness," and "Nuisance Value."

Hemingway marveled at their loyalty to him and their ability to survive bad fights, and he devoted all his tenderness and empty hours them.

"It is wonderful when Marty and/or the kids are here but it is lonesomer as a bastard when I'm here alone," he told his first wife, Hadley, in late November. "I have taught Uncle Wolfer, Dillinger and Will to walk along the railings to the top of the porch pillars and make a pyramid like lions and have taught Friendless to drink with me (Whisky and milk) but even that doesn't take the place of a wife and family." Hemingway complained that he had "never had so much time to think in my life, especially nights on the water and here when I can't sleep from having lost the habit."[116]

Hemingway had by now come to terms with the fact that he had lost another habit even more dear to him than sleep; yet, he had become resigned to the idea that he would be incapable of writing any fiction until the war was over, writing Maxwell Perkins in late February 1944, "When I am through with this war will have to get in training and shape again to write."[117]

So after five years of hedging and remonstrating about an unworthy war, Hemingway was like the lone dancer standing in the center of a ballroom after all the other girls have been taken.

He was desperately in need of a war, any kind of war, and through Martha's connections with the British Air Ministry, on May 17, 1944, Hemingway flew from New York to London to cover the Royal Air Force for Martha's magazine, *Collier's*. Little had changed for Hemingway since World War I, when he sought out war as much to relieve boredom as any other motive. In a 1919 *New York Sun* article entitled "Has 227 Wounds, but Is Looking for Job," one of countless early hyperbolic newspaper articles promoting Hemingway's image as a tough death-defier, a reporter had written: "He did not give up war work when he got rid of those thirty-two slugs. Weary of doing nothing, he obtained permission to go to the front again in October, staying there until armistice."[118] In a different time and place, this is exactly what Ernest Hemingway did in a world war the second time around.

A week after arriving in London, Hemingway's military jeep crashed into a water tank in Lowndes Square during a blackout. Hemingway spent four days at the London Clinic, where his treatment for a severe concussion required him to remain flat in bed with his head braced and immobile. After his release from the hospital on May 29, 1944, he remained plagued by excruciating headaches. Thus, in an instant, the war had not only provided formal permission "not to think," but an injury which facilitated forgetting.

His head injury kept him from beginning his tour with the RAF, but the invasion of Normandy was expected any day, and with headaches, swollen knees, and all, Hemingway instantly got the kind of exalted drama which he craved. On the early morning of June 6, 1944, he found himself on an amphibious landing ship, alongside troops of the U.S. Fourth Infantry Division, surging through mined waters toward the Normandy coast on D-day. When the only map of the coast in the commander's possession blew overboard, the crew could not identify the beach they were supposed to land on. The commander ignored Hemingway's warning that machine-gun fire was coming from the pillboxes on the beach, and gunfire rained on the crew as the ship careened toward the beach. They skirted stakes fastened with contact mines and eventually landed on Utah Beach under the protection of a Navy destroyer. A disappointed Hemingway, however, never made landfall. With tanks burning in the distance, his LCVP (Landing Craft, Vehicle, Personnel) took the wounded and survivors off the beach, ferried them to a nearby destroyer, then returned to land their troops and materiel, "and that was that," as Hemingway wrote afterward.[119]

Back in England, he returned to the field, flew in an RAF B-25 as it bombed German launching sites in France, and characteristically rendered a stoical, yet fervent portrait of the heroic fighting man, who despite the aid of the most advanced military hardware, is often vulnerable to forces out of his control. Though Hemingway was to complain that the censor's pen gutted the most interesting parts of his articles, he reveled in the details of war—the make and model of a gun, the strategy required to shoot down a certain type of airplane. Ironically, though he castigated propaganda strenuously, his war coverage rang of it, exuberantly celebrating Western military might. Unfortunately for him, however, Hemingway found the military hardware more interesting than the assignment itself. He was anxious for more excitement than the RAF offered, and after six weeks in England, Hemingway transferred to France on July 18, where he attached himself to the Fourth Infantry Division's 22d Regiment through most of the summer of 1944, as Allied troops liberated the country.

The fighting was intense. Hemingway's regiment came under heavy tank attack as they pushed rapidly along the main roads leading southward from St. Lo to Avranches on the Brittany coast, at times launching one attack a day. On Saturday, August 5, Hemingway coaxed his friend, *Life* photographer Robert Capa, who was taking photographs around the nearby coastal resort of Granville, to join him and the 22d Regiment for the attack on the village of St. Pois. On the way, Hemingway sat in the sidecar of his captured German motorcycle, with Capa and the public relations officer assigned to Hemingway following behind in a captured Mercedes. Suddenly they came smack up against a German patrol. Hemingway's motorcycle driver slammed on the brakes as it came around a sharp curve in the road, and Hemingway careened into a shallow ditch, but not without hitting his head on a boulder and sustaining his second concussion in two months. While Capa and the others crouched safely behind the curve, Hemingway lay in the ditch for two hours as he was sprayed by antitank machine guns. At one point, two Germans armed with machine pistols stood ten feet away, and Hemingway pretended to be dead to fool them. When it was over, Hemingway was more furious with Capa than with his German attackers, accusing the photographer of lying in wait to get a photograph of his dead body.[120] After the incident, his back hurt, and he was urinating blood, but the grinding headaches had temporarily subsided. He was sleeping again. He was also in love.

Until his hospitalization in London, Hemingway had continued to delude himself that only the war divided him from Martha—writing to her in Italy, trying to arrange meetings in London between their hectic schedules, mentioning her in family letters as though everything were fine. Her failure to nurse him while he was recuperating from his jeep accident not only stpipped him of illusions, but turned submerged resentment into raw hatred. In fact, Martha did visit him in the hospital, where she discovered, to her disgust, that the accident had occurred on the way home from an all-night drinking party at Capa's apartment. Hemingway saw only that she had abandoned him, and he accused her of not doing "anything for a man that we would do for a dog."[121] Overnight, the effusions of a warm, loving husband became the sniping of a bitter, neglected man. He pilloried Martha, calling her, among other names, "Prima-Donna," which he applied to a woman as contemptuously as he applied "coward" to a man. Certainly it was a far more derogatory epithet than "rich-bitch" and "whore"—his names for Pauline after the end of their marriage. At the time of the Normandy invasion, Hemingway had told a fellow correspondent, "Hell, I had to go to war to see my wife," and when he reflected on the marriage a few months later, Hemingway decided that he had made a "very great mistake" by marrying Gellhorn.[122] Yet, he rationalized that it wasn't his fault, because after they had wed, she had transformed into a completely different person from the wonderful "Marty" he had been with in Spain. The shame of it, he felt, was that he had wasted so much time and effort teaching Martha how to "shoot and write well."[123] In October, Hemingway summed up the circumstances surrounding the demise of his marriage in a letter to Max Perkins: "Funny how it should take one war to start a woman in your damn heart and another to finish her."[124]

Hemingway could not have discarded Martha so fast, had not the kind of earth-shattering luck befallen him that in his fiction made the difference between life and death, success and failure. Just days after arriving in London, Hemingway met Mary Welsh, a thirty-six-year-old writer for Time-Life-Fortune. A Minnesotan originally, she was married to an Australian journalist working in London and having an affair with Irwin Shaw, a young private who later achieved fame as the author of such novels as *The Young Lions* and *Rich Man, Poor Man*. It was Shaw, attached to the same documentary film unit as Hemingway's younger brother Leicester, who introduced Hemingway to Welsh.[125]

With the possibility of death at any moment and the probability that love discovered in wartime had no future, war was the best matchmaker for a man who had a habit of idealizing love, sex, and women—that is, until he was married to one for a while. The perfect Hemingway woman throws herself at her man with her entire being. She is willing to be anything and do anything for him. Maria in *For Whom the Bell Tolls* epitomized this ideal to the hilt, telling Robert Jordan she wants to be his "servant." Hemingway yearned above all to attain his ideal of being one in body and spirit with his lover, especially as each successive marriage failed. "We will be as one animal of the forest and be so close that neither one can tell that one of us is one and not the other," Maria tells Robert Jordan in *For Whom the Bell Tolls*, as the lovers lie beside each other in the cold snow beneath their makeshift sleeping bag. "Can you not feel my heart be your heart? I am thee and thou art me and all of one is the other." The pillow talk nauseated critic Edmund Wilson, who described this in his 1941 book *The Wound and the Bow* as "the all-too-perfect felicity of a youthful erotic dream."[126]

In the summer of 1944, Mary Welsh appeared to Hemingway like an angel of mercy. At forty-five, he received her with a passion no less intense than when, as a nineteen-year-old wounded veteran in Italy, he reveled in the love of his night nurse Agnes Von Kurowsky, or when as a thirty-eight-year-old in Spain he arranged weekends with Martha Gellhorn. With Hemingway suffering painful headaches from his London jeep crash and Mary eager to nurse him, they met secretly in hotel rooms whenever he could get away from his division.

As with his other wives, Mary Welsh stood in stark contrast to the woman she supplanted. She was a nurturing caretaker whom Hemingway first nicknamed "Papa's Pocket Rubens," then "Pickle"—the name which stuck. Hemingway liked the fact that Mary was "an eater," and admired her "sound, un-lying competent head." She was physically active, known after the war for welcoming guests to La Finca Vigia's swimming pool in the nude, and she released in the thrice-married, middle-aged Hemingway a torrent of romantic love and sexual passion. "Dearest lovely Pickle in the yellow bed jacket with the magic lovely mouth and the figure heads of all my ships and the place that knows exactly what it wants to do and has, lying beside you, its partner who wants to do that and no other. I love you very much."[127]

Hemingway lamented from the field how much he missed her, and wrote how grateful he was to be dead tired so that he barely had time for yearning. "I miss you so I am hollow and to fill the hollow I put war in day and night. But it is a lousy substitute; like drinking worcester sauce instead of what? Instead of what? Instead of being happy I guess."[128]

Undoubtedly, war did fill up the hollow. As Patton's newly organized Third Army advanced rapidly on Paris in August 1944, Hemingway traveled along the same countryside he had ridden by bicycle and car as a young writer in the 1920s. His familiarity with the terrain, knowledge of battle, as well as his ability to speak French, made him valuable to the commanders of the Fourth Infantry Division, who welcomed him as warmly as Lucasz and Heilbrun had in Spain. He reveled in the responsibility and camaraderie. The "general and I are good friends and we lie on the same blanket when he is dead, dust, impossible tired at the end of the day," he reported to Mary.[129] Relieved from ravaging boredom and loneliness and absolutely gushing in his love for Welsh, Hemingway's mood was positively buoyant: "Actually we have a very jolly and gay life full of deads, German loot, much shooting, much fighting, hedges, small hills, dusty roads, metalled roads, green country, wheat fields, dead cows, horses, new hills, dead horses, tanks, 88's, Kraftwagens, dead U.S. guys, sometimes don't eat at all, sleep in the rain, on the ground, in barns, on carts, on cots, on one's ass and always moveing, moveing [sic]."[130]

All that summer of 1944, Hemingway repeated the pattern of observer-participant he had long established, whether it meant getting into the ring to write about boxing, killing big game in order to write about killing, or bearing a gun during a battle to write about soldiering. As the American army converged to liberate Paris, Hemingway did whatever he had dreamed, imagined, or desired to do in past wars. As in Spain, he had plenty of detractors in competing journalists who found him childish and pretentious, quick with his liquor and a punch, and bizarre in his penchant for carrying a gun and acting like a soldier. But Hemingway could feel like a winner, in fact, for the first time. He had gotten everything he wanted: a war, a woman, and a gun.

In August 1944, knowing the Americans were advancing on Paris, the Germans had cleared out of the town of Rambouillet, twenty-five miles southwest of the capital, but they were still scattered amid the Rambouillet forest north and south of the Americans, and had installed machine-gunners in wheat stacks. Heavy fighting broke out between Rambouillet and Versailles. Hemingway had friends inside the French Resistance, and in the third week of August he broke off from his regiment with permission from Fourth Infantry Division General Raymond Barton, and went to Rambouillet with the intention not only of being the first journalist on the scene, but of helping to identify German positions. The forest was filled with French Maquis resistance fighters—Louis Pasteur's grandson among them—who were collecting information on German strength and position in preparation for the advance on Paris the next day. On August 20, 1944, Hemingway, in concert with the head of the Office of Strategic Services in France, Colonel David Bruce, established the Hotel du Grand Veneur, outside Rambouillet, as the center of the intelligence gathering and defense of the town, which Hemingway expected the Germans to try to retake at any moment.

To safeguard himself against the likely assertion that he was violating the Geneva Convention's ban on journalists carrying guns or leading soldiers, Bruce provided Hemingway with a handwritten order, which he wore inside his shirt when he went out on patrols with Major James W. Thorton of the Second Infantry Regiment of the Fifth Division. The Maquis stored their arms in his bathtub, and Hemingway himself carried a Tommy gun, much to the shock and fury of journalists who arrived after him, only to find that with Colonel Bruce's tacit approval, Hemingway had commandeered their hotel rooms to store bazookas, grenades, and other weapons. William Hearst Jr. was among those who arrived at the hotel and got into a brawl with Hemingway at the hotel bar after chastising Hemingway for telling a GI courier that he was the officer in charge of the press billet. According to Hearst, who was covering the war for his father's newspaper, the *Journal-American*, and later wrote about the incident in his memoir, Hemingway faked reaching into his left shirt pocket to produce his credentials, then sucker-punched him. According to Hearst, Hemingway "slugged down the last of his drink, and swaggered out of the bar like a four-star general," leaving Hearst lying on the floor. The son of one of America's more famous egomaniacs, Hearst nevertheless found Hemingway's megalomania astonishing. "He was the Press Papa—Eisenhower, Bradley, Patton, and Montgomery rolled into one," Hearst later wrote.[131] After Hearst's group arrived in Paris the day after General Jacques Leclerc and his French Armored Second Division entered Paris and the Germans surrendered, he encountered Hemingway at the bar of the Scribe Hotel, where he was "holding court" among the other newsmen who had converged upon the city. Hemingway seemed more concerned that Hearst had told others about the sucker punch than he was apologetic, and Hearst showed no willingness to forgive him. But as in countless other instances where journalists had found Hemingway "a pompous stuffed shirt," he ignored his colleagues' disrespect, or even contempt.[132] For one week of his life, America's number one novelist at the time, whose poor eyesight had kept him from really being a soldier, whose many bumps and scars came almost entirely from clumsy accidents, and who had declared after World War I that "all the real heros are dead," *was* a real American military hero. He had taken off his journalist badge and patroled the town with a gun, conducted interrogations with Colonel Bruce and the Maquis leader, and provided intelligence information which Colonel Bruce gave to General Jacques Leclerc, who was leading his French Second Armored Division into Paris.

As the U.S. Army advanced toward the city on August 24, 1944, on a road littered with bodies, Hemingway was behind in his Willys jeep, carrying a carbine, and wearing a shirt with the Fourth Infantry division shoulder patch. It had rained heavily, and muddy wheat fields were riddled with machine-gun fire as Germans attacked them nearly the whole way. Hemingway later wrote in his *Collier's* article, "How We Came to Paris," "My own aim at this moment was to get into Paris without getting shot."[133]

About ten miles outside of the city, Germans attacked the lead tank. Having left their jeeps in the narrow, muddy road, Hemingway and correspondent Andy Rooney, writing for the army newspaper *Stars and Stripes*, hid behind a stone wall for over an hour as the combat division tried to locate German gun positions. While Rooney trembled with fear, he remembered that Hemingway, carrying a pistol, "honestly was enjoying the whole operation. It was a toy war for him at that point."[134] A couple of days earlier when the newsmen had been in the dining room of their hotel outside Rambouillet, Rooney had witnessed Hemingway's futile attempt to goad a fellow journalist into a fight, and he had found Hemingway's behavior shockingly "childish." Now, as Hemingway happily babbled about himself and German gun positions while the Germans threatened to knock out the division's tanks, Rooney was confused by his impressions of Hemingway, because it seemed as though the writer had no real appreciation of the danger. Rooney was unaware that Hemingway had a superstitious fatalism about dying, often remaining in the center of a shelling as everyone else took cover, because he believed he would be killed when it was time, and then nothing and no one could save him.

As Hemingway's column entered Paris, they ran for cover from German tank and sniper fire near the Bois de Bologne, and again near the Arc de Triomphe, where shooting erupted among the crowds of ecstatic French when a grenade was suddenly thrown—probably by a Fascist—as the liberating troops took some prisoners away. For the next ten minutes, there was shooting, including tank fire. The Arc was badly damaged, German prisoners were kicked and beaten by the French, and when it was over, all the prisoners were dead. Hemingway's division had arrived with a bang—just the way he liked it.

Weeks later, with childlike glee, Hemingway boasted that his actions on the way into Paris were "straight out of Mosby," referring to the famous Confederate ranger John Singleton Mosby, whose independent raids on Union bases and camps were so successful that part of north central Virginia became known as "Mosby's Confederacy."[135] Hemingway claimed to have killed "122 krauts" during the Rambouillet assault, an assertion that was never proven and widely doubted. According to eyewitnesses, Hemingway did drive his jeep toward enemy lines to draw their fire, and when he fired his machine gun back at them, he may well have killed some Germans. In print, he was cautiously coy, and described his contribution as being limited to his translation of the Resistance fighters' account of German activities. He criticized American troops for their condescending treatment toward the Maquis, whom they referred to as "that guerilla rabble," whereas he found them, like all other freedom fighters, courageous and admirable.

As in the case of his adventures on the *Pilar*, Hemingway's unorthodox actions in Rambouillet came under official scrutiny, although with the army, and not the

FBI, directing the investigation, Hemingway received a judgment more to his liking. On October 6, Colonel Parks, the Inspector General of Patton's Third Army, interrogated Hemingway at army headquarters in Nancy, on a charge of breaking the Geneva Convention by acting as a noncommissioned person leading a military group into battle. Hemingway was both amused and honored by the charge. He wanted recognition for what he considered were his courageous actions, but an admission that he commanded the Maquis unit would have led to his release from assignment, perhaps even to his being sent to prison. He was definitely not ready to go home.

Under oath, he denied all the charges, and he was exonerated. He attributed most of his actions to the gathering of material for his stories, and told the inspector general that he only gave advice to troops when he knew it did not contravene the Geneva Convention. He explained that he was the sole person who could act as a translator for two carloads of French guerrilla fighters he had met on their way from Rambouillet to the 22d Regiment's outpost near Maintenon, and told Parks that it was only after the guerrillas became "very impatient," waiting around to be joined by an American mine-clearing and reconnaisance detail to return to Rambouillet, that they "placed themselves under my command ignorant of the fact that a war correspondent cannot command troops, a situation I explained to them at the earliest moment."[136]

In private afterward, Hemingway gloated how he had fooled the investigators, or as he termed it, "Beat rap."[137] Indeed, many of his answers seem comical in retrospect, and reflect Hemingway's skill in bending the truth to suit his own purposes. The only times he ever removed his correspondent's insignia, he testified, was when the weather was warm and he wore shirtsleeves; if he was ever referred to as a "colonel," it was as an empty term of respect and affection, he said, as in the case of a "Kentucky colonel," or as the Chinese refer to a longtime military man as "general."[138]

In the months and years after the incident, Hemingway flip-flopped on what really happened on the forward drive to Paris, at first denying, then accepting responsibility. He joked that his unconventional leading of the Maquis was due to the fact that his brain had "been seriously impaired" in the London jeep accident. He never wavered, however, on how much the drive into Paris meant to him. "That summer from Normandy into Germany was the happiest I ever had in spite of it being in war," he recalled two years later. "[R]e-taking France and especially Paris made me feel the best I had ever felt."[139] The Rambouillet incident came to a final, ironic end, when the military rewarded Hemingway for his ultimate fantasy come true by bestowing on him the Bronze Star on June 16, 1947, at the U.S. embassy in Havana, for his work done in World War II with the French Maquis.

The liberation of Paris on August 25, 1944, gave the free world the solid hope that victory was at hand. Parisians were euphoric. Streets stained in blood, trodden for four years by Nazi jackboots, suddenly swelled with joyous dancing, singing, and drinking. Though Hemingway was an American and not even a soldier, the liberation was especially sweet for him. The happiest time of his life had been in Paris with Hadley during the early 1920s—a period he would later describe as "the time of innocence and the lack of useless money and still being able to work and eat."[140] Despite having been broke and struggling as a writer, he had lived exuberantly among the era's most dynamic artists and writers, including Picasso, Braque, Miró, Gris, Joyce, and Pound, and without the burden of being "a property," as he had come to think of himself after his father's suicide left him the sole provider for his mother and younger siblings.

Now Hemingway arrived with the first of the liberators, and felt as though he were one of them. As he strolled through the Travellers Club and the Hotel Ritz, whose Imperial Suite had been the Paris home to Nazi leader Hermann Goering, Hemingway felt a sense of personal liberation and victory that had eluded him since boyhood, when war was an imaginary game he played but enemies seemed real. "Why don't you ever think of how it is to win?" Robert Jordan asks himself in *For Whom the Bell Tolls*, expressing Hemingway's deep pain at always feeling like the loser. For that moment in Paris, in the flurry of exultation and victory, "all so improbable that you feel like you have died and it is all a dream," as he wrote to Mary, Hemingway's feelings of failure and defeat were exorcised.[141] During his champagne and brandy-filled week-long stay at the Ritz, he cooked on a GI gas stove in his room for guests like Jean-Paul Sartre and Simone de Beauvoir, entertained American Army officers, and managed to see other old friends like Pablo Picasso. When he wrote to his son Patrick that he felt he had "never been happier nor had a more useful life,"[142] Hemingway carefully avoided the fact that part of his bliss in just-liberated Paris came from a rendevouz with Mary.

After the liberation, Hemingway rejoined the 22d Infantry Regiment, Fourth Infantry Division, in the town of Houffalize, forty miles southeast of Liège in southeastern Belgium. In Rambouillet, he had acquired a new bodyguard-driver from the ranks of the French resisters, and during his brief stay in Houffalize, townspeople took him for an American general. Hemingway did not dispel their impression, but rather told them he had only made captain's rank because he was illiterate.[143] The comic respite in Houffalize was brief, however. In the thick Ardennes forest laced with mines and concealed pillboxes, American forces were about to lose all their technological superiority and suffer one of their worst reverses in northwest Europe. In what became the last autumn of the war in Europe, Hemingway witnessed the American army's heaviest fighting yet.

In late August 1944, Allied forces had rolled back the shreds of the tattered German army in Belgium, and moved across the virtually unmanned Siegfried line, the German chain of steel forts and concrete tank barriers that ran along the Franco-German border. In early September, American army commanders poised for a massive offensive to end the war either by moving into the Ruhr Valley and across Germany to Berlin, as Montgomery wanted, or by advancing broadly toward the Rhine River, as Eisenhower was recommending. The commanders then agreed to attack from the north at Arnhem in Holland, but after ten days of fighting, the attempt failed miserably in late September, when airborne troops landed in the midst of two panzer divisions and received inadequate support from the south.

Throughout September and October, German forces bitterly fought the American First Army west of the Rhine, and although Aachen, less than thirty miles from Liège over the German border, fell to the Americans on October 24, the Germans prevented them from crossing the river. Fierce battles raged in and around the wedge-shaped Ardennes where Hemingway thought he might die in

September during the fight at Schnee-Eifel, and in the Huertgen Forest, where his Fourth Division was bivouacked throughout a bitterly cold November and part of December waiting for relief from the U.S. 9th and 28th Divisions, which had launched the devastating offensive to break through the German defenses south of Aachen, and cross the Rhine.[144] In November, the Ninth Army Division alone lost 4,500 men advancing just 1.8 miles. Hemingway's 22d Regiment sustained almost 2,700 casualties.[145]

With its thick pine canopy and needle floor, the Belgian Ardennes reminded Hemingway of boyhood vacations spent in Upper Michigan, but the Huertgen, just northeast of the Ardennes, in Germany, was like Wyoming, he wrote, filled with similar deer, hare, fox, and wild pigeon. The forests' richness delighted the naturalist in Hemingway, but artillery and mortar fire were unremittingly heavy and that reminded him of the sepulchre of World War I. "This is one of the bitterest and worst fights in history," he wrote to Mary on November 20. "Everyday in the woods is like Custer's last stand if that distinguished leader had fought his way out of it and slain the red men."[146]

Despite the terrible toll on Lanham's regiment, Hemingway thrived. He felt he was part of history—that he was bearing witness to that kind of rare, immense, and legendary battle he had included in *Men at War*. The region's unique hilly terrain and bitter winter weather made it the most difficult of the entire western front. November and December were marked by raw, harsh winds, heavy mist, and rains. Flooded, yellow muddy streams reached to the men's waists, and sometimes as much as a foot of snow fell in one day. Prior to World War I the region had seen no significant bloodshed, as army movements chose to encircle the forest rather than pass through it. When in mid-November it snowed and rained for days, mines became impossible to detect, and roads and terrain became impassable with mud and snow, Hemingway found that predicting the strategy for an impending battle in this "fine wild beautiful impractical country" became his "favorite thing." The fighting invigorated him and made him feel young again. He wrote to Mary, "I get the old feeling of immortality back I used to have when I was 19—right in the middle of a really bad shelling—not the cagey assessment of chances—nor the angry, the hell with it feeling—nor the throw away everything feeling—none of those—just the pure old thing we used to operate on—It doesn't make sense—But it's a lovely feeling."[147]

Hemingway treasured the intensive, round-the-clock companionship with the other men and especially his 22d Infantry Regiment commander, Colonel Charles T. Lanham, with whom he shared an intimate, highly rewarding, and complex friendship. Lanham respected and admired Hemingway's knowledge and bravery, but Hemingway idolized Lanham. He repeatedly referred to the colonel as the bravest and sanest man alive, and in describing Lanham to others, the usually vitriolic Hemingway poured out a stream of affection such as he normally reserved for lovers.

In the hours between fighting, the two men evaluated battles fought and those still to come. They told jokes to each other and played poker, and Hemingway read aloud to him and the other men. Lanham and Hemingway's latest jeep driver, Archie "Red" Pelky, were among his most willing playmates and took part in the crazy antics of "Task Force Hemingway," as the group called themselves. At the smoking ruins of a farmhouse in the Huertgen, Hemingway and his friends took turns using the "mortar" he had constructed out of a length of stove pipe and a toilet seat, with champagne corks as projectiles. The group took aim at improvised targets such as cigarettes, but sometimes fired at each other, and Hemingway once hit Pelky behind the ear.[148] Hemingway felt that he had found the bravest and most devoted friends in all his life among the weary but fun-loving soldiers of the 22d Regiment. The young men revered his worldliness, his calm in the face of the intense German onslaught, and not least, his ability to slug down cognac from his canteen. In this group, Hemingway was never lonely. They dined together, lived together, worked together—even went to the bathroom together. As a child, Hemingway had been frightened by the dark, but here, at night, "dog-tired," he slept happily in a sleeping bag, inches away from a soldier sleeping beside him. His feeling of belonging slaked his terrible loneliness and cured his insomnia.

The fun of making "chickenshits wish they were never born" did not diminish Hemingway's awareness that he was taking a big risk to see war this close.[149] On November 16, the very day the U.S. First Army launched the Huertgen offensive, Hemingway requested that his *Collier's* editor name "Mary Welsh of Life and Time Inc., 4 Place de la Concorde" his sole life insurance beneficiary in place of Martha G. Hemingway, with whom he had already worked out a property settlement in preparation for divorce.[150] Hemingway had made up his mind about his "darling lovely beautiful dearest always Pickle" with the quickness of a teenager swept away by an all-consuming crush. He wanted her as his wife.

Hemingway ached to be enveloped in the kind of physical, emotional, and intellectual oneness with Mary that would make him feel loved, nurtured, and safe, but love was bound up in Hemingway's credo with profound responsibility, and much of the couple's wartime romance, especially the longer he endured the raging battle that winter, consisted of Hemingway's heart-wrenching promises to be the "perfect husband" who would provide them with the "perfect" future in which they would do nothing but write, make love, eat and drink, and fish. In the winter of 1944–45, as Europeans endured a renewed show of German tenacity which culminated in Hitler's massive offensive in France and Belgium beginning in December 1944, Hemingway, too, could see the future beyond German defeat, and that was what frightened him. For all his bravado, he was like the little boy in his story "Fathers and Sons," who wishes that his whole family can be buried alongside each other so they can be together in eternity. Finding in Mary Welsh a woman who "wants to stick around with me and let me be the writer of the family," a woman who "[s]ince childies have to be in school am not going to be lonely to die and not able to work," Hemingway poured forth boundless gratitude to Mary like a dying man who had found the cure.[151] He expressed his vision of oneness to Mary and his hopes for the future, but rather than being earthy, sexually unfettered, and exuberant, it bleat pitifully with its sad, underlying cry against aloneness. Hemingway wasn't afraid of death, he had told her, but of reaching London and "finding you were gone somewhere."[152] He promised to stay alive, cut down on his drinking, and write good books that would make her proud of him. Yet, the closer he came to leaving Europe, the more encompassing became his fear of the future. So long as he was in Germany, or "Krautland," as he called it, watching Germans getting killed, which was "the most pleasurable thing a man

could do," he felt protected by the love of a woman, which he said was "as necessary to me as a compass." He professed to look forward to their new life together,
but when he thought about it too hard, the fairy-tale picture turned nightmarish.
Daily his mood swung between joy in the morning when he awoke flushed with
the prospect of battle, and despondency by afternoon as he broke under the weight
of the challenge to be a good husband. Waking to a new day of fighting, he told
Mary he was "happy as always, but then started to think about how wanted our
life together and had a real défaillance . . . so did 50 belly exercises and had one
eighth bottle of Scotch left so drank that in four drinks with water and no left at all
and then piled out into the rain and the rain washed it all away."[153]

What the rain could not wash away was Hemingway's underlying awareness
that he had been largely to blame for the failures of his marriages, despite his
windy protests to the contrary. In 1936, in "The Snows of Kilimanjaro," he came
as close as he would ever come to expressing his sense of culpability when his
dying writer acknowledges, "with the women he loved he had quarrelled so much
they had finally, always, with the corrosion of the quarrelling, killed what they
had together. He had loved too much, demanded too much, and he wore it all
out."[154] Hemingway had never stopped loving his first wife, Hadley; he had never
stopped feeling guilty about hurting her by committing adultery, nor had he
stopped feeling remorseful that his three children had grown up in broken homes.
Courting Mary Welsh in 1944, Hemingway's relentless avowals that he would
make her a fine husband, blended with the effulgent outpouring of love and desperate promises, express his fear that the relationship would end badly, in bitterness and meanness, like the others. The couple promised not to be critical of the
other, and to Mary he frankly acknowledged his dependence on liquor, which he
now called "the Giant Killer," because it was so destructive at the same time that
"loved it, needed it so much."[155] With crippled pride, he detailed the "toughest
day" of fighting, together with the proud report that he had not had a drink for two
days, and he labored to profess confidence that in the perfect life he had planned
for them, they would be "so happy and tired and fine feeling we wont have to
drink in the night."[156]

But Hemingway seemed to know he could only lose if he made his struggle
with alcohol yet another test of his strength, character, and success as a husband.
Sobriety could not last, promises could not be kept, so long as the alcoholic kept
his three military-issue water canteens filled with wine, premixed martinis, or
cognac, and hiatuses at the Ritz were drenched in brut champagne. As the time
grew closer for him to leave the war and return to his civilian writer's life in Cuba,
Hemingway was almost as anxious as he had been before he left that lonely life to
plunge into what was for him the magnificent maelstrom and escape of war.

Hemingway had been at work on *For Whom the Bell Tolls* when he expressed
in the most cogent terms to his publisher Charles Scribner his ambivalence about
the act of writing. "Charlie there is no future in anything. I hope you agree. That
is why I like it at a war. Every day and every night there is a strong possibility that
you will get killed and not have to write. I have to write to be happy whether I get
paid for it nor not. But it is a hell of a disease to be born with."[157] Hemingway
loved writing more than anything else he did, but there was part of him that hated
it too, because he made the stakes so high. Those times when he was confident he

had achieved his exacting standard of good writing, Hemingway momentarily felt redeemed of being the heathen who had disgraced his orthodox parents by being a writer, a drinker, and a divorcé. When in 1927 he was still modest enough to plead for their forgiveness and understanding, he urged his father to see that he did not pander "to the lowest tastes," as his mother charged, but rather attempted to portray life as it really was. "You could if you wanted be proud of me some-times," Hemingway begged, "not for what I do for I have not had much success in doing good—but for my work, ... you cannot know how it makes me feel for Mother to be ashamed of what I know as sure as you know that there is a God in heaven is not to be ashamed of."[158]

Because leaving the war to begin his wonderful new life also meant writing fic-tion again, Hemingway's extreme ambivalence toward his work reared with a vengeance in the waning months of his term in Europe. In large part he had gone to war because he needed a new story to write about, and just as he had hoped, ideas for a novel began flowing in his imagination almost immediately after he arrived. One more time he was bolstered by a new love and the sound of small machine-gun pistols going "trrrrrrutt—Trrrrut—like a kittycat purring but hard and metallic."[159]

When Hemingway described to Mary during the Huertgen battle the glory of killing and in the next breath stated his burning desire to make love to her, he was expressing what was for him a natural joining of sex, love, and death, a symbiosis which was the source of intense creativity. Like his weak-kneed character Francis Macomber, Hemingway always found release from his fear of death and cow-ardice in danger and risk of death, and for him, killing or—in the case of the Ardennes and Huertgen battles in the winter of 1944–45—witnessing killing was an affirmative act of creation, like writing or sex, which is why Hemingway always said it made him feel so alive.[160]

Hemingway had been in Europe less than two months when he felt a story tak-ing shape based on his experiences in Normandy with the Fourth Infantry Division as it broke through above the city of St. Lo and pushed east toward Paris. By the middle of October, he could report to editor Max Perkins from the Siegfried Line, "We hit very fine pay dirt on this prospecting trip."[161] The war had given him a story to tell, but Hemingway wanted to write something more pro-found than the traditional "war book." His novel would have to be about things more basic than politics, personal ambitions, or national agendas, which he believed repeated themselves endlessly, ignorantly, and pointlessly. For a writer who had always been deeply affected by the mysterious, sometimes merciless, always magnificent powers of nature, and who had been toying with the idea of a novel about the sea since 1940, Hemingway's recent experiences flying the skies with the RAF and stalking the battered countryside with the American infantry had given him the impetus he needed. "Have stuff for wonderful book," Hemingway told Perkins. "Want to write novel—not war book. It should have the sea and the air and the ground in it."[162]

The exuberance Hemingway showed to Perkins, however, belied his private ter-ror. He despaired of failing, and confided to Mary that no matter how hard he tried he would not be able to "write what I want." He felt pressure to earn a lot of money, since he had not made much in five years, and he also felt pressure not to repeat himself, since he had written two war novels already. He told Mary he was "trying to see and notice all the things I haven't fooled with"; nevertheless, he was feeling old, jaded, and threatened by young, new writers coming up behind him, like J. D. Salinger and William Saroyan, whom he had recently met during their military tours in Europe. "I will just take my small piece of a tiny part of it and buttress it with the forgotten sometimes punchy knowledge and the new will work the mess so the old magic will work—and then we will have a book one day at a time."[163]

In the meantime, however, there was still plenty of battle to absorb for a novel. A delusionary Hitler had refused to see the ignominious defeat his commanders recognized as a certainty, and instead believed that if his troops redoubled their assault against the U.S. First Army, the Allied western front might collapse. In extreme secrecy deep within the Ardennes, Hitler refurbished guns and tanks, assembled twenty-eight divisions of 250,000 men, and under the nominal command of the seventy-year-old, semiretired Field Marshal Gerd von Rundstedt, launched a massive offensive in the region on December 16, 1944. Hitler's plan—though even von Rundstedt was appalled at the risks—was to divide the Allied army, which had been weakened in the Ardennes, into three sections, recapture its vital supply port at Antwerp, Belgium, and thereby force the British off the continent as had been achieved at Dunkirk in 1940. German forces would then be freed to stop the Soviet offensive expected at the Danube Valley in the coming spring.

Bad weather and the element of surprise enabled the Germans to gain an advantage at the Belgian cities of Liège, Saint-Vith, and Bastogne, but reinforced Allied forces under Field Marshal Sir Bernard Montgomery, General Omar Bradley, and Lieutenant General George Patton battered the German forces and halted their advance by the beginning of January. When the Battle of the Bulge ended in mid-January of 1945, Americans accounted for 77,000 of 81,000 Allied casualties, the worst toll in American history.[164]

Sick with a temperature of 104 degrees, Hemingway accompanied the 22d Infantry Regiment during the Battle of the Bulge and the ensuing defense of Luxembourg at the end of December, although he was working solely on his own at this point. In November during the Huertgen battle, he and *Collier's* had come to a messy parting of the ways over what he termed their "mutilation" of the six articles he wrote for them. The clincher came when he gave a story to a *Life* magazine writer for free rather than to *Collier's*, whereupon the magazine abruptly stopped paying his expenses. Hemingway considered this an act of disloyalty for which he never forgave *Collier's*.

When the Luxembourg defense ended, Hemingway returned to his base at the Ritz Hotel. Though Paris was his favorite city in all the world, his imagination had already left Europe for Cuba where he envisioned Mary at La Finca Vigia comforting and arousing him during any and all hours not filled writing his new novel. He eagerly awaited his departure, and passed the time in a state of general alcoholic merriment, entertaining guests such as Marlene Dietrich, with whom he had become good friends the previous autumn.

Knowing he needed a "wife who will be in bed at night instead of in some different war," Hemingway exacted a promise from Mary which he believed would cement their beautiful future.[165] Though he had acknowledged responsibility for his drinking, this did not diminish Hemingway's belief that love was ruined nearly as often by forces completely out of the lovers' control—nature's wrath, aging and infirmity, money problems, death—as by a couple's own selfishness and cruelty. In this case, Hemingway was afraid that the uncontrollable "force" was Mary's journalism career, and so before he left Europe, he asked Mary to agree that when they set up house together in Cuba, she would become Mrs. Ernest Hemingway.[166]

Hemingway flew from Paris to New York on March 6, 1945, on the first leg of his trip home. Mary, who still needed to arrange for her divorce, planned to join him in Cuba as soon as possible. Hemingway promised he would remain faithful to her "in my heart in my mind and in my body."[167] Hemingway summoned all his bonhomie to quell a propensity for seeing women as "bitches" and "whores," but the malicious vision was never far below the surface and always threatened to throw him off kilter. Just months earlier he had told Mary he would dedicate his new novel to her even if she were unfaithful to him "altho might add," he wrote her then with his grim brand of sexual humor, "F—K her the Persian Harlot in parenthesis."[168] Upon leaving Paris for New York, Hemingway reiterated to Mary the urgency of rushing her personal affairs so they could begin their life together. It is likely that his sense of desperation was aggravated by the guilty feelings which always followed a particularly humiliating blunder on his part. Just a few weeks earlier, Mary had almost ended their relationship when Hemingway, in a drunken frenzy, had taken her husband's photograph into her bathroom at the Ritz and machine-gunned it, along with the toilet bowl, sending water gushing to rooms below.[169]

The photographs which captured the homecoming of Cuba's most famous and flamboyant foreign resident as he stepped off the plane at Havana Airport on March 25, 1945, show a forty-six-year-old Hemingway, aged more than twenty years in a scant four. For all his exuberant love of war and danger, the years had taken their toll: the smiling, youthful-looking Hemingway captured by camera in 1941 on the patio of La Finca Vigia with his arm around the waist of Martha Gellhorn was no more. His boyishly cropped black hair was streaked with white. His eyes had narrowed, become old, with spidery lines coursing from the corners. His belly, which had long resisted the telltale alcoholic's paunch, had grown flabby, protruding over the belt which carried his signature miniature Zeiss binoculars and his liquor-filled canteens.

The writer's hulking body had taken an unusual battery of hits over the years— war wounds, hunting accidents, car crashes, parasitic fevers, and fistfights spawned of drunken insanity; Hemingway was like a scarred cavorting Bacchus. But the corporeal scars were nothing compared to the internal demons which plagued him. The rigors of fiction-writing aggravated a relentless, lifelong boredom and loneliness. An obsessive fear of failure as a writer and as a man competed with another, more frightening fear—that he would become the coward his father was and that like his father, he would kill himself someday to relieve his pain.

A man could prove himself in war as in nothing else. If in war you fought bravely, you were brave. If you saved others, you were valiantly selfless and courageous. But if you fought with your wife, lied, whored, and drank, you were just ruining the two of you. And if you wrote a good book and made a lot of money, you proved nothing. Daily life, utterly devoid of the rush of passion under fire or the possibility of heroic death, was boring to Hemingway. The words "bored" and "boring" reappear constantly in his private descriptions of himself and his life, though they seem remarkable to the outsider looking at the larger-than-life big game hunting, bullfighting, and deep sea fishing so ebulliently celebrated in magazines like *Life, Collier's*, and *Cosmopolitan*. When others might have trembled twenty yards from the German offense or cowered from a lion ready to spring, Hemingway felt alive. Where he felt terror was in the quiet shades of gray of everyday life, with a wife, his work, and just plain living. The Huertgen battle was "a fight such as has been fought very few times ever in the world," but the more natural process of aging and, worse, finding oneself alone with only the blank page were fights almost too hard for Hemingway to bear.

Thus, when he returned home to Cuba near the end of the Second World War, the art of fiction-writing reared up as the enemy more frightening than any German. Searing and painful, Hemingway believed the process of writing novels held up an unforgiving mirror to his shortcomings and failures, and yet he was compelled to write. Hemingway had described in *For Whom the Bell Tolls* the "[r]idding of self that you did in war"; at home, far from a war, there were no fox-holes in which he could hide.[170]

Hemingway was home less than a week before "the Black Ass," as he called depression, caught him in its grip.[171] He complained of feeling "lonely and use-less," and "absolutely homesick" for the men of the 22d Regiment, especially Colonel Lanham, whom he missed terribly. Being apart from Mary made him "sick," he wrote Lanham on April 2, though perhaps the worst part of his struggle against the depression was that he could not fall back on his old companion, liquor, in his earnest attempt to stick to his promise to Mary. He had not cut out drinking entirely, but he was not downing two bottles of Perrier Jouet while he shaved as he had at the Ritz when on leave from his battalion. "The son of a bitch is home," he groused to Lanham, speaking about himself. "He's out of it. He ought to be happy. He isn't. When Mary comes it will be different. I'll just try to use this dull time to get in good shape for her and to work."[172]

But Hemingway could not work. Intermittent headaches, ringing in the ears, and stroke-like "slowness" and "loss of verbal memory" from the numerous head injuries he had sustained in Europe had dogged him throughout his European tour, and though he attributed his inability to begin his novel to being sorely out of practice, Hemingway feared that his injuries would prevent him from ever writing again.

Hemingway looked for every excuse he could to avoid sitting down and work-ing, and having been away from his beloved Cuba, house, and boat for nearly a year, this was not hard to do. La Finca Vigia had sustained extensive damage from a hurricane which had swept through the island on October 19, 1944, with 180 MPH winds, and Hemingway threw himself into renovations so that the house and gardens would be at their best for Mary's arrival. He spent time in old haunts with old friends—fishing, playing tennis, and pigeon-shooting—although he tried to avoid settings like the Club de Cazadores del Cerro—his gun club—where there was apt to be heavy drinking. Anyway, he found that killing a pigeon didn't rate with killing a "kraut," so he didn't mind not going.

While he desperately awaited Mary's arrival, Hemingway reiterated his intention to be a good husband, and if he succeeded at that, he told her, he would "be a good writer."[173] To retrieve the discipline of writing in order to ready himself for the novel, Hemingway began writing letters to anyone he could think of—his children, Mary, Perkins, Lanham, ex-wives—often more than five in a day, but he still found himself desperately lonely for Mary, and unable to sleep or work. He counted the days until she was due to arrive in late April, calling this time "Limbo," just as he had the terrible period after Martha left in 1943, and he found himself wishing he could hire someone else like James Thurber "to write what I have learned instead of haveing [*sic*] to write it myself."[174]

Around the middle of April, Hemingway's old friend, Dr. Sotolongo, offered the writer a magnificent gift by providing a medical reason for his inability to concentrate. Sotolongo examined Hemingway's wounded head and found that he had received grossly inadequate treatment in Europe, but expressed the opinion that the symptoms would dissipate with rest and time. Moreover, Hemingway felt greatly relieved by the doctor's suggestion that instances of abhorrent ill humor were attributable to the effects of brandy and gin on his injured brain and not his basic nature as a human being. Sotolongo advised Hemingway to refrain from intensive concentration during his recuperation, which was a good thing, since by now Hemingway had fallen into a deep morass, telling Lanham that he didn't "give a damn about writing and would rather be back with you. This goddamn boreing civil life is wonderful I know but I am bored right through the marrow of all the old bones."[175]

For Mary's sake he had managed to maintain a celibate, mostly abstemious life—he had even turned down a tempting offer to open a brothel, in spite of the fact he thought it "would be a lovely place to go in afternoons when bored." But feelings of loneliness, boredom, uselessness, and trepidation engulfed him.[176] His sarcastic quip that at La Finca Vigia his command merely included four gardeners, a butler, a maid, and a Chinese cook betrayed mournful feelings of uselessness now that he had no Maquis to lead into brave battle. He worried, too, over lack of any word regarding his eldest son, John, who had joined the Office of Strategic Services in July 1944, been severely wounded and captured in Germany the previous October, and was interred in a prisoner-of-war camp. Hemingway kept insisting that his depression would lift as soon as his life with Mary began, and admitted to Lanham that while he waited for her arrival, he felt he was "just killing days and wishing I were a soldier instead of a chickenshit writer. Old worthless wish."[177]

The long days of waiting finally came to an end when Mary arrived in Cuba in the first week of May 1945, and the glorious "new life" for which he craved seemed to begin auspiciously. The Germans surrendered on May 7, and his son John, despite a serious injury to his right arm and weight loss, was otherwise fine after his release from a Nuremberg prisoner-of-war camp. Yet, that spring day, so festive for millions around the world, included an incident in Hemingway's life which demonstrated that the end of the war, rather than being a great new beginning, was in fact the beginning of his slow end. He and Mary were celebrating the end of the war in Europe at La Floridita, when a poor amateur artist unwittingly provoked him by sketching a portrait in hopes that Hemingway would give him some money. Hemingway destroyed the sketch, threw its remnants on the floor, and cruelly insulted the artist, who then fled the bar. As always when Hemingway created a humiliating scene, remorse set in after the crestfallen man left the bar. Hemingway left a message of apology, accompanied by a twenty-dollar bill.[178]

In the autumn of 1945 Hemingway finally got down to work on his novel, his first in more than five years. In many respects, the physical changes in him between 1941 and 1945 marked a chasm of aging, from youth to old age, although at forty-six Ernest Hemingway was merely middle-aged. One of his greatest works, *The Old Man and the Sea*, a spare, monumental, overwhelmingly sad tale of one man's quest to meet his greatest challenge, was yet to come, but the years of Hemingway's top production and critical success were behind him when war broke out in Europe. The novel that Hemingway finally began writing in the autumn of 1945 was not a war book, nor was it even the novel he had planned to write when he was covering the Schnee-Eifel and Huertgen battles. The novel he began, *Garden of Eden*, was not even published during his lifetime. Despite continuous rewriting, he never finished this most bizarre and most personal of all his works.

Garden of Eden gave vent to Hemingway's closest demons during his courtship of Mary when soon he would have to leave the cocoon of military life and return to Cuba as a civilian, husband, and writer. There were no heroes in *Garden of Eden*; in fact, there was barely the semblance of rational behavior. Hemingway's continued reworking of the book over the next thirteen years suggests the highly personal nature of the writing, as well as his probable suspicion that its graphic, unorthodox sexuality, involving bisexuality and sexual transference, was too provocative for public taste. *Garden of Eden* reads as if it were secret notes Hemingway wrote at night when liquor failed as a soporific, and in fact, the novel was pieced together from more than a thousand handwritten pages for publication by Scribner's in 1988.

The story of newlywed writer David Bourne was filled with Hemingway's usual, and increasingly consuming, obsessions—redemption through animal killing, the suicide of a father, who had humiliated and punished him as a youth, alcoholism, lying, and the quest for complete love with a woman. To reach that love, David and his new wife, Catherine, want to obliterate the sexual roles that alienate men and women. However, Catherine, jealous of her husband's writing talent and fame, becomes increasingly bizarre in her sexual and emotional desires. Bourne, at first willing to do anything to please his wife, is driven to despair by Catherine's weird games. Like all of Hemingway's protagonists, David Bourne is the victim of his own weakness, as well as the selfish, often indiscriminate interests of others. Though in the end David finds the perfect love he craves—with his wife's female lover—it is not before Catherine destroys his writings to coerce him into writing about her.[179] In the story, writing is an escape from a troubled marriage, but the better the writing goes, the worse becomes the estrangement between husband and wife. David, like Hemingway, recognizes his inability to reconcile his conflict between writing, which requires isolation, and marriage, which offers companionship, but, for Hemingway and his fictional heroes inevitably resulted in hysterical jealousy and torment. Each day spent in the Garden of Eden harbors the potential for dizzying change and emotional upheaval.

When Mary arrived in Cuba in the spring of 1945, Hemingway felt torn between the novel he wanted to write and his overwhelming need to fulfill his sense of obligation to please her. (The couple married on April 11, 1946.) He had promised her she would adore his island and home as he did, and when she failed to warm up to her new surroundings readily, Hemingway was deeply disappointed. Like David and Catherine, who move about continuously between hotels in Spain and southern France, as though by moving they could keep from ruining each other, by September of 1945 Hemingway was telling Mary, who had returned temporarily to the States to visit her parents, that he could write his novel in some other place of her liking. "[I] can work in Basque country, in Paris, anywhere in the hills, in Spain (am only mentioning where have worked good)," he offered.[180] Paris seemed the best choice, for there Hemingway hoped they could recover the sexual, romantic perfection of their time at the Ritz during the war, and that he could recapture the productivity he achieved as a young writer during the halcyon 1920s, before his father's suicide in 1928.

That event lingered like the ghost that refused to go away. In *Garden of Eden*, Hemingway explored his father's suicide more skillfully and intimately than in any other earlier work. As the tumultuous marriage is being played out, David, whose previous novel was about war, is writing a story about his father and himself when he was six and the two went on safari together. By writing the story, David hopes to understand what his father felt at the moment he died, but in writing it, David also resuscitates the feelings of guilt, betrayal, inadequacy, and persecution his father inspired in him. As soon as young David locates the elephant that his father intends to shoot, he is overcome by a sense of guilt and identification with the hunted animal. In a stark admission of Oedipal conflict, the boy thinks for an instant, "They would kill me and they would kill Kibo too if we had ivory." When his father tells David to finish off the dying elephant, David can't, and he chokes with hate for his father and grief for the animal.

The war had exhausted and depleted Ernest Hemingway, as though it had been the apex of his life, and he bided his time until he ended his life by his own hand, a prospect he had entertained intermittently since the traumatic breakup with Hadley in 1926. In the years immediately following the war, Hemingway's fame grew to immense proportions, and his income grew along with it. The attacks on him continued to be personal and unsparing. Critics obviously knew his vulnerability on the score of bravery, and when anyone challenged his record or truthfulness, he always told them to go ask now-General Lanham or Marlene Dietrich to vouch for him, although the only knowledge Dietrich possessed was what he himself had told her. In 1947 he actually asked Lanham to defend his bravery in a letter to William Faulkner after the latter had mildly critized Hemingway for failing to experiment more in his writing. The Rambouillet and Huertgen experiences took on mythic significance, proof to himself as he sat drunk, despondent, and wistful in Cuba, that he had really had been brave and honest. He became mired in minute alarmist details concerning his health, weight, diet, and bowels, keeping careful records of his blood pressure and temperature and any foods or activities which might explain fluctuations. This obsessive medical bent was likely an inheritance from his father, who maintained his medical office in the family home and frightened his children with horror stories of insanity, blindness, and death, which he often connected with sex. About this time, Hemingway also became obsessed with controlling the growing body of biographical material being written about him, under his fierce conviction that "Any man's autobiography is his own property,"[181] and he described biographers or journalists seeking information on him as "FBIing around."[182] His narrow view of men narrowed further. Someone who had fought in the war and been wounded deserved a measure of sympathy no matter how low a character he might be. Anyone who hadn't been wounded deserved no consideration. In May 1950, Hemingway entertained the idea of inviting Senator Joseph McCarthy to the Finca Vigia to box him so that the senator, "a shit," could vent whatever was eating at him at Americans' expense. "Some of us have even seen the deads and counted them and counted the numbers of McCarthys," he wrote in a letter. "There were quite a lot but you were not one and I have never had the opportunity to count the number of your wounds."[183]

After the war, Hemingway the artist became lost to Hemingway the little boy who had been afraid of the dark. Writing became more of a challenge than it had ever been, and with the terrible effort came dissatisfaction, more unfinished manuscripts and writing that lost its vigor, as Hemingway abandoned free imagination to delve deeper and deeper into his own fears and remorse for the failure of his marriages to Hadley and Pauline and the cost to his children.[184] He was no longer satisfied with depicting external "reality," even if that reality were molded by an intriguing, idiosyncratic personal perspective. He had told Perkins during the war that his ambition was to write something bigger than he had ever done, by penetrating the essence of nature, and to this end, when it worked, his postwar writing was like a late Degas or Matisse, achieving a purity and depth of emotion with simpler lines. In Hemingway's case, however, the "lines" are sadder as well as simpler—his heroes no longer courageously pursue an ideology or a cause. His postwar protagonists were still drunks, isolated, alone, struggling desperately for some measure of dignity and personal achievement—to do what is right, to be brave—but for no other reason than their own survival. Like the heroes in earlier work who identify with the animals they stalk and kill, Hemingway's late heroes increasingly recognize that their fate is "[t]o be hunted and to die. Nothing more," as Pablo, the guerrilla leader in *For Whom the Bell Tolls* expects. In that novel, something as monumental as a righteous war robs Jordan and Maria of their chance for a future together. In *Garden of Eden*, a man and woman are torn apart by plain and ugly selfishness and their inability to be kind to each other.

When Hemingway's long-awaited World War II novel, *Across the River and into the Trees*, finally appeared in September 1950 to devastating reviews, it was a world apart from the heroic, romantic story of war Hemingway had depicted in *For Whom the Bell Tolls*. In fact, Hemingway was not able to write the magnificent novel about human struggle which he had envisioned in 1944, "with the sea, air and ground in it," until *The Old Man and the Sea* in 1952, which was not about war at all. Stuck in writer's limbo, he returned to Italy in late 1948 to survey World War I battle sites, including Fossalta di Piave, where he had sustained the trench mortar wounds whose scars he had worn henceforth like badges of honor. That he went back at all was a measure of how disgruntled with the present he had become. In 1922 he was filled with hope for a boundless future when he returned with Hadley to Fossalta to find it clean and prettified with no sign of war, and afterward told a former Red Cross colleague, "We can't ever go back to old things or try and get the 'old kick' out of something or find things the way we remembered them."[185] Now, married to Mary and settled into unextraordinary routine, Hemingway did try in Italy to retrieve the old times, fell madly in love with nineteen-year-old Adriana Ivancich, and returned to Cuba to write his "World War II" novel during one of the most emotionally difficult—and besotted—periods of his life.

The protagonist of *Across the River and into the Trees*, Colonel Richard Cantwell, is an embittered ex-army regular, defeated by a tidal wave of uncontrollable forces which have conspired to ruin him. Having found Renata, the greatest love of his life, based on Adriana, Cantwell succumbs to the infirmity of his worn-out, sick soldier's body, and dies of a heart attack. Readers would find no sense of salvation through heroic personal sacrifice in this "war novel." From the West's great battle against fascism, America's great novelist had taken only sadness and defeat. Like his fictional Colonel Cantwell, Hemingway had succumbed to morbidity under the incessant grip of alcohol and the feeling of being hunted and defeated, and his reputation and ego took a major blow when the novel was savaged by reviewers.

Interviewed by the *Kansas City Star* on September 10, 1950, Hemingway defended his novel. "It's different, of course. You can't go on writing about a bunch of people on a hill in a war. I'd say the new book is about love and death, happiness and sorrow and the town of Venice."[186] He answered critics who complained that "nothing happened" in the book by faulting their insight. He defended himself, raging, "In writing I have moved through arithmetic, through plane geometry and algebra, and now I am in calculus. If they don't understand that, to hell with them."[187]

Two years later, when *The Old Man and the Sea* appeared in *Life* magazine, however, critics *did* finally "understand," and they marveled at Hemingway's effort to reduce characters to their expressionistic essence. Sixteen years after he first wrote about a lone fisherman, and eight years after he formulated the artistic ambition to write in a more transcendental style, Hemingway achieved artistic perfection in this pared-down story of struggle, love, and sacrifice between just one man and one fish. The opening paragraph said volumes about its author's state of mind when there was no war to fill up the hollow: "He was an old man who fished alone," it began, and ended with a description of his boat's tattered sail, which "looked like the flag of permanent defeat."

In *The Old Man and the Sea*, for which he won the 1952 Pulitzer Prize, Hemingway paid his ultimate tribute to the animal kingdom, which he admired for its nobility and dignity, but also for its "endurance which outmeasured man's." Contemplating the wonders of the animal world, he concluded that "[m]an is not much beside the great birds and beasts," but in *The Old Man and the Sea*, both man and beast fall prey to terrible forces beyond their control, and here, Hemingway's long-term identification with the hunted animal reached its apotheosis. Santiago, the old fisherman, and the big fish he hunts "become joined." He finally catches the fish after a journey which nearly kills him, and when sharks began to rip through the fish, Santiago suffers "as though he himself were hit." Santiago proves his skill by catching the fish, but as in most of Hemingway's works, success is tainted with loss. When the sharks tear into the fish lashed to his boat, Santiago feels regret and shame. He wonders whether it is a sin to kill the animal you love, and finally decides that the act was a necessity and it is best not to think about it. Santiago returns to his village feeling defeated and dreaming of lions, animals that endure beyond all others.

Hemingway himself endured until 1961, but not well. On an average day he consumed three or four bottles of whiskey with a few friends, and at night between dinner and bedtime he consumed two bottles of wine. His old self-delusion that exercise "boiled out" the effects of drinking gave way to new cures: vitamin B_1 capsules and methyltestosterone pills "for gloom."[188] In 1955, the year after he won the Nobel Prize for literature, he contracted hepatitis, and because he already had hypertension, his doctors ordered that he limit his drinking to two ounces a day. Writing became impossible.

Though Hemingway had courted death in an effort to conquer his fear of it, in the end his life became exactly what he had feared most since the age of six—not physical pain, for which he had great tolerance—but days filled with boredom, emptiness, and depression, with his "body worn out and old and illusions shattered."[189] In the year before he died he lost more than fifty pounds. Prone as he was to hypochondria, he now believed he had leukemia, although his doctors said otherwise. During his final years his health was ravaged by a host of illnesses, including diabetes, as well as high blood pressure and headaches such as had plagued his father before his suicide. He suffered memory loss, and became paranoid and delusional, convinced that the FBI was after him.

Before leaving Cuba for medical treatment at Minnesota's Mayo Clinic, which included electric shock therapy, Hemingway informed his old friend and gardener that his father had committed suicide, telling him, "Animals and human beings should not die in bed, they shouldn't be allowed to suffer or make others suffer."[190] On July, 2, 1961, Hemingway put an end to his misery by killing himself with a shotgun blow inside his mouth. The blast obliterated the upper half of his head. The carnage was as gruesome as any battle scene he had ever witnessed or written about.

Had he been able to conquer his private demons, Hemingway might have lived to give America a Vietnam novel. Lieutenant William Calley's order to massacre civilians at Mei Lai was the quintessence of official military arrogance and power gone awry, scarcely different from the story of the Republicans' massacre of fascists in *For Whom the Bell Tolls*. In Vietnam, Hemingway might have hitched a ride on a Huey medivac helicopter ferrying the wounded to Saigon. He might have fallen in love again with a woman who could give him that feeling of safety and indomitability he so craved. He was only sixty-two when he killed himself and easily could have lived to write as pointedly about Johnson, Westmoreland, McNamara, and Nixon as he had about Churchill, Roosevelt, and Montgomery.

"I know that all the real heroes are dead," a young Hemingway had declared in 1919 with false modesty after recuperating from his mortar attack wounds.[191] But in the end, heroics had nothing to do with it.

CHAPTER SIX

Ezra Pound

THE TRAINS RAN ON TIME

If you can understand the cause, or causes of one war, you will understand the cause or causes of several—perhaps of all. But the fundamental causes of war have received little publicity. School-books do not disclose the inner workings of banks. The mystery of economics has been more jealously guarded than were ever the mysteries of Eleusis. And the Central Bank of Greece was at Delphi.

"America and the Second World War," 1944

When the United States entered World War II on December 7, 1941, Ezra Loomis Pound, born in Hailey, Idaho, in 1885, had not lived in America for over thirty years. In 1908, the twenty-three-year-old Pound had fled to the literary London of Ford Madox Ford and W. B. Yeats to make his way as a poet, since Pound felt that America had no "conception of poetry, The Art."[1] There had been nothing and no one holding Ezra Pound in America. In 1907 his fiancée's father terminated the engagement when Pound was fired from a teaching post at a small Presbyterian college after hosting the star of a visiting burlesque troupe in his room. Pound, the son of a U.S. Mint worker, had no money and even fewer options. In 1906 his doctoral fellowship was revoked at the University of Pennsylvania by professors who had tired of his condescending attitude and trouble-making. Pound had attributed their ridicule to his "unusual agility of mind," when in fact they could not have thought worse of him—one faculty member called him "a weed."[2] He possessed a grating personality marked by intellectual arrogance and acid intensity, coupled with a set of rigid principles about art and thought that many found excessive and exhausting.

Though Pound left America, America had never left Pound. American to the bone, he had made it his supreme goal to save the nation from the mediocrity and ignorance in which he felt it had been mired since the late eighteenth century, when political and cultural leaders had turned mistakenly to Europe for grace and beauty. As a result of this supposed egregious error in judgment, Pound viewed his birth country as a poisoned body in an attenuated death throe, stuck in the dark ages. Its economics was based on a feudal system, he claimed, and in order to eradicate European influence, Pound envisioned an American Renaissance. He set forth its basic tenets in his seminal companion essays, "Patria Mia" and "America: Chances and Remedies," written between the fall of 1912 and spring of 1913. "A Risorgimento means an intellectual awakening," Pound stated plainly. "This will have its effect not only in the arts, but in life, in politics, and in economics."[3]

Pound listed the requirements for his Risorgimento—namely, a great leader and "propaganda" necessary for moving a society toward a common good. "[T]here is what is called an 'age of art' when men of a certain catholicity of intelligence come into power. The great protector of the arts is as rare as the great artist, or more so," Pound wrote.[4] He reminded readers that New York and Philadelphia had approximately the same climate as Florence and Rome, and he charged that America would never be a great nation until it produced a great city like Rome, "to which all roads lead, and from which there goes out an authority."[5]

Pound's vitriolic rhetoric drew quick fire from American critics, who chided him for his expatriation and charged that his poetry—steeped in ancient foreign languages and references to obscure historical figures—was unoriginal and foreign, therefore disqualifying him as a credible authority. Pound retaliated with characteristic venom and self-promotion, proclaiming that he was *more* patriotic than they, because he alone had a vision of America's greatness. His Risorgimento was to be epic. His shrill descriptions of its coming employed flowery language, passion, and appeals to nationalism such as Hitler used in addressing the Reichstag, although the Fuhrer preached force to worshipful legions, while Ezra Pound preached art to a minuscule readership. His books were published in numbers of less than a thousand, and his articles appeared in small avant-garde literary magazines. On August 18, 1912, a frothing Pound told publisher Harriet Monroe, "That awakening will make the Italian Renaissance look like a tempest in a teapot! The force we have, and the impulse, but the grudging sense, the discrimination in applying the force, we must want and strive for."[6]

From the outset, Pound's Risorgimento linked America's artistic and intellectual rebirth to radical changes in the American economic system. Though after 1933, his raving obsession with economics embraced agriculture, industrial output, and state credit policy, his early economics were strictly limited to the arts. His frustration with publishers who paid little, late, and sometimes nothing at all, and the fact that poverty drove many of the best artists to work in menial jobs which left them too exhausted to create, stamped on Pound a loathing for a free-market monetary system in which a rare book collector could pay $20,000 for an Edgar Allen Poe manuscript or an oil painting by a dead painter, while the living artist struggled to feed himself, let alone buy ink and paper.

To redress these injustices, Pound lambasted U.S. tariffs on American books exported abroad as unnecessarily harsh, and called for their repeal to open up foreign markets to American writers. He also demanded that the price of an artwork be regulated and based solely on the artist's expenditures in time, materials, and food. In 1915, he set $1,000 as the limit for any painting sold, although at the time he did not specify who or what governing body would be responsible for regulating the art market.

On the surface, many of his prescriptions dating from this time appear sound, though one could hardly separate them from the hysterical rhetorical flame with which he preached them. But even more important to Pound's disastrous future, they grew out of his increasingly murky conception of society as divided into essentially two groups: impoverished artists—the creators of civilization and culture, requiring financial backing, and parasitic consumers—the enemies of civilization, ever threatening the Risorgimento and the artists' rightful place at the apex of society. The art/book collector who rejected the cultural high road of subsidizing the living artist became just such a loutish consumer, and Pound denounced him with characteristic force. His cultural perfidy, Pound asserted, made him one of the many worthless social parasites whose annihilation was justified. One of Pound's poems, his translation of the Confucian poem "Yung Wind," particularly captured his view of this culturally worthless individual and his just fate. Such a man is considered "beneath the rat's modus"; he merely "clutter[s] the earth," and therefore "might quite as well cease to be."[7]

In the meantime, Ezra Pound was finding his own place on earth increasingly problematic. In the winter of 1919–1920, he moved to France from England, which after a decade he had decided was "under a curse." In Paris, he quickly fell into the artistic and literary circles of Picasso, Picabia, and Cocteau, and in 1921 wrote a friend, "Fools . . . are less in one's way here." But before long, France, like England, was filled with rejection and disappointment.[8] His aspiration to resurrect in Paris the *Little Review*—a literary magazine that had folded in London—to publish the best work by French writers fell far short of his ambition. His frustration culminated in a renewed effort to establish a financial subsidy on behalf of writers, which he had tried to do for a decade. Bel Esprit, as the financial plan was called, was to have given those rare artists with the potential of producing "master works" the freedom and security of financial independence through the establishment of a fund of three hundred to five hundred pounds— then about $1,600–2,300 U.S. dollars—solicited from thirty to fifty people committed to art and civilization. T. S. Eliot and James Joyce, both of whom were holding down regular jobs to support their families, were to have been the subsidy's first recipients.[9] "If there aren't 30 or 50 people interested in literature, there is no civilization,"[10] Pound had told his friend Wyndham Lewis, but like most of his other plans, Bel Esprit went nowhere.[11]

Then in May 1923 Pound reported that he had been dropped by New York-based *Dial* magazine after writing a denunciation of contemporary art patrons in his regular column, "Paris Letter." "[M]y communication with America is over. I.e., public communication. The last link severed," he declared.[12] Pound seemed to be battling with everyone over his work, including his new Paris publisher, the American William Bird of the tiny, but highly reputed Three Mountains Press. Bird was producing an expensive, limited, hand-printed, vellum edition of Pound's epic poem, *The Cantos*, loosely based on Homer's *Odyssey* and Dante's

Divine Comedy, which Pound had begun in 1915 and which would consume him for the rest of his life. While Pound despised the publishers' practice of appealing to collectors, he blamed the United States economic system and the Federal Penal Code for stifling the artists' financial and creative freedom. "Nobody can pay 25 dollars for a book. I know that," he told the critic R. P. Blackmur, adding, "I didn't make the present economic system."[13]

But by 1925 Pound had indeed begun to see his role as a "remaker" of the U.S. economic system which he so abhorred. His zeal had shifted from the economic plight of artists, which clearly he had been unable to improve, to the wider subordination of society at the hands of economic policymakers: bankers, Wall Street barons, and politicians. At this time Pound did not yet deem himself to be the expert he took himself to be a decade later, when he sought to advise President Roosevelt and the U.S. Congress. Yet, already he was confident enough to demand that government keep out of its citizens' private affairs and limit its scope and budget to public works. "A good state is one which impinges least upon the peripheries of its citizens," he wrote that year. "The function of the state is to facilitate the traffic, i.e., the circulation of goods, air, water, heat, coal (black or white) power, and even thought; and to prevent its citizens from impinging on each other."[14] Since Pound had defined his concept of humanity as early as 1917 as a "collection of individuals, not a whole divided into segments or units," in which a man must never allow himself and his creative intellect to become "the slave of the State (i.e. of the emperor)," it followed in Pound's evolving economic dogma that the state and its economy existed to serve those special individuals— intellectuals and artists like himself—rather than the other way around.[15] Failure of the state to keep to this narrow sphere had led, he charged, to the current "plague" afflicting democracy.

Pound's writing continued at a brisk pace, but his grandiose plans foundered. Although the poet Horace Gregory termed Pound "the minister without portfolio of the arts," the title was hollow.[16] America had not of course established a Ministry of Beaux Arts with poet Ezra Pound at the helm, one of his many prerequisites for returning to his native country. England, he wrote in his 1920 poem, "Hugh Selwyn Mauberley," was "an old bitch gone in the teeth, . . . a botched civilization."[17] Harriet Monroe, his own collaborator at the *Little Review*, had rejected many of his poems, calling them "unprintable," while taking the work of other writers he brought her. Now, Paris had revealed itself to be little better than accursed England. There was nowhere to go but to Italy, land of the great cities of Rome and Florence—the land where modern civilization, he proclaimed, had begun.

"Fascism is not a political party but a specific concept of life and attitude toward man, love, and work," Wilhelm Reich wrote in his classic study, *The Mass Psychology of Fascism*, published in Germany in 1933.[18] If Reich was correct, then Ezra Loomis Pound was a fascist decades before he publicly avowed the greatness of fascism from a radio pulpit in Rome. Pound despised people, the public, politicians, bankers, fellow writers, industrialists, magazine and book publishers, and just about everyone, except for his few friends and many long-dead figures of history—poor, misunderstood, and isolated visionaries—whom he revered and whose personae he adopted in his poetry.

Long before he ever marveled at Mussolini's smoothly functioning fascist state, Pound was bent on telling the ignorant and contemptible public who "keep their ostrich heads carefully down their little silk-lined sand-holes" how and what to think, and to teach the artist striving for perfection how and what to write, laying down his prescription in a steady stream of spirited essays and books such as *Pavannes and Divisions* (1918); *"How to Read"* (1931); *ABC of Reading* (1934); and *Make It New* (1934). Pound saw the world as encompassing extremes of good and bad, with the middle ground signifying the horror that was mediocrity. If ever there was a political ideology to satisfy a misanthropic elitist with a Messianic complex, that was fascism. And when glorious Italy of "ancient libraries," of Catullus, and Dante—and Benito Mussolini—welcomed the American Ezra Pound with open arms, Pound responded to his new home like a grateful guest who polishes the silver, makes the beds, and pleads never to leave. In Italy of the 1920s, Pound thought he had finally found a base from which he could change America and thus, the world.

Little more than a week after arriving in late November 1924, Pound told Wyndham Lewis that leaving England for Paris had rejuvenated him by fifteen years and now he had "added another ten years of life by quitting same."[19] Pound neglected to mention to Lewis that before he had left Paris he had spent two days in the American Hospital. Pound complained of a painful appendix, but according to his friend Ernest Hemingway, the problem was more on the order of a "small nervous breakdown."[20]

When Benito Mussolini became Italy's sixtieth premier on October 30, 1922, Italy was in a state of social, economic, and political chaos, and on the verge of a Socialist-inspired revolution. The country was riven by violent class warfare. Inflation and mass unemployment pitted peasants and industrial workers against an increasingly militant middle-class elite and a bourgeois class impatient after the end of World War I for Italy to take its place among Europe's leading powers. Concessions to Socialists had been minor, and violent agricultural and factory strikes—more than 2,000 work stoppages in 1920 alone—hobbled the nation.

On June 19, 1920, Ezra Pound had become stranded in prefascist Italy while returning from vacation to his home in Paris when a railroad strike began half an hour after he arrived in Milan. One can only imagine his chagrin. In 1917 Pound had quoted Kipling's sentence "Transportation is civilization," in his own essay "Provincialism the Enemy." "Whatever interferes with the 'traffic and all that it implies' is evil," Pound had written. "A tunnel is worth more than a dynasty."[21]

With the Fascists' win in Italy in 1922, a loose affiliation of industrialists, bankers, large landowners, veteran soldiers, and the middle class wrested control from centrist factions in the government. In cities and the countryside, Fascists, whose name came from the ancient Roman symbol for the government's power of life and death, won elections through a campaign of extortion, murder, destruction of socialist facilities, and voter fraud. (In Latin, a *fascis* was an ax tied up with a bundle of rods borne before the chief Roman magistrates as a symbol of their authority.)

The surface aim of Mussolini and the Fascists was to wrest control from the militant work force, but their larger plan was to vanquish democracy and socialism and to reassert Italy's historic greatness. These Fascists, who since 1920 raised their arms in the salute of Roman legionnaires when they bashed and bloodied and chanted "Eja, eja, alala," the so-called war cry of Aeneas and his Trojan soldiers, were now elected officials. "The century of democracy is over," the Fascists had declared in August 1922, after quelling a general strike by Socialists.[22]

From the outset, Mussolini seemed like a miracle worker to Italy and to the world. A former journalist and editor of *Il Popolo*, the socialist newspaper in the Italian-Austrian border city of Trent, Mussolini fulfilled his aims to reduce the deficit, balance the budget, reform the strike-ridden and inefficent railways, and increase worker productivity.[23] Strikes were outlawed and factory wages and productivity became regulated by the government, as were the hiring and firing of all workers. He squelched the Mafia's hold on businesses by arresting Mafia bosses. This primarily agrarian nation of vineyards, wheat fields, and olive and lemon groves went on the move. By 1932 Mussolini's Fascist government spearheaded the construction of about four hundred new bridges, four thousand miles of new roads, aqueducts, telephone lines, ocean liners, speedier trains, and airplanes. In one giant land reclamation project alone, 180,000 acres of useless Pontine marshland south of Rome became a booming network of towns, farms, roads, and canals.[24] And Mussolini managed all this while cutting the workday to eight hours.

In his own country, Mussolini's name and image became plastered on everything from women's bathing suits and perfumed soap to school room crucifixes, a mountain, and a newly hybridized black carnation. Abroad, admiring nations ignored the more distasteful realities of fascist leadership to lionize Mussolini as a great statesman, a problem-solver of magical proportion, a wunderkind, a "man of action," a Caesar. A young Adolf Hitler saw him as a model and felt indebted to him, but even the pacifist politician Mahatma Gandhi called him "a superman," and Thomas Edison, who had brought the world into the modern age, extolled Mussolini as "the greatest genius of the modern age." Thirteen years before England declared war on Italy, the aristocratic Winston Churchill, then the Chancellor of the Exchequer, praised Mussolini, a blacksmith's son, for his "struggle against the bestial appetites of Communism."[25]

There was of course a dark underside to the children's summer camps and orphanages and the fight against crime. Il Duce's Italy—"strong, prosperous, great and free"—was anything but free. To aid Mussolini in establishing this new, streamlined Italy, an army of 680 agents of the OVRA (Organizzazione di Vigilanza e Repressione dell' Anti fascismo), the Organization for Surveillance and Stamping out of Antifascism, monitored the public's telephone calls and mail, and resorted to terror and murder to implement fascist policy. Antigovernment political parties and publications were prohibited and the jury system was replaced with tribunals headed by a military judge. "Book and Musket, the Perfect Fascist," became the government's dictum for millions of Italian schoolchildren.

In early 1925 Pound and his wife, Dorothy Shakespear, settled permanently in the village of Rapallo, a well-known European artists' retreat, about twenty miles north of Genoa on the Italian Riviera. Almost instantly, Pound found himself treated as the celebrity he felt he deserved to be, exulting when Manlio Torquato Dazzi, the director of the Malatestine Library in Cesena north of Rimini, praised

Pound's Hell Cantos as the work of "a vigore propriamente (outspoken) Americano."[26] These were the exceptionally harsh Cantos XIV and XV which depicted London at the time Pound fled in the winter of 1919–1920 as hell. Dazzi also gave Pound the extraordinary compliment of displaying a copy of the Three Mountains Press edition of *Draft of XVI Cantos* in the library. Around Rapalla Pound came to be known as "Il Signor Poeta."

Such adulatory reception was the kind of respect Pound had thought was unattainable in a world of "stupidities," "vulgarities," and "imbeciles" such as he had described in his poem, "Salvationists."[27] Pound, who always seemed to make a concerted attempt to hurt and reject others before they could hurt and reject him, believed he had found in Italy not merely an antidote to Anglo-French bourgeois anti-intellectualism, but an entire system filled with people like himself—"the lovers of perfection alone."[28] Thus, for once in his chiaroscuro life, Pound had nothing to criticize and everything to extol. Italy became a boundless "foreign fastness" such as the wandering, lonely speaker in his poem "The Seafarer" seeks. To Pound, Italy was a land of alien people whose foreignness made them preferable to the familiar, especially since in too-familiar Paris, the expensive Three Mountains Press edition of *Draft of XVI Cantos for a Poem of Some Length* had proved a commercial flop.[29] After a year and a half of production, the work had appeared in January 1925, but by December not a single copy had sold at Paris's Shakespeare & Co. Bookshop, the major local outlet for books from Three Mountains Press. Pound's other Three Mountains Press book, *Antheil and the Theory of Harmony*, about Pound's friend, the American-born composer George Antheil, sold just thirty-eight books in the low-priced edition and one copy in the deluxe. A general interest book that Bird himself wrote about French wine sold sixty-eight copies, the most of any book published by Three Mountains Press, including Hemingway's first published collection of short stories, *in our time*, which sold just twenty-five copies at Sylvia Beach's bookstore, Shakespeare & Co.[30] Pound was adamant never again to publish a book with an English or American publisher.

Faced with perhaps his worst rejection thus far, Pound, living in an Italy policed by blackshirts, did not have to look far to see the effectiveness of strong-arm tactics in fighting one's enemies, as opposed to the futility of breast-beating and sending angry letters. In late 1926, while observing a bitter dispute between his friend James Joyce and New York publisher Samuel Roth over the latter's unauthorized publication of uncopyrighted sections of *Ulysses* in his *Two Worlds Monthly* magazine, Pound recommended as effective retaliation "a gang of gunmen to scare Roth out of his pants," adding, "I don't imagine anything but physical terror works in a case of this sort." Short of such draconian measures, Pound advised Joyce to mount "a firmly abusive campaign in the press."[31] As it turned out, Pound refused to take part in a protest against Roth, but in any case, by 1930, Joyce was world-famous and no longer needed Pound's help. *Ulysses* was banned in the United States and England, but Germans and French could read all of Joyce's fiction in translation and some of his work appeared in Russian, Swedish, Polish, and Japanese, while Ezra Pound saw his fortunes wane even further, admitting wryly to friend H. L. Mencken in 1928, "the State of Pound . . . is the only state in which I have any preponderant authority or even influence."[32] Pound became even less willing to cooperate with people who could help him, and even cavalier about his misfortune, boasting that in Italy he had found a tonic for his economic failure. At last he had arrived in a land where money did not matter. Life in Liguria, he explained, sheltered him from the shame of being poor as well as laid bare contemporary America's hideous arrogance rooted in money and politics. In truth, Pound was not poor when he moved to Italy, because Dorothy inherited a sizeable income in 1923 after her father's death. Italy had no central bank like England's Bank of England, the first bank founded specifically to extend credit to a national government, and this fact alone convinced Pound that Italy was morally pure and superior.[33] Pound had come to believe that debt to bankers and foreign governments lay at the heart of war and society's ruin, and with the Italian government stressing budgetary restraint, he proclaimed Italy to be the only Western civilization where the bank did not have "a corner on money."[34]

"Poverty here is decent and honorable," Pound wrote to Harriet Monroe on November 30, 1926, explaining his refusal to make a lecture tour in America. "In America it lays one open to continuous insult on all sides, from the putridity in the White House down to the expressman who handles one's trunk."[35]

Italy's fascist government seemed to Pound to be perfectly designed to rule millions of incompetent, ignorant, and greedy human beings, keep the church in its place, and at the same time nurture the few great artists like himself. As dictator, Mussolini was not subject to the whims of vote-hungry politicians who, Pound asserted, wrung nations dry with their costly public projects tailored to win votes. Pound believed that, from his perch above the masses, Mussolini was able to see truth and do what was right for the republic.

But in Mussolini himself, Pound had found the leader of a government whose voice loudly echoed his own—the kind of great leader he had described in "Patria Mia" as necessary for a nation's excellence, and which America, still held captive by bankers and politicians, refused to elect. "Personally I think well of Mussolini," he told Monroe in 1926. "If one compares him to American presidents (the last three) or British premiers, etc., in fact one can NOT without insulting him. If the intelligentsia don't think well of him, it is because they know nothing about 'the state,' and government, and have no particularly large sense of values. Anyhow, WHAT intelligentsia."[36]

Pound saw Mussolini as a man of refined tastes and sensibility. Not only had Mussolini turned broken-down, chaotic Italy into a sleek machine where land was tilled instead of wasted, and where taxes on invested capital were eliminated, but he was a man whose ambition was to cultivate the finest in art and music.[37] For Pound, there was never any dark side to imperialist Italy; he believed that a nation's well-being justified any oppression or injury to the individual, informing Harriet Monroe in 1931, "The intelligence of the nation [is] more important than the comfort of any one individual or the bodily life of a whole generation."[38]

On January 30, 1933, the very day Adolf Hitler won popular election as Germany's new chancellor, Ezra Pound met Benito Mussolini for the first time through a music impressario and solo violinist named Olga Rudge, with whom Pound began having an affair shortly after they met in Paris in 1923. Rudge, an eccentric woman who for a time dyed her hair red to match Vivaldi's, had met

Mussolini in 1927 when she enlisted his help to arrange a concert for Pound's friend George Antheil.

"Muss[olini] prefers [musical] classics," Pound reported to publisher William Bird several weeks later.[39] This was greatly to Mussolini's credit since Pound believed that the classics protected one from dispiriting mediocrity. "You read Catullus to prevent yourself from being poisoned by the lies of pundits," Pound once explained, and "you read Propertius to purge yourself of the greasy sediments of lecture courses on 'American Literature.' . . . The classics, 'ancient and modern,' are . . . the antiseptics. They are almost the only antiseptics against the contagious imbecility of mankind."[40] Like Pound, Mussolini's favorites included the Roman poets Virgil and Catullus, and he, too, idolized Dante, calling him "the immortal father of our race."[41]

Pound believed he sensed in Mussolini a kindred spirit who, like himself, saw the arts and not the church as "the acknowledged guide and lamp of civilization."[42] Pound believed that in America, venal, petty bureaucrats had succumbed to Christian evil, and would keep the nation from attaining greatness until "patient, plodding, unfrivolous people like myself . . . free the country of the curse."[43] Pound believed that Italy had been freed of just such a curse because Mussolini rejected Christianity and rebuked priests and popes for their historical corruption. In his 1909 novel, *The Cardinal's Mistress*, Mussolini had depicted Papal Rome as giving off "a putrid stink of all the vices," and called the Papacy a "senescent institution."[44] When he came to power, Mussolini swiftly took on the church, dismantling some two thousand Catholic youth organizations, and proclaiming his superiority over the Pope, although throughout his reign he granted the church concessions to keep it pacified.

Since Pound saw religion as the "root of all evil, or damn near all," with Christianity the most destructive of all religions, Mussolini's rebuke to the church demonstrated another example of the dictator's rational thinking and visionary leadership.[45] Pound believed such great leadership was demonstrated only in rare cases throughout history and was exemplified best by Sigismundo Malatesta, the fifteenth-century Italian condottiere, military engineer, art patron, and poet who was excommunicated after he challenged papal authority and spent his life defending his domain against superior forces; and by Pound's ultimate hero, Confucius, the sixth-century B.C. Chinese philosopher and minor provincial official.[46] It is therefore all the more fascinating that despite Pound's resounding emphasis on secular rule and intellectualism, he endowed Mussolini with the mystical, omnipotent power of a god, and like the unwavering follower that he was, he stubbornly glorified Mussolini long after his other minions burned him in effigy. Pound's rationalism often took just such an absurd turn, but in this case, the erudite poet with the irritating personality and urge to command shared not only ideas, but a surprising number of personality traits and biographical circumstances with his idol.

Stubborn, single-minded, ruthless, tyrannical, jealous, suspicious, energetic, and ideological are all adjectives which apply equally to Mussolini and Pound. As young men, both had suffered humiliation and rejection because of their arrogance and iconoclasm, and Mussolini, also a voracious reader who had eked out a meagre living by writing literary and social commentary for socialist newspapers before becoming the powerful (and vengeful) editor of the socialist newspaper *Il Popolo*, also saw writing as a powerful propaganda tool to vanquish enemies and disseminate their personal truths. At the same time Pound was espousing Nietzschan views as an editor of the *Little Review* in London, Mussolini was writing commentary which reflected a similar anti-Christian, antichurch (and anti-Austrian) perspective. Both came to see themselves as leaders of their great, rejuvenated nations, with Mussolini outstripping even Pound's grandiosity by predicting as a soldier in 1917 that he would someday be "master of the world."[47]

As the 1930s progressed and Adolf Hitler became the dark, dominant force in Europe, self-deception fed by hubris convinced both Mussolini and Pound that shimmering destinies as master of their respective worlds lay before them, though for Pound, Mussolini's success seemed crucial to stem the tide of his failure.

By 1934 Ezra Pound had stopped searching for that "new voice, some Rabelais" who could explain the subtleties of human behavior. Inspired by Italy's promise under Mussolini and driven by an explosive fanatical conviction, he concluded that the solution to civilization's problems lay not in the arts, but in the realm of economics. Every great age in culture from Europe to Asia, he announced, was built on sound economic policy, whereas nations in economic chaos were mired in corruption, censorship, religious fanaticism and persecution, and war. Taking an antiwar position in World War I, Pound had called war "the symptom of the disease"—the result of "Atavism and the loathsome spirit of mediocrity cloaked in graft."[48] True civilizations, he believed, abolished violence, so as to free men up to be constructive—that is, to build railroads or create artworks.[49] In evidence of how broadly his ideology evolved between the two world wars, Pound had first believed that the subject of war was not within the poet's purview, and during World War I he urged poetry magazines to refrain from commentary. Despite the death of friends—the sculptor Gaudier-Brzeska and the English philosopher and poet T. E. Hulme—and the wounding of Wyndham Lewis, Pound's main gripe during World War I concerned government censorship of reading material under the guise of protecting national security. Above all, Pound had seen World War I as a nuisance which disrupted his ability to publish. But in a reflection of his dual nature which at once despised and respected strict authority, Pound granted full authority to a government at war. In 1917 he wrote Harriet Monroe: "it is legal for a government to do almost anything in war/time. That is, anything short of military law itself may be regarded as a palliative or substitute for military law."[50]

By the time Adolf Hitler was elected chancellor of Germany in 1933, Pound believed ever more devoutly that war was "the symptom of the disease," but not so much of mediocrity as it was the product of economic miasma and nations' enslavement by monied interests. "If a nation will master its money," Pound wrote over and over, war could become obsolete, and yet he had become convinced that American and English bankers were doing everything they could to foment conditions for a war. It seemed entirely reasonable to the increasingly rabid Pound that as the only writer in the English language who understood the evil relationship between money, banking, and war, it was his job to prevent that war.

Pound's vision of economics as the motivating force or explanation of human behavior was neither new nor exceptional for an American writer at that time. The era in which Pound came of age as a man and writer reverberated with Marxian-Leninist doctrine which attempted to explain to an economically divided, late-nineteenth-century industrializing world just how the monied class controlled the poor workers. American writers and artists who ignored economics—especially after the Russian Revolution—were regularly denigrated by their peers as oblivious of reality, dangerously romantic, or callous. What separated Ezra Pound from most of his fellow American artists was that not only did he have no interest in helping the common man attain self-rule (though he believed his ideas would free him from economic slavery), but he despised him and called him too imbecilic to make his own decisions. In an era when many of his fellow, impoverished writers were striving for a "new, rational social order," based on economic equality, as Wilhelm Reich stated the goal of the aching masses, Pound sought control of the masses by one supreme ruler, whom Pound invested with idealized gifts of intellect, perception, and aesthetic sensibility. It made no difference whether sound economic policy was drawn by "an intelligent democracy" or by an "omniscient despot," Pound wrote in 1933 in "ABC of Economics," reflecting the complex nature of both his own leanings and the Italian Fascist movement itself, which grew out of socialist sympathies, but then embraced capitalism and imperialism.

It was as though the antiecclesiastical Pound had received religious illumination. Once perceiving himself as the leader of the cultural Risorgimento, Pound now saw himself as responsible for an even larger mission—the economic and cultural salvation of the United States of America. Since he had long believed it was the poet's place to "make certain horrors appear horrible," because no one else was prepared to tell the truth, Pound was certain that his distance, objectivity, and wide erudition made him the one artist who could *save* America from the monstrous parasites leading it to misery and doom.[51] In his self-appointed mission to translate the complexities and nuances of money, banking, and economics to a contemptible public, Pound merely shifted his social focus from perfection in the arts to perfection in money.

Pound launched his crusade to enlighten Americans. This one-time college instructor who vilified the American university system as a storehouse for unimaginative lemmings and had formulated an alternative curriculum for anyone who wanted it, devised a similar economic education for the American public based on Social Credit economics, a short-lived economic movement which sought redress for the chronic deficiency in purchasing power among the working class under existing Western capitalist systems.[52]

The theorist behind Social Credit was a former British engineer named C. H. Douglas, whom Pound met in London in 1918, two years before Douglas laid out the main principles of his theory in his first book, *Economic Democracy*. Douglas maintained that under capitalism purchasing power is often less than prices set by factories, which also set wages. This problem could be solved, according to Social Credit principles, if the money circulated were equal only to what is produced by labor—goods like wool, grain, and bricks, for example. What appealed to Pound was Social Credit's dictum that only the government, and not the banks, could extend credit, or "REAL MONEY," as Pound called it. Under Social Credit's vision, taxes were unnecessary; moreover, the government paid citizens a dividend out of the interest it received for extending credit.

On the basis of Douglas's anti-Semitic-shaded economic writings, together with those of Silvio Gesell, a contemporary German money-theorist once tried, but acquitted for high treason, Pound concluded that states whose economies were predicated upon Social Credit economics—that is, used money solely for long-term capital investment in bridges, roads, canals, etc., to benefit the polity—would become "the country of Utopia."[53] As part of his utopian vision, Pound demanded that stamp scrip rather than money be used to purchase goods.

Just as Pound had translated classic Noh plays from the Japanese, and Provençal, Latin, Greek, and Chinese poetry into modern English, he began translating into essays and poetry the theories and principles of Douglas and Gesell, as well as those of German cultural anthropologist Leo Frobenius, Thomas Jefferson, and A. Overholser, whose book, *History of Money in the United States*, Pound considered the bible of economic truth when it appeared in 1936. Nearly fifty now, Pound began to endorse this new covey of truth-sayers with an indefatigable, impassioned gusto that surpassed even that with which he had tried to build an audience for modern poetry. While more mainstream economists like John Maynard Keynes lacked Pound's unqualified confidence in Social Credit, Pound considered C. H. Douglas another in a long line of sages misunderstood by the rabble. He had decided it was his moral obligation to make Social Credit lucid for government leaders and the public, although the real effect of his increasingly prolix, abstruse, and bizarrely caustic essays was to make Social Credit economics accessible only to those readers who might not require a bromide after ingesting a rhinoceros, horn first.

In practical terms, Pound's rejection of and by America seemed final by the early 1930s. A volume containing the literary essay "How to Read" (1931) and part of *The Spirit of Romance* (1910) was published in France in 1932, but Pound still could not find an American publisher for his prose. When the editor of *Americans Abroad*, an anthology published in Paris in December 1932, asked for Pound's biographical sketch to accompany his work, Pound submitted the following: "The reader wishing information re Mr. Pound's bio-bibliography will have to consult the English 'Who's Who' as his name has been removed from the American one."[54] In England, Faber and Faber finally brought out a collection of his prose in 1934, but in a concise summary version titled *Make It New*. He still refused to compromise his standards, and continued insulting the editors of American literary magazines; in one instance, Pound rejected a $25 offer to be included in the *Saturday Review of Literature*.

With each rejection, his resolve only hardened, for his optimism had surged after he met Mussolini for the first time on January 30, 1933. "With the dawn of the year XII of the present era"—in 1931 he began dating his letters by the fascist calendar—"the chronicler's old sap moves again; for the first time since we were that way ourselves, I am ready to take rash chances, to put my money on this year's colts."[55]

Pound was writing fast and furiously. Invigorated by his meeting with Mussolini in January (when he returned to Rapallo, he was greeted by the town band), the following month he wrote the essays "ABC of Economics" and "Jefferson and/or Mussolini," both of which demonstrated Pound's zealous adulation for fascism and its leader. While admitting that the "details" of Mussolini's "surfaces" are "un-Jeffersonian," he contended that the similarity became clear if one viewed Mussolini as an "artist . . . driven by a vast and deep 'concern' or will for the welfare of . . . Italy."[56] When he declined to write an article on James Joyce in late 1934, he explained, "There is too much future, and nobody but me and Muss/and half a dozen others to attend to it."[57]

In the past Pound had complained that his essays, written to "set the people straight in their thinking," took precious time away from his poetry. Beginning in the 1930s they became the very stuff of his poetry. As a result, he was writing his Cantos more quickly. Thirty had been completed between 1919 and 1934; in the next six years he wrote forty-one more as they became the poetic outlet for the ideas he developed in economics, government, history, and religion: *Cantos XXXI–XLI*, for instance, were the poetic counterpart of "Jefferson and/or Mussolini."

Pound was bursting with excitement at the sudden realization that Dante, his idol, had put "money-power at the root of Evil" in his poem *Inferno*, and Pound's creativity flowed.[58] When Harriet Monroe, his publisher at the extinct *Little Review*, objected to the economic turn his Cantos were taking, he retorted, "I admit that economics are in themselves uninteresting, but heroism is poetic, I mean is a fit subject for poesy . . . an epic includes history and history ain't all slush and babies' pink toes."[59]

As in the past, when he had instructed poets to use concrete words and no abstractions, Pound now applied the same literary formula to economics. "I have to get economic good and evil into verbal manifestation, not abstract, but so that the monetary system is as concrete as fate and not an abstraction etc.," he explained to a young poet seeking literary advice.[60] As a result, dozens of succinct images and verse phrases from his essay work found new life in his Cantos. "Popolo . . . ignorante" (ignorant populace), for example, from Canto XLI, first appeared in "Jefferson and/or Mussolini"; the phrase "Free Speech without radio" which appeared in *The Pisan Cantos*, LXXVI, was first seen in prose in *Townsman* magazine in June 1940, more than a year before he began broadcasting pro-fascist diatribes over Rome Radio.

In Rapallo, Pound became an unpaid unofficial advisor to *Egoist* magazine, where T. S. Eliot was an editor, but Pound no longer counted on literary magazines which had been his lifeblood—and his battlefields—and which he believed ultimately failed him. He began writing his hodgepodge of social credit economics and conservative and fascist ideas almost exclusively for anticommunist magazines and Social Credit journals like A. R. Orage's *New English Weekly*, which shared a considerable anti-Semitic readership with C. H. Douglas's *Social Credit*. Douglas's book described the spurious "Protocols of the Elders of Zion" that Hitler claimed proved Jewish world domination and justified crimes against Jews.[61] Pound read American Social Credit magazines like *New Democracy*, and in 1934 he began penning a column, "American Notes," for the *New English Weekly*, drawing from American newspapers he received and the *Congressional Record*. Under the pseudonym "Alfred Venison, the Poet of Titchfield Street," Pound held bankers accountable for fluctuations in the stock market and accused them of being more powerful than knights, lords, or even the king of England. And war, he asserted, was the rotten fruit of a state's economic policy which cared nothing for helping artists build real culture, but encouraged capitalist monopolies to reap huge profits from scarce goods and services. His body of strange, electrifying essays on economics was growing: "ABC of Economics" (1933), "Social Credit" (1935), and "What Is Money For?" (1939) were just a few of the many hyperbolic treatises in which he sought to explain how national economic abundance freed up money and enabled the state to become the artist's collaborator, rather than enemy.

Pound was appalled that President Roosevelt was borrowing huge sums of money to feed the hungry and unemployed, and he lambasted the United States for borrowing on anything but long-standing capital projects. Roosevelt became for Pound the incarnation of evil government, the worst kind of leader who sacrificed the security of the best in *Res Publica* for the comfort of the worst. Pound long believed democracy was unreasonable, because "There is no more equality between men than between animals," as he wrote in a "manifesto" entitled *National Culture* that he published in 1938, and Roosevelt's New Deal gave unwarranted support to the "rabble . . . the filthy, sturdy, unkillable infants of the very poor" whom he had spit upon in his poem "The Garden"—and to the Jews.[62]

In Canto XLVI Pound railed against Roosevelt and the expanded role of the U.S. government:

> FIVE million youths without jobs
> FOUR million adult illiterates
> 15 million 'vocational misfits', that is with small chance for jobs
> NINE million persons annual, injured in preventable industrial accidents
> One hundred thousand violent crimes. The Eunited [*sic*] States ov [*sic*]
> America
> 3rd year of the reign of F. Roosevelt.[63]

Anyone who had been acquainted with Pound and his ideas in London in 1912 or in Paris in 1921 would have recognized this economic vision as a progression from his Risorgimento and Bel Esprit. It was a very short leap from telling the ignorant what they must read, think, and write to prescribing how they must tear down the contemporary banking systems and democracy. Indeed, when the question of Pound's sanity arose after his arrest for treason in 1945, many who had known him years before said he was no different than he had ever been. In his 1912 poem "New York," Pound had written of an empty and spiritless city: "I will breathe into thee a soul/And thou shalt live for ever." Now the message had expanded into something like: I will breathe into thee a soul by telling thee how the bankers have strangled the lifeblood from America, how the munitions manufacturers make war, and how America can do right and shall live forever in a civilized utopia where master artists are compensated for their genius. Pound's earlier diatribes against U.S. tariffs on books were repackaged to challenge interest rates and taxes on unprofitable goods and services. His harangues against manuscript collectors and the high prices they paid found their equivalent in dizzying diatribes against the unproductive aristocracy and capitalism. The emperor simply wore new—if neon-colored and wildly embroidered—clothes.

In England, T. S. Eliot, one of Pound's most loyal supporters, found his friend's material increasingly difficult to sell to his colleagues at Faber and Faber, and Pound was unable to find a publisher for "Jefferson and/or Mussolini" until 1935.

But ironically, not until war came did Pound find even begrudging acceptance among those he most respected—the Italian fascist leadership. Throughout the 1930s, Pound repeatedly requested to be allowed to come to Palazzo Veneziato to enlighten Mussolini on Gesell stamp-scrip economics—"the New Economy," as he called it—but was ignored.[64] Mussolini's ministers, whose staff handled a flow of Pound communications, had decided he was "mentally unbalanced," with a "nebulous mind devoid of any sense of reality."[65]

As usual, Pound was undaunted by his lack of success. He would save the world, even if no one was listening. The January 10, 1935, issue of the *New English Weekly* carried Pound's updated statement of his mission, reaffirming the Messianic impulse which in the past had moved him to promote himself as the savior of modern poetry. "I write treatises because I am a species of pachyderm, I am a porter of teak, I am a beast of burden because the circumjacent literati are weaklings, they are piffling idiots that can't get on with the job. . . . It is necessary for me to dig the ore, melt it, smelt it, to cut the wood and the stone, because I am surrounded by ten thousand nincompoops and nothing fit to call an American civilization or a British civilization."[66]

If Pound's language—electric and venomous since youth—seemed affronting and vile to English-speaking libertarians of the 1910s and 1920s, it suddenly suited the European temper of the early 1930s. Hitler's National Socialists came to power in 1933 on a platform of German racial and nationalist supremacy, Mussolini marched in lockstep, and a demoralized Europe seemed eager to follow. In 1936, Spain's right-wing monarchists rallied behind fascist General Francisco Franco in a bloody civil war which ravaged Spain for more than two years. Spain's fate did not befall France, which nevertheless boasted numerous right-wing organizations, including the 800,000-member Union Nationale des Combattants, which in 1934 called for a fascist revolution in France. Fascistic French youth found an outlet in the royalist association, Camelots du Roi, Jeunesses Patriotes, and the refined perfume magnate François Coty headed yet another group, the Solidarité Française. In addition, there were the four million French war veterans organized in the Fédération des Anciens Combattants. In Paris throughout the 1930s, the Chamber of Deputies, Place de la Concorde, and Champs-Élysées were all scenes of regular, deadly confrontations between government police and fascist and communist mobs.

Even in England, a monarchy steeped in constitutional law, more than ten thousand Londoners packed the Albert Hall on September 9, 1934, to hear Sir Oswald Mosley tell why he should be dictator of England. "Nazism had become fashionable in London's West End," William Manchester wrote. "Ladies wore bracelets with swastika charms; young men combed their hair to slant across their foreheads."[67] Though many British intellectuals abandoned Mosley's fascist platform after his blackshirts beat hecklers at the Albert Hall in June, and British support for Nazism diminished as Hitler's aggression became less excusable, Germanophilia became a "hidden obsession" among members of the British ruling class, according to Martin Gilbert and Richard Gott in their book, *The Appeasers*. The prestigious London *Times* pandered to the private fetish of Nazi-loving aristocrats, continuously celebrating "the joint Saxon heritage shared by pure-blooded Britons and German Aryans."[68]

By the 1930s, Pound had long since stopped using the word "Risorgimento" to describe his vision. He began speaking about the "Revolution" begun by men such as Jefferson and Adams, which in his view had been destroyed after 1830 by bankers and politicans. He harped on the "poisoning" of his native land—a favorite word of Europe's right-wing nationalists. His reviled politicians, whom he perceived as trespassing against the founding fathers and the U.S. Constitution, were Pound's equivalent of Hitler's demon Austrian dynasty responsible for abandoning "the German fatherland to slavization" and Mussolini's Austrian devil. Pound's propaganda traded on the very myth of impure/foreign elements pushing out pure/native/original elements which Hitler and Mussolini so successfully—and sinisterly—exploited.

The extreme nationalism which engulfed Europe in the late 1920s furnished the perfect atmosphere for Ezra Pound's extreme views toward his native America, and thus, his ideas became even more radical in the years leading up to World War II. But Pound did not focus on contemporary America, which he regarded as hopelessly mediocre. Rather, he leaped back to the America of the Revolution, when her smartest and best-educated men led the fight to break away from Europe and establish an independent culture, law, and economy—before bankers like the Rothschilds, munitions manufacturers like the Du Ponts, and politicians like Alexander Hamilton ruined her, as he was convinced they had. Pound dreamed of a nascent, pure, and grand America of the eighteenth and early nineteenth centuries, with leaders like Thomas Jefferson, John Quincy Adams, and Martin Van Buren, who had supported Andrew Jackson in his war against the banks during the Panic of 1837—an America with no national debt and no greedy bankers reaping giant profits through speculation and "USURA," Pound's preferred word for "interest."

Pound may have seemed on the surface the unlikeliest flag-waver, given his expatriation, harsh critique of America, and immersion in ancient foreign history and language; yet, beneath the cosmopolitan literary Pound was the native Idahoan whose maternal Yankee ancestors were whalers and Wadsworths, and whose paternal grandfather Thaddeus, a three-term U.S. congressman, farmer, and silver mine owner, built a railroad across the Wisconsin prairie and lost three fortunes pursuing a variety of doomed schemes. Pound's economic focus on agriculture and land as symbols of national well-being reflected a romanticized, sanitized American heritage of which Pound became increasingly protective as his own fortunes declined.[69] In 1942, he would declare in a radio broadcast that "the Kike" was "against all that is decent in America, against the total American heritage," and yet Pound, whose poetry was filled with hundreds of references to ancient cultural myths built on conflicts between good and evil, ally and enemy, darkness and light, had always seen complex life in just these simplistic, moralistic terms, no matter how elaborately and learnedly he adorned his reasoning.[70] And like countless Germans, Italians, Spanish, French, and Japanese who in the 1930s followed their fascist dictators' call to right historical wrongs and resuscitate their nations' past greatness, Pound, living in Italy, in the very heart of fascism, equated "love of country" with a dire sense of mission to restore the old in order to attain the new. As he had done in his poetry, he took the ideas and sentiments of others and transformed them into the personal expressions of a man who loathed nearly everything and everyone. What Pound always lacked, however, was the fundamental understanding which both Mussolini and Hitler intuitively grasped and which accounted for their success. Though they held the masses in contempt, they clearly understood that their power lay with the mob, and they appealed to their people in primitive, yet ennobling terms which they could readily embrace. For all his belief in propaganda, Pound never really understood this. He used inscrutable language to abuse the public, and then he expected it to listen.

At the same time Ezra Pound was reveling in his mission to bring economic enlightenment to America and Italy, his hero, Benito Mussolini, was struggling to decide whose political bed he should be sleeping in. Until the 1935–36 Abyssinian War, which not only promised him armies of slaves and much-needed raw materials to fuel his big-budget projects at home—but was also intended as a warning to Hitler to keep out of Austria—Mussolini had attempted through his foreign policy to align Italy with Britain. However, by May 1936, when he triumphantly added the east African terrority to Italian Somaliland and Eritrea, Mussolini concluded that his best countermeasure to Britian's antifascism was a strong alliance with Germany. The British had reacted strongly against his invasion of Abyssinia—Anthony Eden called for sanctions against Italy in the League of Nations, though members ultimately backed down, more out of fear of upsetting Hitler than of antagonizing Mussolini—and Mussolini suspected that the British were positioning themselves to divide Italy and Germany before reaching a détente with Germany. Mussolini's hard feelings toward England were fueled by the colorful dispatches of his London emissary, Count Dino Grandi. Grandi's critical observations of a strange, cold, fiercely antifascist British people who favored their pets over people read like the testimony of an awestruck traveler to another planet. Grandi's dispatches persuaded Mussolini to see that Germany and Italy actually shared much in their grand historical passion for music and art, while Italy and Britain shared nothing. This conclusion ignored the strong historic ties between Italy and Britain that reached back to Britain's support of Italy against Napoleon. These ties had been strengthened when the British came to Garibaldi's aid in the fight against Austrian domination and, more recently, during World War I when Britain and Italy were allies against Germany.

For both Pound and Mussolini, the Abyssinian war crystalized their hatred for the British. Pound had come to view his eleven-year stay in England as a creative waste, during which he wrote only three Cantos, but like Mussolini, he specifically despised the ruling class and the cabinet, whose members he blamed for leading the West to the brink of war. In "ABC of Reading" he attributed the decline of Greek and Latin studies in modern times to British domination of the world since the Napoleonic wars, and his 1938 *Guide to Kulchur*, a discursive treatise attacking contemporary culture, bankers, eighteenth-century literature, and especially Greek philosophy, was even more scathing toward British leaders, or, as Pound sneered, "the gang now ruling England." (Publication of the book by Faber and Faber was delayed a month to July 1938 so that some of Pound's more stinging phrases could be softened.)[71]

By now his essays were rarely appearing in Europe's literary magazines, and the American ones had all but closed their doors to him. He was studying ancient Chinese ideograms, "the bedrock" of language, as he called them, aided by a Japanese poet and literary magazine editor named Kituo Kitasono, who sent the poems composed of them to Rapallo from Tokyo. Pound complained of not being paid for his Cantos, but when he was offered $2,500 by a British publisher to write a biography of the British author and caricaturist Max Beerbohm, he insulted the publisher, and the offer was withdrawn.

Pound remained fixated on his image of Italy as a renewed empire, and Mussolini as the greatest leader since Confucius. In the winter of 1936–1937, he had written "The Jefferson-Adams Letters as a Shrine and a Monument," an essay that once more justified actions taken by a totalitarian government. "A totalitarian state uses the best of its human components."[72] He could not see that it was Hitler who was winning the totalitarian race to power, manipulating Mussolini's Abyssinian quest and reducing him henceforth to the status of pawn. Though Mussolini invaded Abyssinia to warn Hitler away from Austria, when German units invaded Austria in March 1938, Mussolini sent no troops to the Brenner Pass to stop them. Italy's resources were depleted after the Abyssinian campaign and another Hitler-fueled war, the Spanish Civil War. The Italian fleet was obsolete; there were not enough officers to man the submarines. When Germany's Minister for War and Commander-in-Chief of the German Armed Forces, Field Marshal Werner von Blumberg, was asked after surveying Italian military maneuvers in 1937 who would win a war, he answered, "Whichever country doesn't have Italy as an ally."[73]

The Munich Crisis left Pound more certain than ever that politicians and bankers were succeeding in drawing Europe into war. In his mind the deepening turmoil—and subsequent war—never had anything to do with Hitler or German aggression, and he continued more fervently on his racially shaded economic track. He felt that his message had never been more pressing, and a month after the crisis, while in London to oversee the affairs of his mother-in-law who had just died, Pound made a futile attempt to obtain a meeting with British Prime Minister Chamberlain "to TELL Chamberlain what he was headed for."[74] When that failed, he decided to use money from his wife Dorothy's recent inheritance to try to prevail upon his native "Amurika," as he referred to the United States, to use her influence to keep Europe out of war. On April 13, 1939, the writer who derided wealth and materialism sailed first class for New York on a self-appointed mission to Washington to see President Roosevelt and to save the world from war.

Pound never felt more patriotic than on the eve of his American adventure. "And as to 'am I American': wait for Cantos 62/71 now here in rough typescript," he told critic Hubert Creekmore shortly before he left.[75] Known as the John Adams Cantos, numbers LXII–LXXI recount John Adams's efforts to forge a United States government wholly independent from Britain and France. Pound cast Adams, the second president of the United States, as a the real "pater patriae," partly because he advocated "eternal neutrality in all the wars of Europe,"[76] and dared to stand up to bankers and their nefarious ally, Alexander Hamilton, "the Prime snot in ALL American history."[77]

In Washington, Pound received less than the red-carpet treatment he antici-pated. His request to meet with Roosevelt was denied, and according to biogra-pher Humphrey Carpenter, Pound "never referred again to this failure of his central hope for the trip."[78] Pound nevertheless thrust himself upon official Washington, managing brief encounters with an array of politicians, including Henry A. Wallace, Roosevelt's Secretary of Agriculture, and meeting others randomly through his usual dogged persistence as he went "wandering around more or less blindly" through the halls of Congress.[79]

The most startling of his encounters involved Senator William E. Borah, from Idaho, Pound's birth state. Pound asked Borah, a longtime anti–League of Nations man, to assist Pound in obtaining a position of official service to the United States government, but Borah rebuffed him, saying, "Well, I'm sure I don't know what a man like you would find to DO here." Inasmuch as Pound had spent the past fifteen years spewing vitriol against the government and its bureaucrats, his overture to Borah revealed him as the perennial outsider who rejects those on the inside, yet still wishes he could come in. Ironically, Pound would not again be surrounded by so many influential Americans until he was brought back to Washington under threat of execution for treason in 1945.[80]

Despite its ineffectiveness, Pound's visit to America on the eve of World War II was both significant and fateful for him. It marked the first time he was recognized beyond the tiny circle of literati within which he had been living and working in frustration for decades, by the larger world whose attention he so deeply craved. Even before he disembarked from his steamship, Pound had a taste of the celebrity he would attain after the war.

On March 15, 1938, Hitler invaded Czechoslovakia despite his promise to Mussolini not to, and when Pound was met by the press in the ship's lounge when it docked in New York on April 21, he was asked for his prognostications on war. He responded that the answer lay with bankers and munitions manufacturers. When asked about Mussolini, he told a reporter that the Italian leader "has a mind with the quickest uptake of any man I know except Picabia," adding for those who might not be familiar with the artist that Picabia was "the man who ties the knots in Picasso's tail."[81] (Ironically, Mussolini was beginning to feel like he was the man who ties the knots in Hitler's tail. When the German dictator took Czechoslovakia, Mussolini bellowed, "Every time Hitler occupies a country he sends me a message."[82])

With war in Europe in the offing, Americans were suddenly interested in what Pound had to say, not because he was recognized as a great American poet, but by virtue of the fact that he was an American writer who lived in Italy and had met Mussolini personally. At the time his fascism and anti-Semitism were not widely known in America, but neither was his poetry. In November 1937, Farrar and Rinehart in New York published his latest Cantos XLII-LI, entitled *The Fifth Decad [sic] of Cantos*, yet his body of poetry was difficult to obtain in America, and then comprehensible only to those readers able and willing to interpret verses like the following from Canto XLIII:

Ob pecuniae scarsitatem

S.P. SENEN[sis] ac pro eo amplissim

Balia Collegium civices vigilantiae
totius civitatis
Urban VIIIth of Siena, Ferd. I mag duce d° no°
felicitatem dominante et Ferd I
Roman Emperor as elected.
1251 of the Protocols marked also

X, I, I, F, and four arabic
OB PECUNIAE SCARSITATEM
because there was shortage of coin, in November
because of taxes, exchanges, tax layings and usuries[83]

Pound's early books were out of print, and his prose appeared in American magazines more and more rarely, causing him to complain to Wyndham Lewis that "There is also a lot of my econ. writing available," and to wonder why "the blighters never print me."[84] In real terms, until *Time* magazine wrote an article about Pound upon his arrival in 1939, he was a nobody to the American public.

Ezra Pound's immediate reaction to the outbreak of war was at the same time blasé and dramatic. He continued writing poetry and studying the ancient classics, and in his letters he made only offhand references to war insofar as it affected the interruption of postal communications and publishing, as he did during World War I. The German invasion of Poland on September 1, 1939, received no mention in a letter that Pound wrote the next day to an American interested in starting a new literary magazine, whereas he decried the "dryrot and redflannel in American letters."[85] Until the spring of 1940, when public music performances were suspended in Rapallo, he and Olga Rudge were still organizing concerts in the town. As ever, Pound's concern remained the support of the best composers of the era, as he insisted on performances only of "Grade A stuff."[86]

Yet, the advent of war constituted a profound rejection for Pound. It had broken out, he believed, because no one, including Mussolini, had listened to C. H. Douglas, Gesell, Overholser, or Ezra Pound. For fifteen years apparently, no one had paid him any heed. When war erupted, Pound recognized his failure to influence, and for the first time a tone of sadness, frustration, and weariness surfaced in his letters.

"I don't propose to deal with dead matter and negations. In fact the younger generation ought to do the killing and carrying away of corpses," he wrote on November 3, 1939. "I've got my time cut out now for positive statements. My economic work is done (in the main). I shall have to go on condensing and restating, but am now definitely onto questions of BELIEF. Re econ: I can depute the rest to Overholser. Nobody knows what I have done."[87]

"Belief" referred to Pound's intensifying interest in religion, although in fact it had little to do with spirituality or self-reflection. Pound had decided that religion, like the arts, was the result of certain underlying racial and economic characteristics. He had long been revolted by the Catholic and Anglican religions, and as his frustration with Italy and world events intensified, he became more drawn to the East—to ancient classic Chinese belief and philosophy as expressed in the teachings of Confucius and his follower Mencius.[88] His ideal of the ancient Chinese Empire, where money benefited the state and the arts blossomed, mirrored the vision he had of Italy in the 1920s and 1930s under Mussolini, and Confucian principles which emphasized peace and humanity represented to him the apex of human intellect, spirituality, and reason. Although Pound continued to support Mussolini and fascism, his Italian utopia was turning out to be less than perfect, and he began to conceive of a new utopia, based on the ancient Chinese Empire.

Yet, if he longed to enter a Confucian "dimension of stillness," as he claimed in Canto XLIX from the *The Fifth Decad [sic] of Cantos*, Pound's roar was never louder than after war was declared, although for nearly two more years he continued to be rebuffed by Italian propaganda officials in Rome who did not share his interest in a government-sponsored campaign to make fascism more appealing to Americans, who were not yet in the war. In December 1939, Luigi Villari, a minister of popular culture whom Pound had unsuccessfully lobbied, called him "a dreamer who also wants to be involved in economic and financial matters about which he has some pretty fantastic notions." Villari observed that Pound's economic writings were not taken seriously in the U.S.; therefore, "an initiative originating from him would not carry much weight."[89] (After Pound's broadcasts began, Villari himself went on Rome radio to persuade listeners that Pound was "insane.")

As usual, Pound was undeterred by rejection. He made several trips to Rome in 1939 and 1940 to convey his desperate hope that Americans be told that their president, "Stinkie Roosenstein," was allowing bankers and Jews to steer America into a war in which they should remain neutral. Leaping a gap in logic, Pound also blamed England and France for leading America to war by dominating U.S. policy, just as they had dominated American arts and letters. America's avoidable entry into war was largely the message of his latest Cantos, LII–LXXI; however, since they were published in London by Faber in January 1940 in an edition of only one thousand copies, few heard it.

Then in March 1940, one of those minute, seemingly insignificant events that can change one's life happened to Ezra Pound. Pound had been writing articles on economics for the fascist periodical *Meridiano di Roma* for nearly six months when an old friend from Paris, the infamous American expatriate Natalie Clifford Barney, left Pound a radio as a gift.

Though by now the war had interrupted communication with old friends like T. S. Eliot in London, Pound's initial reaction to the radio was to criticize it as a "God damn destructive and dispersive devil of an invention," and to deride its millions of listeners as a passive "mass of apes and worms."[90] Pound was nevertheless quick to appreciate radio's enormous power. In his 1938 *Guide to Kulchur* he had asserted that "Lenin won by Radio," and that a "Representative ('democratic') government cannot survive unless the jaw-house is put on the air."[91] While he accused the BBC of spewing "bilge" and lies as he wrote in Canto LXXVI, he also told publisher Ronald Duncan "what drammer or teeyater wuz, radio is."[92] Since "contemporariness" had always been one of Pound's artistic goals despite his interest in the ancient past, it was natural that he should look to radio as a new outlet for truth, especially since so many old outlets were now closed to him. "It seems such a waste to grind out new prose when there is such a lot of my stuff out of print," he had explained to T. S. Eliot during his futile effort to get his 1938 essay "The Ethics of Mencius" reprinted in *Criterion* magazine.[93]

Between the time that France fell to the Germans in June 1940 and Pearl Harbor was attacked by the Japanese in December 1941, Katue Kitasono, Pound's poet-friend in Tokyo, was his primary non-Italian correspondent. Even before war broke out, a number of Pound's old American friends such as E. E. Cummings had become repelled by his anti-Semitism and economic harangues. Cummings decided that

Pound was either "a spy or merely schizo, but ... incredibly lonesome."[94] By the autumn of 1940, war had even cut Pound off from his remaining American friends, like Wyndham Lewis, who had left Europe and returned to the U.S. in late 1939.

In September 1940 *Cantos LII–LXXI* were published in America by James Laughlin's New Directions in an edition of one thousand copies, but, isolated in Italy, Pound complained, "I don't even know whether Jas [James Laughlin] has got out the Am. edtn. 52/71 Cantos."[95] In the past Pound had endorsed Italian press censorship, writing in "Jefferson and/or Mussolini" (and Canto XLI, lines 113–115), "As the Duce had pithily remarked: 'Where the Press is "free" it merely serves special interests.' " Now he bemoaned the limitations on reading material coming to him in Italy, ignoring the fact that he had been reading and writing for fascist publications almost exclusively since the late 1930s.

Though cut off from friends, nowhere did Pound mention feeling lonely. Friendships, marriage, and parenthood—the civil violation or death of millions under fascism—were all subordinate to the intransigent "idea," as Pound escaped as always into raw intellectualism as an outlet for his emotional chaos. He rarely, if ever, acknowledged his inner turmoil in bald emotional terms, because he was preternaturally afraid of emotion and fled difficult personal situations altogether. He had sent both his children away at birth to be raised by women other than their mothers. His daughter by Olga Rudge, named Mary, lived with a foster family in the Tyrolean village of Gais and visited her parents only on school vacations. She did not know that her father had a wife who was not her mother. Pound's son by Dorothy, named Omar, lived at boarding school in England. Pound had not seen him since birth, and he, too, knew nothing of his father's second family.

Despite the rebuff by Italian propaganda officials, Pound continued to work on his next group of Cantos, and as he had been doing since the mid-1920s divided his time between the two women in his life, spending five nights a week with his pro-Hitler, anti-Semitic English wife, Dorothy, in one part of Rapallo, and spending two nights with Olga Rudge in another part of town, in a small house about a mile up the hill in Sant' Ambrogio. With food in his stomach, a roof over his head, a typewriter, and plenty of reading material, war remained for him the outer world's economic debacle, the result of basic human ignorance, greed, and mediocrity. Two weeks after Japan joined in a tripartite pact with Germany and Italy, granting Japan's right to "establish a new order in Eastern Asia," Pound advised his friend Kitasono that Japanese world conquest could be facilitated if Japan adopted the Roman alphabet, as England had done. "You will invade much better by giving us the sound of your verse in these Latin signs that are understood from the Volga to the West Coast of Canada, in Australia, and from Finland to the Capes of Good Hope and Horn," Pound counseled.[96]

As Hitler steamrolled over Europe—without consulting his former mentor—Mussolini wavered between support, deep resentment, jealousy, and fear that Italy would be Hitler's next victim. Mussolini had hoped to use Hitler's conquest of Europe to accomplish his own ambition to rule the Mediterranean and surrounding regions, but with the Italian military grossly unprepared, Mussolini had not planned on going to war before 1942. As a result, he was an uneasy and unpredictable ally of Hitler, who had clearly relegated him to the status of a junior partner.

On March 31, 1940, less than two weeks after the two dictators met at the Brenner Pass to discuss a three-way entente with the Soviet Union to crush Britain, Mussolini sent a top-secret internal memorandum, in which he recognized that if Italy were to desert Germany and join the Allies, "She would not avoid an immediate war with Germany."[97] Indeed, Italy's entry into war on the Axis side on June 10, 1940, was a harbinger of Hitler's absolute domination over Mussolini and Italy.

Nevertheless, Mussolini acknowledged no such reality, and in October 1940 the vacillating dictator demanded a southern empire to match Hitler's northern model: part of southern France, Corsica, Malta, Tunisia, part of Algeria, an Atlantic port in Morocco, French Somaliland, and the British territory in Egypt and Sudan. After Hitler took complete control of Romania in early October in violation of his promise to Mussolini, the latter, against the advice of his three chiefs of staff, retaliated by sending his troops to invade Greece on October 28.

The invasion of Greece proved a disaster for Italy's small, weak forces. Its three divisions were quickly overrun in fierce fighting against a poorly equipped, but impassioned Greek army. Then, on the night of November 11–12, the British sank three Italian battleships at Taranto in the first of a series of major Italian humiliations.[98] In December and January 1941, General Sir Archibald Wavell's combined force of British, Indian, Australian, New Zealand, French, and Polish units conquered a five-hundred-mile swath from Egypt to Libya, destroying an Italian army six times its own size. When the Germans landed in Greece in April to prevent a British invasion, they saved Italy from failure, but they could not save Mussolini from ignominy. Allied advances on El Alamein, Morocco, and Algeria reversed all Italian gains, and a physician attending Mussolini in the fall of 1942 reflected the turncoat mood of the country when he described the dictator as "a failed journalist with ulcers."[99] The modern Roman Empire was over before it ever began.

Pound had loudly preached for decades that war laid the state open to stronger foreign powers, but ironically, Mussolini's subjugation to Adolf Hitler became Ezra Pound's golden opportunity to disseminate his message. Like Pirandello's six actors in search of a play, Pound yearned for a forum in which to be heard, and Hitler's war provided him his stage.

After Italy joined Germany's war against the Allies, Italian propaganda bureaucrats looked with a fresh eye upon the eager American with the rapier tongue who seethed with hatred for Franklin Roosevelt, his allies, bankers, and the Jews— even if Italian officials did harbor reservations about Pound's sanity and motives. On January 21, 1941, Pound transmitted his first radio broadcast from the top floor of Rome's Ministry of Popular Culture, where the Italian broadcasting service had set up a studio. He was paid 350 lire, the equivalent of $17 per broadcast. His wartime radio work produced his steadiest income since his teaching days at Wabash College and was his primary source of income at a time when most of his assets were frozen and nearly all other sources of income had dried up.

At long last, Ezra Pound's voice and message went out over shortwave transmission to Britain, Europe, the Pacific, and his "Eunited States of Amurkia." After decades of his being restricted to a small select group of sympathetic readers, Pound now reached millions, and, for the first time in more than twenty years, he stopped work on his Cantos. At the age of fifty-six, the poet whom reviewers had called talentless and publicity-hungry had found his "maximum utility" as a disseminator of fascism's grotesque rhetoric.[100]

If ever there was an artist perfectly suited to writing hate-inflamed propaganda, Ezra Pound was that one. Art, he had pronounced as a young man, was meant to be didactic, because "revelation is always didactic," and as early as the 1910s he promoted propaganda as a "necessity" if the artist was to get his truth across to an ignorant public. No matter that his writing had been incomprehensible to most; his poisonous intolerance and hatred dripped from his words. Since propaganda shuns truth and reason in order to stoke listeners' deepest fears and anxieties, ironically it was probably the format which best suited his unique talent, which combined a brutally powerful—and dazzling—command of word and language with inexhaustible energy and a zealous desire to convert his listeners. Perhaps most importantly, Pound believed in the credo of propagandists. In a statement that could have come from Nazi propaganda minister Joseph Goebbels himself, Pound wrote in 1922: "Humanity is malleable mud. . . . Until the cells of humanity recognize certain things as excrement, they will stay in [the] human colon and poison it."[101]

Pound read his fiery scripts as part of a news, music, and commentary program called the "American Hour," and twice a week until the Allied invasion of Italy in September 1943, he broadcast in an exaggerated burlesque-English the same vivid economics lessons and "anti's" he had been preaching for decades. (He stopped broadcasting for two months after Pearl Harbor and again from August through October 1942.) If Pound couldn't stop the war from starting or keep America neutral, he was going to clarify for the world what it had done wrong and why. At his request, he was introduced as "Doctor Pound." The title had some validity, since Pound had received an honorary doctorate from his alma mater, Hamilton College, on his trip to America in 1939.

"You do not know what has HAPPENED," he warned his audience on May 28, 1942.

> And the first thing to DO about it is to pull OUT of this war—a war that you never ought to have flopped into. Every hour that you go on with it is an hour lost to you and your children. And every sane act you commit is committed in HOMAGE to Mussolini and Hitler. Every reform, every lurch towards the just price, toward the control of the market is an act of HOMAGE to Mussolini and Hitler. THEY are your leaders however much you are conducted by Roosevelt or sold up by Churchill. . . . You follow Hitler and Mussolini in EVERY CONSTRUCTIVE act of your Government. Damn you, you follow Mosely, go back and read over his programmes.[102]

If Pound asserted anything new to his public in his broadcasts, it was his admiration for Hitler as the great leader of the well-ordered German fascist state. He had essentially ignored Hitler throughout the 1930s, as though he were a bit player on the European stage while Mussolini was John Barrymore. Now Pound disregarded Germany's trampling on Europe and murder of millions. Roosevelt, Jews, the Bolsheviks, the English, and the bankers were the "VERMIN"—not Hitler. As he had done with each of his heroes, he painted Hitler as a truth-saying victim, fighting against a huge tide of ignorance and misunderstanding, and he distilled

Mein Kampf's murderous agenda into a model of hygiene, good breeding, historical perception, and political responsibility. Even Mussolini, who privately disdained his own anti-Jewish laws of 1938, was more realistic about Hitler than Pound.

American troops who listened to his colorful broadcasts thought that "Dr. Pound" was a joke, with his accented delivery and rolling R's. His words, however, did not amuse officials of the Federal Communications Commission, who began monitoring his broadcasts after America's entry into the war in December 1941, or the Justice Department, which began building a case against him for treason in 1942. Yet, Pound never imagined he would get into trouble for his broadcasts, and later told the American poet Donald Hall that he was "completely surprised" by his arrest, because he never advised soldiers to mutiny. He conducted his broadcasts under the assumption that he was a patriotic defender of America, exercising his constitutional right to free speech as an American citizen. Moreover, Pound believed his broadcasts could change the future, because he alone was providing the truth to young men, "build[ing] their souls, or at least their minds for tomorrow."[103] In 1945, he proudly and adamantly insisted that his message was personal and that he was not the tool of the Italian government. He argued he was not "sending axis propaganda but my own," a point he later used to defend himself against the treason charge.[104]

In the winter of 1943 Italy was beset with communist uprisings, high inflation, and worker strikes—the very conditions which had brought Mussolini and the Fascists to power in 1922. (After the fall of El Alamein in October 1942, the Banca d'Italia printed 40 billion lire to end a run on the national bank.) On April 3, 1943, Mussolini attempted to placate striking workers by promising substantial wage increases and bonuses. It was a far cry from the early days of his power, when Fascists strong-armed strikers and Mussolini balanced his budget.

Mussolini's domestic opposition, tired of war and terrified of Hitler, was wide and deep, including Fascist party members, Communists, and anti- and promonarchists. Within his own government, a faction led by his son-in-law, Count Galeazzo Ciano—one of the "half-baked amateur/or mere scoundrels" described by Pound in Canto LXXX—called for a coup to oust Mussolini so that Italy could break with the Germans and negotiate a separate peace plan with the Allies. Mussolini held on, kept in power by loyal Fascists who guarded him twenty-four hours a day. But he was not the same man as before. Aides described his behavior as insane, saying that he seemed to have lost "all semblance of logic."[105]

Pound could not fathom that his leader's grandiose dreams and fundamental weaknesses were largely responsible for Italy's mess; like Mussolini, he blamed others for the country's problems. As Pound continued broadcasting, old friends like Ernest Hemingway and Archibald MacLeish read copies of transcripts and were convinced that he, too, had gone insane. In early May of 1943, Hemingway wrote MacLeish, "He has certainly lived with very little dignity for a man who gave his allegiance to a government simply because under that government he was treated seriously."[106]

On July 16, 1943, Allied forces landed on Sicily. Since November the Italian air force had lost 2,190 planes, and the entire Italian military defense of Sicily consisted of a mere seven infantry divisions (without tank protection), three battleships, and seventy fighter planes. On July 19, at a meeting between Hitler and Mussolini in the seventeenth-century Villa Gaggia outside Feltre, near the Austrian border, a battered Mussolini, who had lost fifty pounds in six weeks that summer, sat mostly silent as Hitler harangued against Italy and her troops and announced that he would take complete control and reorganize the decimated Italian army in southern Italy. Less than a week later, on July 25, 1943, Mussolini was arrested at King Emmanuel III's palace in Rome in a coup led by the king, Ciano, and General Pietro Badoglio, who had hated Mussolini since the disastrous Greek campaign. As his wardens took him away, Mussolini was delusionary, still believing he could bring an end to the war if Hitler could only be persuaded to forget about Russia.

The day after Mussolini's arrest, Ezra Pound was indicted "in absentia" along with seven others, on charges of treason against the United States.[107] For the first time in Ezra Pound's life, his own country was taking him very seriously. The *New York Times* carried the news on the front page of its July 27 edition. Pound was specifically named in the headline, along with Jane Anderson, an art and music critic who had been broadcasting from Berlin, while the six others appeared merely as "Other Expatriates." If convicted, Pound faced a sentence ranging from imprisonment for a period of at least five years to death.

In the confusing, panicky aftermath of Mussolini's arrest and imprisonment, General Badoglio ordered carabinieri to occupy Radio Italia headquarters, its outlying radio stations, post offices, telephone exchanges, and the Ministry for Home Affairs. Before Mussolini's arrest, Pound had returned from Rome to Rapallo, where he heard about the indictment over the BBC, but he had no intention of discontinuing his broadcasts for the Ministry of Propaganda, which continued its shortwave transmissions. He wrote several more scripts in August 1943, although these, his last, were attributed to someone else. Then in early September, he traveled from Rapallo to Rome with the aim of getting back on the radio.

On September 4, General Badoglio signed a secret unconditional surrender with General Eisenhower ("September treason," Pound called it in Canto LXXII), fully expecting the Allies to send troops to Rome to defend the city against the Germans, who were engaged in vicious fighting with the American Fifth Army at Salerno and Naples. When the Americans decided not to commit troops to Rome, in order to save its forces for the Normandy invasion, Badoglio, his government, and the king fled the city. Germans troops occupied Rome on September 10, 1943.

That morning, Pound expected that the Americans would occupy the city and arrest him, so he left Rome on foot and headed for Rapallo, about 350 miles to the north. Contemplating his journey later, he saw himself on his walk to Rapallo as Theseus on his hazardous journey to Athens. In Canto LXXVII, Pound recalled snippets of conversation with peasants who helped him on his journey. Wearing snowshoes provided by the son of his Italian translator, Riccardo Umberti, Pound took trains part of the way, worrying at German checkpoints whether he would be caught and arrested as an American spy.[108] He walked through Bologna and stopped in Milan, where he saw the ruins of churches destroyed by bombs. Rather than going first to Rapallo, he decided to seek out his eighteen-year-old daughter, who was still living in Gais. When he arrived, he told her for the first time about his other family. His confession was in no way the result of pangs of guilt; with his capture and/or execution an imminent possibility, he wanted her to know as a practical measure. In the coming months, however, the Germans, Italians, and Americans had more pressing business than Ezra Pound.

Mussolini was abducted from his Italian guards by German airborne commandos and returned to Italy as a virtual prisoner of the German occupying forces. Hitler warned him that "Northern Italy will envy the fate of Poland if you do not agree to honor the alliance," and then imprisoned him in the Villa Feltinelli on the western shore of Lake Garda near the town of Salo, five hundred miles north of Rome.[109] In Canto LXXIV Pound associated Mussolini with Catullus, one of his ancient literary heroes, who also lived for a time on the lake. Though Mussolini was guarded night and day by a force of thirty or more Germans, Hitler disseminated a story that he was the head of an indomitable Republica di Salo, a government still loyal to the ideals of Italian Fascism.

On September 22, 1943, Hitler's commander in charge of procuring slave labor from occupied Europe, Gauleiter Fritz Sanckel, proclaimed that 30,000 Italians required for obligatory "work service" would be rounded up by military patrols. Eventually, the German army shipped 600,000 Italian soldiers in cattle cars to forced labor camps in Germany, where they worked in factories and mines and lived in appalling conditions. Upwards of 200,000 Italians were conscripted into the new republican army and served directly under German command. Imprisoned Italian soldiers were starved, beaten, and denied medical treatment. Diseases like tuberculosis, pneumonia, and malaria were rampant in the camps, and bodies lay unburied for weeks.[110]

On the whole, Italians received worse treatment than French, German, or Russian prisoners, possibly as a result of Hitler's belief, stated in *Mein Kampf*, that "all Mediterranean peoples are tainted by Negro blood." Perhaps their mistreatment was retribution for Hitler's humiliation on his first visit to Rome in 1934, when Mussolini, donning dress uniform with gold braid detail, ordered the men of his Fascist militia not to shave, press their uniforms, or march in step. The tables had completely turned in a mere four years. In May 1938, Hitler returned triumphantly to Rome, Mussolini roared "Viva il Fuhrer" and imitated Hitler's goosestep with a similar *Romano paseo* at a $5 million gala, and afterward the Mussolini government issued an "Aryan Manifesto" limiting employment and education for the nation's 57,000 Jews, a move that ran counter to Italy's longstanding tolerance and Mussolini's acceptance of Jews. Pound saw the new antiJewish laws as another testament to Mussolini's rational leadership, rather than as an act of subservience to Hitler.

As their fates were slowly sealed, both Pound and Mussolini still expected victory, as though through some magical force. In December 1943, Pound began writing broadcasts again for transmission from German-occupied Milan. They reprised his Roman scripts, although he now celebrated the Salo Republic and condemned those who were responsible for the July coup. "In the north the fatherland is reborn," Pound wrote in Canto LXXIII in 1944, having resumed work on them after a three-year hiatus.[111] He traveled more than once to Lake Garda, where he spoke with the Salo minister of affairs about Social Credit, still hoping to influence Mussolini.

Pound's own situation was dismal under German occupation. Though he was earning income from articles for fascist magazines, his financial condition was desperate. Before war was declared, he had converted his American money into Italian government bonds, which were now worthless. Food was scarce—just like Mussolini, he had lost some fifty pounds—and in May 1944 after the Germans evicted Pound and his wife, Dorothy, from their apartment, they moved in with his mistress, Olga Rudge. "[H]atred and tension permeated the house," Pound's daughter, Mary, told biographer Humphrey Carpenter.[112]

Pound kept busy on his Cantos and another Confucian text, *The Unwobbling Pivot*, which was published in Italian by the Salo Ministry of Propaganda in February 1945. In the face of Italy's defeat, he continued writing about an Italy rising like a phoenix under Mussolini's valiant leadership, although with Hitler firmly in control of the northern half of Italy through the spring of 1944, most Italians thought Mussolini was dead. "The dead are not dead," Pound answered doubters in Canto LXXIII. In truth, about the time American forces entered Rome in June 1944, a depressed Mussolini was spending long hours reading Socrates and Plato. "He's not a dictator any more, he's a philosopher," remarked one German who knew him at that time.[113]

On April 28, 1945, Mussolini was savagely executed by communists, who then controlled more than half the arms, funds, and transport in northern Italy. Days before, Mussolini was still planning to reign over an Italy cleansed of its German occupiers. He had ordered the bones of Dante, his—and Pound's—hero, disinterred in Ravenna and brought to him at his hideout in Milan. Only twelve Old Guard Fascists remained to accompany him to Val Tellina, a mountain redoubt eighty-five miles north of Milan and the intended home of his new government. The rest had fled in fear of the advancing partisans.

On March 8, German military leader Karl Wolff, believing the war was lost, had met in secret with Allen Dulles, head of the U.S. Office of Strategic Services, and promised to withdraw German troops from northern Italy and to disarm Fascist units before the Allies arrived in Milan.[114] As American forces under General Mark Clark's Fifth Army neared Milan on April 25, 1945, hoping to capture Mussolini before the communists got him, Mussolini fled under German guard with his long-time mistress, Claretta Petacci, toward Lake Como, thirty miles north. He was headed for his imagined seat of power and safety at Val Tellina, but he never reached it. Partisans captured Mussolini with the intention of bringing him to trial, but he and his captors were ambushed by a rogue band of communists under separate orders to execute him. As he was about to be shot, a frantic Mussolini cried out, "Let me live and I will give you an empire."

On May 7, 1945, the Germans unconditionally surrendered to Allied commanders at Reims, France. As Pound expected, the communists seized control of Italy, and partisans—"maggots," he called them in Canto LXXIV—executed hundreds of "traditore" all over Italy. Italian communists went about calling in old debts, and in the chaos which ensued Pound and his mistress, Olga Rudge, were arrested by anti-American communist partisans on May 2, although they were released after a few hours. Feeling left out when American liberators failed to summon him, a disappointed Pound came of his own volition two days later to the American Counter Intelligence Center in Genoa. Pound later explained, "I expected to turn myself in and to be asked what I had learned."[115]

Over the course of the next days it became apparent that he was deluding himself. Pound realized he was not going to be summoned to Washington as an expert on European affairs, and more, that with the 1943 treason charge looming, he faced death or imprisonment. He felt bewildered and uncertain. Later he said that he had been "puzzled over having missed a cog somewhere."[116]

After two weeks of interrogations by a Rome-based FBI agent, during which Pound delivered his customary denunciations at Churchill and Roosevelt, and tributes to Mussolini, Pound was transferred on May 24 to a detention training camp in Pisa. With his hands shackled, Pound was put in isolation in a small cell, a "gorilla cage" as he later called it. In the middle of June he was moved out of isolation after a medical examination concluded that he was headed for a nervous breakdown. He remained at the camp for nearly the next four months, during which American officials of the Justice Department made plans to bring him to the United States.

After consorting with the most innovative thinkers and artists of the early twentieth century, Pound was now surrounded by members of the plebeian masses whom he had spent a lifetime denigrating. The prisoners were mostly black soldiers—"niggers," he called them in *The Pisan Cantos*—many with surnames of American presidents like Washington and Jefferson. Perhaps the irony struck Pound, with his mania for American historical figures and his stereotypical race theories. Whatever his prejudices, he must have kept them to himself, since many prisoners showed him preferential treatment contrary to their orders. One, a soldier named Henry Hudson Edwards, fashioned a writing table for him out of a packing box. Pound was lent an old Remington typewriter, and in the camp's medical tent he assembled *The Pisan Cantos*, the latest installment of his epic poem. After a lifetime, it was his turn to become the protagonist in a grueling and lonely Odyssean journey.

Watched over by armed guards, Pound became the embodiment of his own persecuted, isolated Men of Truth whose personae he had adopted in poems about Renaissance renegades and martyrs such as Sigismundo Malatesta, whom he lionized in *Cantos VIII–XI*; those persecuted for their religious beliefs, like the Manicheans and Joan of Arc; and American statesmen like Jefferson, John Quincy Adams, and Martin Van Buren, hounded for their political beliefs. His art had become his life, and his life in turn became his art. Like his hero Odysseus caught in the power of Circe or the Cyclops, Pound was "a man on whom the sun has gone down," as he described himself in Canto LXXIV.

Yet, in prison, Pound's extraordinary mind burst with creative energy, and for the first time, his rage and frustration seemed to flow like tears from his heart, rather than emerge like the overly calculated product of his mind. He recalled the great artists and creators of his lifetime—"Degas, Manet Guys unforgettable"—and cried as though from the bottom of his soul: "I don't know how humanity stands it / with a painted paradise at the end of it / without a painted paradise at the end of it."[117] Like Odysseus, Pound recognized the magnitude of the ordeal he faced, knowing full well that he, like the black panther in the Roman zoo cited in Canto LXXIV, might also "die in captivity."

The Pisan Cantos, the greatest artistic achievement of Pound's life, represented a shift away from history and economics to an utterly personal and immediate struggle of a man seeking to understand how he had arrived in such terrible trouble, and to find through Confucian philosophy an inner peace and balance which would allow him to survive. Confucian philosophy placed man in the middle, in balance between earth, or nature and heaven, or spirit. Under its influence, Pound had yearned during the 1930s and early 1940s for a paradise more permanent and reliable even than Mussolini's Italy, but he was still bellicose then, as though the spiritual, peaceful Confucian side of him was battling his violent fascist sensibility, which categorically refused to surrender. When millions died and fascism crumbled and the victors cast him as a traitor, Pound realized that something had gone terribly wrong, either in his thinking or in theirs, or both, and he became guided by the Mencian parable: "An archer having missed the bullseye does NOT turn round and blame someone else. He seeks the cause in himself."[118] Though Pound had always blamed anyone *but* himself, he now realized that life's answers must come from within. Like Pound's own journey, *The Pisan Cantos* move from a wider circle of worldly events—Hitler, Mussolini, Fascism, etc.— inward to Pound's spiritual and artistic essence. The reader participates in the fluid "process" Pound writes of—a Confucian concept of life flowing, with no beginning and no end, and of man attaining "full humaneness" through the divine processes of heaven and earth. *The Pisan Cantos* were the expression of an overwrought, bereft, war-weary Pound, eager to let himself be the conduit for nature's fluid, luminous, peaceful divinity.

The change which took place in Pound as a result of his mounting troubles and imprisonment was vast and clearly visible in his postwar work. It can be illustrated in any number of examples, but one in particular from *The Pisan Cantos* makes it crystal clear: Pound's translation of the Chinese ideogram for "middle," which he rendered here as "unwobbling pivot." Before the war, he had applied the term "pivot" to money. In a *Townsman* article published in April of 1939, he had written in typical Pound money-speak: "the moment in fact that there is a common denominator of exchange, that money the denominator, the measure, i.e., money becomes the PIVOT of all social action." When Pound wrote *The Pisan Cantos* in 1945 he shed the monetary association and gave "pivot" an essential place in a spiritual philosophy.

The ten *Pisan Cantos* deliver an exquisite and amazing sense of immediacy and thus offer a poetic recording of the actual events of Pound's stay at the detention camp, as well as providing a window into Pound's psyche during the summer of 1945. They commemorate a piece of a man's—and an artist's—life more sharply than any photograph, and taken as a whole resemble Monet's impressionist masterpiece, the twenty-six views of Rouen Cathedral. Pound recorded subtle changes in the Pisan sky as he whiled away hours at the camp, the rampant cursing by prisoners, popular American songs played over the loudspeaker, and the doings of minute ants and wasps which crawled and buzzed about his cell and medical tent where he wrote the poems. When he looked out the window of his jail cell, Pound saw the mountains surrounding Pisa in the distance, which reminded him of Mount Taishan, a sacred mountain of China in Shantung Province near Confucius's birthplace, and an ancient Chinese symbol of balance, intellect, and illumination. Like Mussolini dreaming of Val Tellina from Lake Garda, Pound dreamed of Mount Taishan as a symbol of safety, peace, and power, at a time when he began to think he might be executed for treason against America.

In writing *The Pisan Cantos*, Pound worked from a 1923 Shanghai edition of *The Four Books of Confucius*, which he had stuck in his pocket when he was arrested at his house in Rapallo, a copy of the Bible, and *The Pocket Book of Verse*, which he found at the camp, as well as a few copies of *Time* magazine and some issues of *Stars and Stripes*. As a fatigued, sometimes despairing Pound searched his memory for phrases of Virgil, Homer, Dante, Aristotle, Shakespeare, and dozens of others for inclusion in his poetry, he also recorded that in the "shit-house" he heard that the war with Japan ended, that Winston Churchill was defeated as Prime Minister on July 26, 1945—a fact over which he rejoiced—and that on August 14 a court sentenced Henri Philippe Pétain, the former Vichy leader, to execution by a vote of fourteen to thirteen. Pound watched the clover growing near his cage and saw the birds sitting on the barbed wire from his tent, and their flights and landings were music to him. Accordingly, Canto LXXV consists of a rendering of Clement Janequin's violin and piano version of *Song of the Birds* by German composer Gerhart Munch, whom Pound greatly admired and arranged concerts for in Rapallo in the 1930s. Snippets of dialogue uttered by black prisoners were recorded in all their colloquial color. Among the more memorable of the prisoners was a sergeant known as "the ripper"—a philosopher of sorts, who explained to Pound that Hitler had not started the war, which instead had been man's or nature's answer to "excess population."

Pound's penchant for the precise recording of his surroundings gave rise to an amusing circumstance. In a 1978 interview, the camp commander, John L. Steele, told a researcher, Michael King, that camp censors at first suspected that the numbers appearing in the poems were part of a secret spy code employed by Pound. They were particularly nervous about the lines from Canto LXXX: "contract W, 11 oh oh 9 oh/now used as a wardrobe/ex 53 pounds gross weight." Pound eventually was able to convince them that the numbers referred to the stencil markings on a bacon box into which a hungry cat had stepped.[119]

The Pisan Cantos distilled Ezra Pound's autobiography in lyric form. He recalled days as a youth in New York City at his Uncle Ezra's boardinghouse on East Forty-Seventh Street. His Aunt Frances Weston who had taken Pound abroad in 1892 and 1898 was immortalized in Pound's reference to her love of alabaster bric-a-brac and "coloured photographs of Europe" (Canto LXXIV). He remembered inns and restaurants he had visited as a young man, and the instructor at Cheltenham Military Academy who had introduced him to the *Iliad* by reciting long passages. He recalled evenings of exciting talk and dancing at salons and cafés in London, Paris, Vienna, and New York, with artists like Picasso, Yeats, and Cocteau. He remembered the battle waged by artists around 1912 against turgidity and romanticism, and a dealer's response that "we couldn't sell anything modern" was scalded into his memory and reproduced in Canto LXXIV. On the whole, the memories were as fine as aged brandy. Though he had hated the ugly rich, Pound mourned the passing of that time of furs and rich gowns. While it had been a time of bitter personal battles, frustration, rejection, and poverty, Pound had nevertheless expected that with his intellect and rhetorical skill he could change art and society. Now the "era of croissants," as he called the pre–World War I time in Canto LXXX, was long dead. He missed deceased friends like A. R.

Orage and Ford Madox Ford, and pleaded, "de mis soledades vengan" ("Out of my solitude let them come"). He felt old and wondered whether he would ever again be free to enjoy the pleasures he cherished. He missed Dorothy and Olga, and worried that they would be left widows if he were executed. "O lynx, guard my vineyard/As the grape swells under the vine leaf," he wrote in Canto LXXIX. "This is my Agamemnon, my husband, dead by my right hand," Pound quotes a grieving Clytemnestra in Canto LXXXII.

The stream-of-consciouness catalog of joyful memories of youth and artistic freedom, coupled with the reader's knowledge of his troubles, and the underlying tone of frustration as Pound yearned both to understand his predicament and to feed his creative impulses in prison, make *The Pisan Cantos* the most humane, emotional, and powerful poetry Ezra Pound ever created. The exquisite phrase "Beauty is difficult" summed up Pound's plight, punctuated by a Greek chorus of "weeping" and "tears" that shriek his suffering. At the end of Canto LXXVI, Pound warned of "woe to them that conquer with armies/and whose only right is their power," but *The Pisan Cantos* as a whole weep for all the ostracized, persecuted, lonely purveyors of truth and beauty who died believing they were wronged. Woe unto Confucius, Odysseus, Sigismundo, and Thomas Jefferson. Woe unto Mussolini. Woe unto Ezra Pound, who seemed to have taken literally the Confucian idea he translated from Mencius in Canto LXXIV: "A man on whom the sun has gone down/[. . .] first must destroy himself ere others destroy him."

At times during the five months he was held at the detention camp, Pound felt confident that the future would be bright, especially with Churchill's defeat and the expectation that the new prime minister from the Labour Party, Clement Attlee, would nationalize the Bank of England, which he did. At times during his imprisonment, Pound appeared to be more at peace than he had ever been, now that he had come to fully understand Confucius's belief that a man, "coming to rest, [is] . . . at ease in perfect equity." But Pound's mood and thoughts fluctuated during his detention, and the poems mirror the ebb and flow, sometimes saying opposing things. At times he felt panic, and saw chaos and defeat beyond the camp's gates— "the gates of death," as he called them. The poems reach several epiphanic crescendos, the most chilling of which comes at the end of Canto LXXXII. After powerfully evoking the Greek theme of death and regeneration, Pound interrupts himself because, suddenly, "the loneliness of death came upon me/(at 3 P.M., for an instant)." The lyrical mood is instantly broken, and the reader feels as though he is standing inside the gorilla cage beside a terror-stricken Pound.

In no way were *The Pisan Cantos* Ezra Pound's apologia, however. Despite his affirmation of man's humbling before Nature in the cry of "Pull down thy vanity, I say pull down" (Canto LXXXI), and the admission of his own mistakes, he was not about to go away quietly in shackles when there was so much blame left to go around. Laval and Pétain were still "gli onesti" (the honest ones), Churchill was still a "squeak doll," and Roosevelt, a "snotty barbarian." Pound painted Mussolini as a victim of internecine corruption and bureaucracy, stabbed in the back by his son-in-law Ciano, whom Pound termed a "two-faced bastard," and a bevy of other scoundrels and traitors. Whereas in reality Mussolini endured humiliation and resounding defeat while he lived on Lake Gardone, Pound romanticized "poor old Benito" reigning at "Gardone/to dream the Republic."[120]

Rising through the Confucian humility was Pound's same old wail that, like Cassandra, he had been given the gift of prophecy, but was cursed never to be believed. He was indomitable, but also "a lone ant from a broken ant-hill/from the wreckage of Europe, ego scriptor" ("I, the writer"). Canto LXXXI ended with Pound proclaiming his innocence and defending his mistakes, because action of any kind, no matter how flawed, was still preferable to a man doing nothing. "[T]o have done instead of not doing/this is not vanity," he wrote, ending Canto LXXXI with the resounding lines: "Here error is all in the not done/all in the diffidence that faltered . . ."

In a profound way, Pound had come full circle as an artist. *The Pisan Cantos* harked back to a spiritual essence found in Pound's Cantos prior to 1933, before he became obsessed with economics. In those early Cantos, tracing his hero's perilous journey through the gates of hell toward paradise, Pound proclaimed that intelligence was the manifestation of divine spirit. Especially in the Cantos written prior to the early 1920s, Pound explored the theme of beauty as reflected in the arts, and the artist's divinity through creation was expressed in a multitude of symbols involving mysticism and Neo-platonism. After Pound's move to Italy and his febrile infatuation with Mussolini and obsession with economics, this spirituality was lost in brittle lessons and crazed harangues. *The Pisan Cantos'* call to action, no matter the cost, echoed an idea that Pound had set forth in Canto VII, in the winter of 1920–1921, when disillusionment with England forced him to emigrate to Paris. Pound felt that he was fleeing hell and the living dead, and he alluded to Dante's *Inferno, III*, to the souls of those who were never alive, because they took no action—good or bad—and are thus scorned by both heaven and hell.[121] If action alone promised escape from purgatory, Pound should have felt he had saved himself, having moved beyond the parameters of the written word to the active world of radio and propaganda.

No longer substituting the feelings of obscure, maligned and misunderstood historical figures for his own, Pound finally achieved his poetic quest in the intense moment-by-moment poetry of *The Pisan Cantos*. In his 1910 *Spirit of Romance*, a twenty-five-year-old Pound had defined the ideal when he wrote: "art becomes necessary only when life is inarticulate and when art is not an expression, but a mirroring, of life; it is necessary only when life is apparently without design. . . . Art that mirrors art is unsatisfactory. . . . No poem can have as much force as the simplest narration of events themselves."[122]

On November 18, 1945, Ezra Pound returned to the United States, handcuffed and accompanied by a three-man armed guard, including two colonels. His celebrity, which had begun in 1943 with his indictment in absentia, was now established. Journalists met him at the marshal's office where he was brought after his plane landed. But Pound did not return to the wealthy America of industrialists, bankers, and usurers he had denounced for decades. As it happened, Pound himself needed no money in his hermetic world of wood-paneled courts, psychiatric rooms, jail cells, and finally, St. Elizabeth's Psychiatric Hospital in Washington, D.C. His increasingly Kafkaesque circumstances demonstrated that a nation's truths can be perceived from diametrically opposed positions, pursued with equal fervor, and in the end, decreed by whatever individual or group holds the power. Pound had been judged to be free of "psychosis or neurosis" by every medical examiner beginning with the army's own psychiatrists; indeed, one psychiatrist's conclusion that Pound lacked "personality resilience" seemed to be the worst diagnosis. Yet, Pound became the pawn of forces beyond his control.[123] On one side were Justice Department lawyers, anxious to punish him, but increasingly doubtful that they had sufficient evidence to convict on the treason charge. (The constitutional requirement of two witnesses to the treasonable action was the sticking point.) On the other side was the director of St. Elizabeth's, Dr. Wilfred Overholser, who out of eagerness to keep such an interesting and infamous inmate, pressured his own hospital psychiatrists to diagnose psychosis when in fact they concluded that Pound merely demonstrated feelings of superiority, egotism, and infallibility. In the middle, as though handpicked to serve Dr. Overholser rather than Pound, was Pound's lawyer, Julien Cornell, a Yale Law School graduate, civil liberties specialist, and Quaker, who held his own medically unsubstantiated belief that Pound was insane.

Considering that his *Cantos* repeatedly invoked Sigismundo Malatesta's motto, "Tempus loquendi, Tempus tacendi" ("There is a time to speak, there is a time to be silent," from Ecclesiastes), it was one of the great ironies of Pound's life that the one time when it was imperative that he speak, he stood mute. Frazzled, fatigued, and confused over what was happening to him, Pound abided by Cornell's advice and stood silent with his head down when District Court Judge Bolitha Laws asked him at a hearing on November 27, 1946, whether he was entering a plea of guilty or not guilty. It may have been the only time in Pound's life when he went along with what someone else was telling him.

At a second hearing on February 13, 1946, a jury took just three minutes to find Pound unable to stand a criminal treason trial by virtue of insanity. Journalists from newspapers and magazines swarmed the courthouse to hear the verdict. It was the first time an accused war criminal escaped trial because of alleged insanity. Pound was taken to St. Elizabeth's, not expecting to remain for the rest of his life, yet fully aware that a treason charge stands as long as the defendant is alive.

Pound began his incarceration in 1946, and his case became one of the dozens of such causes célèbres as postwar, paranoid America had a penchant for creating. In the end, the same U.S. government which Pound blamed for so much destructiveness took him far more seriously than longtime friends and colleagues, and thus built his fame more successfully than the best public relations department could have. While Pound insisted throughout his twelve-year internment that he wanted his freedom, St. Elizabeth's became as a sacred shrine to Pound's growing, loyal following of young writers, literary scholars, and academics from around the world who condoned his wartime activities and anti-Semitism as the product of an eccentric poetic genius.

Especially after Pound was awarded the Bollingen Prize for *The Pisan Cantos* in 1949, articles in mainstream publications like *Time*, *Newsweek*, and *Life* celebrated his early efforts on behalf of many of the century's finest writers. Pound was credited with having been perhaps the single most important influence upon modern poetry between 1905 and 1918, because of his intransigent demand for poetic terseness, and his emphasis on sound and rhythm. Works long out of print or never printed in the United States began to appear. A collection of his letters was published in 1950; biographies and more prestigious accolades followed. His poetry became part of the American university curriculum which he had vilified throughout his life as a course of study rooted in "mediocrity . . . set to crush out all impulse and personality, which aims to make not men but automata."[124] In earlier years, Pound had taken the offensive against any reader who could not understand *The Cantos*, writing in 1917 that Carl Sandberg's criticism revealed the "complex of the uneducated in the same way class hatred works on the basis of money." Now, at the age of sixty-one, he was clearly tired of obscurity and deigned to do whatever he could to bring his writing to the public.[125] The young brash Ezra Pound who had written in 1916 that "friendly critics/Do not set about to procure me an audience" had become an eager participant in the expanding myth of Ezra Pound, poet-fascist-victim.[126] He allowed a young professor named Hugh Kenner access to his notebooks, and as a result of their relationship, Kenner, who hired Pound's daughter as his literary translator of sorts, provided crucial exegeses for generations of readers, beginning with classical Latin and Greek annotations to the first enlarged edition of *The Cantos*, published by James Laughlin's New Directions in 1954.

That Pound was fruitful at St. Elizabeth's, despite his age and tribulations, was not really surprising. When he was an undergraduate at Hamilton College, Pound had defined independence as having "a sufficient income to live on so that a man can do what he liked."[127] Locked behind the gates at St. Elizabeth's, Pound was in many ways freer and more secure than he had ever been. He himself observed: "The only time in my life I ever had enough caviar was Xmas day at St. Elizabeths."[128] He continued writing articles and translating ancient poems into modern English idiom, publishing a collection of Chinese poetry under the title *The Classic Anthology* in 1954, and *Sophocles' Women of Trachus (Trachinaiai)* in 1955. That same year he finished the latest installment of *The Cantos*, published as "Section: Rock Drill." (Canto CXX, Pound's last, was published in 1969, when he was eighty-four.)

As Pound sanguinely sat for interviews—and cultivated a relationship with a sycophantic anti-Semite named John Kasper—his old friend Archibald MacLeish led a frustrating decade-long effort to convince the U.S. government that Pound was no threat to anyone and the treason charge should be dropped. Ernest Hemingway, who wrote MacLeish in 1943, "If Ezra has any sense, he should shoot himself. Personally I think he should have shot himself somewhere along after the twelfth canto, although maybe earlier," nevertheless joined MacLeish in his efforts along with Robert Frost and T. S. Eliot. All of these writers perceived Pound as an egoist with misplaced loyalties who had taken out his own personal frustration on the government, but they all felt deeply indebted and morally obligated to rescue him. Hemingway, who as a young writer in Paris learned much about precise language from Pound, swore that he would have gone up on the gallows with Pound if he were hanged.

As Pound's confinement dragged on year after year, many in the international community besides his friends came to regard him as a political prisoner. Several secret internal Justice Department memoranda which expressed doubt that Pound's broadcasts could meet the judicial standard for treason seem to give credence to their suspicion.[129] Privately, his friends agonized over his tragedy, despite misgivings about Pound as an individual, and they believed his incarceration was an embarrassment to America which would escalate into a scandal if he were to die at St. Elizabeth's. MacLeish, a well-known Roosevelt Democrat and former lawyer, lobbied successive Republican attorneys general and State Department officials in Washington, but to no avail. FBI Director J. Edgar Hoover and the Justice Department concluded that Pound was a threat to national security—that he was bound to return to Italy and become a communist agitator. Evidently, they were unfamiliar with Pound's arch anticommunism, but Pound's own continued rantings fueled their assessment of him as a security risk. As late as December 1955 he refused a MacLeish-brokered deal with the Justice Department unless it included a presidential pardon and an indictment of Roosevelt. In 1957 he wrote to a British author: "the present state of the u.s. govt., etc. is 7 times worse/not only idiocy but pusillanimity, 90 out of 96 senators cowering in abject terror before a few lousy kikes."[130]

On April 18, 1958, fifteen years after the initial treason indictment against him, the charge was dropped by the same judge who presided over the original hearings. Dr. Overholser of St. Elizabeth's remained fixed in his opinion that Pound was "permanently and incurably insane," but he also concluded that further institutionalization would be pointless. Judge Laws deemed Pound no danger to "the safety of other persons or the officers, the property, or other interests of the United States," after Pound's new lawyer, Thurmon Arnold, told the judge he represented "the world community of poets and writers" in seeking the dismissal of the indictment.[131] Pound was seventy-three.

He was released from St. Elizabeth's on May 7 (V-E Day), 1958, and he and Dorothy sailed to Italy on June 30. He was excited about his return home after so many years, and at a port call in Naples, he gave the fascist salute. Soon after his return, however, Pound realized that after finally attaining the recognition he had coveted for a lifetime, despite his avowals to the contrary, he could not fully bask in it, because his fame rested in America. Part of him wanted to return; yet, half a century spent living away from the hustle and bustle of his native country had made life there seem impossible for him. He didn't even drive a car.

Except for several short trips abroad, Pound spent the remainder of his life in Italy with Dorothy and Olga, struggling to cope with freedom, old age, a sense of failure, and the realization that he was separated from the fame he had won at such a high cost to his freedom. In 1960, during his interview with the poet Donald Hall, a depressed and often confused Pound said he wished he could return to America.

"Europe was a shock. The shock of no longer feeling oneself in the centre of something is probably part of it. Then there is the incomprehension, Europe's incomprehension, of organic America. There are so many things which I, as an American, cannot say to a European with any hope of being understood. Somebody said that I am the last American living the tragedy of Europe."[132]

Ezra Pound died on November 1, 1972. More than forty years before, a profile of Benito Mussolini contained a line about the dictator's career that aptly describes that of his extraordinary American disciple, Ezra Pound: "When he crossed the frontier he plunged into Italian politics and his purely literary career was ended."[133]

CHAPTER SEVEN

Thomas Mann
DISILLUSIONMENT

What a glorious gift is imagination, and
what satisfactions it affords!

Confessions of Felix Krull, Confidence Man, 1954

The fight between good and evil had been fought and won. Germany's
Mephistopheles had been vanquished. The "prince with the soul of a
waiter," as Thomas Mann had called Adolf Hitler in 1933, in the end blew
out his brains to escape ignominy and punishment. After twelve years nearly too
horrible to fathom, Germany was free from the dark underworld.

Thomas Mann's Germany lay at war's end like a corpse. The previous March,
Hitler's troops had begun carrying out the dictator's "scorched earth" policy,
destroying bridges, mines, industrial installations, and transportation and communication lines in fulfillment of the dictator's belief that if Germany lost the war, its
people "had no right to live." Hitler's old friend and armaments minister Albert
Speer was able to persuade him to rescind the decree after two weeks of destruction, but together with the Allied bombing in the final months of the war, Germany,
wrote one American observer, had been returned "to the Bicycle Age."[1] Its cities,
which had for the most part remained intact after World War I, were either obliterated altogether, like Nuremberg, Mannheim, Cologne, Darmstadt, and Koblenz; or
half ruined, like Munich, Berlin, Dresden, Hamburg, Mainz, and Frankfurt. City
streets were heaped with rubble rising twenty feet high, deathly quiet, and largely
devoid of men, with so many dead, missing, or swept into Allied prisoner-of-war
camps. Starving women went scavenging for food and fuel in the half-deserted

suburbs, leading horse-drawn carts or walking. Many homeless sought refuge in cellars or on the upper floors of hollowed-out buildings such as Mann's former house at 1 Poschingerstrasse, Munich.[2] And soapbox fortune-tellers did a brisk business as defeated Germans put their future in the hands of fate.

Only three cities, Heidelberg, Celle, and Flensburg, remained in good condition. Though Lübeck, Mann's ancient birth city, emerged relatively undamaged, its citizens were nonetheless scarred and unforgiving even of their own kind. Demobilized German soldiers swarming in from territory that had reverted to Polish control found Lübeck's citizens belligerent and conveniently forgetful in their dealings with former Wehrmacht soldiers, whom they now labeled "refugees." Many refused to sell them food or rent them a room and posted signs on their doors that read, "Tuberculosis Cases Here," to turn them away.[3]

Thomas Mann had despaired at the destruction of Germany, but he did not blame the Allies. Rather, he condemned Hitler for having done this to the German people, and the German people for having done it to themselves. Mann had put his hope for Germany's rehabilitation in his white knight, Franklin Roosevelt, whom he had solemnly trusted to bring about Hitler's defeat as early as 1935, and whose 1944 reelection campaign he had aided. On April 12, 1945, Mann's beloved president died at age sixty-three from a cerebral hemorrhage. When Mann had become an American citizen the previous June, he had expressed the sentiment that it was "Roosevelt's America" to which he took his oath of devotion. Now he was grief-stricken. Roosevelt's death was more than a personal loss. Mann recognized that an American era had come to an abrupt, sad, and defining end. "Roosevelt—let me not speak of it," Mann grieved. "This is no longer the country to which we came. One feels orphaned and abandoned."[4]

Only days after Roosevelt's death, Harry Truman made it clear that with the victorious end of the war against Germany within sight, the time was ripe for a major change in American policy toward the Soviet Union. Communists had not wasted any time filling the power vacuum left by German defeat. Bloody, broad-based communist shifts of power took place in Italy, Greece, Turkey, Albania, Yugoslavia, Czechoslovakia, Romania, and Bulgaria after Nazi troops began evacuating pockets of occupied territory. Careful not to incite his allies, Stalin refrained from overt subversion of satellite governments and insisted that Russia was only interested in installing friendly governments in regions which might threaten Soviet security. Nevertheless, especially in Italy, Greece, and Yugoslavia, the American and British governments had good reason to worry about Communist takeovers. Communist insurgencies increased as ethnic peoples, starved and ruined under the Nazi yoke, showed themselves ready to die rather than be forced to return to their prewar lives of privation and hardship. British forces had put down the Greek civil war in April 1944 using infantry, tanks, and planes, but with Communists numbering two million out of seven million at the time of liberation, Greek's rugged Communist forces were not about to go away quietly into the night.

As the Allies looked to the future at the Yalta Conference in February 1945, Stalin was a colossal force with which to be reckoned. His troops were still needed to finish off the Nazis, and his promise to join the Americans' war against Japan gave him a powerful bargaining chip. At Yalta, Roosevelt and Churchill agreed to let Russia annex nearly half of Poland's prewar territory, and also promised Stalin the Kurile Islands, the southern part of Sakhalin Island, and railway rights in Manchuria. Roosevelt returned from the conference on Russian soil saying he and the Soviet leader had had a meeting of the minds, unaware that Churchill the previous October had concluded a secret agreement with Stalin, apportioning most of the Balkans to the Soviets and leaving Greece in British hands.

When Truman took up residence in the White House, American policy toward the Soviets went from conciliation to confrontation. At the new president's first cabinet meeting he was informed by Secretary of State Henry Stimson that government scientists had nearly perfected an atomic bomb. Although the bomb had been developed as a defensive weapon against Germany, Truman conceived of an America with atomic capability as no longer needing Soviet help to fight the Japanese. He did not share Stalin's overriding interest in preventing the rapid recovery of Germany, which had devastated Russia twice in a quarter century.[5]

In late July 1945 the Potsdam Conference, intended to formalize Yalta agreements, was so bitterly divisive that participants could barely agree on any issue, large or small. Truman refused to recognize Communist governments in the Balkans, and Stalin, who had installed a Communist-controlled government in Poland in June, refused to guarantee nonintervention in Poland's expansion of its borders far west to the Oder and Neisse Rivers, into one of Germany's richest territories. The belligerent conference terminated in a stalemate, with Truman, who halfway through received word that the atomic bomb had been successfully tested, concluding that "Force is the only thing the Russians understand."[6]

Truman had felt well-armed at Potsdam to play his trump cards against the Soviets, but even without the atomic bomb, America was emerging from the war as an economic megaforce with power to wield any way its conservative, free-market economy policymakers chose. With only six percent of the world's population, America in 1945 had three-fourths of the world's invested capital and two-thirds of its industrial capacity. Late in the war the United States extended to its allies—including Russia—billions of dollars in loans under terms almost unilaterally dictated, but these loans had merely jump-started Europe's war-strapped economies. American leaders who possessed the single-minded vision of postwar America as Europe's golden egg recognized the imperative of creating a politically stable, economically growing, capitalist Europe, importing vast quantities of American goods, not only to sustain America's booming wartime economy, but to propel it to even higher levels. Therefore, U.S. policymakers believed that as long as the United States could control Europe's political destiny, a rebuilt, free-market Germany held mind-boggling commercial potential. Largely to this end, Truman and his colleagues aimed their strongest efforts at establishing political and economic superiority over the Soviets, a scheme which involved keeping them out of Asia.

On August 6 and August 9, 1945, the United States dropped atomic bombs on Hiroshima and Nagasaki, Japan. The spate of books published to commemorate the fiftieth anniversary of the bombings reaffirmed the complex motives behind Truman's decision, but it can be said without debate that he wanted to end the war as soon as possible with the smallest loss in American lives. Despite obvious defeat, in the days prior to the attack, the Japanese government and military still refused to surrender, and an American invasion of Japan at Kyushu—known as "Operation Olympic"—was to be three times the size of the Normandy invasions, with projections of casualties of Americans alone ranging from thirty thousand to one million. Truman, a man of quick decision and little inclination to hand-wringing, was not certain the Japanese would *not* have surrendered without the bomb, but he was unwilling to take the chance.

With the atomic bombings of Japan, the kind of peace which Thomas Mann had predicted in early 1944 could only come as the result of "physics" had been won, and with more devastating effects than he or anyone else could have imagined. The cities of Hiroshima and Nagasaki and their civilian populations were burned beyond recognition with more than 200,000 gruesomely dead and many more burned and maimed. The world as it had been known by statesmen, scientists, philosophers, theologians, artists, children, and streetsweepers, from Topeka to Tanganyika, was no more and would never be again. The machine gun and the iron tank of Mann's First World War seemed mere Tinkertoys compared to the vast killing power of the A-bomb. "A cloud of anxiety of a totally new sort hangs over mankind," Mann wrote to Agnes E. Meyer on August 25. "[W]hat a terrible shame that life might have to seek another refuge in the cosmos because it took so wrong a course on earth!"[7]

How could it be that peace had finally come, but with no relaxation in fear and hate? Now that new demons threatened humanity's basic existence on earth, it was almost as though the Nazi era had been the first part of a horrible epoch that was to culminate in absolute self-destruction. In the struggle against Hitler, good and evil were clearly delineated. One either opposed fascism with all one's might or one became a smarmy accomplice, like Mann's former friend, Ernst Bertram, whom Mann had once wrongly assumed stood for freedom and humanity simply because he was a writer and an intellectual. Even "Bolsheviks"—capitalist Western Europe's bogeymen throughout the 1920s and 1930s—had never threatened to incinerate Europe and her people into a heap of ash.

After August 6, 1945, the rules in this "new world," as Mann called the postatomic era, seemed to have changed altogether, and Mann, who kept to his same moral code which forgave human error but demanded goodness too, was left feeling mournful and more alienated than at any time in his life. Perhaps the written word was still the language of mankind, as he once asserted, but it had not made man more humane, nor had it been powerful enough to spawn new worlds. Brute force alone conquered the multitude of foreign evils, not any humanitarian awakening to fascism's attack on freedom, justice, and decency. The leaders were different in name, but not in spirit, and their tactics remained the ancient, tried and true ones. What had really changed history, it seemed to Mann, was a single new weapon of catastrophe, the A-bomb.

In *Joseph the Provider*, Thomas Mann's fictionalized Egypt anticipated America's postwar role as "granary to the world." Egypt became sole provider to its neighboring peoples during the biblical seven-year famine. The final volume of the Joseph story, published in America in 1944, also portrays the underside of ancient Egypt's wealth and generosity in its descriptions of the cleverly calculated exploitation of its debtors. For with Egypt's dispensing of its "magic store" came restrictions on immigration, the drawing up of "lists" of recipients, and the annex-ation of provincial land to the pharaoh's domain. In many ways, this ancient Egypt was a fictional counterpart of postwar America, when in the name of national security and protection against the "Red" demon, lies, smears, and viola-tions of basic democratic rights became the law of the land. Mann realized that he had been lured into the kind of "roseate" illusions about America to which he assumed he was immune, and the realization was very hard for him to take.

As early as 1943, when the the war began to turn in the Allies' favor, Mann had sensed the chilly change in the American atmosphere, but because he did not want his antifascism wrongly taken for support of communism, he was careful to dis-semble his newfound conviction that blame for the war lay with rich capitalists and power brokers. His confidence in America had become a defensive psycho-logical posture toward the end of the war; just as he had clung to his vision of Germany as a democratic nation even after Hitler took over, Mann could hardly face the possibility that America's moral and democratic foundations would crumble just when Germany and the rest of the world required justice more than ever. For the most part, Mann was able to lay aside his fears for the future, and he took it as a given that America, as the most democratic nation the world had ever seen, would always exhibit characteristics of fairness, equity, and humanity. An article Mann wrote shortly before Germany's defeat called "The End" and an address, "Germany and the Germans," allowed him to comment on Germans' unique "tragic" character, while concealing his more anxious feelings about American and Soviet antagonism.

Thomas Mann had been the American government's dream in the propaganda war against Hitler and fascist evil. His becoming an America citizen on June 23, 1944, was a U.S. public relations coup, covered with great fanfare in newspaper articles and magazines around the country. Quintessentially German and a Nobel Prize winner, Mann was internationally known as a lover of freedom, morality, and civilization. He had indefatigably vilified Hitler to millions around the world in print and over the BBC, barnstormed the U.S. with the gusto of a Bob Hope, writ-ten articles commissioned by the Office of War Information, helped refugees find work and housing, and, perhaps most symbolic, assumed the position as German Consultant to the Library of Congress in Washington, under the aegis of its Chief Librarian, Archibald McLeish, another freedom lover, idealist, democrat, and soon-to-be-casualty of the new order in America.[8] At the august Library of Congress, Mann's wartime addresses were introduced by the nation's most impor-tant Democratic politicians, including Roosevelt's vice president, Henry Wallace, a renowned New Deal liberal and humanitarian. Mann, a symbol of German patri-cian tradition and intellectualism, took the stage and held forth on the essence of democracy with a stupendous oratorical flair. Audiences were often brought to tears by the great writer's gripping message of hope and freedom, if and only if human beings fought the temptations of sin and remained moral and righteous.

As long as America at war needed Mann, its leaders overlooked the writer's praise of socialism as a "humanistic" ideology. Throughout the 1930s Mann boldly urged the democratic nations to ally themselves with Russia against Hitler on moral grounds and chastised them when they did not. In his widely dissemi-nated address of 1938, "The Coming Victory of Democracy," for example, Mann told Americans that socialism was a "civilized and humanitarian idea" and "an entirely moral impulse."[9] Nevertheless, Mann's soft line on Russia and her ideology was disregarded by Americans in their appreciation for his resounding praise of America as "the classic land of democracy."[10]

It was not until the Cold War was in full swing that Americans, fearing Soviet domination of their hearth and home and reviling anything and anyone remotely "Red," could recall Thomas Mann telling them in 1938: "Whatever one may think of socialism from the point of view of economic and political individualism, one must admit that it is peace-loving, pacifist even to the point of endangering itself. . . . [I]t must be admitted that the moral nature of all real socialism is substantiated even in the case of Russia; one must recognize it as a peacefully disposed nation and admit that, as such, it constitutes a reinforcement of democracy."[11] If Mann, like so many others, had a blind spot toward Soviet ambition in the years before World War II, it was owing to his devouring hatred of fascism and his recognition that without Russia, Hitler could not be defeated. Once the war was over, statements like these would come back to haunt him.

In the immediate jubilation over the end of the war in Europe, Mann seemed welcomed by the Truman government. He delivered a lecture at the Library of Congress on May 29, 1945, and the Office of War Information recommended that the address, "Germany and the Germans," be distributed throughout Europe. The American government still loved Thomas Mann, even if conservative Democrats were disinclined to listen to Mann's warning that the victors must differentiate between "good" Germans and "bad" ones.

In retrospect, the reception at Agnes and Eugene Meyer's home after Mann's Library of Congress lecture was like the Last Supper for New Deal Democrats. Among the guests, Francis Biddle, Roosevelt's longtime attorney general, had already resigned to become one of two United States representatives on the International Military Tribunal at the Nuremberg Trials. Archibald MacLeish, who late in the war left his Library of Congress post to become Assistant Secretary of State for Cultural and Public Affairs, was gone as of August 17.[12] He and another guest, Elmer Davis, journalist, author, popular radio commentator, and the first director of the Office of War Information, would both be targeted by Wisconsin Senator Joseph McCarthy when he drew up a list of books written by so-called "fellow travelers" of the Communists.

By the end of 1946, Thomas Mann felt that the American government on which he had rested all his hopes for the world's future was no more. Under pressure from southern conservative Democrats, the Republican-controlled House and Senate, and his own low public approval ratings, President Truman fired or forced out all of Roosevelt's cabinet members and policymakers and replaced them largely with career military men and Wall Street financiers. Among the most notable casualties was Mann's friend, Henry Wallace, Truman's Secretary of Commerce, whose calls for close ties with the Soviets had made him persona non grata within the Truman cabinet as a "fellow traveler."

Truman's new colleagues shared the president's vision of postwar America as the world's leading economic and political power, as well as his fierce conviction that America and the Soviets could not peacefully coexist. Truman's domestic policy concentrated on building big business through lower taxes, halting immigration, and diminishing the influence of organized labor through the most drastic strike-breaking, union-busting tactics since the 1920s. In May 1946, after Truman's proposal for a labor settlement was rejected by the railroad engineers and trainmen unions, Truman drafted a law to empower him to declare a state of national emergency and draft strikers into the armed forces. Over the objections of Attorney General Tom Clark, the legislation came close to being passed, but was blocked in the Senate by conservative Senator Robert A. Taft of Ohio, who charged that the law violated the U.S. Constitution and took America down a path to "Hitlerism, Stalinism, totalitarianism."[13]

In late 1946, as Mann wrote the final pages of his novel *Doctor Faustus*, his lament for Germany and Europe, he was in mourning for the America of Franklin Roosevelt. His brush with death earlier that year from a cancerous lung tumor and the continuing battle to write *Doctor Faustus* no doubt aggravated his somber mood, but Mann saw no demons which were not actually lurking within the new America. New Deal philosophies which had shaped American politics during the fascist reign in Europe were undone by lawmakers who believed they were an impediment to American free enterprise, global leadership, and national security. "Peace has to be built on power," President Truman told Congress that summer. Mann sadly felt that he had held a romanticized vision of America, and in October 1946 he reported to Hermann Hesse in Switzerland, "blind, anachronistic forces are struggling with malignant obstinacy . . . and will probably cause the country to repeat all the experiences of Europe."[14]

Mann's fears that European-style fascism would come to America were heightened when in November a jittery and disgruntled public delivered a landslide win to Republicans in congressional and gubernatorial elections. Many who came into office were extreme conservatives like Senator Joseph McCarthy, who assailed opponents, liberals, and labor supporters as agents of a Communist conspiracy. In vicious substance and hateful tone, their mantra was all too eerily reminiscent of the "Leftist enemy" diatribe used by German nationalists during the 1920s. As Mann pondered the growing atmosphere of xenophobia and repression in America, he wrote to Agnes Meyer on December 1, 1946, "I fear having to go through the whole disaster, somewhat modified, once again. And then there would be no further exile—for where would I go?"[15] At the time he found consolation in knowing that America was in a diametrically different position economically and historically from Germany after World War I, and he attributed some of his intense angst to what he called his German inclination "toward pessimism."[16]

When Mann finished *Doctor Faustus* in January 1947 he was physically, emotionally, and spiritually exhausted. In the spring he wrote a painful essay on Nietzsche's exploitation by the Nazis, which he used as a vehicle to condemn postwar politics and the atom bomb. Mann wrote that governments did not have it within their power to make a "new order," and could only hope to transform the world's "spiritual climate" if human beings recognized "the mystery, difficulty and nobility of man."[17] He delivered the essay, "Nietzsche's Philosphy in Light of Recent History," together with readings from *Doctor Faustus*, at the Library of Congress and in New York in the spring of 1947. Mann sailed to Europe—his first trip back since war broke out in 1939—and repeated the address that summer in London, Bern, Basel, and Zurich. He purposely steered clear of Germany under the assumption that a visit would be profoundly controversial, if not dangerous, but he was so graciously received at the same Zurich Schauspielhaus where he had read excerpts from *Lotte in Weimar* in 1938 "that the whole nine intervening years of life seemed to have vanished."[18]

After the three-month tour, the Manns vacationed in Switzerland, Italy, and Holland. When he returned to California on September 14, 1947, Mann began a humorous novella entitled *The Holy Sinner* and contemplated resuming the Felix Krull project which he had abandoned twice, most recently in 1943, to write *Doctor Faustus*. He had vowed never to write another long novel, explaining, "I am not longer fit for Atlaslike tasks," and he found great pleasure in comic works.[19] Mann had always leaned on humor, or "self-mocking" as he liked to call his particular brand of comedy, to leaven his tragic side, and now "[c]omedy, laughter, humor seem to me more and more soul's salvation."[20] He was adamant about not letting himself get depressed over the mood of the country. He claimed still to be "an American patriot"; nevertheless it was impossible for him not to compare circumstances in America with prewar Nazi Germany.

In the spring of 1947, President Truman launched his own anticommunist campaign under political pressure from the new Republican majority as well as out of the government's fear that Soviet spies had stolen American atomic secrets. He appointed a committee to study individuals' loyalty in the workplace, which led directly to the passage of the National Security Act later that summer. The Central Intelligence Agency, the National Security Council, and the Joint Chiefs of Staff were also established. Such official "committees," "councils," and "acts" struck Mann as hallmarks of right-wing hysteria in the name of national security such as he had seen before in Germany, where nationalist mythology, religion, and morality were invoked to support government suppression of the press, persecution of political enemies, and blacklists. Around the same time, his daughter Erika's application for American citizenship was being withheld because of her liberal politics and lesbianism.[21]

Throughout 1947 the world grew scarier by the week as the Americans and Soviets engaged in showdown after showdown. In March Truman's $400 million economic and military aid package to Greece and Turkey sailed through Congress despite criticism from liberals that the Truman Doctrine would lead to war, or at least "a century of fear." In Germany, occupiers had squabbled over the country's economic and political fate since taking over on July 1, 1945.[22] The new American Secretary of State, George Marshall, demanded German unification over fierce objections by the French and Russians, and then squeezed the Russians hard by halting war reparations to them altogether in May. Now America moved aggressively to keep Europe out of the Soviet sphere of influence. Marshall introduced his plan to infuse billions of dollars in economic aid into East and West Europe to oust socialist and communist governments. After President Truman and Assistant Secretary of State Dean Acheson noted that early drafts of the plan made it sound like "an investment prospectus," Marshall appealed to the American public by stressing the "Communism vs. Democracy" theme.[23] The Soviets responded by seizing valuable oil and art assets in their German occupation zone, and in October, Communists from nine nations formed the Comintern to fight American "imperialist hegemony."

By the end of 1947, it seemed more reality than perception that an "Iron Curtain" divided the world, with the Communists controlling Eastern Europe and the Balkans, and making serious inroads in China, Korea, and Latin America.[24] Greece remained caught in a bloody tug-of-war. After the bankrupt British government pulled out in March 1947, Communist rebels fought a significant American military operation using dive bombers and napalm. Germany, especially the joint Soviet-American–controlled Berlin, also remained a potential powder keg. The majority of Americans, who had assailed Truman's anti-Soviet stance in 1945 and 1946 as fear-mongering and militaristic, answered "yes" to a poll asking whether Russia was out to rule the world. But if the American public remained uncertain as to the United States' proper role in the fight against Communism, their right-wing leaders clearly were not. American Soviet-policy guru George Kennan in February of 1946 had provided the intellectual basis for direct U.S. intervention to "contain" Soviet geopolitical influence. Using the same sort of apocalyptic buzzwords that made Nazi propaganda so effective, Kennan wrote that "Providence" had given Americans "the responsibilities of moral and political leadership that history plainly intended them to bear."[25]

Understandably, Thomas Mann feared where America's anti-Communist hysteria would lead. In Washington, power over domestic issues was being wielded by men like Republican Congressman John Rankin of Mississippi, an ardent white supremacist and anti-Semite, and his successor on the House Committee on Un-American Activities, John Parnell Thomas of New Jersey, a man who equated the New Deal with "the socialism of Hitler, that of Mussolini and the Communism of Stalin."[26] In mid-October 1947 Mann expressed his fears to Agnes Meyer "in a low voice": "We can already see the first signs of terrorism, tale-bearing, political inquisition, and suspension of law, all of which are excused by a state of emergency. As a German I can only say: That is the way it began among us, too."[27]

Mann's three-month trip to Europe in the summer of 1947 had made him feel nostaligic and sad. War-scars and all, Europe's lingering beauty and gentility deeply touched Mann's nineteenth-century bourgeois psyche, and there was part of him that felt upon his return to the United States "as if Europe, after all, has again become home for me and my work."[28] He had been feted at luxurious country homes, visited with old friends, attended a Strindberg play and a performance of Wagner's *Götterdämmerung* conducted by one of the signatories to the 1933 Wagner protest. In Noordwijk, he and Katia returned after an eight-year hiatus to the Huis ter Duin hotel, which Mann still called "the most beautiful seaside hotel in the world."[29] Upon his return from Europe, Mann felt that America's foreign policy reflected its unseemly transformation from humanitarian leader to crass mercantilist. The country, Mann observed, had "resolved to buy" the world, rather than lead it, as a result of the kind of supreme national power, wealth, and arrogance that his fictionalized Egypt embodied in *Joseph the Provider*.[30]

Mann was back at home in Pacific Palisades when in October 1947 the House Un-American Activities Committee held more hearings on the so-called Communist infiltration of the Hollywood film industry. (His friends Charlie Chaplin and the German composer Hanns Eisler had been summoned to testify before the committee in 1946, and Eisler was ordered not to leave the United States.) On November 25, motion picture industry representatives caved in to fears of persecution and voted to ban ten individuals accused by Congress of being Communists from work in the film industry unless each "is acquitted or has purged himself of contempt and declares he is not a Communist."

"Europe seems far away," Mann wrote wistfully to Hesse on November 27, 1947, "like a dream." Five years earlier, when the fight against Hitler invigorated him and gave him a sense of his place in the world, Mann had put all his faith and hope for the future into making his California house his home for the remainder of his life. In the fall of 1947 a disillusioned Mann admitted to his friend, "It's been a long time since I've known what 'home' really means."[31]

Given the xenophobic climate in America, it was not surprising that Mann had begun to feel more conscious of his "Germanness." Although he had always had the highest regard for America, citizenship had been a calculated public move to repay the many influential Americans who helped him during the war.[32] In late January 1947 in a statement widely disseminated in Germany, Mann confessed to the dean of Bonn University: "my 'de-Germanization,' to use Nietzsche's word, has not progressed very far after all. On the contrary, I find that in these happier foreign parts I have become all the more conscious of my Germanism."[33] Mann attributed part of his feeling of Germanness to writing *Doctor Faustus*. The work was "so utterly German," Mann explained, that he worried how it would translate into other languages.[34]

Ironically, Mann's growing alienation came in no small part from his devout conviction that while he was no longer happy in America, neither could he live in Germany. Mann's carefully worded, very diplomatic praise for Bonn University upon its reinstatement of his honorary doctorate had belied his darker feelings for Germany which were sparked by the immediate resumption of the internecine battles among German intellectuals who were again free to squabble. The conciliatory and symbolic move by the Bonn faculty was undoubtedly part of the serious game of German fidelity in which Thomas Mann, as usual, found himself a very public pawn.

Under Allied occupation, Germany's "rebuilding" became nearly the national obsession that "Aryan supremacy" had been in the 1930s.[35] German artists and intellectuals who had acquiesced to fascism and remained untouched by the Nazis, like composer Hans Pfitzer who had signed the April 1933 protest against Mann, and Walter von Molo, former president of the Prussian Academy, now condemned Mann for not returning to participate in Germany's rebuilding. Von Molo's open letter to Mann printed on August 4, 1945, in the *Hessische Post* and sent to Mann by the Office of War Information was only the beginning of the postwar dual between German intellectuals and Thomas Mann. Prompted by Mann's reply to von Molo, novelist Frank Theiss launched a vicious attack on Mann in the *Münchener Zeitung*. Theiss had already come out against exiles for having watched German suffering "from comfortable box seats abroad," and now charged that Mann could no longer count himself a German writer because he not only hated Nazism but Germany as well.[36] Mann fared no better among returning exiles such as his old friend Alfred Doblin, who also condemned Mann for staying away and accused him of abandoning his country.

Mann had little good to say about these former colleagues who seemed to have suddenly made it their mission to rebuild Germany—and publicly cast him in a bad light—when they had done nothing to bring Hitler down. In his open reply to Walter von Molo, Mann defended his exile, blaming it on the Germans themselves who had allowed fascism to take root. He admitted that he did not want to return because he was "scared of German ruins—not only rubble but people."[37] Privately, he sneered at Germans' demands that he "serve as psychiatrist to the nation,"[38] and charged that these attacks were the result of petty jealousy over his ability to keep working, earn a good living, and speak out freely against Hitler, while staying safely moored in America. Mann thought it ironic that "in 1933 they were only too glad to be rid of me, though today they pretend to be mortally offended at my not going back."[39]

It hardly helped Mann's situation in Germany or at home in America that Germans in the Soviet-occupied zone enthusiastically embraced him and his work out of their institutional lust to condemn fascism and the West. Given the anti-Communist climate in America, these were the voices Mann was most cautious not to attract. He answered the endless official and private requests that he come to Germany by saying that he preferred to let *Doctor Faustus*, rather than Thomas Mann, speak to Germans. The novel, which was published in Stockholm on October 17, 1947—his first new book to appear in Germany since 1935—only added to the controversy over Thomas Mann and his "Germanness."

Doctor Faustus expressed Mann's belief that Germany could not heal itself if it did not face its past sins, as it had failed to do after World War I. It soon became clear, however, that many Germans under Allied occupation wanted no part of "German guilt," and hence no part of Thomas Mann. Polls taken soon after the war showed that the German people's greatest criticism of Nazism was that it had been poorly executed. The Nuremburg war crimes trials began in November 1945 and for the next eleven months exposed German evil to its shattered people against their will. Many more Germans lamented their plight at the hands of the Allied victors than under Hitler's rule, and by the end of 1946, the defeated Germans' initial shock and apathy yielded to anger and violence. Minor rioting broke out against local German police by demonstrators carrying pro-Nazi posters threatening death to "Those Who Betray Germany." In the spring of 1947, a writer friend of Mann's, Ernst Wiechert, who had been interred in a Nazi concentration camp, had rocks thrown through his windows and was branded "a traitor" after he alluded to German "guilt" in a Swedish newspaper interview. Mann felt he had good cause to wonder what terrible fate might befall him if he visited Germany on an upcoming summer lecture tour. Friends like Hermann Hesse warned Mann to avoid the country because of the strong possibility there would be an attempt on his life; Mann's friend Eric von Kahler agreed, and so did Mann's daughter Erika.[40] "Am I to go around Munich with an M.P. bodyguard?" a piqued Mann wondered.[41] When he finally made the painful decision to exclude Germany from the tour, Mann launched an open attack on Germany and her people, clearly angry that they had impinged on his freedom to travel as he pleased.

While still aboard the *Queen Elizabeth* en route to London, Mann accused the Germans of "self-pity and an inability to see the chaos in neighboring countries."[42] When he arrived in London, he gave a blistering press conference accusing Germany again of "self-pity" and of "misusing her liberty and democracy." He reiterated comments like these over the BBC and in a separate broadcast for

German radio before German journalists counterattacked several days later. In a particularly vitriolic attack, a Bremen newspaper carried an article alleging that in 1933 Mann had written to Hitler's Interior Minister, Wilhelm Frick, pleading to be allowed to return to Germany. Mann disputed the existence of such a letter, and openly demanded that the writer of the article, Manfred Hausmann, produce it for verification. Mann was vindicated six weeks later when the letter was unearthed among ministry papers and revealed more mundane contents regarding Mann's passport application and Munich property.

In addition to the journalists' attacks, Mann resented the countless requests by Nazi complicitors for his help in reducing their punishments. Both struck him as nauseating attempts to use him to commit yet a new swindle in the name of the fatherland.[43] The more Germans overestimated his power and influence, as he felt they did, the more blame they wanted Thomas Mann to shoulder, and the bigger scapegoat he became. In truth, Mann felt less empowered as a political being than at any time in his career, and when he spoke out now about Germany his remarks brimmed with anger and resentment, instead of the empathy he had felt toward Germany even late in the war. Mann thought Germany's sins had cost him too much, and when pressed to play the role of influence-peddler, especially on behalf of Germans with short-term memories, he bristled. When, for example, the brother of Hans Blunck, who was Nazi Reichsschrifttumskammer (Chamber of Writers) president from 1933–1945, requested that Mann lobby the British military for leniency for his brother who was awaiting trial, Mann wrote to Hans directly in an English prison camp: "I do not have the power to bind and loose, you know. . . . Everyone must try to settle with his own conscience."[44] Neither infuriated critics nor refused supplicants appreciated the profound sadness and sense of alienation that Mann suffered as a result of their demands.

In November of 1948 President Truman surprised even Thomas Mann and recaptured the presidency. Fearing that Republican Thomas E. Dewey would win, Mann had lent his support to his old friend, Henry Wallace, who led a splinter party called the Progressive Citizens of America. Wallace had found support among other intellectuals like Albert Einstein and Frank Lloyd Wright, and by early 1948 polls showed his party would garner ten percent of the vote. But Wallace was always more a man of principle than of shrewd backroom politics, and he made the mistake of publicly welcoming the support of the American Communist Party. In the months prior to the election, both Truman and Dewey managed to convince the American public that the Progressive Citizens of America was dominated by Communists, whose twelve leaders were then under federal indictment for conspiring to overthrow the U.S. government. By October Wallace's popularity waned to about four percent.

Though Mann had considered Truman merely the lesser of two evils, he was nevertheless positively gleeful that a Democrat had won. After the Soviet seizure of Czechoslovakia in February and the blockade of Berlin in June, anti-Communist hysteria reached a new fever pitch in the United States. Alger Hiss, the head of the Carnegie Endowment for International Peace, was accused of passing State Department secrets to the Soviets, and his protracted case became the rallying point for Red-baiters bent on eliminating all Communist espionage in the United States. To this end, the House Un-American Activities Committee set its sights on alleged Soviet spies among former Roosevelt administration members, such as Harry Dexter White, the former assistant secretary of the Treasury. Mann acknowledged hating the spy-chasing committees "almost as much as I once hated Hitler,"[45] and felt reassured that Truman's win signified "a clear victory for F.D.R. and a clear expression of the people's desire to continue to be governed in his spirit."[46] Mann hoped, too, that Truman's win would lead to an end to the political persecution, since Truman had recently denounced the spy hunting as demoralizing to the country.

After Truman's reelection, however, America's right-wing paranoia only worsened, and Mann, who had largely receded from the domestic political spotlight, was reeling on all fronts. *Doctor Faustus* received a bashing by several respected reviewers just before Knopf brought it out in November. Hamilton Basso's piece in the October 30 issue of the *New Yorker* was perhaps the most damaging—and the most accurate—calling the novel, "a thick, heavy pudding." Mann was so outraged that he wrote to the magazine's editor the following week, accusing Basso of being "stupid like a tenor."[47] Already certain that America was in the monstrous grip of "bankers and generals," Mann reacted to the poor reviews of a novel he felt had been written in his "heart's blood" with an increased sense of alienation.[48] Then, in November 1948, Mann's children Klaus and Erika became enmeshed in the net when they were accused by a Munich newspaper of being "leading agents of Stalin in the U.S.A."

With Mann's fear mounting that America's all-consuming hatred for the Soviet Union was leading to a third world war, he no longer cared to be a well-behaved guest, and he began to take more direct offensive action. In March 1949 he protested to Secretary of State Dean Acheson against what he construed to be the State Department's nefarious efforts to cast the upcoming International Cultural and Scientific Conference for World Peace at New York's Waldorf Astoria as a Communist vehicle. He complained to Acheson that the State Department was purposely denying travel visas to non-Communist Western European and South American delegates. Mann's concerns were confirmed by the April 2 issue of *Life*, which published an article on the conference dinner accompanied by photographs of fifty important individuals, including Mann, under the caption, "Dupes and Fellow Travelers Dress Up Communist Fronts." Mann had not even attended the dinner.

In reality, Mann had no illusions that the American government would portray peace initiatives with the Soviets as anything but "criminal," but by now he barely cared. Since his 1947 lecture tour to Europe, he had been wistful about his life in Switzerland, and that visit had only served to heighten his sense of his life in America as citizen-exile. He was nearly seventy-four, and plagued by the ills common to a man his age, all of which had relegated him to a sofa in order to write. Though he liked to boast that he appeared as robust as a man twenty years younger, deep down he felt like "an old man, somewhat wearied by a life work at which I have labored hard, and by the shocks the times have inflicted upon us."[49] Superstition had prompted him at thirty to predict his death at seventy, and he was growing increasingly anxious about death—a feeling separate from, though not unrelated in psychology to his son Klaus's latest suicide attempt in July 1948. There were also the continued public attacks from composer Arnold Schoenberg, who had charged Mann with stealing his twelve-tone musical system for *Doctor Faustus*. Schoenberg's persistent churlishness so rankled Mann that he had even interrupted work on the novella *The Holy Sinner* just to exonerate himself by writing *Story of a Novel: The Genesis of Dr. Faustus*, published in Germany in April 1949.[50]

By mid-1949 Mann was suffering from the kind of deep, sad world-weariness that causes one to take risks regardless of the consequences, and for the first time in his life, Mann entered a brutal political fray without any real optimism that he could change the course of history. Life and work had become joyless and irritating. So, in the summer of 1949, Mann took a public step potentially as irrevocable and dangerous as his 1936 letter to Eduard Korrodi aligning himself with Germany's Jewish exiles: he traveled to Frankfurt and Weimar in the Soviet zone to accept Germany's most prestigious literary award, the Goethe Prize—and 20,000 marks (about $4,700)—at the anniversary celebration commemorating Goethe's two-hundredth birthday.

Mann might have seemed the errant son coming home, but after this son had emptied his luggage and hung up his clothes, he was itching to make trouble for the West Germans.

On May 23, 1949, the Federal Republic of Germany was founded, formally dividing Germany into two separate nations. The Soviets did not proclaim their German Democratic Republic until October 12, and Mann, who was roundly beseeched not to go to Weimar, looked on the visit as an opportunity to argue for the reunification of Germany and rapprochement with the Soviets. First in Frankfurt, where he was accompanied by municipal police escorts, Mann gave numerous inflammatory interviews and, when he refused to visit the former Buchenwald concentration camp being used by the Soviets to imprison twelve thousand political dissidents, many in the West German press saw it as just one more sign that Mann was a Communist.

Riding in a Soviet military vehicle and accompanied to the eastern zone by the East German minister of culture, Mann received a veritable hero's welcome in Weimar. After he gave his speech, "Goethe and Democracy," he participated in a parade through the city's streets, replete with flowers, bands, and schoolchildren raising flags in his honor. Though Mann in an extemporaneous interview accused the Soviets of using the same repressive methods to implement their revolution as the czars, he returned to America highly impressed with the "pure idealism" and intellectual and cultural exuberance he encountered among the people in the eastern zone, as opposed to the moral and spiritual lassitude and confusion he observed in West Germany, which he was certain remained a Nazi stronghold.[51] The nearly three-month European leg of Mann's lecture tour also included Sweden, Denmark, and Switzerland, and Mann found many European intellectuals expressing his same somber view of American leaders as power-hungry "colonizers" who were leading the world into another war. As it turned out, what Mann gained in self-possession by openly criticizing America and West Germany, he lost in self-sacrifice.

On May 21, 1949, Klaus committed suicide in Cannes. He had been despondent over the political bloodletting among Europe's intellectuals, and particularly over the accusation of being a Communist agent by Munich's *Echo der Woche* weekly newspaper.[52] Clearly, Klaus lacked his father's leavening sense of humor in the midst of human suffering, but suicide ran in the Mann family—Mann's sister Carla took her life in 1910 and sister Julia in 1927—and Klaus, a homosexual with a long history of depression, morbidity, and drug use, bore the additional and gargantuan burden as the writer-son of the one of the century's acknowledged greatest writers.

As with all remote relationships, theirs was extremely complex and made more so by underlying sexual confusion on both their parts, and filial jealousy. Thomas Mann was brutally critical of Klaus's achievements; an unsparing critic, his high praise was always undercut by his aloof and stinging criticism of Klaus's work as "flawed" and showing a "certain sloppiness."[53] Though Mann reacted coolly to Klaus's death as he had to his sisters' suicides and saw it as a betrayal, he also admitted feeling sad and guilty.[54]

When Mann returned to California from the Weimar trip in August 1949, he allowed his frustration and bitterness to erupt recklessly. Swiss journalist Paul Olberg had written an open letter accusing Mann of repudiating his former democratic principles, and on August 27 Mann fired back with extraordinary rancor. After clearly stating yet again that he was not a Communist, but merely a missionary of peace, he made the egregious mistake of condoning violence in the name of peace. "Violence is of course an evil thing, and concentration camps a terrible educational method," Mann wrote, alluding to the Buchenwald camp which he had avoided on his tour. "But attempts to bring about socialism without violence, such as Beneš made, have also failed; and the English experiment in socialism is running into every kind of opposition."[55]

Not surprisingly, Mann's letter to Olberg found its way back to America, and with Truman announcing on September 23 that the Soviets had detonated an atomic bomb within the U.S.S.R., it was only a matter of time before the Communist label stuck so fast that Mann became just as much persona non grata in America as he had been in Germany. In December 1949, the Beverly Wilshire Hotel in Los Angeles refused to rent its hall for a dinner of the Arts, Sciences and Professions Council because Mann was supposed to be one of the speakers. The hotel reversed its decision after heavy public protest, but Mann was ill when the council convened and did not speak. When Mann's brother Heinrich died on March 12, 1950, in Santa Monica, Mann lamented, "The way things are going aboveground, we need not so especially mourn his passing."[56]

Just days after Mann buried his brother, Luther Evans, Librarian of Congress, notified Mann that his upcoming Library address was canceled. Mann had called the lecture "a historic act" during its wrenching preparation because, though it ended with a repudiation of communism, it boldly criticized America as a hegemonic colonizer of non-Communist countries. Privately, Mann even compared the lecture's power to his 1932 speech at Berlin's Beethoven's Hall after which he and Katia were forced to escape from rioting Nazis.

Mann delivered the lecture in April and May to overflowing audiences in Chicago, New York, Stockholm, Amsterdam, Paris, and Zurich, but the significance of the Library of Congress cancellation was all too obvious. Mann had come full circle back to 1933, at the beginning of his exile. He even sought emotional sanctuary in Montagnola with Hermann Hesse after the tour, just as he had during the first tremulous days of the Nazi regime. On March 25, 1950, Mann confided to an old friend, "Things are happening and things are being prepared which would previously have been unthinkable in a country where Fascism had not yet broken out fully and openly. The 'cold war' is ruining America physically and morally."[57] Fittingly, his lecture was entitled "The Years of My Life."

In June 1950 Communist North Korea invaded South Korea and by August 1, American troops were fighting in a new foreign war. On November 5, Communist China entered the conflict and in a press conference on November 30, President Truman said the Americans would use the atom bomb against the Chinese if necessary. Mann shuddered at the possibility and endorsed the principles issued by the American Peace Crusade, wondering how America could prefer "for the world to end than for it to become Communist?"[58] Mann was also asking himself how he and Katia could "get away now?" That previous September Congress overrode President Truman's veto and passed the McCarran Act, one of the most restrictive and repressive pieces of legislation in American history. Members of so-called Communist organizations were required to register with a Subversive Activities Control Board, whereupon they lost the right to travel, work in defense plants, or hold government jobs. If members were aliens they would be deported. Most horrifying, the Act established six "detention centers"—concentration camps—for political dissidents.[59]

In the remainder of 1950 and 1951 Communist hysteria, fanned by a maniacal Senator Joseph McCarthy, finally claimed Mann in a way fascism never could. Still young and idealistic in 1937 when he came to America and was treasured by the free world, in 1951 Mann was old, sickly, embittered, and—worst of all—disillusioned when publication after publication denounced him as a Communist and his peace efforts as "Communist-front activities." On June 20, 1951, California Congressman Donald Jackson denounced him as "one of the world's foremost apologists for Stalin and company."[60] When his daughter Erika was interrogated by the FBI in October, Mann feared it was only a question of when he would be formally charged as a Communist by the House Un-American Activities Committee. Even without knowing that his FBI dossier was eight hundred pages long, having lived and suffered long enough to have seen history's wide, catastrophic swell, Mann envisioned having his passport and property confiscated by the new Eisenhower administration.

Though at times now he was seized by acute depression, grieving that the world had become a horrible hopeless place "from which there is no longer escaping," Switzerland still beckoned as a safe haven as it had in the early days of the Third Reich.[61] It was close enough to Germany for him to imbibe the German culture and speak the language, but free from the trouble, pain, and chaos of his native homeland. Audiences there still loved him and treated him like a literary god and paragon of humanity, and he could easily travel to other countries in Europe where literary honors and monetary prizes were again being bestowed upon him. There was also a financial factor. Whereas life in postwar, booming California was expensive, the annual rent on a nice house in Switzerland with a view of Lake Zurich approximately equaled the pay of Mann's housekeeper in California.

On June 24, 1952, Thomas Mann and his wife, Katia, left Franklin Roosevelt's America on a European lecture tour and never returned. (Mann's old friend,

Charlie Chaplin, was named a Communist by McCarthy's committee and emigrated to Switzerland in April the following year.) Erika, suffering deep depression, insomnia, and intestinal pains, accompanied her parents to Switzerland.

For a long while after the move, Mann felt nostalgic for his Pacific Palisades home, Seven Palms House. In Switzerland, which he assumed would be his last stop, he lived a peripatetic, busy life, yet with a depressing awareness that he had a limited amount of time left to keep working. He and Katia inhabited a succession of houses around Zurich, and he mourned to Hesse shortly before moving into what was to be his last home, "There has been too much wandering in my latter years."[62]

Still, Mann did not look back. After this emigration, when responding to domestic political questions from American journalists, he kept the kind of cautious silence he had maintained as an exile in Switzerland in the 1930s, declining interviews or giving abstract, uncritical answers about his commitment to peace to avoid having his words twisted to the left. He knew that in Cold War America, there was no place for his brand of didactic intellectualism, as there was no place for a man such as he who in 1945, after the war ended, preferred that a fund collected by international immigrants to show their appreciation be donated to the starving children of Europe rather than used to buy a portrait of George Washington. Nothing more dramatically demonstrated the anti-intellectual, anti-humanitarian spirit of America at the time Mann left than the 1951 best-seller *Washington Confidential*. With the blind prejudice of any good Nazi, its author asserted "where you find an intellectual, you will probably find a Red."[63]

In the end, Mann was a victim not of World War II, but of the ardent nationalism which he saw as the underlying cause of every war since the nineteenth century. His return to Switzerland was a measure of his bitter disillusionment with a postwar America turned dark and foreboding, but it was also his assertion of a simple right to live on earth in peace—to be left alone to live and write, which he did until the last days of his life.

World War II had freed his world from the fascist evil of Hitler, elevated Roosevelt's New Deal America to world greatness, but then, out of a stark fear of an ally turned mortal enemy, America's new leaders came dangerously close to creating the kind of sinister society their predecessors had fought to destroy. Through sheer force of will, foresight, and monumental talent, Mann had come through the reign of Hitler and the war scarred, but ever eager to move onward to the new. Despite dwindling energy and uncharacteristic dissatisfaction with his fictional works after *Doctor Faustus*, Mann nevertheless survived and flourished as a writer. A novella, *The Black Swan* (*Die Betrogene*), was published in September 1953, and his greatest international success, *Confessions of Felix Krull, Confidence Man*, appeared one year later, when he was seventy-eight. Politics and nationalism had broken his earthly spirit, but they could not kill the pure, inborn creative force of the artist. Mann danced forward with a vengeance. In the final months of his life he lived as he had for decades: paying tribute to art, beauty, and humanity, and decrying the sins of nationalism, in an address he wrote to commemorate the 150th anniversary of the poet Friedrich Schiller's death. Mann told audiences in the spring of 1954 in East and West Germany, Switzerland, and the Netherlands that Schiller had been right to call on a politically divided world to unite "under the banner of truth and beauty,"[64] for unless mankind remembered to honor the human race first and foremost, Mann declared, it was doomed, "not only morally but physically as well."[65]

At the time of his death on August 12, 1955, in a Zurich hospital, Thomas Mann was working on a plan to have the world's intellectuals appeal to governments to become more humanistic. Though he expected nothing concrete to come of the plan, the eighty-year-old Mann was still hoping to exercise "quiet influence over the spirits of men."[66]

Notes

Chapter One

THOMAS MANN

On a Mission from God

1. Richard and Clara Winston, eds. and trans., *Letters of Thomas Mann* (Berkeley: University of California Press, 1970), p. 67. Thomas Mann to Heinrich Mann, 18 September 1914.

2. Ibid., p. 69. Mann to Richard Dehmel, 14 December 1914.

3. Ibid., p. 75. Mann to Ernst Bertram, 18 August 1916.

4. *Professor Unrat* was made into the Hollywood movie *The Blue Angel* in 1930, starring the German-born actress Marlene Dietrich.

5. *Letters of Thomas Mann*, p. 86. Mann to Karl Strecker, 18 April 1919.

6. Ibid., p. 78. Mann to Ernst Bertram, 25 November 1916.

7. Ibid., p. 90. Mann to Gustav Blume, 5 July 1919.

8. Ibid., p. 92. Mann to Count Hermann Keyserling, 18 January 1920.

9. Hermann Kesten, ed., Richard and Clara Winston, trans., *Thomas Mann Diaries, 1918–1939* (New York: Harry N. Abrams, Inc., 1982), p. 12. Diary entry, 5 October 1918.

10. William L. Shirer, *The Rise and Fall of the Third Reich* (New York: Simon & Schuster, 1960), pp. 61–62.

11. Anni Carlson and Volker Michels, eds., Ralph Manheim, trans., *The Correspondence of Hermann Hesse and Thomas Mann, 1910–1955* (New York: Harper & Row, 1975), p. 22. Hermann Hesse to Thomas Mann, 4 June 1933.

12. It is interesting to speculate whether the era's nationalist German writers lost to oblivion would have garnered the international acclaim won by German antifascist writers had Hitler won the war.

13. Klaus Mann, *Mephisto*, trans. Robin Smythe (New York: Random House, 1977), p. 142.

14. Mann's income from book sales in Germany never approached anything like Hitler's success as the author of *Mein Kampf*. Hitler's autobiography and blueprint of his vision for himself and Germany appeared in two volumes in 1925 and 1926 and sold a million copies in 1933, making him richer than Mann ever was.

15. Thomas Mann, *Young Joseph*, trans. H. T. Lowe-Porter (New York: Alfred Knopf, 1935), p. 6. First published as *The Tales of Jacob*, S. Fischer Verlag, Berlin, 1933.

16. Mann's patrician family background in north Germany could not have been less like Adolf Hitler's in the south. Born in Austria's rural Braunau am Inn across the border from Bavaria, Hitler was descended from itinerant peasants. His father—himself illegitimate—sired two illegitimate children before marrying his third wife, Hitler's mother, a housemaid. As much as Mann's cultured youth in Lübeck inspired his burning love of the Republic, Hitler's disenfranchisement led him to despise it.

17. Klaus Mann, *Mephisto*, p. 87.

18. In Switzerland, Hesse lived as a kind of literary/cultural Buddha, but he was no hermit; admirers, soul-searchers, and writers sought audiences with him, and he had remained tied, if very loosely, to literary affairs in Germany.

19. *Correspondence of Hesse and Mann*, p. 11. Hesse to Mann, 20 February 1931.

20. Mann was unusually connected for a writer. At one time or another, he belonged to such organizations as the PEN Club, the Munich Rotary Club, the League of Nations Comité permanent des Lettres et des Arts, the German Writers' League, where he was a member of the executive committee, and the German Academy for the Cultivation of Germanism Abroad, founded in Munich in 1925.

21. Katia Mann, *Unwritten Memories*, eds., Elisabeth Plessen and Michael Mann, trans. Hunter and Hildegard Hannum (New York: Alfred A. Knopf, Inc., 1975), p. 86.

22. *Correspondence of Hesse and Mann*, p. 9. Mann to Hesse, 27 November 1931.

23. Ibid., p. 10.

24. Ibid., p. 17. A decade of murder later, on May 25, 1943, in a BBC radio broadcast to Germany, Mann recalled the charred "gift," calling it "an individual prelude . . . to the ceremonial mass burning of books, undertaken by the Nazis on May 10, 1933" (note 5).

25. Ibid., p. 17.

26. Thomas Mann, "The Sufferings and Greatness of Richard Wagner," reprinted in *Essays of Three Decades*, trans. H. T. Lowe-Porter (New York: Alfred A. Knopf, Inc., 1947), p. 314.

27. Ibid., p. 346. In his youth, Wagner was a Socialist and took part in the Dresden uprising during the German Revolution in 1849. He fled Germany for Switzerland to avoid arrest and remained in exile until 1861. Later, in a life of extreme ups and downs, he turned away from socialistic ideas and took a more metaphysical, world-renouncing view under the influence of German philosopher Arthur Schopenhauer (1788–1860), another of Mann's heroes.

28. Ibid., p. 343.

29. *Thomas Mann Diaries*, p. 140. Diary entry 30 March 1933. As late as January 26, 1933, President von Hindenburg told the Reichswehr commander-in-chief that he would never appoint Hitler chancellor. It took just three more days for the fear of civil war between the German army, the Nazis, and the political left to persuade von Hindenburg that Adolf Hitler was the only candidate.

30. According to Peter Hoffman, author of *The German Resistance 1933–1945,* the German Communist Party was a complete failure in opposing fascism. Soviet leadership held the view that a fascist government would self-destruct, paving the way for a Communist regime, but Stalin also discouraged the instigation of revolutions around the world, contrary to Trotsky's mandate. Peter Hoffman, *The History of the German Resistance 1933–1945*, trans. Richard Barry (Cambridge: The MIT Press), 1977, p. 5.

31. Thomas Mann, *This Peace*, trans. H. T. Lowe-Porter (New York: Alfred Knopf, 1938), p. 44. This specific commentary comes from Mann's November 9, 1938, address to the American Booksellers' Association.

32. *Mann Diaries*, p. 128. Entry 15, March 1933.

33. Ibid., p. 127.

34. Ludwig Fulda, a literary translator evicted from the Prussian Academy in 1933 for being a Jew, eventually returned to Berlin out of homesickness and committed suicide in 1939.

35. *Mann Diaries*, p. 130. Entry 18, March 1933.

36. Throughout his life, Mann resorted to sedatives during particularly stressful periods. In the next few months his medicine chest expanded to include a veritable pharmacopeia of sedatives, sleeping pills, and stomach relaxants: Adalin, Evipan, Phanodorm, Luminol, and Eumydrin. Often these pills were no match for his nervous anxiety.

37. Ibid., p. 139. Entry 29, March 1933. Dachau lay just fifteen miles outside the city of Munich.

38. Ibid., p. 136. Entry 27, March 1933.

39. Ibid., p. 135.

40. Ibid., p. 150. Entry 13, April 1933.

41. Ibid., p. 144. Entry 3, April 1933.

42. Ibid., p. 129. Entry 17, March 1933.

43. By mid-October 1933, about 600 Germans had been murdered and over 26,000 Germans had been arrested. According to official data reviewed by Peter Hoffman, between 1933 and 1945 about three million Germans were kept in concentration camps or

prisons for political reasons—some for the entire twelve years. Hoffman, *The German Resistance*, p. 16.

44. *Letters of Thomas Mann*, p. 123. Mann to Joseph Ponten, 21 January 1925.

45. *Mann Diaries*, p. 143. Entry 2, April 1933. Mann viewed Martin Luther, the founder of the sixteenth-century Christian Reformation in Europe, as the quintessential historical symbol of the demonic German revolutionary spirit prior to Hitler. Interestingly, in the early days of the Hitler regime, many evangelical pastors embraced the Lutheran vision of an anti-establishment Germany, and supported the nationalistic "German Christian" movement, in opposition to Marxism, Judaism, and other so-called threats to the Christian faith.

46. Ibid.

47. Ibid., p. 145. Entry 5, April 1933.

48. Strauss was perhaps the world's leading living composer when the Nazis elected him the first president of the Reich Music Chamber from 1933–1935. A political naif who underestimated the Nazis, Strauss experienced his own problems with them in 1935 when they ordered his new opera, *Die schweigsame Frau* (*The Silent Woman*) closed after its fourth performance in Dresden. The libretto was written by eminent novelist and poet, Stefan Zweig, an Austrian Jew and pacifist. Strauss also had a Jewish daughter-in-law, and his long time librettist, Hugo von Hofmannsthal, who died in 1929, was a Jew. Zweig, incidentally, was forced by the Nazis to leave Austria in 1934, lived in London until 1940, and committed suicide with his wife in 1942 in Brazil.

49. From a poem, "Taking Stock" ("*Besinnung*"), Hesse sent Mann in November 1933. The poem was published separately in February 1934 in *Die Neue Rundschau* and was included in the volume *Vom Baum des Lebens*, published by Insel-Verlag, Leipzig in 1934. The collection of sixty-five poems was reissued in 1942 in a special edition for the German armed forces. Farrar, Strauss and Giroux published an American edition in 1970.

50. *Thomas Mann Diaries*, p. 154. Entry 30, April 1933. In truth, Mann's Munich lawyer, Valentin Heins, withheld a considerable portion of Mann's private papers. When Mann later tried to get them, Heins told him they were lost when his office was bombed during the war. Mann never believed him.

51. Ibid., p. 155. Entry 3, May 1933.

52. Ibid., p. 158. Entry 10, May 1933.

53. *Letters of Thomas Mann*, p. 170. Mann to Albert Einstein, 15 May 1933. Einstein, a Jew and pacifist, suffered a decade of intellectual persecution by nationalist scientists after winning the Nobel Prize in 1921. Like Mann, he had been away from Germany when Hitler seized power. He settled in Princeton, New Jersey, where he became a neighbor of Mann.

54. Thomas Mann, *Joseph in Egypt*, trans. H. T. Lowe-Porter (New York: Alfred A. Knopf, Inc., 1938), p. 457.

55. *Thomas Mann Diaries*, p. 172. Entry 1, October 1933.

56. Mann characterized Italian Fascism in his 1930 novella *Mario and the Magician* as a transitory state, "something rather like an illness."

57. *Thomas Mann Diaries*, p. 164. Entry 23, June 1933.

58. Thomas Mann, *Young Joseph*, p. 17.

59. Mann had not even prepared to publish of any part of the Joseph story prior to Hitler becoming German chancellor. He left the manuscript at home in Munich, and Erika brought it to him in Arosa. The behind-the-scenes turmoil surrounding the publication of *The Tales of Jacob* (*Joseph and His Brothers* in the United States) was rife with politics and uncertainty. In fact, the book was published in Berlin in October 1933 by S. Fischer Verlag, but Gottfried Bermann Fischer took the precaution of obtaining a commitment from the Amsterdam publisher Querido Verlag, in the event the Nazis blocked publication at the last minute. Querido had added a special department of exile literature in 1933, and was publisher of Klaus Mann's *Die Sammlung*. Querido's owner, Emmanuel Querido, died in the Auschwitz concentration camp in 1943.

60. *Letters of Thomas Mann*, p. 181. Mann to Alfred Knopf, 20 January 1934.

61. Perhaps Mann's greatest miscalculation of the era was his early prediction that Hitler's persecution of Jews would "subside" as the result of world pressure. Mann, whose

wife was Jewish, regarded Jews as a "morally superior" people (*Mann Diaries*, p. 177, Entry 15, October 1933), and atrocities committed against them nauseated him. Nevertheless, he harbored deep stereotypes concerning Jews, and early in the Hitler regime, he found himself glad that Jews were removed from participating in the legal system. Thoughts such as these surprised and upset him. He called them "[s]ecret, disquieting, persistent musings" (*Diaries*, p. 150, Entry 10, April 1933).

62. Ibid., p. 167. Entry 26, July 1933.

63. *Mann Diaries*, p. 169. Entry 7, September 1933.

64. Ibid., pp. 170–171.

65. Ibid., p. 170.

66. Thomas Mann, *Joseph and His Brothers*, trans. H. T. Lowe-Porter (New York: Alfred A. Knopf, Inc., 1934), p. 147.

67. Thomas Mann, *Story of a Novel: The Genesis of Dr. Faustus*, trans. Richard and Clara Winston (New York: Alfred A. Knopf, Inc., 1961), p. 19.

68. Thomas Mann, *Young Joseph*, p. 50.

69. Mann, *Story of a Novel*, p. 21.

70. Mann, *Young Joseph*, p. 43. Mann's God of the Joseph story was the Almighty One, but he still required a partnership with special men like Abraham, Jacob, and Joseph (and Mann)—thinkers, dreamers, and writers. Abraham, Mann wrote, is like God's father because "He had perceived Him and thought Him into Being." This expressed the essence of Mann's concept of the artist as god.

71. The pressure was intense on individuals with lesser Aryan features. German writers had to prove Aryan blood at least four generations back in order to be published or performed. But even marriage to a non-pure Aryan qualified as "racial profanation." Hitler blamed such marriages for contributing to "liberal" tendencies.

72. Klaus Mann, *Mephisto*, p. 187.

73. A panoply of divisions were established in 1933 under a Reich Cultural Chamber, which fell under the aegis of the Reich Ministry of Propaganda: a Reich Press Chamber, Radio Chamber, Theater Chamber, Music Chamber, and Chamber of the Visual Arts.

74. Mann had written in *Young Joseph* (page 27) of Jacob's similar repugnance of state-sponsored edicts: "The service of the state, which obviously conditioned all things in that country [Egypt], offended his hereditary sense of independence and personal responsibility. . . . He called the land of mud down there not Kemt or Mizraim but Sheol, hell, the kingdom of the dead. His disgust, on grounds both ethical and intellectual, extended to the exaggerated respect which, as he had heard, was paid there to letters."

75. *Mann Diaries*, p. 222. Entry 5, August 1934.

76. *Correspondence of Hesse and Mann*, p. 41. Mann to Hesse, 7 August 1934.

77. *Letters of Thomas Mann*, p. 191. Mann to Bertram, 30 July 1934.

78. *Mann Diaries*, p. 202. Entry 20, March 1934.

79. In November 1935 Mann and his publisher decided to divide the ever-growing manuscript, already nearly six hundred pages long, into two volumes. *Joseph in Egypt*, the third volume, was originally published in German in 1936. *Joseph the Provider*, the fourth, was originally published in 1943. As published, the work constitutes a tetralogy, not a quintet.

80. Thomas Mann, *The Coming Victory of Democracy*, trans. Agnes E. Meyer (New York: Alfred A. Knopf, Inc., 1938), p. 30.

81. *Letters of Thomas Mann*, p. 110. Mann to Ida Boy-Ed, 5 December 1922.

82. Ibid., p. 202. Entry 20, March 1934.

83. Ibid., p. 222. Entry 5, August 1934.

84. Mann, *The Coming Victory of Democracy*, p. 31.

85. Ibid., p. 12.

86. Ibid., pp. 28–29.

87. In *Young Joseph*, Joseph's brothers try to exonerate themselves from guilt by drawing just such a subtle distinction. Too cowardly to kill Joseph themselves, they put in place all the machinery so he will die. "But what had happened had been just a happening, it was not an act, not a deed, you could not call it so. It had come about, indeed, through them, but

they had not done it, it simply happened to them. . . . And that was a world-wide difference; it was all the difference between an act and an occurrence." Indeed, at the Nuremberg trials after the war, the defendants commonly expressed their amazement that Nazi hate propaganda against Jews had really been implemented. Mann, *Young Joseph*, p. 198.

88. G. M. Gilbert, *Nuremberg Diary* (New York: Farrar, Strauss & Co., 1947), p. 289.

89. *Letters of Thomas Mann*, p. 185. Mann to Rene Schickele, 2 April 1934.

90. Ibid.

91. *Correspondence of Hesse and Mann*, p. 107. Mann to Hesse, 8 February 1947.

92. Mann contrasted the Roosevelt-inspired construction of housing for millions with the colossal public structures Hitler had built in Berlin, Munich, and Nuremberg at a time when hundreds of thousands of Germans needed homes. In his 1938 essay, *The Coming Victory of Democracy*, Mann called Hitler's titanic buildings "monster structures," the product of "depravity" and "decadence" (p. 39), whereas Roosevelt's building plans "aimed at the needs and the reasonable well-being of the population" (p. 40).

93. *Mann Diaries*, p. 244. Entry 29, June 1935.

94. *Letters of Thomas Mann*, p. 196. Mann to Louise Servicen, 23 May 1935.

95. Ironically, it was not politics per se, but race hatred that ended publication of Mann's books in Germany during the Hitler era. In February 1935, Jewish publishers, including S. Fischer Verlag, were ordered to liquidate their businesses. A few weeks later, the regime issued a declaration that all non-Aryan members of the Kulturkammer, the Reich Chamber of Culture, were prohibited from pursuing literary activity. Gottfried Bermann Fischer had managed to stay in business until that point, although with foreigners boycotting German books and the German public mostly buying "patriotic" literary works, his company's output had greatly diminished. Fischer's story was a microcosm of the experience of exiles during Hitler's reign. He was forced to sell to an Aryan in November 1935, relocated the company to Vienna, fled after the Anchluss to Stockholm, and emigrated to the United States in 1940 after being expelled for anti-Nazi activity. After the war he returned to Europe.

Mann's last book to be published in Germany until *Doctor Faustus* in 1946 was a book of essays, *Leiden und Grosse der Meister* (*Sufferings and Greatness of the Masters*) on March 28, 1935. The book was published in America as *Freud, Goethe, Wagner*, trans. H. T. Lowe-Porter (New York: Alfred A. Knopf, 1937).

96. *Mann Diaries*, p. 255. Entry 3, February 1936.

97. *Letters of Thomas Mann*, p. 186. Mann to Rene Schichele, 2 April 1934.

98. Mann formally expressed this concept in the lecture "Humaniora und Humanismus" at the Commission Internationale de Coopération Intellectuelle in Budapest on June 9, 1936.

99. Mann delivered a private reading of the lecture, "Freud and the Future," to the ailing Freud in his Vienna home on June 14, 1936. At the time, Freud's doctor was so indignant about events in Germany that he refused to use German medicines to treat his patient.

Earlier in the tour, Mann met with Czech President Beneš in Prague on May 11. Beneš expressed optimism about English policy and the Sudeten Germans, whose loyalty to Konrad Henlein, the Sudeten German Party leader, Beneš doubted. Mann concluded after the meeting that Beneš "shows little understanding of the spirit of nazism" (*Mann Diaries*, p. 260. Entry 13, May 1936). Indeed, Mann was right. When the English sacrificed Czechoslovakia under the one-sided terms of the Munich Pact and German troops occupied the Sudetenland on October 5, 1938, Henlein personally greeted Hitler in the city of Eger.

Mann's Freud lecture was subsequently published by S. Fischer Verlag in Vienna in 1936, and in America in *Freud, Goethe and Wagner*, trans. H. T. Lowe-Porter and Rita Matthias-Reil (New York: Alfred A. Knopf, Inc., 1937), and in *Essays of Three Decades*, trans. H. T. Lowe-Porter (New York: Alfred A. Knopf, Inc., 1947).

100. M. Lincoln Schuster, ed., *The World's Great Letters* (New York: Simon & Schuster, 1940), p. 514. The Dean of Bonn University to Thomas Mann.

101. Mann's "Open Letters" were eagerly greeted by antifascists in Europe, if in secret in Germany. For example, in just a few weeks, more than 20,000 copies of his reply

to the dean of the philosophical faculty at Bonn University were distributed in several languages.

102. *Mann Diaries*, p. 274. Entry 5, March 1937.

103. Thompson wrote: "Wherever men love reason, hate obscurantism, shun darkness, turn toward light, know gratitude, praise virtue, despise meanness, kindle to sheer beauty; wherever minds are sensitive, hearts generous and spirits free—there is your home. In welcoming you, a country but honors itself. And of your future in history we have no doubt." Thompson, a foreign correspondent in Berlin from 1924–1934 was the first American citizen to be deported by the Nazis. Schuster, *World's Great Letters*, p. 522.

104. *Correspondence of Hesse and Mann*, p. 63. Mann to Hesse, 17 October 1936.

105. *Mann Diaries*, p. 284. Entry 27, November 1937.

106. Mann, *The Coming Victory of Democracy*, p. 9.

107. Ibid., pp. 56–57.

108. Freud, eighty-one and too sick to climb stairs, resisted leaving his native Austria until a friend compared his situation to that of the second officer of the Titanic. When officially asked why he abandoned the ship, he answered, "I never left the ship, Sir; she left me." In the weeks prior to Freud's emigration to London in early June 1938, his physical safety in Vienna was ensured through the intervention of an impressive coterie of protectors, including President Roosevelt, who authorized Secretary of State Cordell Hull, Assistant Secretary Sumner Welles and the American ambassadors in Vienna, Berlin, and Paris to personally appeal to the German authorities. Peter Gay, *Freud: A Life for Our Times* (New York:Anchor Books/Doubleday, 1989), pp. 623–629.

109. *Mann Diaries*, p. 295, 20 March 1938.

110. *Letters of Thomas Mann*, p. 224. Mann to Erich von Kahler, 26 May 1938.

111. The Thomas Mann Gesellschaft based in Prague and Zurich primarily helped German exiled intellectuals obtain work. The Prague office closed when Czechoslovakia fell to the Nazis in October 1938.

112. *Letters of Thomas Mann*, p. 224. Mann to Unknown, 21 May 1938.

113. Throughout the 1930s, the Garden was the site of many mass rallies both pro- and anti-Nazi. At a German-American Nazi rally held there five months after Mann's address, Bund leader Fritz Kuhn denounced Jews to more than 22,000 adherents. Like their German counterparts, American Nazis were keenly aware of the power of national myths: a poster of George Washington decorated the hall along with pro-Nazi banners.

114. Ibid., p. 229. Mann to Erich von Kahler, 19 October 1938.

115. Mann, *This Peace*, trans. H. T. Lowe-Porter (New York: Alfred A. Knopf, Inc., 1938), pp. 10 and 21.

116. Ibid., p. 8.

117. Ibid., pp. 21–22.

118. Ibid., p. 47. Mann's November 9 address, together with the essay "This Peace," were published by Alfred Knopf in one volume on November 21, 1938, under the title *This Peace*. A second printing was issued in December 1938.

119. *Correspondence of Hesse and Mann*, p. 98. Mann to Hesse, 25 November 1945.

120. Mann severed his ties to the League in December 1939 after its November bulletin ran an article criticizing France for yielding to fascistic corruption. In a complete about-face since WWI, Mann had become archly pro-France and called the article by League member Elliot Paul a piece of Stalinist propaganda.

121. In *Lotte in Weimar* (in the U.S. retitled *The Beloved Returns*), Mann described just this kind of character transposition in relation to Goethe and his former secretary, Reimer. Explains Mann's fictional Reimer: "for years I have carried on his correspondence, not only to dictation but also quite independently, or rather as though I were he, in his place and in his name and spirit. You see, the independence rises to such a height that it turns dialectically as it were into its opposite, it is abrogated, the surrender is of such a kind that I am not present at all, and he speaks out of me." Thomas Mann, *The Beloved Returns* (New York: Alfred A. Knopf, Inc., 1940), p. 75.

122. Ibid., pp. 70 and 78.

123. *Letters of Thomas Mann*, pp. 122–123. Mann to Josef Ponten, 21 January 1925.

124. *Mann Diaries*, p. 342. Entry 26, October 1939.

125. Ibid., p. 327. Entry 28, April 1939.

126. Thomas Mann, *The Beloved Returns*, trans. H. T. Lowe-Porter (New York: Alfred A. Knopf, Inc., 1940), p. 88.

127. Ibid., pp. 247 and 335.

128. *Mann Diaries*, p. 319. Entry 14, February 1939.

129. Ibid., p. 324. Entry 24, March 1939.

130. Shirer, *The Rise and Fall of the Third Reich*, p. 460.

131. *Mann Diaries*, p. 336. Entry 25, August 1939.

132. In their memoirs, both Katia (*Unwritten Memories*) and Erika Mann (*The Lost Year of Thomas Mann*) related the story of their escape from Sweden. On the flight from Malmö, in southern Sweden, to Copenhagen, Denmark, a stewardess told them that Nazi fliers were coming close to planes, looking through the windows for individual "enemies," and shooting at them. The press had reported Mann's departure for America, and with the Nazis probably on the lookout for him, a nervous Katia asked Mann, who was sitting in a window seat and not privy to her conversation, to exchange seats with her.

133. Ibid., p. 341. Entry 19, September 1939.

134. *Letters of Thomas Mann*, pp. 249–250. Mann to Golo Mann, 3 November 1939. The final manuscript of *Lotte in Weimar* reached Gottfried Bermann in Stockholm via Portugal in Swiss diplomatic mail. It was published originally in German in December 1939.

135. Thomas Mann, *This War*, trans. Eric Sutton (New York: Alfred A. Knopf, Inc., 1940), p. 54.

136. *The Transposed Heads: A Legend of India* (*Die vertauschten Köpfe: Eine indische Legende*) was published by Bermann-Fischer Verlag in 1940 and by Alfred Knopf in 1941, trans. H. T. Lowe-Porter.

137. *Letters of Thomas Mann*, pp. 268–269. Mann to Erich von Kahler, 8 July 1940.

138. Klaus Mann, born in 1906, was a prolific playwright, novelist, essayist, and left-leaning journalist who was targeted by the German Right. After his journal, *Die Sammlung*, suspended publication in August 1935, Klaus, in exile in Amsterdam, published his third novel, *Mephisto*, in 1936, a scathing depiction of the decadent Weimar drama world and the willingness of German artists and intellectuals to accept Nazi takeover. The novel, thinly veiled, was the story of his sister Erika's first husband, Deutsches Theatre director and actor, Gustaf Grundgens, who was promoted by the Nazis to the Berlin State Theatre in 1934. Klaus moved to London in 1936 and later to New York, where he founded *Decision: A Review of Culture*. The magazine which lasted from January 1941 to February 1942 was sponsored by Sherwood Anderson, W. H. Auden, Eduard Beneš, and Somerset Maugham among others. In 1942, Klaus joined the U.S. Army and saw action in Italy. He committed suicide in 1949.

139. The youngest Mann children, Elisabeth, or "Medi," born in 1918, and Michael, or "Bibi," born in 1919, were still in school in Munich when the family left Germany. After escaping Germany, they continued their studies in Zurich, and moved to America with their parents. Michael became a concert violinist who performed around the world, and during the war he lived with his Swiss wife in Carmel, California. He committed suicide in 1977 at the age of fifty-eight. In November 1939 Medi married Italian-American literary historian, Giuseppe Antonio Borgese, who had emigrated to America in 1931. Almost three times her age and an arch antifascist, Borgese was a professor at the University of Chicago during the war years.

140. Erika's marriage to Gustaf Grundgens lasted from 1925–1928, and in 1933 she opened a political cabaret in Munich called The Peppermill. The Nazis closed it down, but she successfully reopened it under the same name in Zurich a year later.

141. Thomas Mann, *Joseph the Provider*, trans. H. T. Lowe-Porter (New York: Alfred A. Knopf, Inc., 1944), p. 24.

142. *Letters of Thomas Mann*, p. 273. Mann to Agnes E. Meyer, 24 September 1940.

143. *Correspondence of Hesse and Mann*, p. 86. Mann to Hesse, 17 July 1941.

144. Peter Calvocoressi and Guy Wint, *Total War* (New York: Pantheon Books/Random House, 1972), p. 196.

145. Correspondence of Hesse and Mann, p. 81. Mann to Hesse, 2 January 1941.

146. *Letters of Thomas Mann*, p. 193. Mann to Hedwig Fischer, 2 November 1934.

147. Because of the war, Mann's appointment came under some fire. Making the announcement on January 16, 1942, Librarian of Congress Archibald MacLeish was careful to note that Mann's "devotion to the cause of democracy led him to self-imposed exile from Nazi Germany." Mann's annual salary, which he waived in 1944, was underwritten by Agnes and Eugene Meyer. Mann held the honorary post until his death. Scott Donaldson, *Archibald MacLeish: An American Life* (Boston: Houghton Mifflin Company, 1992), p. 325.

148. *Letters of Thomas Mann*, p. 295. Mann to Erich von Kahler, 31 December 1941.

149. *Correspondence of Hesse and Mann*, p. 89. Mann to Hesse, 15 March 1942.

150. The line, from Mann's novel *Doctor Faustus*, quoted Keats's "Ode to a Nightingale," and reads in full: " 'the consolations of a sunny world, which make one forget the weariness, the fever, and the fret Here, where men sit and hear each other groan.' " Thomas Mann, *Doctor Faustus*, trans. H. T. Lowe-Porter (New York: Alfred A. Knopf, Inc., 1948), p. 264.

151. *Letters of Thomas Mann*, p. 299. Mann to Agnes E. Meyer, 22 January 1942.

152. Ibid., p. 263. Mann to Bruno Frank, 4 June 1940.

153. Ibid., p. 328. Mann to Bertolt Brecht, 10 December 1943.

154. Ibid., p. 305. Mann to Agnes E. Meyer, 20 August 1942.

155. Ibid., p. 306.

156. Mann, *This War*, p. 9.

157. Mann, *Young Joseph*, p. 263.

158. Scott Donaldson, *Archibald MacLeish: An American Life*, p. 325.

159. Mann, *Story of a Novel*, p. 14.

160. Ibid., p. 17. Mann's novella, written in German with the title *Das Gesetz* (*The Commandments*), was first published as a separate volume by Bermann-Fischer Verlag, Stockholm, in 1944. Alfred A. Knopf, Inc., published the novella in English in 1945 under the title *The Tables of the Law*, translated by H. T. Lowe-Porter.

161. In the fall of 1940 Mann began delivering radio broadcasts to Europe over the BBC from the NBC studios in Los Angeles. Twenty-five of Mann's BBC broadcasts were published in 1942 in *Deutsche Horer!* by Bermann Fischer, Stockholm. Alfred Knopf published the book in 1943 as *Listen, Germany!* Mann's last radio broadcast eulogized Franklin Roosevelt.

162. Thomas Mann, *The Tables of the Law*, trans. H. T. Lowe-Porter (New York: Alfred A. Knopf, Inc., 1945), p. 12. The narrator repeatedly calls the Israelites "formless humanity," and "raw material." Like the novelist who shapes formless ideas and emotions into characters in a story, Moses faces the task of "shaping" and "forming" souls.

163. Ibid., pp. 52–54.

164. *Letters of Thomas Mann*, p. 328. Mann to Bertolt Brecht, 10 December 1943.

165. Thomas Mann, *Doctor Faustus*, p. 30.

166. Thomas Mann, *Story of a Novel*, p. 17.

167. *Correspondence of Hesse and Mann*, p. 121. Mann to Hesse, 27 November 1947.

168. In his portrayal of hell in Chapter XXV, Mann brilliantly captured Germany during the Nazi era: "Every compassion, every grace, every sparing, every last trace of consideration for the incredulous, imploring objection 'that you verily cannot do so unto a soul': it is done, it happens . . . far down beneath God's hearing, and happens to all eternity . . . yea, that hell is to be defined as a monstrous combination of suffering and derision, unendurable yet to be endured world without end." *Doctor Faustus*, p. 245.

169. Mann, *Doctor Faustus*, p. 236.

170. Mann, *Story of a Novel*, p. 55.

171. The article was probably "How to Win the Peace," published in the *Atlantic Monthly*, February 1942.

172. Mann, *Story of a Novel*, p. 6.

173. Mann's main musical advisor for *Doctor Faustus* was Theodor Wiesengrund-Adorno, a dialectic composer of modern music and a former philosophy teacher at

Frankfurt am Main University. Adorno was another casualty of the Nazi era, expelled from his teaching post in 1933. His non-nationalistic, "radical" music alone qualified as a sin committed against the Fatherland, but Adorno was also the son of a German-Jewish father and Italian-descended mother, which made him a definite "enemy of the German people." Adorno lived in Los Angeles, heard about Mann's work-in-progress, and in July 1943 appeared at Seven Palms House bearing his treatise, *Inspiration in Musical Creation*. In *Story of a Novel* (pp. 44–45). Mann freely admitted that Chapter XXII is taken completely from Adorno's critical analysis of Arnold Schoenberg's twelve-tone technique.

174. Mann, *Doctor Faustus*, p. 45.

175. Mann, *Story of a Novel*, pp. 37–38.

176. *Letters of Thomas Mann*, p. 323. Mann to Agnes E. Meyer, 2 June 1943.

177. Ibid., p. 325. Mann to Conrad Kellen, 19 August 1943.

178. Ibid., p. 327. Mann to Bertolt Brecht, 10 December 1943.

179. Ibid., p. 325. Mann to Conrad Kellen, 19 August 1943.

180. Mann, *Story of a Novel*, p. 51.

181. Interestingly, Hesse was not among the authors whose works were banned in Germany by the Nazi authorities. He continued to be published by his and Mann's old Berlin firm after its sale to a non-Jew in 1935. And while his books were classified as "undesirable" and many were out of print, reading them was not a punishable offense. His 1942 novel, *The Glass Bead Game*, about an artistic utopia at a time in the future when there are no more wars, was printed in Zurich because of Germany's paper shortage. Coincidentally, both *The Glass Bead Game* and *Doctor Faustus* were fictionalized biographies involving music and one's yearning to balance high intellect with nature. Hesse based the character Thomas van der Trave upon Thomas Mann.

182. Mann, *Story of a Novel*, p. 55. Despite Mann's goal of "universality," *Doctor Faustus* paints a thoroughly German picture of evil, with occasional moments of humor. "Speak only German," the Devil orders Adrian in Chapter XXV, in a scene of quintessential Mann tragicomedy.

183. *Letters of Thomas Mann*, p. 327. Mann to Berolt Brecht, 10 December 1943.

184. Ibid., p. 333. Mann to Harry Slochower, 18 February 1944.

185. Ibid., p. 327. Mann to Bertolt Brecht, 10 December 1943.

186. Mann, *Doctor Faustus*, pp. 252–253.

187. Mann, *Story of a Novel*, p. 14.

188. *Letters of Thomas Mann*, p. 335. Mann to F.W. Bradley, 20 May 1944.

189. Ibid., p. 337 Mann to Klaus Mann, 25 June 1944.

190. Ibid., pp. 337 and 350, Mann to Erich van Kahler, 1 May 1945; *The Story of a Novel*, p. 87.

191. Thomas Mann, *Doctor Faustus*, p. 118.

192. *Correspondence of Hesse and Mann*, p. 122. Mann to Hesse, 26 October 1947.

193. *Doctor Faustus*, p. 485.

194. Ibid., p. 180.

195. Ibid., p. 166.

Chapter Two

JOHN STEINBECK

America Against Itself

1. John Steinbeck, *Journal of a Novel: The East of Eden Letters* (New York: Viking Press, 1969), p. 103.

2. Steinbeck always prided himself on his mechanical ingenuity. His inventiveness was not merely limited to fixing cars, water heaters, and gas lines, however. When he

worked at a fish hatchery in 1928, he devised prophylactics out of preserved fish skins. Jackson J. Benson, *The True Adventures of John Steinbeck, Writer* (New York: Viking Press, 1984), p. 132.

3. Elaine Steinbeck and Robert Wallsten, eds., *Steinbeck: A Life in Letters* (New York: Viking Press, 1975), p. 70. To Carlton A. Sheffield, 21 June 1933.

4. Ibid., p. 72. John Steinbeck to Carlton A. Sheffield, 21 June 1933.

5. Ibid. Steinbeck arrived at his phalanx conclusions while isolated at home in northern California. In Berlin, William L. Shirer, the American journalist who witnessed Hitler's earliest days in power and published his important book *Berlin Diary* in 1941, observed Steinbeck's ideas in shocking practice. On September 4, 1934, Shirer, newly arrived in Berlin, watched "solid phalanxes of wildly cheering Nazis." Nazi party officials, he wrote three days later, shed "their individual souls and minds . . . until under the mystic lights and at the sound of the magic words of the Austrian they were merged completely in the Germanic herd." William Shirer, *Berlin Diary* (New York: Alfred A. Knopf, 1941), pp. 16 and 21. Steinbeck and Shirer became friends when they met in London in 1943 covering World War II.

6. Adolf Hitler, *Mein Kampf*, Ralph Manheim, trans. (Boston: Houghton Mifflin Company, 1971), p. 450. Volume one was published in the fall of 1925. Hitler's business manager, Max Amann, alleged sales of 23,000, but historians remain dubious. Even Hitler's National Socialist Party colleagues found the book "silly." Volume two was published in December 1926 and had even fewer sales. Sales began to rise about 1930, and when Hitler came to power in 1933, every German citizen was required to buy a copy. During the years while he was in power, only the Bible sold more copies.

7. Hitler wrote in *Mein Kampf*, "Nature . . . puts living creatures on this globe and watches the free play of forces. She then confers the master's right on her favorite child, the strongest in courage and industry" (p. 134).

8. When Hitler made a tour of his occupying troops in the Rhineland in March 1936, he asked that a recording of Wagner's *Parsifal* be played. He remarked that he had built his religion out of that opera and said, "You can serve God only as a hero." John Toland, *Adolf Hitler* (New York: Ballantine Books, 1976), p. 298.

9. John Steinbeck, *The Grapes of Wrath* (New York: Compass Books Edition/Viking Press, 1962), p. 175.

10. *Steinbeck: A Life in Letters*, p. 124. To George Albee, late 1936.

11. John Toland, *Adolf Hitler* (New York: Ballantine Books, 1976), p. 342. Goering continued at the Nuremberg rally: "This miserable pygmy race [the Czechs] without culture—no one knows where it came from—is oppressing a cultured people and behind it is Moscow and the eternal mask of the Jew devil."

12. Robert DeMott, ed., *John Steinbeck, Working Days: The Journals of the Grapes of Wrath 1938–1941* (New York: Viking Penguin Inc., 1989), p. 70. Diary entry 69, 12 September, 1938.

13. Ibid., p. 77. Diary entry 79, 26 September 1938.

14. Ibid., p. 70. Diary entry 68, 9 September 1938.

15. Ibid., p. 92. Diary entry 99, 25 October 1938.

16. Ibid., p. 56. Diary entry 52, 16 August 1938.

17. *Steinbeck: Letters*, p. 143. John Steinbeck to Mr. and Mrs. Joseph Henry Jackson, January 1938. The extremes of Steinbeck's career are best illustrated by the publication history of *The Red Pony*. Steinbeck wrote the five stories comprising *The Red Pony* between 1933 and 1934 during his parents' illness, and at the time he had tremendous difficulty getting them published. By 1937 when the first edition of the book was published in novel form, Steinbeck was famous enough to merit an expensive limited edition.

18. Ibid.

19. DeMott, *Working Days*, p. 38. Diary entry 29, 5 July 1938.

20. Ibid., p. 106. Diary entry 101, 16 October 1939.

21. In the 1939 film *The Wizard of Oz*, Dorothy chanted, "There's no place like home." Two years earlier, Margaret Mitchell's *Gone with the Wind*, dramatizing a woman's abiding connection to her ancestral home and land, became a best-seller and

Pulitzer Prize winner. Fictional stories of disenfranchisement, even if they took place during the distant Civil War or in the fantasy land of Oz, spoke a common language to Americans of the 1930s.

22. *Steinbeck: A Life in Letters*, p. 175. To Chase Horton, date unknown.

23. DeMott, *Working Days*, p. 106. Diary entry 101, 16 October 1939.

24. Ibid.

25. Benson, *The True Adventures*, pp. 401–402.

26. DeMott, *Working Days*, p. 106. Diary entry 101, 16 October 1939.

27. Ibid., p. 109. Diary entry 103, 19 October 1939.

28. Ibid., p. 108.

29. Ibid., p. 106. Diary entry 101, 16 October 1939.

30. *Steinbeck: A Life in Letters*, pp. 181–182. To Carlton A. Sheffield, 13 November 1939.

31. *Of Mice and Men* was directed by Lewis Milestone. Russian-born, Milestone collaborated with Joris Ivens the next year on the documentary film, *Our Russian Front*. Milestone was one of Hollywood's most socially conscious directors and made two Hollywood war films, *All Quiet on the Western Front*, in 1930, and *A Walk in the Sun*, in 1946, which told the story of war through a soldier's eyes. Milestone also directed the 1949 film version of Steinbeck's *The Red Pony*.

32. *Steinbeck: A Life in Letters*, p. 184. To Elizabeth Otis, 15 December 1939.

33. John Steinbeck, *The Log from The Sea of Cortez* (London: Mandarin Paperback, 1958), p. 68.

34. Even before the boat left port, Carol's presence provoked trouble. As designated cook, she was so frugal that she ordered only enough food to last a week and refused to pay for any more. When the crew threatened to quit, the captain promised to reimburse her for any leftovers worth more than fifty dollars, but Carol's anger lingered, and she locked herself in her room for a day and a half after the boat sailed. Benson, *The True Adventures*, pp. 438–441.

The conflict may have lingered in Steinbeck's mind. In *The Log from The Sea of Cortez* (p. 72), he wrote, "It is amazing how much food seven people need to exist for six weeks," and then went on to list the galley's cornucopia of food stocks.

35. DeMott, *Working Days*, p. 110. Diary entry 106, 4 January 1940.

36. Steinbeck, *The Log from The Sea of Cortez*, p. 246.

37. Ibid., p. 70.

38. *Steinbeck: A Life in Letters*, p. 188. To Elizabeth Otis, 26 March 1940.

39. Steinbeck, *The Log from The Sea of Cortez*, p. 273.

40. A few months after this trip, Steinbeck went to Washington and urged President Roosevelt to order that counterfeit German money be printed and dropped over Axis and occupied countries. The plan was rejected.

41. DeMott, *Working Days*, p. 113. Diary entry 109, 12 January 1940.

42. Though *The Sea of Cortez* was the product of Ricketts's and Steinbeck's joint venture aboard the *Western Flyer* (as well as years of collaborative thinking), and they shared credit for the book, Steinbeck spoke of the book privately as though he were its sole author.

43. DeMott, *Working Days*, p. 121. Diary entry 118, 29 September 1940.

44. Steinbeck, *The Log from The Sea of Cortez*, p. 159.

45. Ibid., p. 150.

46. Ibid., p. 305.

47. Ibid., pp. 207–213.

48. DeMott, *Working Days*, p. 122. Diary entry 119, 12 December 1940.

49. *Steinbeck: A Life in Letters*, p. 207. To Pascal Covici, 1 January 1941.

50. DeMott, *Working Days*, pp. 124–125. Diary entry 120, 20 January 1941.

51. Materialism was an evolutionary mutation that would lead the human species to extinction, Steinbeck wrote in *The Log from The Sea of Cortez*. He equated Henry Ford with Adolf Hitler and wrote that mass production was, in evolutionary terms, like the "thickening armor of the great reptiles." Note: Fascist Ezra Pound equated Henry Ford with the Great Flaubert.

52. Steinbeck, *The Log from The Sea of Cortez*, p. 132.

53. *Steinbeck: A Life in Letters*, p. 192. To Joseph Hamilton, Spring 1940.

54. DeMott, *Working Days*, p. 42. Diary entry 34, 12 July 1938.

55. Allan Winkler, *The Politics of Propaganda: The Office of War Information, 1942–1945* (New Haven: Yale University Press, 1978), p. 16.

56. *Steinbeck: A Life in Letters*, p. 222. To Webster F. Street, 25 November 1941.

57. Ibid., p. 223. John Steinbeck to Webster F. Street, 8 December 1941.

58. Executive Order 9066 empowering the military to relocate residents of "military areas" was signed by President Roosevelt on February 19, 1942. On March 2, the western states of Washington, California, and Oregon were declared strategic areas from which residents of Japanese descent must be excluded. Ultimately, more than 110,000 of these residents, sixty-four percent of whom were American citizens, were forced to abandon homes and businesses and move to ten relocation centers.

59. Benson, *The True Adventures*, p. 498.

60. *Steinbeck: A Life in Letters*, p. 222. John Steinbeck to Webster F. Street, 25 November 1941. *The Sea of Cortez* had set forth the differences between two kinds of thinking: teleographic, based on emotions and prejudices, and nonteleographic, based on impartial analysis. The book alleged that many of the world's problems resulted from teleographic or prejudiced thinking. *The Moon Is Down* exemplified Steinbeck's conviction that teleographic thinking was fatal.

61. The Pulitzer Prize committee named no "Best American Play" for the 1942 drama season. The highly regarded playwright Maxwell Anderson also received poor reviews for his play, *Candle in the Wind*, a love story that took place in occupied France and carried the popular message that the righteous win wars.

62. *Steinbeck: A Life in Letters*, pp. 229–230. To Webster F. Street, 8 April 1942.

63. Steinbeck, *The Log from The Sea of Cortez*, p. 54.

64. Ibid., p. 55.

65. Benson, *The True Adventures*, p. 508.

66. Ibid., 509.

67. DeMott, *Working Days*, p. 176. Editor's note 114.

68. One senior league member, Midwestern fiction writer Meridel LeSueur, declared, "Such conferences of writers and artists are the living glowing nuclei of a new life within the maggoty body of a social corpse." This was not the kind of language upon which the FBI looked with favor. Daniel Aaron, *Writers on the Left* (New York: Columbia University Press, 1992), p. 307.

69. Herbert Mitgang, *Dangerous Dossiers: Exposing the Secret War Against America's Greatest Authors* (New York: Ballantine Books, 1989), p. 53.

70. In his 1967 autobiography, Rickenbacker partly attributed the crew's survival to the twice-daily prayer meetings the men held. This fact confirmed Steinbeck's belief that men needed prayer to fend off their deepest fears.

71. Donald Spoto, *The Dark Side of Genius: The Life of Alfred Hitchcock* (New York: Little Brown & Co., 1983), pp. 266–267. Though Steinbeck sold several of his novels to Hollywood in the 1930s, he resisted writing scripts for the studios, whose people had their own ideas on how to adapt his novels. In 1938, when he refused to write a script for *Of Mice and Men* with a different ending from the novel, producer Myron Selznick accused him of wanting to be "writer and director and producer." Benson, *True Adventures*, p. 373.

72. *Steinbeck: A Life in Letters*, p. 234. To Webster F. Street, 15 March 1943.

73. Ibid., p. 218. To Elizabeth Otis, 18 July 1941.

74. Ibid., p. 228. To Webster F. Street, 14 February 1942.

75. Ibid., p. 239. To Webster F. Street, 9 April 1943.

76. Benson, *The True Adventures*, p. 517.

77. John Steinbeck, *Once There Was a War* (New York: Bantam Books, 1960), p. 6. Dispatch date, 22 June 1943.

78. For security reasons, Steinbeck concealed Fairbanks's identity in the Ventotene dispatches and referred to him as "commodore."

79. *Steinbeck: A Life in Letters*, p. 246. To Gwyndolyn Steinbeck, 22 September 1943.

80. Ibid., p. 82. To Carl Wilhelmson, 9 August 1933.

81. Steinbeck, *Once There Was a War*, pp. vi and xiv from the Introduction.

82. Ibid., p. x.

83. *Steinbeck: A Life in Letters*, p. 352. To Elaine Scott, 16 August 1949.

84. Ibid., p. 256. To Carlton A. Sheffield, 27 September 1944.

85. Ibid., pp. 255–256; Benson, *The True Adventures*, p. 543.

86. Carol had performed similar high jinks during the Great Depression to keep her husband from despondency. If Carol was Steinbeck's source for Mary Talbot, then it was Steinbeck who was responsible for her lunacy. In fact, after their divorce, Steinbeck often blamed himself for the change in Carol.

87. John Steinbeck, *Cannery Row*, in *The Short Novels of John Steinbeck* (New York: The Viking Press, 1953), pp. 408–409.

88. Benson, p. 541.

89. *Steinbeck: A Life in Letters*, p. 255. To Carlton A. Sheffield, 27 September 1944.

90. Ibid., p. 258. To Pascal Covici, November 1944. Steinbeck's fictional families dwindled in size during the war years as the writer's sense of alienation grew. Danny's band in *Tortilla Flat* was a boisterous six. The big Joad brood lost members to death and trouble, but a core of six remained. At the end of *The Pearl*, only Kino and his wife Juana are left.

91. Ibid., p. 263. To Pascal Covici, Spring 1945.

92. Ibid., p. 261. To Pascal Covici, Christmastime 1944.

93. Ibid., p. 263. To Pascal Covici, Spring 1945.

94. Steinbeck cited his commitment to *The Pearl* project when he declined an offer to cover the Nuremberg war crimes trials for the *New York Herald Tribune*. Given that he loathed his recent war coverage from Europe, it is unlikely he would have accepted the offer even if he had not been so occupied.

95. Ibid, p. 269. To Jack Wagner, early 1946.

96. Steinbeck's use of the toilet bowl to represent life in America is one of his most subtle and brilliant images. Just one decade before the time of *The Wayward Bus*, *The Grapes of Wrath* had shown the Joad children seeing a flush toilet for the first time when they arrive in a government-sponsored labor camp. In one of the novel's funniest scenes, the children innocently press the lever, see the torrent of water, and panic for fear they have broken it.

97. John Steinbeck, *The Wayward Bus* (New York: Viking Press, 1947), p. 611.

98. *Steinbeck: A Life in Letters*, p. 378. To Pascal Covici, Midsummer 1950.

99. John Steinbeck, *East of Eden* (New York: The Viking Press, 1952), p. 27.

100. *Steinbeck: A Life in Letters*, p. 352. To Elaine Scott, 16 August 1949.

101. Ibid., p. 336. To John O'Hara, 8 June 1949.

102. Ibid., p. 383. To Bo Beskow, September 1950.

103. Ibid., pp. 454–455. To Elizabeth Otis, 17 June 1954.

104. Ibid., p. 467. To Elizabeth Otis, 29 September 1954.

105. Ibid., p. 465. To Elizabeth Otis, 17 September 1954.

106. Ibid., p. 556. To Professor and Mrs. Eugene Vinaver, 27 June 1958.

107. Ibid., p. 520. To Elizabeth Otis and Chase Horton, 26 April 1957.

108. Ibid., p. 609. To Joseph Bryan III, 28 September 1959.

109. Ibid., p. 658. To Pascal Covici, July 1961.

110. Ibid., p. 627. To Elizabeth Otis, June 1960.

111. John Steinbeck, *The Winter of Our Discontent* (New York: The Viking Press, 1961), p. 81.

Chapter Three

VIRGINIA WOOLF

The Outsider's Lament

1. Leonard Woolf, *The Journey Not the Arrival Matters: An Autobiography of the Years 1939–1969* (New York: A Harvest Book/Harcourt Brace Jovanovich, 1969), pp. 45–46.

2. Ibid., p. 46.

3. Ibid.

4. Virginia Woolf, *Three Guineas* (New York: A Harvest Book/Harcourt Brace Jovanovich, 1966), p. 17.

5. Ibid., p. 13.

6. Ibid., p. 11.

7. Nigel Nicholson and Joanne Trautmann, eds., *The Letters of Virginia Woolf, 1936–1941*, vol. 6 (New York: Harcourt Brace Jovanovich, 1980), p. 354. To Vita Sackville-West, 29 August 1939.

8. Virginia Woolf, *The Years* (New York: Harcourt, Brace & Company, 1937), p. 410.

9. *Letters of Virginia Woolf*, p. 219. To Ethel Smyth, 18 March 1938.

10. Virginia Woolf, *Mrs. Dalloway* (New York: Harcourt, Brace, & World, Inc., 1925), p. 15.

11. Ibid., p. 13.

12. Arthur Marwick, *The Deluge: British Society and the First World War* (New York: W. W. Norton & Co., 1965), pp. 289–303.

13. Leonard Woolf, *Downhill All the Way: An Autobiography of the Years 1919–1939* (New York: Harcourt Brace Jovanovich, 1967), p. 9.

14. The anger felt by the English lower classes toward the ruling class was so deep that during the London Blitz in the autumn of 1940, M.P.s quipped that revolution would have broken out had the Germans not bombed wealthy areas of London as well as poor. Harold Nicolson, *The War Years 1939–1945*, vol. 2, ed. Nigel Nicolson (New York: Atheneum, 1967) Diary Entry 17, September 1940, pp. 114–115.

15. *Letters of Virginia Woolf*, p. 366. To Edward Sackville-West, 25 October 1939.

16. Ibid., p. 383. To Ethel Smyth, 20 February 1940.

17. The anonymous comment appeared in *Time and Tide*, 25 June 1938.

18. Q. D. Leavis writing in the September issue of *Scrutiny* magazine.

19. *Letters of Virginia Woolf*, p. 267. To Ethel Smyth, 29 August 1938.

20. Ibid., p. 235. To Ethel Smyth, 7 June 1938.

21. Ibid., p. 259. To Ling Su-Hua, 27 July 1938.

22. Ibid., p. 277.

23. Ibid.

24. Ibid., pp. 275–276.

25. Harold Nicholson, *The War Years*, p. 52. Diary Entry 31, December 1939.

26. *Letters of Virginia Woolf*, p. 327. To Ling Su-Hua, 17 April 1939.

27. Ibid., p. 262. To Ethel Smyth, 7 or 8 August 1938.

28. Virginia Woolf, *Roger Fry: A Biography* (London: Hogarth Press, 1940), p. 52.

29. Ibid., p. 231.

30. Leonard Woolf, *The Journey Not the Arrival Matters*, p. 43.

31. Ibid.

32. Virginia Woolf, *Roger Fry: A Biography*, p. 59.

33. *Letters of Virginia Woolf*, p. 354. To Vita Sackville-West, 29 August 1939.

34. Marwick, *The Deluge*, p. 306.

35. *Letters of Virginia Woolf*, p. 327. To Ling Su-Hua, 17 April 1939.

36. Ibid., p. 357. To Vita Sackville-West, 8 September 1939.

37. Ibid., pp. 365–366. To Edward Sackville-West, 25 October 1939.

38. Virginia Woolf, *Between the Acts* (New York: Harcourt Brace & World, Inc., 1941), p. 115.

39. Ibid., p. 358. To Ethel Smyth, 12 or 13 September 1939.

40. Ibid., p. 432. To William Plomer, 15 September 1940.

41. Ibid., p. 361. To Philippa Woolf, 29 September 1939.

42. Ibid., p. 401. To Ethel Smyth, 9 June 1940.

43. Ibid., p. 352. To Ethel Smyth, 20 August 1939.

44. Ibid., p. 431. To Ethel Smyth, 12 September 1940.

45. Ibid., p. 359. To Ethel Smyth, 26 September 1939.

46. Ibid., pp. 444–445. To Ethel Smyth, 14 November 1940.

47. Virginia Woolf, *Mrs. Dalloway*, p. 182. In his autobiography, *The Journey Not the Arrival Matters*, Leonard Woolf wrote that the massacres of Armenians by Turks and Kurds in 1894 when he was fourteen awakened his political sensibilities. The Armenian cause became the raison d'être of his schoolteacher, a Mrs. Cole, whose horror stories gave the young Leonard for the first time "a dim understanding of the difference between civilization and barbarism." Undoubtedly, Virginia Woolf borrowed from her husband's childhood memories for the scene in *Mrs. Dalloway*.

48. *Letters of Virginia Woolf*, p. 436. To Angelica Bell, 1 October 1940.

49. Virginia Woolf, *Roger Fry*, p. 233.

50. Ibid., p. 215.

51. Ibid., p. 49.

52. Virginia Woolf, *Between the Acts*, p. 178.

53. Ibid., p. 180.

54. For an excellent source on the fall of the Low Countries, Chamberlain's resignation, and Churchill's appointment as prime minister, see William Manchester, *The Last Lion: Winston Spencer Churchill/Alone 1932–1940* (Boston: Little, Brown & Company, 1988), Part Six, Cataclysm.

55. Ibid., pp. 683–684.

56. *Letters of Virginia Woolf*, p. 422. To Ben Nicholson, 24 August 1940.

57. Ibid., p. 425. To Mrs. G. E. Easdale, 3 September 1940.

58. Nicholson, *The War Years 1939–1945*, pp. 115–116. Diary Entry 19 September 1940.

59. *Letters of Virginia Woolf*, p. 429. To Ethel Smyth, 11 September 1940.

60. Ibid., p. 433. To Ethel Smyth, 20 September 1940.

61. Leonard Woolf, *The Journey Not the Arrival Matters*, p. 59.

62. *Letters of Virginia Woolf*, p. 433. To Ethel Smyth, 20 September 1940.

63. Nicolson, p. 114. Diary Entry 17 September 1940. Churchill told a secret session of the House of Commons on September 17 that England could expect half a million Germans to land in England.

64. *Letters of Virginia Woolf*, p. 439. To Ethel Smyth, 12 October 1940.

65. Leonard Woolf, *The Journey Not the Arrival Matters*, p. 71.

66. *Letters of Virginia Woolf*, p. 439. To Ethel Smyth, 12 October 1940.

67. Ibid., p. 442. To Angelica Bell, 26 October 1940.

68. Ibid., p. 444. To Ethel Smyth, 14 November 1940.

69. Ibid., p. 431. To Ethel Smyth, 12 September 1940.

70. Ibid., p. 449. To Edward Sackville-West, 1 December 1940.

71. Leonard Woolf, *Beginning Again: An Autobiography of the Years 1911–1918* (New York: A Harvest Book: Harcourt, Brace Jovanovich, 1964), pp. 91–93. Virginia Woolf took pains to refute the charge that she was an ivory tower aristocrat, especially since the Stephen family always worried about finances. "Would that I could make the visit [to the U.S.] pay in return and bring back 30,000 pounds à la Dickens," Leslie once lamented to his friend, Oliver Wendell Holmes. Frederic William Maitland, *The Life and Letters of Leslie Stephen* (New York: G. P. Putnam's Sons, 1906), p. 202.

72. *Letters of Virginia Woolf*, p. 454. To Ethel Smyth, 24 December 1940.

73. Ibid., p. 478. To Ethel Smyth, 10 March 1941.

74. Ibid., p. 458. To Dr. Octavia Wilberforce, 9 January 1941.

75. Studies conducted by Steven Stack cite factors which make the mentally ill prone to suicide: major disruptions in friendships, isolation, the necessity of forming new relationships, changes in diet, residence, and routine, and family turmoil. ("The Effect of Immigration on Suicide: A Cross National Analysis," *Basic and Applied Social Psychology* 2, 3 (1981): 205–218; and "Comparative Analysis of Immigration and Suicide," *Psychological Reports* 49 (1981): 509–510).

Additional factors include fear of the unknown and prior suicide attempts. Interestingly, suicide rates among both the military and civilian population decreased strikingly during both world wars, supporting a theory posed by E. Durkheim in *Suicide: A Study in Sociology* (1897), that "a popular war reflects stronger social integration which results in lower suicide rates" among the non-mentally ill civilian and military population. See "Suicide in the U.S. Army: Epidemiological and Periodic Aspects," by Joseph M. Rothberg, Ph.D, and Col. Franklin D. Jones, MC, USA, in *Suicide and Life-Threatening Behavior*, vol. 17 (2) summer 1987.

76. Leonard Woolf, *Downhill All the Way*, p. 57.

77. *Letters of Virginia Woolf*, p. 448. To Vita Sackville-West, 29 November 1940.

78. Leonard Woolf, *The Journey Not the Arrival Matters*, p. 88.

79. Ibid.

80. *Letters of Virginia Woolf*, p. 460. To Ethel Smyth, 12 January 1941.

81. Leonard Woolf, *Beginning Again*, p. 80.

82. Ibid.

83. Ibid., p. 79.

84. Interview with Joseph M. Rothberg, Ph.D., civilian research mathematician in the Walter Reed Army Institute of Research, Department of the Army, and Adjunct Associate Professor of Psychiatry, F. Edward Hebert School of Medicine.

85. Leonard Woolf, *The Journey Not the Arrival Matters*, p. 78.

86. *Letters of Virginia Woolf*, p. 460. To Ethel Smyth, 12 January 1941.

87. Ibid., p. 445. To Vita Sackville-West, 15 November 1940.

88. Ibid. p. 467. To Ethel Smyth, 1 February 1941.

89. Ibid., p. 466.

90. Leonard Woolf, *The Journey Not the Arrival Matters*, p. 44.

91. Ibid., p. 91.

92. Virginia Woolf, *Between the Acts*, p. 209.

93. Ibid., p. 219.

94. *Letters of Virginia Woolf*, p. 464. To Shena, Lady Simon, 25 January 1941.

95. Ibid., p. 472. To Mary Hutchinson, 10 February 1941.

96. Ibid., p. 479. To Elizabeth Robins, 13 March 1941.

97. Ibid., pp. 467–468. To Desmond MacCarthy, 22 February 1941.

98. Ibid., p. 411, note 1.

99. Ibid., p. 414. To Benedict Nicolson, 13 August 1940. Woolf quotes Nicholson's letter to her.

100. Ibid. pp. 414–415.

101. Ibid., p. 420. To Ben Nicolson, 24 August 1940.

102. Ibid., p. 475. To Ethel Smyth, 1 March 1941.

103. Ibid., p. 478. To Ethel Smyth, 10 March 1941.

104. Ibid., p. 483. To Lady Cecil, March 21, 1941.

105. Ibid., p. 368. To Dorothy Bussy, 5 November 1939.

106. Ibid., p. 475. To Ethel Smyth, 1 March 1941.

107. Ibid., p. 483. To Lady Tweedsmuir, 21? March 1941.

108. Ibid., p. 466. To Ethel Smyth, 1 February 1941.

109. Ibid., p. 483. To Lady Cecil, 21 March 1941.

110. Ibid., p. 485, note 2, concerning a letter from Vanessa Bell to Virginia Woolf, 20 March 1941.

111. Ibid. To Vanessa Bell, 23? March 1941.

112. Harold Nicholson, *The War Years 1939–1945*, p. 159.

Chapter Four

COLETTE

The Survivor

1. Colette, *My Apprenticeships (Mes Apprentissages)*, trans. Helen Beauclerk (New York: Farrar Straus Giroux, 1978), p. 19.

2. Colette, *Evening Star (L'Étoile Vesper)* (New York: Bobbs Merrill Company, Inc.), 1973), p. 76.

3. Colette, *Claudine in Paris*, in *The Complete Claudine*, trans. Antonia White (New York: Avenel Books, 1976), pp. 332–333.

4. In a thinly veiled description of what had happened to her, Colette wrote in her second novel, *Claudine in Paris*, "The physical horror of seeing the furniture moved and my little possessions packed up made me shivery and cross, like a cat in the rain. Having to watch the departure of my little ink-stained mahogany desk and my narrow walnut four poster bed and the Norman sideboard that serves me as a linen cupboard nearly threw me into hysterics. . . . I've never detested [my father] so much as I did that day" (p. 214).

5. Colette, *Cheri*, trans., Roger Senhouse (Garden City, New York: The International Collectors Library, 1974), p. 27.

6. Colette, *Duo* and *Le Toutonier (The Divan)*, trans. Margaret Crosland (London: Peter Owen, 1976), p. 185.

7. Ibid., p. 146.

8. Ibid., p. 176.

9. Robert Phelps, ed. and trans., *Letters from Colette* (New York: Farrar Straus Giroux, 1980), p. 144. To Helen Picard, 25 January 1933.

10. Ibid.

11. *Letters from Colette*, p. 89. To Marguerite Moreno, end of May 1925. Colette possessed an uncanny talent for describing in her fiction situations before they happened to her in her own life. *Cheri*, published before she met Maurice, told the story of a love affair between Lea, a much older woman, and young Cheri, whose lonely childhoods make Lea call the two of them "sort of orphans, you and I." Colette was married to a man ten years older when she described in Cheri: "complete trust on the part of her young lover, a self-surrender to confessions, candors, endless secrets—those hours in the depths of the night when, in almost filial gratitude, a young man unrestrainedly pours out his tears, his private likes and dislikes, on the kindly bosom of a mature and trusted friend. . . ." This could have precisely described the intense, nighttime conversations she and Maurice shared when they later met. *Cheri*, p. 29.

12. Elizabeth Sprigge and Jean-Jacques Kihm, *Jean Cocteau, The Man in the Mirror* (New York: Coward-McCann Inc., 1968), p. 167.

13. Maurice Godaket, *The Delights of Growing Old: An Uncommon Autobiography*, trans. Patrick O'Brien (New York: Farrar, Straus and Giroux, 1966), pp. 107–108.

14. Ibid., pp. 80; and 112.

15. Ibid., p. 84.

16. Sprigge and Kihm, *Jean Cocteau*, p. 139.

17. *Letters from Colette*, p. 161. To Renee Hamon, 25 February 1938.

18. Ibid., p. 172. To Renee Hamon, 27 August 1939.

19. Ibid., p. 171. To Helen Picard, 21 August 1939.

20. Maurice served in WWI as a volunteer in the Belgian/Dutch contingent of the French Foreign Legion. After his experiences in that war, which included being shot in the leg, he concluded, "All wars are monstrous imbecilities." Godaket, *The Delights of Growing Old*, p. 64.

21. Larry Collins and Dominique Lapierre, *Is Paris Burning? How Paris Miraculously Escaped Adolf Hitler's Sentence of Death in August 1944* (New York: A Pocket Cardinal Edition, 1965), pp. 67–68.

22. Colette, *Looking Backwards* (*Journal à rebours* and *De Ma fenêtre*), trans. David Le Vey (Bloomington: Indiana University Press, 1975), p. 7.

23. Ibid., pp. 69–70.

24. *Letters from Colette*, p. 177. To Leopold Marchand, end of June 1940.

25. Colette, *Looking Backwards*, p. 85.

26. *Letters from Colette*, p. 177. To Madame Leopold (Misz) Marchand, 12 July 1940.

27. Maurice Godaket, *Close to Colette: An Intimate Portrait of a Woman of Genius* (New York: Farrar, Straus and Cudahy, 1957), p. 162.

28. Colette, *Looking Backwards*, p. 85.

29. Godaket, *Close to Colette*, p. 162. Colette explained to a friend ten minutes after inventing the title that *La Lune de pluie* referred to the particular kind of moon that has a rainbow-like halo and portends bad weather. (*Letters from Colette*, p. 180).

30. Godaket, *Close to Colette*, pp. 165–168.

31. Colette, *Looking Backwards*, p. 144.

32. Paul Webster, *Petain's Crime: The Full Story of French Collaboration in the Holocaust* (Chicago: Ivan R. Dee, 1991), p. 21.

33. Herbert Lottman, *Colette: A Life* (Boston: Little, Brown and Company, 1991), p. 43.

34. Ibid., p. 95.

35. Colette's two divorces and the risqué subject matter of her novels did not make her a favorite with the church. When she died, she was refused Christian burial rites. Colette is buried in Père Lachaise cemetery and was the first woman in France to be granted a state funeral. Her childhood memories of the church as institutionalized boredom were well-captured in her early work, *Claudine in Paris* (1901).

36. *Letters from Colette*, p. 182. To Renée Hamon, 1 January 1941.

37. Lottman, *Colette: A Life*, p. 255.

38. Years after Colette followed her second husband to the front at Verdun, she wrote in *Le Toutonier* (*The Divan*), "We never resist a man. Death is the only place where we don't follow him" (p. 207).

39. Colette, *Evening Star*, p. 45.

40. *Letters from Colette*, p. 172. To Helen Picard, early September 1939, p. 172.

41. *Letters from Colette*, p. 158. To Helen Picard, 6 December 1937.

42. Ibid., p. 159. To Renée Hamon, 24 December 1937.

43. Colette, *Evening Star*, p. 26.

44. Ibid., p. 47.

45. Ibid., p. 48.

46. *Letters from Colette*, p. 161. To Renée Hamon, 25 February 1938.

47. Colette, *Evening Star*, p. 20.

48. Michael R. Marrus and Robert O. Paxton, *Vichy France and the Jews* (New York: Basic Books, 1981), p. 226, Note 1.

49. Paul Webster, *Petain's Crime*, pp. 94–95. René Blum, the younger brother of left-wing Jewish Prime Minister Leon Blum (June 1936–April 1938), was among the men arrested with Maurice. He died in Germany in 1943.

50. *Letters from Colette*, p. 187. To Marguerite Moreno, 13 February 1942. Colette's description of Cheri's torment during his three-month absence from his lover could have described Colette's pain while waiting for Godaket: "If a door opened, it was Nounoune; the telephone rang, Nounoune; a letter in the garden postbox, perhaps Nounoune. . . . In the very wine I drank, I looked for you. . . . And then at nights . . . Oh, heavens above!" Colette, *Cheri*, p. 112.

51. Colette, *Julie De Carneilhan*, trans. Patrick Leigh Fermor (New York: Farrar, Straus and Young, 1952), p. 163. When the virulently anti-Semitic Paris newspaper *Gringoire* announced the forthcoming serialization of *Julie De Carneilhan*, the announcement ran alongside a cartoon showing the Statue of Liberty holding a Jewish menorah in place of her torch. Four years earlier, on the first day of serialization of Colette's short story collection, *Bella-Vista*, the paper ran an "exposé" on then-Premier Leon Blum, a Jew and Socialist, replete with a cartoon showing trash cans filled with German-Jewish refugees.

52. *Letters from Colette*, p. 184. To Renée Hamon, 23 February 1941.

53. Colette, *The Divan*, p. 176.

54. *Letters fron Colette*, p. 184. To Renée Hamon, 23 February 1941.

55. Colette, *Evening Star*, p. 32.

56. Webster, *Petain's Crime*, p. 87.

57. Yvonne Mitchell, *Colette: A Taste for Life* (New York: Harcourt Brace Jovanovich, 1975), p. 205.

58. Colette, *Evening Star*, p. 21.

59. Colette, *Duo*, p. 98.

60. Colette, *Evening Star*, p. 116.

61. Jean Cocteau, *The Difficulty of Being*, trans., Elizabeth Sprigge (New York: Coward-McCann, 1967), p. 93.

62. Colette, *Evening Star*, p. 70.

63. Ibid., p. 94. In 1939, three years before her arthritis confined her to her divan, Colette wrote *Le Toutonier* (*The Divan*). It was the story of three distraught sisters permanently bound by their terrible experiences with men, who retreat to their huge old English divan as though it were a fortress.

64. Colette, *Gigi*, in *The Colette Omnibus* (New York: International Collectors Library, 1974), p. 239.

65. Colette, *Evening Star*, p. 24.

66. Claude Levy and Paul Tillard, *Betrayal at the Vel d'Hiv*, trans. Inea Bushnaq (New York: Hill and Wang, 1969), p. 95.

67. *Letters from Colette*, p. 191. To Rénee Hamon, 6 November 1942.

68. Colette, *Evening Star*, p. 20.

69. Levy and Tillard, *Betrayal at the Vel d'Hiv*, p. 129.

70. Godaket, *Close to Colette*, p. 184.

71. Mistinguett, the legendary French stage star of the Folies Bergère, became Maurice Chevalier's lover when he became her revue partner in 1909. Just a few years earlier as a novice in the same revue as Colette, Chevalier was too shy to talk to her.

72. Godaket, *Close to Colette*, p. 187.

73. *Letters from Colette*, p. 204. To Marguerite Moreno, 8 September 1944.

74. Ibid., p. 181. To Renée Hamon, 12 December 1940.

75. Despite Nazi atrocities against French women, the occupiers exerted a strong influence on French fashion. The wartime rage in Parisian women's hair styles became the "nordic coiffure" after the hair style of the star of Jean Cocteau's highly successful 1944 film, *L'Éternal Retour*. The hair of both male and female stars of the film was so blond that anti-Fascists condemned the movie.

76. *Letters from Colette*, p. 193. To Renée Hamon, late July 1943.

77. Ibid., p. 198. To Maurice S., 30 October 1943.

78. Colette, *Evening Star*, p. 70.

79. Ibid., p. 62.

80. Ibid., p. 53.

81. In her diary, the writer Marguerite Duras, whose husband was arrested by the Nazis, vividly captured this time when the French waited for liberation: "We're in the vanguard of a nameless battle, a battle without arms or bloodshed or glory; we're in the vanguard of waiting." Marguerite Duras, *The War, A Memoir*, trans. Barbara Bray (New York: Pantheon Books, 1986), p. 35.

82. *Letters from Colette*, p. 206. To Marguerite Moreno, 25 April 1945.

83. Lottman, *Colette: A Life*, p. 298.

84. During the Occupation, Chevalier, who was at the time the most famous music hall performer in France, mimed a song which expressed his loathing of the Germans. As he left the stage, he crossed his arms, patted his sleeves and pronounced, "*Bravo les copains! Les copains au-dela de la manche.*" It was a play on the word "*manche*," which means both "sleeve" and, when capitalized, "the English Channel." Chevalier was congratulating French boys across the Channel. Despite this brazen show, his international fame made him untouchable by the Nazis.

Chapter Five

ERNEST HEMINGWAY

War As an Aphrodisiac

1. Ray Lewis White, ed., *Sherwood Anderson/Gertrude Stein: Correspondence and Personal Essays* (Chapel Hill: The University of North Carolina Press, 1972), p. 73.

2. Carlos Baker, ed., *Ernest Hemingway: Selected Letters, 1917–1961* (New York: Charles Scribner's Sons, 1981), p. 427. To John Dos Passos, 17 December 1935.

3. Ibid., p. 430. To Ivan Kashkin, 12 January 1936.

4. Ibid., p. 431.

5. Jeffrey Meyers, *Hemingway: A Biography* (New York: Harper & Row, 1985), p. 54.

6. Ernest Hemingway, *To Have and Have Not* (New York: Grosset & Dunlap, 1937, reprinted from Charles Scribner's Sons, 1937), p. 238. Hemingway was having fun with critics who had condemned him for ignoring social issues. Based upon Hemingway's friend John Dos Passos, the novel's protagonist, Richard Gordon, is at work on a novel about a strike in a textile plant. Drunk at a bar, he meets an admirer who says that he's a "sucker for anything on the social conflict" and asks Gordon if the novel has a character who is a "beautiful Jewish agitator," which Sylvia Sydney could play in the movie version (pp. 196–197).

7. *Hemingway: Letters*, p. 176. To F. Scott Fitzgerald, 15 December 1925.

8. Responding to Europe's growing crises, the era's most socially conscious documentary filmmakers organized an independent, nonprofit organization known as Frontier Films, in June 1937. Joris Ivens and Archibald MacLeish were both members of the advisory board. Other members included Ralph Steiner, Leo Hurwitz, Malcolm Cowley, John Dos Passos, Elia Kazan, Lillian Hellman, Lewis Milestone, and Clifford Odets. Led by Paul Strand, Frontier Films produced some of the era's most powerful documentaries, including *Spain in Flames*, on which Hemingway consulted, *Heart of Spain*, and *China Strikes Back*.

9. *Hemingway: Letters*, p. 100. To Dr. Clarence Edward Hemingway (C.E.), 7 November 1923.

10. Ibid., p. 398. To Mrs. Paul Pfeiffer, 16 October 1933.

11. Carlos Baker, *Ernest Hemingway: A Life Story* (New York: Charles Scribner's Sons, 1969), p. 275. The article, "Notes on the Next War: A Serious Letter," appeared in 1935 in *Esquire*, September, vol. 4, p. 156.

12. Ibid., p. 314.

13. *Hemingway: Letters*, p. 459. To Mrs. Paul Pfeiffer, 2 August 1937.

14. Norberto Fuentes, *Hemingway in Cuba* (Secaucus, New Jersey: Lyle Stuart, 1984), p. 144. Hemingway and Joris Ivens screened their as yet unfinished film, *Spanish Earth*, for the Writers' Congress audience on June 4, 1937. Besides Hemingway, speakers that evening included Earl Browder, Secretary of the American Communist Party. On July 8, he and Ivens screened the film at the White House for President and Mrs. Roosevelt. Hemingway's main impression of the dinner was of the terrible food, and he thought Roosevelt "very Harvard charming and sexless and womanly." According to Hemingway, the Roosevelts felt the film was insufficiently propagandistic. *Hemingway: Letters*, p. 460. To Mrs. Paul Pfeiffer, 2 August 1937.

15. Lucasz, a Hungarian, was killed in mid-June 1937 in the Huesca offensive, when his Ford drove over a fascist-planted bomb near Aragon. The day after he died, Lucasz's chief medical officer, Dr. Werner Heilbrun, another Hemingway hero, was killed by rebels en route to the Pyrenees.

16. Denis Brian, *The True Gen* (New York: Grove Press, 1988), p. 119.

17. Fuentes, *Hemingway in Cuba*, p. 156.

18. Brian, *The True Gen*, p. 109. The charge was made by Alvah Bessie, a novelist, former newspaper editor and volunteer soldier with the Lincoln Brigade.

After World War I, Hemingway told people he had been attached to an elite Italian troop corps at the time he was wounded during a mortar attack, when in truth, as a Red Cross ambulance driver he handed out chocolate bars and cigarettes to soldiers at the front.

19. *Hemingway: Letters*, p. 471. To Maxwell Perkins, 12 July 1938.

20. At a rate of $500 per dispatch and $1,000 per 1,200-word mailed-in story, Hemingway earned a total of $15,000 from his NANA assignments.

21. Basil Wright, "Land Without Bread and Spanish Earth," World Film News (London), December 1937. Reprinted in Lewis Jacobs, ed., *The Documentary Tradition* (New York: Hopkinson and Blake Publishers, 1972), pp. 146–147.

22. Fuentes, *Hemingway in Cuba*, p. 143. The seventeen-month period during which Hemingway traveled back and forth to Spain was extremely productive. In addition to his dispatches, novel work, and magazine articles, Hemingway also wrote his play about the Spanish Civil War, *The Fifth Column*, as well as numerous short stories which were included in one volume, *The Fifth Column and the First Forty-nine Stories*, published in October 1938.

23. *Hemingway: Letters*, p. 456. Hemingway to Harry Sylvester, 5 February 1937.

24. The early stages of Hemingway's affair with Martha Gellhorn followed the same pattern as his affair with Pauline. Just as he had brought Pauline home to Hadley eleven years earlier, he brought Martha home to Pauline. But since Pauline had been Hadley's best friend in Paris at the time she and Hemingway became involved, she did not make the mistake of fostering an intimacy between herself and Martha. Hemingway would follow the same pattern in the late 1940s when he fell in love with a nineteen-year old Italian girl and brought her home to his fourth wife, Mary Hemingway.

25. Hemingway's by-then nominal marriage to Pauline did not end until Christmastime 1939 after he and Martha had openly vacationed together at Sun Valley, Idaho, and he ignored Pauline's ultimatum to choose between women. Despite the fact that he and Gellhorn had formally set up house in Cuba, and met openly in the United States when Hemingway came to visit Pauline and their two children, Hemingway refused to acknowledge blame for the breakup of the marriage. He and Pauline were finally divorced after a bitter financial dispute, on November 5, 1940. She was awarded custody of the couple's two children, Patrick and Gregory, on the grounds of desertion.

26. *Hemingway: Letters*, p. 484. To Thomas Shelvin, 4 April 1939.

27. Ibid. p. 483. To Maxwell Perkins, 25 March 1939.

28. Baker, *Ernest Hemingway: A Life*, p. 356.

29. Hemingway's unwavering loyalty to the Communists led to a deep rupture in his friendship with John Dos Passos. While Dos Passos found it morally reprehensible that the Republicans executed a professor, José Robles Pazos, whom they alleged to be a Franco informant, Hemingway looked at all such incidents as part of defeating an evil enemy. The friendship suffered irreparable damage after Hemingway wrote a piece for a new anti-fascist magazine called *Ken* in the summer of 1938, airing his opinion of Dos Passos as a political naïf.

30. *Hemingway: Letters*, p. 498. To Maxwell Perkins, 8 December 1939.

31. Hemingway, *For Whom the Bell Tolls* (New York: Charles Scribner's Sons, 1940), p. 129. Hemingway ended *For Whom the Bell Tolls* with its dying hero, Robert Jordan, readying himself to kill fascist Lieutenant Berrendo. Hemingway implied that Jordan's death would not be in vain, because with even one less fascist, the world will be a purer place.

32. William White, ed., *By-line: Ernest Hemingway/Selected Articles and Dispatches of Four Decades* (New York: A Bantam Book Paperback edition, 1970), p. 256. "A Program for U.S. Realism," from *Ken* magazine, August 11, 1938.

33. Ibid., p. 8. "Hemingway Sees Defeat of Franco," from *New York Times*, 19 May 1937.

34. *Hemingway: Letters*, p. 505. To Maxwell Perkins, c. 1 May 1940.

35. Ibid. Britain's monumental failure against Hitler's Scandinavian campaign capped years of inaction and appeasement. The Chamberlain government equivocated on taking action to protect Norway until it was too late, fully aware that Narvik, in northern Norway,

and Baku, on the Caspian Sea, were crucial for keeping Swedish iron ore and Caspian oil out of German hands. Once Hitler attacked, Britain, with French help, responded with shamefully small forces and, in the case of Narvik, Norway's most important port, refused to land troops following victory at sea. Hemingway blamed the disaster on Churchill, whose title at the time was Chairman of the Committee for Coordinating the Fighting Services, and Churchill himself was to admit his culpability in his *Memoirs*, writing, "it was a marvel that I survived." Ironically, the fall of Norway finally brought Chamberlain down as Prime Minister and swept Churchill in to replace him. Harold Nicholson, *The War Years, 1939–1945*, vol. 2, Nigel Nicholson, ed. (New York: Atheneum, 1967), p. 68.

36. *Hemingway: Letters*, p. 476. To Mrs. Paul Pfeiffer, 6 February 1939.

37. Ibid.

38. Fuentes, *Hemingway in Cuba*, p. 319.

39. *Hemingway: Letters*, p. 479. To Maxwell Perkins, 7 February 1939.

40. Ibid., p. 474. To Maxwell Perkins, 28 October 1938.

41. Ibid., p. 484. To Thomas Shelvin, 4 April 1939.

42. Matthew Bruccoli, ed., *Conversations with Ernest Hemingway* (Jackson: University Press of Mississippi, 1986), p. 24. "Back to His First Field," from *Kansas City Times*, 26 November 1940.

43. Martha Gellhorn's novel, *A Stricken Field*, was set against the backdrop of Czechoslovakia's mobilization for war against the Nazis in the summer of 1938. During the period of Martha's coverage of the crisis for *Collier*'s, she and Hemingway, who was then covering the war in Spain, rendezvoused in Paris. Her character, *Old John* was drawn from Hemingway.

44. Baker, *Ernest Hemingway: A Life*, p. 353.

45. Bruccoli, *Conversations*, p. 23.

46. *Hemingway: Letters*, pp. 407–408. To F. Scott Fitzgerald, 28 May 1934.

47. Anderson's innovative novels and short stories, such as *Winesburg, Ohio, The Triumph of the Egg*, and *Horses and Men*, influenced a generation of American writers. In his customary pattern of biting a hand that had fed him, Hemingway returned Anderson's early help by writing a brutal satire of him in late 1925, *The Torrents of Spring*. Hemingway wrote the satire in just six days while awaiting publication in America of *In Our Time*, his first short story collection, by Boni & Liveright. Hemingway claimed his motive was merely to enable readers to differentiate between himself and Anderson, another Boni & Liveright author, whose latest novel, *Dark Laughter*, had just been published, to Hemingway's intense displeasure. A more likely reason had to do with Hemingway's building resentment of Anderson, to whom he was often compared, which was aggravated by his mother's attention to Anderson's career rather than her son's, and her unfavorable comparision of his work to that of "the Master." *Hemingway: Letters*, p. 178. To Archibald MacLeish, 20 December 1925.

48. Ibid., p. 523. To Maxwell Perkins, 29 April 1941.

49. Ibid., p. 506. To Maxwell Perkins, 13 July 1940.

50. The journalist Herbert Mitgang, who obtained the heavily censored Hemingway dossier under the Freedom of Information Act in the late 1980s, concluded that Hemingway was watched by "FBI informants and probably customs officials whenever he crossed an American border or traveled to Africa or Europe." Herbert Mitgang, *Dangerous Dossiers: Exposing the Secret War Against America's Greatest Authors* (New York: Donald I. Fine, Inc.), p. 68.

51. *Hemingway: Letters*, p. 419. To Ivan Kashkin, 19 August 1935.

52. Ibid.

53. Ernest Hemingway, *For Whom the Bell Tolls*, p. 163.

54. Hemingway, *To Have and Have Not*, p. 97.

55. Daniel Aaron, *Writers on the Left: Episodes in American Literary Communism* (New York: Columbia University Press, 1992), p. 50.

56. Ibid., p. 104.

57. Ibid., p. 7.

58. *Hemingway: Letters*, p. 519. To Charles Scribner, c. 21 October 1940.

59. Despite being one of America's better paid fiction writers, Hemingway relied on magazine work between novels to fund his foreign adventures and expensive domestic lifestyle, although during Prohibition he helped pay for trips to Europe and Africa by selling bootleg Cuban liquor in the United States. As in the case of *For Whom the Bell Tolls*, Hemingway was always heavily in debt by the time he finished a novel.

60. William L. Shirer, *The Rise and Fall of the Third Reich* (New York: Simon and Schuster, 1960), p. 871.

61. Auden and Isherwood's 1939 book, *Journey to a War*, offers a fascinating glimpse of Chiang Kai-shek's China on the eve of World War II. Hankow, particularly, where the Chinese government had relocated after the fall of Shanghai, was populated by a bizarre mix of foreigners, many of whom were military advisors and instructors. These included anti-German, anti-Japanese Soviets who were engaged in an ironic effort to prop the weakened Chiang government and to thwart the Chinese Communists from invading Russian territory; and German anti-Communists who had come to China before Hitler and were still training the Chinese military. American, British, and French bon vivants were still enjoying a lazy, expatriate lifestyle, while Catholic missionaries and spies were there in ample number, too. See W. H. Auden and Christopher Isherwood, *Journey to a War* (New York: Paragon House, 1990).

62. Ibid., pp. 253 and 244. Mao Tse-tung always feared a compromise peace between Chiang Kai-shek and the Japanese, and he suspected that his Red Army was persistently denied supplies to keep it from becoming too powerful after a Chinese victory.

63. Shirer, *The Rise and Fall of the Third Reich*, p. 872.

64. William Manchester, *Goodbye, Darkness: A Memoir of the Pacific War* (Boston: Little, Brown and Company, 1980), p. 84.

65. William White, ed., *By-line*, p. 277. Ralph Ingersoll, "Story of Ernest Hemingway's Far East Trip," from *PM*, June 9, 1941.

66. W. H. Auden and Christopher Isherwood, *Journey to a War*, pp. 144–145.

67. William White, ed., *By-line*, pp. 279–280. Ernest Hemingway, "Russo-Japanese Pact," from *PM*, June 10, 1941.

68. Ibid., p. 280.

69. Ibid., p. 295.

70. Matthew Bruccoli, ed., *Conversations with Ernest Hemingway*, p. 8. "Hemingway Sees Defeat of Franco," from *New York Times*, 19 May 1937. Hemingway was as fooled by Japan's conviction to follow its own course against the United States as was Hitler, who persistently attempted, unsuccessfully, to persuade Japan to join Germany in attacking Russia. As both Hitler and Hemingway were shortly to learn, Japan had its own agenda.

71. *Hemingway: Letters*, p. 533. To Charles Scribner, 12 December 1941.

72. There is strong evidence that more than a week before the attack, Washington had obtained from Japanese intelligence the exact date and locus of attack, yet an array of Hawaii's highest ranking military leaders rendered Pearl Harbor absolutely vulnerable.

73. *Hemingway: Letters*, p. 531. To Maxwell Perkins, 11 December 1941.

74. Ibid., p. 532. To Charles Scribner, 12 December 1941.

75. White, *By-line*, p. 256. "A Program for U.S. Realism," from *Ken*, August 11, 1938.

76. Fuentes, *Hemingway in Cuba*, p. 61.

77. *Hemingway: Letters*, p. 533. To Charles Scribner, 12 December 1941.

78. Ibid., p. 536. To Hadley Mowrer, 23 July 1942.

79. *Hemingway: Letters*, p. 523. To Maxwell Perkins, 29 April 1941.

80. Ibid., p. 420. To Ivan Kashkin, 19 August 1935.

81. Fuentes, *Hemingway in Cuba*, p. 258.

82. Peter Golenbock, *Bums* (New York: G. P. Putnam's Sons, 1984), p. 49.

83. Fuentes, *Hemingway in Cuba*, p. 25.

84. *Hemingway: Letters*, p. 535. To Hadley Mowrer, 23 July 1942.

85. Ibid., p. 536.

86. Mitgang, *Dossiers*, p. 62. Led by retired U.S. Army Air Corps Captain A. Chennault, the 100 volunteer pilots of the "Flying Tigers" were so helpful fighting the Japanese over China that the American government wanted them to become part of the

Tenth U.S. Air Force. When their contracts with Chennault expired in July 1942, however, only five pilots stayed on.

87. Ernest Hemingway, ed., *Men at War* (New York: Berkley Mediallion paperback/Berkley Publishing Corporation, reprinted 1960), p. 21. Originally published in 1942 by Crown Publishers.

88. Hemingway, *For Whom the Bell Tolls*, p. 304.

89. *Hemingway: Letters*, p. 538. To Evan Shipman, 25 August 1942.

90. Hemingway, *Men at War*, p. 20.

91. Baker, *Ernest Hemingway: A Life*, p. 382.

92. *Hemingway: Letters*, p. 550. To Allen Tate, 31 August 1943.

93. Hemingway, *Islands in the Stream* (New York: Charles Scribner's Sons, 1970), p. 397.

94. Brian, *The True Gen*, p. 137.

95. Ibid., p. 140.

96. *Hemingway: Letters*, p. 538. To Evan Shipman, 25 August 1942.

97. Hemingway, *Islands in the Stream*, p. 215.

98. *Hemingway: Letters*, p. 543. To Patrick Hemingway, 7 October 1942.

99. Meyers, *Hemingway: A Biography*, p. 9.

100. Richard Whelan, *Robert Capa: A Biography* (New York: Alfred A. Knopf, 1985), p. 150.

101. Brian, *The True Gen*, pps. 139–140.

102. *Hemingway: Letters*, pp. 445–446. To Archibald MacLeish, c. 5 May 1943.

103. Ibid., p. 545.

104. The fight which broke out between them on Hemingway's boat had its source in MacLeish's refusal to accompany the relentlessly competitive Hemingway on his safari earlier that year. Hemingway, feeling rejected, held a deep grudge against MacLeish for a long time.

105. Ibid.

106. Ibid. pp. 545–546.

107. Ibid., p. 546.

108. Ernest Hemingway, "Fathers and Sons," in *The Snows of Kilimanjaro and Other Stories* (New York: Charles Scribner's Sons, paperback reprint 1964), p. 57.

109. *Hemingway: Letters*, p. 549. To MacLeish, 10 August 1943.

110. Ibid.

111. *Hemingway: Letters*, p. 551. To Patrick Hemingway, 30 October 1943.

112. Fuentes, *Hemingway in Cuba*, pp. 340–341. Hemingway to Allen R. May, 31 August 1943.

113. Ibid., p. 22.

114. *Hemingway: Letters*, p. 552. To Patrick Hemingway, 30 October 1943.

115. Ibid., p. 553. To Maxwell Perkins, 16 November 1943.

116. Ibid., p. 555. To Hadley Mowrer, 25 November 1943.

117. Ibid., p. 557. To Maxwell Perkins, 25 February 1944.

118. Bruccoli, ed., *Conversations with Ernest Hemingway*, p. 2. "Has 227 Wounds, but Is Looking for Job," from *New York Sun*, 22 January 1919.

119. White, ed., *By-line*, p. 312. Hemingway, "Voyage to Victory," from *Collier's*, July 22, 1944.

120. Richard Whelan, *Capa*, p. 220.

121. *Hemingway: Letters*, p. 571. To Patrick Hemingway, 15 September 1944.

122. Brian, *The True Gen*, p. 149.

123. *Hemingway: Letters*, p. 571. To Patrick Hemingway, 15 September 1944. Hemingway's criticism was mostly disingenuous and wholly self-serving. While he did influence Gellhorn's style to a degree, Gellhorn is widely regarded as a first-rate reporter. She published more than one hundred magazine articles, mainly covering war, six novels, and several short story and journalism collections. Hemingway was said to be jealous that Martha got closer to the Normandy invasion than he did. She was aboard the first hospital ship to reach the beaches.

124. Ibid., p. 574. To Maxwell Perkins, 15 October 1944.

125. As in his previous extramarital affairs, Hemingway did his best to flaunt his new love to his wife. His first date with Mary Welsh took place one night after Hemingway sent an enraged Martha fleeing from his hotel room after he stripped down naked and pretended he was going to attack her. She was consoled with the help of an old friend, NANA correspondent Ira Wolfert, but when they encountered Mary in the hotel corridor on their way to dinner, Hemingway dumped Martha on Wolfert and left with Welsh.

Leicester Hemingway, like his older brother, fatally shot himself on September 13, 1982, after struggling with depression and diabetes. Baker, *Hemingway: A Life*, p. 393.

126. Baker, *Hemingway: A Life*, p. 369.

127. Fuentes, *Hemingway in Cuba*, p. 373. To Mary Welsh, Christmas night 1944.

128. *Hemingway: Letters*, p. 559. To Mary Welsh, 31 July 1944.

129. Ibid., p. 562. To Mary Welsh, 5 or 6 August 1944.

130. Ibid., p. 561. To Mary Welsh, 1 and 6 August 1944.

131. William Randolph Hearst, Jr., with Jack Casserly, *The Hearsts, Father and Son* (Niwot, Colorado: Roberts Rinehart Publishers, 1991), p. 152.

132. Ibid., p. 156. When Hearst wrote his memoir, he expanded upon criticism he had previously leveled against Hemingway. Interviewed a few years earlier by Denis Brian for his 1988 book *The True Gen*, Hearst told Brian that Hemingway "thought he was the Second Coming and acted like it."

133. White, ed., *By-line*, p. 336. "How We Came to Paris," from *Collier's*, October 7, 1944.

134. Brian, *The True Gen*, p. 162.

135. *Hemingway: Letters*, p. 574. To Maxwell Perkins, 15 October 1944.

136. Brian, *The True Gen*, p. 325. Appendix A, Transcript of the Military's Interrogation of Hemingway in World War II.

137. *Hemingway: Letters*, p. 573. To Colonel Charles Lanham, 8 October 1944.

138. Brian, *The True Gen*, p. 329.

139. *Hemingway: Letters*, p. 608. To Konstantin Simonov, 20 June 1946.

140. Hemingway, *Islands in the Stream*, p. 448.

141. *Hemingway: Letters*, p. 565. To Mary Welsh, 27 August 1944.

142. Ibid., p. 571. To Patrick Hemingway, 15 September 1944.

143. Baker, *Hemingway: A Life*, pp. 423–424.

144. During the 22d Regiment's direct assault in the Schnee-Eifel on September 14 and 15, Hemingway was actually laid up with a bad cold at divisional headquarters. He wrote his *Collier's* piece, "War in the Siegfried Line," based on firsthand accounts of men like Captain Howard Blazzard of Arizona who fought the assault, although Hemingway's description of how the Americans penetrated "the dark forest wall of the Schnee Eifel range where the dragon lived," failed to mention the fact that he was not present. White, ed., *By-line*, p. 346. Hemingway, "War in the Siegfried Line," from *Collier's*, November 18, 1944.

145. I. C. B. Dear, gen. ed., *Oxford Companion to WWII* (New York: Oxford University Press, 1995), p. 546; Baker, *Hemingway: A Life*, p. 438.

146. Fuentes, *Hemingway in Cuba*, p. 357. Hemingway to Mary Welsh, 21 November 1944.

147. Ibid., p. 361. Hemingway to Mary Welsh, 23 November 1944.

148. Norberto Fuentes, *Ernest Hemingway Rediscovered*, Marianne Sinclair, trans. (New York: Charles Scribner's Sons, 1988), p. 50.

149. Fuentes, *Hemingway in Cuba*, p. 355. Hemingway to Mary Welsh, 20 November 1944.

150. The alteration of his life insurance policy came just days after Hemingway and Martha Gellhorn had their final scene. In the second week of November, Martha arrived in Paris and told Hemingway she wanted a divorce. Although he was already planning to marry Mary Welsh, about whom Martha knew little, Hemingway became enraged, telling Martha that she would be the cause of his death in battle and thus be responsible for leaving his children orphans. According to Robert Capa, who had been friends with both

Hemingway and Gellhorn from their days in Spain, Martha was so distraught that when Capa went to her hotel room at four in the morning, she was still crying. Capa told her about Hemingway's affair with Mary Welsh and had her call Welsh's room at the Ritz to prove it. When Hemingway answered the phone, Martha told him she knew about the affair and demanded a divorce. Whelan, *Robert Capa, A Biography*, p. 228.

151. Ibid., p. 576. To Patrick Hemingway, 19 November 1944.

152. Ibid., p. 562. To Mary Welsh, 1 and 6 August 1944.

153. Ibid., p. 354. To Mary Welsh, 20 November 1944.

154. Ernest Hemingway, *The Snows of Kilimanjaro and Other Stories*, p. 15.

155. Fuentes, *Hemingway in Cuba*, p. 360. Hemingway to Mary Welsh, 22 November 1944.

156. Ibid., p. 355. To Mary Welsh, 20 November 1944.

157. *Hemingway: Letters*, p. 503. To Charles Scribner, 24 February 1940.

158. Ibid., p. 259. To Dr. C. E. Hemingway, 14 September 1927.

159. Ibid., p. 562. To Mary Welsh, 1 August 1944.

160. The connection in Hemingway's work between killing, sexuality, and creation was never stronger than in his 1933 story "Fathers and Sons." Out on a hunting trip, Nick Adams has his first sexual intercourse with an Indian girl. As they lie together afterward, she asks Nick, "You think we made a baby?" Instantly, a gunshot is heard, and a black squirrel is killed.

161. Ibid. p. 575. To Max Perkins, 15 October 1944.

162. Ibid., p. 574.

163. Fuentes, *Hemingway in Cuba*, p. 369. Hemingway to Mary Welsh, 29 November 1944.

164. Marcel Baudot, Henri Bernard, Hendrik Brugmans, Michael R. B. Foot, and Hans-Adolf Jacobsen, eds., *The Historical Encyclopedia of WWII* (New York: Facts on File, Inc., 1980) pp. 71–72. First published in France as *Encyclopédie de la Guerre 1939–1945*.

165. Fuentes, *Hemingway in Cuba*, pp. 387–388. Hemingway to his sister Carol, undated, about the time of his divorce from Martha in 1945.

166. Ibid., p. 375.

167. *Hemingway: Letters*, p. 578. To Mary Welsh, c. 6 March 1945.

168. Ibid., p. 568. To Mary Welsh, 11 September 1944.

169. Baker, *Ernest Hemingway: A Life*, pp. 443–444.

170. Hemingway, *For Whom the Bell Tolls*, p. 447.

171. *Hemingway: Letters*, p. 579. To Colonel Charles Lanham, 2 April 1945.

172. Ibid., p. 580.

173. Ibid., p. 582. To Mary Welsh, 9 April 1945.

174. Ibid., p. 583.

175. Ibid., p. 586. To Colonel Charles Lanham, 14 April 1945.

176. Ibid., p. 587.

177. Ibid., p. 589. To Colonel Charles Lanham, 20 April 1945.

178. Fuentes, *Hemingway in Cuba*, p. 227.

179. Hemingway drew on a real-life disaster to evoke David's sense of loss. In December 1922, Hemingway's first wife, Hadley, was en route to Lausanne, Switzerland, to meet Ernest, who was on assignment for the *Toronto Star*, covering the war between Greece and Turkey. At Paris's Gare de Lyon train station, the suitcase that Hadley was bringing to her husband, holding more than two years of his writing, including carbons and duplicates, was stolen. Hemingway had to begin again from scratch.

180. *Hemingway: Letters*, pp. 596–597. To Mary Welsh, 1 September 1945.

181. Ibid., p. 777. To Charles Fenton, 29 July 1952.

182. Baker, *Ernest Hemingway: A Life*, p. 867.

183. *Hemingway: Letters*, p. 693. To Senator Joseph McCarthy, 8 May 1950.

184. In the 1950s, when Hemingway wrote about his sub-hunting activities of 1942–43, the "Friendless" operation was transformed into a sad story of an artist who uses the adventure (and liquor) to drown his sorrow over the death of his eldest son. Hemingway had not had to reach far for the sorrow: he had spent two months fearing that his eldest son, John,

was dead after being captured by the Germans on October 28, 1944. Hemingway could never get the work to come out as he wanted, and it was published only after his death when Mary allowed Scribner's to make it part III of *Islands in the Stream*.

185. *Hemingway: Letters*, p. 85. To William D. Horne, 17–18 July 1923.

186. Bruccoli, ed., *Conversations with Ernest Hemingway*, p. 54. Ben F. Meyer, "Hemingway Novel of Venice Completed at Home in Cuba," from *Kansas City Star*, 10 September 1950.

187. Ibid., p. 62. Harvey Breit, "Talk with Mr. Hemingway," from the *New York Times Book Review*, 17 September 1950.

188. Baker, *Ernest Hemingway: A Life*, p. 753.

189. *Hemingway: Letters*, p. 19. To his family, 18 October 1918.

190. Fuentes, *Hemingway in Cuba*, p. 57.

191. *Hemingway: Letters*, p. 21. To James Gamble, 3 March 1919.

Chapter Six

EZRA POUND

The Trains Ran on Time

1. D. D. Paige, ed., *The Letters of Ezra Pound, 1907–1941* (New York: Harcourt, Brace & Co., 1950), p. 9. To Harriet Monroe, 18 August 1912.

2. E. Fuller Torrey, *The Roots of Treason: Ezra Pound and the Secrets of St. Elizabeth's* (London: Sidgwick & Jackson, 1984), p. 36.

3. Cookson, ed., *Selected Prose.* (New York: New Directions Book, 1973), p. 111. From "Patria Mia." This essay first appeared in eleven installments of *The New Age* magazine from 5 September to 14 November 1912.

4. Ibid., p. 130. From "Patria Mia," Part Two, "America: Chances and Remedies." Originally published in *The New Age* magazine in six installments between 1 May and 5 June 1913.

5. Ibid., p. 101.

6. Ibid., p. 10. Letter to Harriet Monroe, 18 August 1912. See *Mein Kampf* for similarity in tone.

7. Ezra Pound, *The Classic Anthology Defined by Confucius* (Boston: Harvard University Press, 1954), pp. 6–7. From "Yung Wind, VIII: Sans Equity and Sans Poise."

8. *Letters*, p. 166. To Agnes Bedford, April 1921.

9. Eliot worked in a bank to support his family, and he completed his masterpiece, *The Waste Land*, in 1922 under extreme mental and physical stress. James Joyce tutored French while he finished *Ulysses*. Pound edited both Eliot's *The Waste Land* and Joyce's *A Portrait of the Artist As a Young Man*.

10. *Letters*, p. 176. To Wyndham Lewis, 5 April 1922.

11. In 1933 Pound wrote, "Whatever economic passions I now have, began *ab initio* from having crimes against living art thrust under my perceptions." *Selected Prose*, pp. 230–231. "Murder by Capital," *Criterion*, July 1933.

12. *Letters*, p. 186. To Kate Buss, 12 May 1923.

13. Hugh Ford, *Published in Paris* (New York: Collier Books/Macmillan, 1975), pp. 111–112. Pound fulminated specifically against Section 211, which prohibited the import or sale of material classified as "obscene." In his "Program for 1929," Pound called for an amendment of Section 211 to read: "This statute does not apply to works of literary or scientific merit." Eventually laws on controversial literary material were relaxed, but individual judicial review and not statutory change in the law was responsible. Federal Judge John M. Woolsey's famous decision overturning the ban of James Joyce's *Ulysses*, later upheld by the U.S. Supreme Court, was the first of many such illustrious court rulings.

14. Ezra Pound, *Impact: Essays on Ignorance and the Decline of American Civilization*, Noel Stock, ed. (Chicago: Henry Regnery Company, 1960), p. 218. From "Definitions," originally published in *Der Querschnitt*, January 1925.

15. Cookson, ed., *Selected Prose*, pp. 200 and 192. From "Provincialism the Enemy," *The New Age*, 19 July 1917.

16. Forrest Read, ed., *The Letters of Ezra Pound to James Joyce* (New York: New Directions, 1967), p. 3.

17. Ezra Pound, *Personae* (New York: New Directions Book, 1926), p. 191. From "Hugh Selwyn Mauberley," V.

18. Wilhelm Reich, *The Mass Psychology of Fascism*, Mary Higgins and Chester M. Raphael, M.D., eds. (New York: The Noonday Press/Farrar, Straus and Giroux, 1993), p. xxii.

19. *Letters*, p. 190. To Wyndham Lewis, 3 December 1924.

20. Carlos Baker, ed., *Ernest Hemingway: Selected Letters 1917–1961* (New York: Charles Scribner's Sons, 1981), p. 127. Ernest Hemingway to Gertrude Stein and Alice B. Toklas, 10 October 1924.

21. Cookson, ed., *Selected Prose*, p. 199. From "Provincialism, the Enemy," Part Four. First printed in *The New Age* on 2 August 1917.

22. Richard Collier, *Il Duce* (New York: The Viking Press, 1971), p. 62. The Fascists loved Virgil as much as Pound did. The chant was the brainchild of the Italian poet/patriot fighter Gabriele D'Annunzio.

23. Poverty-stricken since youth, Mussolini did not even know what an IOU was when he took out a loan for *Il Popolo*. When he repaid the loan, he was aghast to discover the bank charged him interest, and he called the bankers "robbers" (*Il Duce*, p. 70).

24. Pound hailed the Pontine Marsh reclamation in both the 1933 essay "Jefferson and/or Mussolini" (*Selected Prose*, p. 23), and Canto XXXVIII.

25. Collier, *Il Duce*, p. 93.

26. *Letters*, p. 200. To William Bird, 24 August 1925.

27. Pound, *Personae*, p. 99. From "Salvationists."

28. Ibid., p. 95. From "Ite."

29. Ibid., p. 65. From "The Seafarer."

30. Ford, *Published in Paris*, pp. 114–115.

31. *Letters*, p. 203. To Harriet Monroe, 19 November 1926.

32. Ibid., p. 221. To H. L. Mencken, 3 September 1928. This was a rare statement of painful self-awareness. In a dramatic turn of the tables, in London in 1931, Joyce was soliciticing commercial publishers for Pound's *Cantos* and collected essays, to no avail.

33. In Pound's 1942 essay "The Visiting Card," published first in Italian in Rome, he stated plainly: "The war in which brave men are being killed and wounded our own war here and now, began—or rather the phase we are now fighting began—in 1694, with the foundation of the Bank of England." *Selected Prose*, p. 308.

34. *Letters*, p. 279. To Joseph Gordon MacLeod, 28 March 1936.

35. Ibid., p. 204. To Harriet Monroe, 30 November 1926.

36. Most of Mussolini's early monetary innovations were eliminated, especially after 1935. Salaries of state employees were taxed, and the eight-hour day hailed by Pound was lengthened by the granting of exemptions. Burdensome taxes on dividends, real estate, and business followed.

37. *Letters*, p. 205. To Harriet Monroe, 30 November 1926.

38. Ibid., p. 237. To Harriet Monroe, 27 December 1931.

39. Ibid., p. 208. To William Bird, 4 March 1927. In his 1909 novel, *The Cardinal's Mistress*, Mussolini portrayed his hero Madruzzo as a man squeezed between an evil woman and a corrupt Church. "He read a few urgent papers which dealt with political matters, and then began to recite Virgil. He found comfort and support in the sweet Latin poet. . . . Emmanuel did not write verse, but in the hours of sorrow he went to the great classics as one would go to trusted friends for consolation." Mussolini, *The Cardinal's Mistress* (New York: Albert & Charles Boni, 1928), p. 12.

40. *Letters*, p. 113. To Margaret C. Anderson, June 1917.

41. Collier, *Il Duce*, p. 215. Like all of Pound's heroes, Dante Alighieri, b. 1265, dared to stand up to the powers that be and suffered a harsh sentence of exile as a result. He was an established poet when he became involved with Florentine government and politics. When he challenged Pope Boniface VIII to stay out of Florentine affairs, he was charged with corruption, and when he refused to pay a fine, he was condemned to be burned alive if he ever returned to the republic. He finished *The Divine Comedy* shortly before his death on September 14, 1321, and was buried in Ravenna, where he spent the last years of his life.

42. *Letters*, p. 48. To Harriet Monroe, January 1915.

43. Ibid., p. 98. To H. L. Mencken, 27 September 1916.

44. Mussolini, *The Cardinal's Mistress*, pp. 137 and 213.

45. *Letters*, p. 98. To H. L. Mencken, 27 September 1916.

46. Like Pound, Confucius (551–479 B.C.) was a scholar of poetry and ancient history who saw politics as moral persuasion and wanted to transform society and its rulers. He eventually rose to the office of Minister of Justice in the state of Lu in Shantung Province, but was ostracized for his teachings, one of which called for the creation of a scholarly community of noblemen to serve as the moral vanguard for rulers. He went into self-imposed exile, and suffered at times starvation, homelessness, and violence at the hands of his opposition. At the time of Confucius's death at the age of seventy-three, some three thousand believers adhered to his message that a fragmented society could only be healed if its rulers became more human.

47. Collier, *Il Duce*, p. 51. Perhaps the greatest difference between Pound and Mussolini was the latter's attainment of real power. In ironic testament to the savagery of the times, Ezra Pound might have been more successful had he acted out his violent rhetoric rather than just enunciated it.

48. *Letters*, p. 46. To Harriet Monroe, 9 November 1914. Pound addressed World War I in 1923 when he wrote Canto XVI, in which Dante and Virgil reach Purgatory. Pound recalls friends like Lewis, Brzeska, and Hemingway who took part in the war, and describes it as the pointless, self-cannibalization of Europe.

49. Cookson, ed., *Selected Prose*, p. 197. From "Provincialism the Enemy", first published in *The New Age*, 26 July 1917.

50. *Letters*, p. 126. To Harriet Monroe, 29 November 1917.

51. Ibid., p. 181. To Felix Schelling, 9 July 1922.

52. Social Credit government was short-lived, except in Canada, where the world's first Social Credit government ruled from 1935 to 1971 in Alberta province. The party abandoned nearly all of Douglas's policies by the late 1930s.

53. Cookson, ed., *Selected Prose*, p. 337. From "Gold and Work," first published as "Ore e Lavoro" in Rapallo.

54. Ford, *Published in Paris*, p. 313. *Americans Abroad* carried a stellar group of American writers, including E. E. Cummings, Henry Miller, Gertrude Stein, John Dos Passos, William Carlos Williams, and Ernest Hemingway. Interestingly, editor Peter Neagoe concluded that the writing of these expatriates reflected little or no European influence.

55. Read, ed., *Letters to James Joyce*, p. 254; from "Date Line," *Make It New*, p. 15; *Literary Essays*, p. 83.

56. Humphrey Carpenter, *A Serious Character: The Life of Ezra Pound* (New York: Delta Book/Bantam Doubleday Dell Publishing Group, Inc., 1988), p. 499.

57. Read., ed., *Letters to James Joyce*, p. 254.

58. *Letters*, p. 255. To Laurence Binyon, 6 March 1934. In Paradise XIX of *The Divine Comedy*, Dante wrote about Philip the Fair of France, who falsely manipulated his kingdom's currency to finance his Flemish campaigns in 1302. Pound alluded to this in Canto XXXVIII, which focused specifically on Social Credit economics' criticism of the capitalist system of money distribution. Canto XXXVIII was first published in *New Age* magazine in 1933, and drew largely on C. H. Douglas's 1924 book, *Social Credit*. Pound wrote in Canto XXXVIII that Social Credit was so full of truth that men were not used to it and could not fathom its core: "the light became so bright and so blindin [*sic*]/in this layer of paradise/that the mind of man was bewildered." Ezra Pound, *The Cantos of Ezra Pound* (New York: New Directions, 1972), p. 190.

59. *Letters*, p. 247. To Harriet Monroe, 14 September 1933.

60. Ibid., p. 260. To Mary Barnard, 13 August 1934.

61. Pound's anti-Semitism was not unique among the era's otherwise "enlightened" artists. Poets Vachel Lindsay and Edgar Lee Masters were virulent anti-Semites, but novelist Theodore Dreiser was perhaps the worst. He publicly slandered Jews, warned of their "race" overrunning the country, and in 1922 described New York to his friend H. L. Mencken (another anti-Semite and friend of Pound's) as "a Kyke's dream of a ghetto." In 1933 he called for Jews to be "relocated in some Jewish national homeland." Daniel Aaron, *Writers on the Left* (New York: Columbia University Press, 1992), pp. 276–277.

62. Carpenter, *A Serious Character*, p. 557. In Pound's mind, Roosevelt broke every tenet of Confucian leadership, and he agreed with Confucian follower Mencius who contended that revolution is a moral imperative in the case of an unfit ruler. Pound felt that America could still reach greatness if someone other than Roosevelt were president—namely, Congressman George Holden Tinkham, an anti-Roosevelt, anti–League of Nations Republican from Massachusetts. The two maintained a lively correspondence throughout the 1930s. When Pound visited Washington in 1939, Tinkham wrote him letters of introduction.

63. Ezra Pound, *The Cantos*, p. 235.

64. Gesell proposed a paper money system by which on the first of each month a note would be stamped with a fixed value, based on the actual amount of hard goods produced by the society. Pound first learned of stamp-scrip as a youth, when his grandfather Thaddeus used it in his lumber camps. Pound believed that if nations used stamp-scrip, they could keep free of inflation, debt, speculation, and hence, war.

65. Carpenter, *A Serious Character*, p. 540.

66. Cookson, ed., *Selected Prose*, p. 435. From "Jean Cocteau Sociologist," *The New English Weekly*, 10 January 1935. The strong link between poverty and radical social activism is as clear in Ezra Pound as in Adolf Hitler. Before Hitler discovered anti-Communist, anti-Jesuit politics in Munich around 1913, he had experienced hunger and homelessness during his quest to be an artist in Vienna. When his paintings did finally begin to sell, he attributed his success to there being "no end of stupid people."

In a rare, tempered, and revealing comment on his underlying motivation, Pound told William Bird in 1925: "You can let your fancy play as to the course of modern art if I had had an income, esp. during the 1912–1914 period." One could let his fancy play, too, as to the course of modern history had Hitler the artist earned an income in Vienna. John Toland, *Adolf Hitler* (New York: Ballantine Books, 1976), p. 43. *Letters*, p. 201. To William Bird, 11 November 1925.

67. William Manchester, *The Last Lion: Winston Spencer Churchill Alone, 1932–1940* (Boston: Little, Brown & Co., 1988), p. 190.

68. Ibid. Ezra Pound contributed to both Mosely's *British Union Quarterly* and *Action*, the British Union of Fascists' weekly publication.

69. Pound contended that U.S. history could be written simply by tracing the migrations of New England or Quaker whaling families from about 1630.

70. E. Fuller Torrey, *The Roots of Treason*, p. 19.

71. Carpenter, *A Serious Character*, p. 545.

72. Cookson, ed., *Selected Prose*, p. 158. From "The Jefferson/Adams Letters," *North American Review*, winter 1937–1938.

73. Collier, *Il Duce*, p. 135.

74. Carpenter, *A Serious Character*, p. 555. Though Mussolini believed himself the winner in the Crisis because he had brokered a last-minute deal between Chamberlain and Hitler, he was enraged that Hitler neglected to consult him, and in the end was forced to beg Hitler not to mobilize against Czechoslovakia.

75. *Letters*, p. 322. To Hubert Creekmore, February 1939. Since Pound had resisted many invitations to come to America to lecture and visit during his years in Europe, citing among his reasons the high cost of American restaurants and hotels, it is likely that without Dorothy's recent inheritance he would never have felt bold enough to make the trip. Pound's excoriation of the American poor as an underclass of ignoramuses barely veiled his keen awareness of his own poverty.

76. Ezra Pound, *The Cantos*, p. 410. Canto LXX.

77. Ibid., p. 350. Canto LXII.

78. Carpenter, *A Serious Character*, p. 560.

79. Ibid.

80. Pound probably felt he could better understand bureaucrats if he could observe them close up. In Canto LXXX he wrote, "If a man don't occasionally sit in a senate/how can he pierce the darrk [*sic*] of a /senator?"

81. Carpenter, *A Serious Character*, p. 559.

82. Collier, *Il Duce*, p. 158. While Pound was in the U.S., Mussolini fell into Hitler's trap when he signed the Pact of Steel on May 22, 1939, which committed Italian military support to Germany. The pact ignored German minister Ribbentrop's earlier promise that Italy would have three years to ready for war, and when Hitler invaded Poland in September, Mussolini was forced to comply.

83. Ezra Pound, *The Cantos*, p. 216. Cantos XLIII, lines 40–50. Much of Cantos XLI, XLII, and XLII were a translation by Pound from *Il Monte dei Paschi di Siena e le Aziende in Esso Riunite*, 9 vols., Siena, 1891–1925, and concerned the establishment of a new bank, Il Monte dei Paschi ("Mountain of the Pastures"), by the General Council of Siena in 1624. The bank's original funding was guaranteed by the income from grasslands south of Siena, prohibited long-term debt, and initially restricted foreign imports of grain to protect peasants. Pound held up Il Monte dei Paschi as the moral opposite of the Bank of England, founded in 1694.

84. *Letters*, p. 323. To Wyndham Lewis, 3 August 1939.

85. Ibid., p. 325. To Douglas MacPherson, 2 September 1939.

86. Ibid., p. 344. To Tibor Serly, April 1940.

87. Ibid., p. 328. To Douglas McPherson, 3 November 1939.

88. Pound had studied the ancient Chinese classics since the 1910s; in 1928 he published *Ta Hio*, his translation of the second of the so-called *Four Books of Confucius*.

89. Carpenter, *A Serious Character*, p. 567.

90. *Letters*, p. 342. To Ronald Duncan, 31 March 1943.

91. Ezra Pound, *Guide to Kulchur* (New York: New Directions, 1951), p. 241.

92. *Letters*, p. 342.

93. Ibid., p. 335. Ezra Pound to T.S. Eliot, 18 January 1940.

94. Carpenter, *A Serious Character*, p. 559.

95. *Letters*, p. 346. To Katue Kitasono, 29 October 1940.

96. *Letters*, p. 347. To Katue Kitasono, 15 November 1940.

97. Collier, *Il Duce*, p. 173.

98. The Italian loss at Taranto was a preamble to the sinking of three Italian cruisers and two destroyers in the battle off Greece's Cape Matapan on March 28, 1941. That battle signified the end to Italy's navy as a factor in the war.

99. Collier, *Il Duce*, p. 185.

100. Pound was deeply impressed with the late nineteenth-century concept that each man has a "function," and he used this phrase in 1913 in a letter to his father. Though he disavowed Marx, whom he claimed bestowed "money with properties of a quasi-religious nature" ("Gold and Work"), and he despised the Communists, whom he accused of not understanding the fundamentals of economics, he nevertheless divided society into three classes based on the Mencian model: rulers, manual laborers, and laborers who serve the nobility with their minds. Pound's analysis, however, never resolved a deep conflict between his artistic and intellectual ambition and his anti-intellectual, middle-class roots, which emphasized the moral value of hard physical labor. Isabel Pound chastised her son for his "low diet and sedentary life" and held up his hardworking ancestors to him as proper role models. In 1913 Pound defended his choice to "camp . . . in the fields of the muses," but his poem "Further Instructions," published in 1916 in *Lustra*, reflects and mocks Isabel's Victorian Midwestern didacticism: "You are very idle, my songs./I fear you will come to a bad end./You stand about in the streets,/You loiter at the corners and bus-stops,/You do next to nothing at all." *Letters*, p. 20. To Homer Pound, 3 June 1913; to Isabel Pound, May 1913.

101. *Letters*, p. 181. To Ronald Duncan, 31 March 1943.

102. Carpenter, *A Serious Character*, pp. 609–610.

103. Ibid., p. 590.

104. C. David Heyman, *Ezra Pound, The Last Rower* (New York: The Viking Press, 1976), p. 168.

105. Collier, *Il Duce*, p. 196.

106. Carlos Baker, ed., *The Letters of Ernest Hemingway*, p. 545. To Archibald MacLeish, c. 5 May 1943.

107. The timing of Pound's indictment seems to have been a coincidence. Various government agents had been seeking an indictment as far back as August 1942.

108. Ubaldo degli Uberti was an admiral under Mussolini and translated "The Unwobbling Pivot" into Italian for Pound in 1945. He died in May 1945 from wounds he sustained after being ambushed by a platoon of Russian-German troops who mistook him for a partisan.

109. Collier, *Il Duce*, p. 271.

110. Richard Lamb, *Italy at War, 1943–1945* (New York: St. Martin's Press, 1993), pp. 49 and 55. Deportation of Italian Jews began in late September 1943, and another round of anti-Jewish laws were enacted in November. Concentration camps were set up inside Italy, such as the one at Fossoli near Modena, and at a disused rice factory at San Sabba near Trieste. Out of a total of about 32,000 Italian Jews and 12,500 foreign-born Jews living in Italy, some 7,682 eventually died.

111. Cantos LXXII and LXXIII were printed in a Salo journal, *Marina Republicana* in January and February 1945. By order of Pound's heirs, they were not included in the collected *Cantos* until 1987.

112. Carpenter, *A Serious Character*, p. 636.

113. Collier, *Il Duce*, p. 299.

114. Code-named "Operation Sunrise," Dulles's plan aimed to win German withdrawal from northern Italy without destruction of the region's vital industrial plants.

115. Donald Hall, *Remembering Poets, Reminiscences and Opinions* (New York: Harper Colophon, 1977), p. 239.

116. Ibid.

117. From Canto LXXIV.

118. Cookson, ed., *Selected Prose*, p. 96. From "The Ethics of Mencius," *Criterion*, July 1938; and Canto LXXVII.

119. Carroll F. Terrell, *The Companion to the Cantos*, Vol. II (Berkeley: University of California Press, 1984), p. 434. Editor's note 109, from Michael King: "Ezra Pound at Pisa: An Interview with John L. Steele," *Texas Quarterly*, XXI, 4, Winter 1978.

120. The dream evaporated, Pound explained, because Mussolini never had the time to implement it. In both his *Guide to Kulchur* and *Pisan Canto* LXXXI, Pound recalled H. L. Mencken's statement that man "can't be convinced in anything less than a geological epoch" (*Guide to Kulchur*, p. 182).

121. Terrell, *The Companion to the Cantos*, Vol. 1, p. 35. Editor's note 44, also citing Pound's *Spirit of Romance*, p. 129.

122. Ezra Pound, *Spirit Of Romance* (London: Peter Owen, 1952), p. 129.

123. Carpenter, *A Serious Character*, p. 668. From a report by DTC psychiatrist William Weisdorf; E. Fuller Torrey, *Roots of Treason*, p. 8. From a report by Captain Walter H. Baer.

124. Cookson, ed., *Selected Prose*, p. 132. From "Patria Mia." Little of Pound's poetry is available today off the university campus, whereas one can find numerous biographies of the man and dozens of books written by professors and critics explaining the meaning of *The Cantos* themselves. The collected *Cantos*, first published by New Directions in 1948, is hard to find in used bookstores. Though few have actually read his poetry, Pound is widely identified as the American fascist poet.

125. *Letters*, p. 115. To Harriet Monroe, 21 August 1917. T. S. Eliot best captured Pound's attitude as a writer-thinker when he observed that *The Cantos* read "as if the author was so irritated with his readers for not knowing all about anybody so important as [Martin] Van Buren that he refused to enlighten them." Charles Norman, *Ezra Pound* (New York: Macmillan, 1960), p. 354.

126. Pound, *Personae*, p. 81. From "Tenzone."

127. Noel Stock, *The Life of Ezra Pound*, p. 17.

128. Carpenter, *A Serious Character*, p. 803.

129. Torrey, *Roots of Treason*, p. 180.

130. Carpenter, *A Serious Character*, p. 825. Ezra Pound to Patricia Hutchins, March 1957.

131. Ibid., pp. 842–843.

132. Donald Hall, *Remembering Poets*, p. 244.

133. Mussolini, *The Cardinal's Mistress*, p. x. From "Introduction," Hiram Motherwell.

Chapter Seven

THOMAS MANN

Disillusionment

1. Julian Bach Jr., *America's Germany: An Account of the Occupation* (New York: Random House, 1946), p. 14.

2. Mann's son Klaus visited Munich right after the German defeat as a correspondent for the American Army publication *Stars and Stripes*, and reported to his father that the house had been used by the Nazis as a home for young unmarried Aryan women in Lebensborn, Hitler's program for mass pure race propagation. The home's contents had all been auctioned.

3. Ibid., pps. 16–17.

4. Richard and Clara Winston, eds. and trans., *Letters of Thomas Mann* (Berkeley: University of California Press, 1975), p. 351. To Eric von Kahler, 1 May 1945.

5. Lawrence S. Wittner, *Cold War America* (New York: Praeger Publishers, 1974), p. 9. Soviet casualties, far heavier than those sustained by the other warring nations, multiplied catastrophically as Stalin bitterly waited for the Allies to launch their second front to divert German forces from Russia. All told, the German occupying forces killed an estimated fifteen to twenty million Russians, and completely or partially demolished fifteen large cities, 1,710 towns, and 70,000 villages. Tens of thousands of factories, railroad lines, bridges, power stations, and nearly 100,000 collective farms—together totaling nearly $130 billion in property—were destroyed.

6. Ibid., pp. 13–14.

7. Richard and Clara Winston, *Letters of Thomas Mann*, p. 353. To Agnes E. Meyer, 25 August 1945.

8. The article, "The Camps," concerned the Allied liberation of concentration camps in Weimar, Germany, in April 1945. The Office of War Information had requested the article for inclusion in the United Nations' founding session in San Francisco later that month.

9. Thomas Mann, *The Coming Victory of Democracy*, trans. Agnes E. Meyer (New York: Alfred A. Knopf, Inc., 1938), pp. 37 and 40.

10. Ibid., p. 7.

11. Ibid., pp. 40 and 42.

12. Late in the war, MacLeish's liberalism came under fire from conservative, anti–New Deal Democrats and almost cost him his State Department post. During divisive confirmation hearings before the Senate Foreign Relations Committee in December 1944, Missouri Democrat Bennett Champ Clark tried to portray MacLeish as anticapitalist and pro-Communist. MacLeish's nomination was at first defeated, but he finally won approval through the efforts of Committee Chairman Tom Connally of Texas, who worked to obtain approval for Roosevelt nominees.

13. Wittner, *Cold War America*, p. 19.

14. Anni Carlson and Volker Michels, ed., Ralph Manheim, trans., *The Correspondence of Herman Hesse and Thomas Mann, 1910–1955* (New York: Harper & Row, 1975), p. 102. Thomas Mann to Herman Hesse, 12 October 1946.

15. *Letters of Thomas Mann*, p. 373. To Agnes E. Meyer, 1 December 1946.

16. Ibid.

17. Richard and Clara Winston and Tania and James Stern, *Last Essays* (New York: Alfred A. Knopf, Inc., 1959), p. 177. From "Nietzsche's Philosophy in Light of Recent History."

18. *Letters of Thomas Mann*, p. 388. To Kitty and Alfred Neumann, 14 July 1947.

19. Ibid., p. 378. To Emile Preetorious, 30 December 1946.

20. Ibid., p. 392. To Agnes E. Meyer, 10 October 1947.

21. Ronald Hayman, *Thomas Mann: A Biography* (New York: Scribner's, 1995), p. 539.

22. Germany's designated zones of occupation were as follows: The Russians in the northeast, from Mecklenburg south to Saxony; the Americans in the south, in Bavaria, Hesse, and northern Wurttemberg; the British in the northwest, from Schleswig-Holstein south to Westphalia; and the French, with the smallest zone, running along their border and including the Rhineland, the Palatinate, and southern Baden. Berlin, to be jointly administered by the Russians and Americans, lay in the Soviet zone. In May of 1946 the Americans and the financially strapped British merged into one zone.

23. Wittner, *Cold War America*, p. 33.

24. Winston Churchill first coined the phrase "Iron Curtain" to describe the irreconcilable ideological division between the Soviets and Western capitalist nations, in a speech on March 5, 1946 in Fulton, Missouri.

25. Ibid., p. 17.

26. Ibid., p. 91.

27. *Letters of Thomas Mann*, p. 393. To Mr. Gray, 12 October 1947.

28. Hayman, *Thomas Mann: A Biography*, p. 544.

29. Ibid.

30. *Letters of Thomas Mann*, p. 393.

31. Carlson and Michels, eds., *Correspondence of Hesse and Mann*, p. 121. Thomas Mann to Hermann Hesse, 27 November 1947.

32. *Letters of Thomas Mann*, pp. 336–337. To Klaus Mann, 25 June 1944.

33. Ibid., p. 381. To Dean of Bonn University, 28 January 1947.

34. Ibid.

35. "De-nazifying" the German mind through the press was as much a part of the Allied occupiers' rebuilding of Germany as restarting German factories and opening German mines.

In the American zone, the Information Control Division of the American Military Government maintained absolute control over the German press in the immediate months after the German defeat, but in August 1945 began licensing publications printed by Germans for Germans. Publishers were handpicked by the Americans on the basis of their "active devotion to democratic ideals," and since many of them had been imprisoned in concentration camps for their anti-Hitler stance, they had already proven their devotion beyond a shadow of a doubt.

By November 1945, sixteen German newspapers in the American zone were disseminating news and information to the German public, as long as they kept to their promise not to print Nazi, militaristic, or racial propaganda, or criticism of the Allied Military government or the United Nations. After the Americans relinquished most press control to German publishers, *Die Neue Zeitung*, printed in Munich under the aegis of the ICD, remained the mouthpiece of the American occupiers. Its editor was Hans Habe, head of the ICD Press section, and former anti-Nazi editor in Budapest. During the war, Habe fought in both the French and American armies and became an American citizen.

36. Hayman, *Thomas Mann: A Biography*, pp. 520–521.

37. Ibid., p. 520.

38. *Letters of Thomas Mann*, p. 354. To Agnes E. Meyer, 25 August 1945.

39. *Correspondence of Hesse and Mann*, p. 112. From Mann's essay "Hermann Hesse on His 70th Birthday." Published in *Neu Zurcher Zeitung*, 2 July 1947.

40. *Correspondence of Hesse and Mann*, p. 104. Hermann Hesse to Thomas Mann, October 1946. In 1946, in addition to writing *The Glass Bead Game*, Hesse completed an antiwar treatise, *If the War Goes On*. The book was published in 1946 in Zurich and in 1971 in America. In 1946 Hesse was awarded Germany's most distinguished literary award, the Goethe Prize.

41. *Letters of Thomas Mann*, p. 385. To Viktor Mann, 27 March 1947.

42. Hayman, *Thomas Mann: A Biography*, p. 540.

43. Of all the requests made to Mann to use his influence with the Allied occupiers, the one made on behalf of his old friend, Ernst Bertram, perhaps most provoked Mann. As punishment for his pro-Hitler writings, Bertram was classified after the war as a "Lesser Offender," and lost his professorship and pension at the age of sixty-four. In July 1948 a former student of Bertram's, Werner Schmitz, wrote Mann, asking for help. Though Mann thought Bertram's punishment too severe, he sharply recounted Bertram's offenses one by one to Schmitz, and cited the countless Jewish scholars and professors who were ejected from their positions with no outcry from their Aryan colleagues. Mann wondered why Bertram, who had once been so close to the Mann family that he became godfather to Mann's daughter Elisabeth, would want to teach Germany's young non-Aryans anyway, since he had once referred to them as "termite people." *Letters of Thomas Mann*, p. 403. Thomas Mann to Werner Schmitz, 30 July 1948.

44. *Letters of Thomas Mann*, p. 368. To Hans Blunck, 22 July 1946.

45. Ibid., p. 405. To Agnes E. Meyer, 7 September 1948.

46. Ibid., p. 408. To Klaus Mann, 12 November 1948.

47. Hayman, *Thomas Mann: A Biography*, p. 554.

48. *Letters of Thomas Mann*, p. 398. To Frederic Warburg, 4 March 1948.

49. Ibid., p. 395. To Walter Kolb, 4 January 1948.

50. *Holy Sinner (Der Erwahlte)* was published in Germany by S. Fischer Verlag and by Knopf in America in 1951. *The Story of a Novel: The Genesis of Dr. Faustus* was not published in America until 1961.

Mann submitted to Schoenberg's pressure by crediting him in subsequent editions of *Doctor Faustus*, but not without maintaining his position that his symbolic depiction of the twelve-tone system made it genuinely his own.

51. Ibid., p. 419. To Paul Olberg, 27 August 1949.

52. Klaus Mann's last article, "The Affliction of European Intellectuals," was published posthumously in the *Neue Schweizer Rundschau* in July 1949.

53. *Correspondence of Hesse and Mann*, p. 136. Thomas Mann to Hermann Hesse, 6 July 1949.

54. Ibid. Though Mann held his children to no higher standard than himself, the problem was that none of his children possessed his Olympian talent. Mann's third son and youngest child, Michael, committed suicide in 1977 at the age of fifty-eight.

55. *Letters of Thomas Mann*, p. 418. To Paul Olberg, 27 August 1949.

Eduard Beneš, Mann's old friend, had been president of the Czech Republic when Hitler annexed the Sudetenland in October 1938. Mann here obviously overlooked Beneš later disgust with Soviet policies which prompted him to quit the new Czech government in June 1948, when the Soviets wanted him to sign the new Communist constitution.

56. Ibid., p. 425. To Maximilian Brantl, 19 March 1950.

Heinrich's life in exile was tragic. After emigrating to America in 1940, he worked for a time as a Hollywood scriptwriter. Whereas his brother's fame increased after his move to America, Heinrich's declined dramatically, and he lived in poverty and obscurity. His second wife, an alcoholic and depressive, committed suicide in 1944, on her fifth attempt.

57. Hayman, *Thomas Mann: A Biography*, p. 570.

58. Ibid., p. 577.

59. The emergency provisions of the McCarran Act, formerly known as the Internal Security Act of 1950, were never implemented. The act was finally repealed in 1971.

60. Ibid., p. 585.

61. *Letters of Thomas Mann*, p. 437. To Erich von Kahler, 23 April 1951.

62. *Correspondence of Hesse and Mann*, p. 159. Thomas Mann to Hermann Hesse, 26 March 1954.

63. Wittner, *Cold War America*, p. 100.

64. *Last Essays*, p. 91. From "On Schiller."

65. Ibid., p. 93.

66. Erika Mann, *Last Year of Thomas Mann* (New York: Farrar, Strauss, and Cudahy, 1958), p. 82.

Bibliography

THOMAS MANN

Chapter One: On a Mission from God

Chapter Seven: Disillusionment

American editions in translation published by Alfred A. Knopf, Inc., New York.
Buddenbrooks 1924. Trans. H. T. Lowe-Porter.
Death in Venice and Other Stories 1925. Trans. Kenneth Burke.
The Magic Mountain 1927. Trans. H. T. Lowe-Porter.
Mario the Magician 1931. Trans. H. T. Lowe-Porter.
Joseph and His Brothers. Trans. H. T. Lowe-Porter, 1934.
Young Joseph 1935. Trans. H. T. Lowe-Porter.
Joseph in Egypt 1938. Trans. H. T. Lowe-Porter.
Joseph the Provider 1944. Trans. H. T. Lowe-Porter.
The Beloved Returns (*Lotte in Weimar*) 1940. Trans. H. T. Lowe-Porter.
The Transposed Heads 1941. Trans. H. T. Lowe-Porter.
The Tables of the Law 1945. Trans. H. T. Lowe-Porter.
Doctor Faustus 1948. Trans. H. T. Lowe-Porter.
Nonfiction American editions in translation published by Alfred A. Knopf, Inc., New York.
The Coming Victory of Democracy 1938. Trans. Agnes E. Meyer.
This Peace 1938. Trans. H. T. Lowe-Porter.
This War 1940. Trans. Eric Sutton.
Freud, Goethe, Wagner 1937. Trans. H. T. Lowe-Porter and Rita Matthias-Reil.
Essays of Three Decades 1947. Trans. H. T. Lowe-Porter.
Listen, Germany 1943.
Last Essays 1959. Trans. Richard and Clara Winston and Tania and James Stern.
Story of a Novel: The Genesis of Dr. Faustus 1961. Trans. Richard and Clara Winston.
Reflections of a Non-Political Man. New York: Continuum Publishing Co., 1987.

Bach, Julian, Jr. *America's Germany: An Account of the Occupation*. New York: Random House, 1946.
Brinkley, David. *Washington Goes to War*. New York: Alfred A. Knopf, Inc., 1988.
Calvocoressi, Peter, and Guy Wint. *Total War*. New York: Pantheon Books/Random House, 1972.
Carlson, Anni, and Volker Michels, eds. *The Correspondence of Hermann Hesse and Thomas Mann, 1910–1955*. Trans. Ralph Mannheim. New York: Harper & Row, 1975.
Donaldson, Scott. *Archibald MacLeish: An American Life*. Boston: Houghton Mifflin Company, 1992.
Gay, Peter. *Freud/A Life for Our Time*. New York: Anchor Books/Doubleday, 1989.
Gilbert, G. M. *Nuremberg Diary*. New York: Farrar, Strauss and Company, 1947.
Goethe, Johann Wolfgang von. *Faust*. Trans. George Madison Priest. Chicago: The Great Books, Encyclopedia Brittanica, Inc., 1952.
Hayman, Ronald. *Thomas Mann: A Biography*. New York: Scribner's, 1995.
Hesse, Hermann. *Magister Ludi* (*The Glass Bead Game*). New York: Bantam Books reprint, 1970.

Hoffman, Peter. *The History of the German Resistance, 1933–1945.* Trans. Richard Barry. Cambridge: The MIT Press, 1977.

Kesten, Hermann, ed. *Thomas Mann Diaries, 1918–1939.* Trans. Richard and Clara Winston. New York: Harry N. Abrams, Incorporated, 1982.

Laqueur, Walter. *Weimar: A Cultural History.* New York: Perigee Book, 1974.

Mann, Erika. *The Last Year of Thomas Mann.* New York: Farrar, Strauss & Cudahy, 1958.

Mann, Katia. *Unwritten Memories.* Ed. Elisabeth Plessen and Michael Mann. Trans. Hunter and Hildegarde Hannum. New York: Alfred A. Knopf, Inc., 1975.

Mann, Klaus. *Mephisto.* Trans. Robin Smyth. New York: Random House reprint, 1977.

Robinson, Armin L. *The Ten Commandments: Ten Short Novels of Hitler's War Against the Moral Code.* New York: Simon & Schuster, 1943.

Schuster, M. Lincoln, ed. *The World's Great Letters.* New York: Simon & Schuster, 1940.

Shirer, William L. *The Rise and Fall of the Third Reich.* New York: Simon & Schuster, 1960.

Toland, John. *Adolf Hitler.* New York: Ballantine Books, 1976.

Winston, Richard, and Clara Winston, eds. and trans. *Letters of Thomas Mann.* Berkeley: University of California Press, 1975. Abridged edition.

Wittner, Lawrence. *Cold War America from Hiroshima to Watergate.* New York: Praeger Publishers, Inc., 1974.

Chapter Two

JOHN STEINBECK

America Against Itself

Works by John Steinbeck

Tortilla Flat. New York: Bantam Book reprint, 1962.

In Dubious Battle. New York: Bantam Books reprint, 1961.

The Forgotten Village (book of film). New York: The Viking Press, 1941.

The Grapes of Wrath. New York: Compass Books Edition/Viking Press, 1962.

The Sea of Cortez (in collaboration with Edward F. Ricketts). New York: Viking Press, 1941.

The Log from The Sea of Cortez. London: Mandarin Paperback, 1958.

The Moon Is Down (novel). New York: The Viking Press, 1942.

The Short Novels of John Steinbeck. New York: The Viking Press, 1953.

The Wayward Bus. New York: The Viking Press, 1947.

East of Eden. New York: The Viking Press, 1952.

Once There Was a War. New York: Bantam Books, 1960.

The Winter of Our Discontent. New York: The Viking Press, 1961.

Travels with Charley. New York: The Viking Press, 1962.

Journal of a Novel: The East of Eden Letters. New York: Viking Press, 1969.

The Acts of King Arthur and His Noble Knights. New York: Del Ray/Ballantine Paperback reprint, 1980.

Aaron, Daniel. *Writers on the Left: Episodes in American Literary Communism.* New York: Columbia University Press, 1992.

Benson, Jackson J. *The True Adventures of John Steinbeck, Writer.* New York: Viking Press, 1984.

Dear, I. C. B., gen. ed. *Oxford Companion to WWII.* New York: Oxford University Press, 1995.

DeMott, Robert, ed. *John Steinbeck: Working Days The Journals of the Grapes of Wrath, 1938–1941.* New York: Viking Penguin Inc., 1989.

Donaldson, Scott. *Archibald MacLeish: An American Life.* Boston: Houghton Mifflin Company, 1992.

Ferrell, Keith. *The Voice of the Land.* New York: M. Evans, 1986.

Hitler, Adolf. *Mein Kampf.* Trans. Ralph Manheim. Boston: Houghton Mifflin Company, 1971.

Israel, Lee. *Miss Tallulah Bankhead.* New York: G. P. Putnam's Sons, 1972.

Katz, Ephraim. *The Film Encyclopedia.* New York: Thomas Y. Crowell, Publishers, 1979.

Mantle, Burns, ed. *Best Plays, 1941–1942.* New York: Dodd, Mead and Company, 1942.

Mitgang, Herbert. *Dangerous Dossiers: Exposing the Secret War Against America's Greatest Authors.* New York: Ballantine Books, 1989.

Rickenbacker, Edward V. *Rickenbacker.* London: Prentice Hall International, 1967.

Spoto, Donald. *The Dark Side of Genius: The Life of Alfred Hitchcock.* New York: Little, Brown & Co., 1983.

Steinbeck, Elaine, and Robert Wallsten, eds. *Steinbeck: A Life in Letters.* New York: Viking Press, 1975.

Stott, William. *Documentary Expression and Thirties America.* New York: Oxford University Press, 1973.

Toland, John. *Adolf Hitler.* New York: Ballantine Books, 1976.

Winkler, Allan. *The Politics of Propaganda: The Office of War Information, 1942–1945.* New York: Yale University Press, 1978.

Chapter Three

VIRGINIA WOOLF

The Outsider's Lament

Works by Virginia Woolf
A Room of One's Own. New York: Harvest/HBJ Book, 1981.
To the Lighthouse. New York: Harvest Book, 1955.
Mrs. Dalloway. New York: Harcourt, Brace & World, Inc., 1925.
The Years. New York: Harcourt, Brace & Company, 1937.
Three Guineas. New York: Harvest/HBJ Book, 1966.
Roger Fry: A Biography. London: The Hogarth Press, 1940.
Between The Acts (Pointz Hall). New York: Harcourt, Brace & World, Inc., 1941.

Annan, Noel. *Our Age: English Intellectuals Between the World Wars.* New York: Random House, 1990.

Bell, Anne Oliver, ed. *Virginia Woolf: A Moment's Liberty, The Shorter Diary.* New York: Harcourt Brace Jovanovich, 1990.

Maitland, Frederic William. *The Life and Letters of Leslie Stephen.* New York: G. P. Putnam's Sons, 1906.

Manchester, William. *The Last Lion: Winston Spencer Churchill Alone, 1932–1940.* Boston: Little, Brown & Company, 1988.

Marwick, Arthur. *The Deluge: British Society and the First World War.* New York: W. W. Norton & Co., 1965.

Nicolson, Nigel, and Joanne Trautmann, eds. *The Letters of Virginia Woolf,* vols. I–VI. New York: Harcourt Brace Jovanovich, 1975–1980.

Rothberg, Joseph M., and Franklin D. Jones. "Suicide in the U.S. Army: Epidemiological Periodic Aspects." *Suicide and Life Threatening Behavior,* 17 (2), 1987, pp. 119–121.

Stack, Steven. "The Effect of Immigration on Suicide: A Cross National Analysis." *Basic and Applied Social Psychology*, 2, 3 (1981), 205–218.

―――. "Comparative Analysis of Immigration and Suicide." *Psychological Reports*, 49 (1981), 509–510.

Woolf, Leonard. *Autobiography*, vols. I–VI. New York: Harvest Book/Harcourt Brace Jovanovich, 1960–1969.

Chapter Four

COLETTE

The Survivor

Works by Colette in English translation

Gigi; Julie de Carneilhan; Chance Acquaintances. Trans. Roger Senhouse. New York; Farrar, Straus and Young, 1952.

Julie de Carneilhan. Trans. Patrick Leigh Fermor. New York: Farrar, Straus and Young, 1952.

My Mother's House. Trans. Una Vicenzo Troubridge and Enid McLeod. *Sido*. Trans. Enid McLeod. New York: Farrar, Straus & Giroux, 1953.

Break of Day. Trans. Enid McLeod. New York: Farrar, Straus and Cudahy, 1961.

The Pure and the Impure. Trans. Herma Briffault. New York: Farrar, Straus & Giroux, 1967.

Evening Star. Trans. David Le Vay. New York: The Bobbs-Merrill Company, Inc., 1973.

The Colette Omnibus: Cheri. Trans. Roger Senhouse. New York: The International Collectors Library, 1974.

Looking Backwards (*Journal à rebours* and *De ma fenêtre*). Trans. David Le Vay. Bloomington: Indiana University Press, 1975.

The Complete Claudine. Trans. Antonia White. New York: Avenel Books, 1976.

Duo and *Le Toutonier*. Trans. Margaret Crosland. London: Peter Owen, 1976.

My Apprenticeships. Trans. Helen Beauclerk. New York: Farrar Straus & Giroux, 1978.

Cocteau, Jean. *The Difficulty of Being*. Trans. Elizabeth Sprigge. New York: Coward-McCann, Inc., 1967.

―――. *My Contemporaries*. Ed. Margaret Crosland. London: Peter Owen, 1967.

Collins, Larry, and Dominique Lapierre. *Is Paris Burning?* New York: Pocket Books, 1965.

Crosland, Margaret. *Colette: The Difficulty of Loving*. New York: The Bobbs-Merrill Company, Inc., 1973.

Duras, Marguerite. *The War: A Memoir*. Trans. Barbara Bray. New York: Pantheon Books, 1986.

Goudeket, Maurice. *Close to Colette: An Intimate Portrait of a Woman of Genius*. New York: Farrar, Straus and Cudahy, 1957.

―――. *The Delights of Growing Old*. Trans. Patrick O'Brian. New York: Farrar, Straus & Giroux, Inc., 1966.

Knopton, Ernest John. *France: An Interpretive History*. New York: Charles Scribner's Sons, Inc., 1971.

Levy, Claude, and Paul Tillard. *Betrayal at the Vel d'Hiv*. Trans. Inea Bushnaq. New York: Hill and Wang, 1969.

Lottman, Herbert. *Colette: A Life*. Boston: Little, Brown and Company, 1991.

Marrus, Michael R., and Robert O. Paxton. *Vichy France and the Jews*. New York: Basic Books, 1981.

Mitchell, Yvonne. *Colette: A Taste for Life*. New York: Harcourt Brace Jovanovich, 1975.

Phelps, Robert, ed. and trans. *Letters from Colette*. New York: Farrar, Straus & Giroux, 1980.

Richardson, Joanna. *Colette*. New York: Franklin Watts, Inc., 1984.

Sarde, Michele. *Colette: A Biography*. Trans. Richard Miller. New York: William Morrow and Co., 1980.

Sprigge, Elizabeth, and Jean-Jacques Kihm. *Jean Cocteau: The Man and the Mirror*. New York: Coward-McCann Inc., 1968.

Webster, Paul. *Petain's Crime, The Full Story of French Collaboration in the Holocaust*. Chicago: Ivan R. Dee, 1991.

Chapter Five

ERNEST HEMINGWAY

War As an Aphrodisiac

Works by Ernest Hemingway

To Have and Have Not. New York: Grosset & Dunlap, 1937.

For Whom the Bell Tolls. New York: Charles Scribner's Sons, 1940.

Men at War. New York: Berkley Medallion Paperback/Berkley Publishing Corporation, 1960 reprint.

Across the River and into the Trees. London: Jonathan Cape, 1952.

The Old Man and the Sea. New York: Charles Scribner's Sons, 1952.

The Snows of Kilimanjaro and Other Stories. New York: Charles Scribner's Sons paperback reprint, 1964.

Islands in the Stream. New York: Charles Scribner's Sons, 1970.

Garden of Eden. New York: Charles Scribner's Sons, 1986.

Aaron, Daniel. *Writers on the Left: Episodes in American Literary Communism*. New York: Columbia University Press, 1992.

Auden, W.H., and Christopher Isherwood. *Journey to a War*. New York: Paragon House, 1990.

Baker, Carlos, *Ernest Hemingway: A Life Story*. New York: Charles Scribner's Sons, 1969.

Baker, Carlos, ed. *Ernest Hemingway: Selected Letters, 1917–1961*. New York: Charles Scribner's Sons, 1981.

Baudot, Marcel, Henri Berhard, Hendrik Brugmans, Michael R. B. Foot, and Hans-Adolf Jacobsen, eds. *The Historical Encyclopedia of WWII*. New York: Facts on File, Inc., 1980.

Brian, Denis. *The True Gen: An Intimate Portrait of Ernest Hemingway by Those Who Knew Him*. New York: Grove Press, 1988.

Bruccoli, Matthew, ed. *Conversations with Ernest Hemingway*. Jackson: University Press of Mississippi, 1986.

Bruccoli, Matthew, and Margaret Duggan, eds. *The Correspondence of F. Scott Fitzgerald*. New York: Random House, 1980.

Cole, Hugh M. *U.S. Army in WWII: The Ardennes, Battle of the Bulge*. Washington, D.C.: Center for Military History, 1994.

Dawson, William Harbutt. *The German Empire 1867–1914 and the Unity Movement*, vol. I. New York: The Macmillan Company, 1919.

Dear, I. C. B., gen. ed. *Oxford Companion to WWII*. New York: Oxford University Press, 1995.

Donaldson, Scott, with R. H. Winnick. *Archibald MacLeish: An American Life*. Boston: Houghton, Mifflin Company, 1992.

Fuentes, Norberto. *Hemingway in Cuba*. Secaucus: Lyle Stuart, 1984.

———. *Ernest Hemingway Rediscovered*. Trans. Marianne Sinclair. New York: Charles Scribner's Sons, 1988.

Golenbock, Peter. *BUMS*. New York: G.P. Putnam's Sons, 1984.

Hearst, William Randolph, with Jack Casserly. *The Hearsts, Father and Son*. Niwot, Colorado: Roberts Rinehart Publishing Group, 1991.

Jacobs, Lewis, ed. *The Documentary Tradition*. New York: Hopkinson and Blake Publishers, 1971.

Manchester, William. *Goodbye, Darkness: A Memoir of the Pacific War*. Boston: Little, Brown and Company, 1980.

Meyers, Jeffrey. *Hemingway: A Biography*. New York: Harper & Row Publishers, 1985.

Mitgang, Herbert. *Dangerous Dossiers: Exposing the Secret War Against America's Greatest Authors*. New York: Donald I. Fine, Inc., 1988.

Nicholson, Harold. *The War Years, 1939–1945*, vol. 2. Nigel Nicholson, ed. New York: Atheneum, 1967.

Paret, Peter. *Clausewitz and the State*. Princeton: Princeton University Press, 1985.

Rollyson, Carl. *Nothing Ever Happens to the Brave, the Story of Martha Gellhorn*. New York: St. Martin's Press, 1990.

Shirer, William L. *The Rise and Fall of the Third Reich*. New York: Simon & Schuster, 1960.

Whelan, Richard. *Robert Capa: A Biography*. New York: Alfred A. Knopf, Inc., 1985.

White, Ray Lewis, ed. *Sherwood Anderson/Gertrude Stein: Correspondence and Personal Essays*. Chapel Hill: The University of North Carolina Press, 1972.

White, William, ed. *By-line: Ernest Hemingway/Selected Articles and Dispatches of Four Decades*. New York: Bantam Book Paperback Edition, 1970.

Winnick, R.H. ed. *Letters of Archibald MacLeish, 1907–1982*. Boston: Houghton Mifflin Company, 1983.

Chapter Six

EZRA POUND

The Trains Ran on Time

Works by Ezra Pound

Spirit of Romance. London: Peter Owen, 1952/1910.

Personae: Collected Shorter Poems. New York: New Directions Book, 1926.

How to Read. New York: Haskell House Publishers Ltd., 1971/1931.

Guide to Kulchur. New York: New Directions, 1938.

The Cantos of Ezra Pound. New York: New Directions, 1972.

Literary Essays of Ezra Pound. Ed. T. S. Eliot. New Directions Book, 1935.

The Classic Anthology Defined by Confucius. Boston: Harvard University Press, 1954.

Impact: Essays on Ignorance and the Decline of American Civilization. Ed. Noel Stock. Chicago: Henry Regnery Company, 1960.

Confucius to Cummings: An Anthology of Poetry. Ed. Marcella Spain. New York: New Directions, 1964.

Ezra Pound: Selected Prose, 1909–1965. Ed. William Cookson. New York: New Directions Book, 1973.

Aaron, Daniel. *Writers on the Left: Episodes in American Literary Communism*. New York: Columbia University Press, 1992.

Baker, Carlos, ed. *Ernest Hemingway: Selected Letters, 1917–1961*. New York: Charles Scribner's Sons, 1981.

Calvocoressi, Peter, and Guy Wint. *Total War*. New York: Pantheon Books/Random House, 1972.

Carpenter, Humphrey. *A Serious Character: The Life of Ezra Pound*. New York: Delta Book/Bantam Doubleday Dell Publishing Group, Inc. 1988.

Collier, Richard. *Il Duce*. New York: The Viking Press, 1971.

Creel, H. G. *Confucius and the Chinese Way*. New York: Harper Torchbooks/The Cloister Library, 1960.

DeGrand, Alexander. *Italian Fascism: Its Origins and Development*. Lincoln: University of Nebraska Press, 1982.

Ford, Hugh. *Published in Paris*. New York: Collier Books/Macmillan, 1975.

Hall, Donald. *Remembering Poets: Reminiscences and Opinions*. New Yorker: Harper Colophon, 1977.

Heyman, C. David. *Ezra Pound: The Last Rower*. New York: Citadel Press Book/Carol Publishing Group, 1992.

Hofstadter, Richard, William Miller, and Daniel Aaron, eds. *The American Republic Through Reconstruction*, vol. 1. Englewood Cliffs: Prentice-Hall, Inc., 1970.

Lamb, Richard. *Italy at War, 1943–1945*. New York: St. Martin's Press, 1993.

Manchester, William. *The Last Lion: Winston Spencer Churchill Alone, 1932–1940*. Boston: Little, Brown & Co., 1988.

Mussolini, Benito. *The Cardinal's Mistress*. New York: Albert & Charles Boni, 1928.

Norman, Charles. *Ezra Pound*. New York: Macmillan, 1960.

Paige, D. D. *The Letters of Ezra Pound, 1907–1941*. New York: Harcourt, Brace & Co., 1950.

Rauchenbus, Stephen. *The March of Fascism*. New Haven: Yale University Press, 1939.

Read, Forrest, ed. *The Letters of Ezra Pound to James Joyce*. New York: New Directions, 1967.

Reich, Wilhelm. *The Mass Psychology of Fascism*. Mary Higgins and Chester M. Raphael, eds. New York: The Noonday Press/Farrar, Straus & Giroux, 1993.

Shirer, William L. *The Rise and Fall of the Third Reich*. New York: Simon & Schuster, 1960.

Spahr, Walter E., ed. *Economic Principles and Problems*. New York: Farrar & Rhinehart, Inc. 1934.

Stock, Noel. *The Life of Ezra Pound*. New York: Routledge and Kegan Paul/Pantheon, 1970.

Terrell, Carroll F. *The Companion to The Cantos*. vols. 1 and 2. Berkeley: University of California Press, 1984.

Toland, John. *Adolf Hitler*. New York: Ballantine Books, 1976.

Torrey, E. Fuller. *The Roots of Treason: Ezra Pound and the Secrets of St. Elizabeth's*. London: Sidgwick & Jackson, 1984.

Wiegand, G. Carl. *Economics: Its Nature and Importance*. New York: Baron's Educational Series, 1968.

Winnick, R. H., ed. *Letters of Archibald MacLeish, 1907–1982*. Boston: Houghton Mifflin Company, 1983.

Chapter Seven

THOMAS MANN

Disillusionment

See Chapter One bibliography.

Index